# Schoolhouses, Courthouses, and Statehouses

# Schoolhouses, Courthouses, and Statehouses

## SOLVING THE FUNDING-ACHIEVEMENT PUZZLE IN AMERICA'S PUBLIC SCHOOLS

Eric A. Hanushek
and
Alfred A. Lindseth

PRINCETON UNIVERSITY PRESS    PRINCETON AND OXFORD

Copyright © 2009 By Princeton University Press

Published by Princeton University Press,
41 William Street, Princeton, New Jersey 08540

In the United Kingdom: Princeton University Press,
6 Oxford Street, Woodstock, Oxfordshire OX20 1TW

All Rights Reserved

Library of Congress Cataloging-in-Publication Data

Hanushek, Eric Alan, 1943–
    Schoolhouses, courthouses, and statehouses : solving the funding-achievement
puzzle in America's public schools / Eric A. Hanushek and Alfred A. Lindseth.
        p.      cm.
    Includes bibliographical references and index.
    ISBN 978-0-691-13000-2 (hardcover : alk. paper)
    1. Public schools—United States—Finance. 2. Academic achievement—
United States. I. Lindseth, Alfred A. II. Title.
    LB2825.H25 2009
    379.1'220973—dc22                                            2008053718

British Library Cataloging-in-Publication Data is available

This book has been composed in Sabon

Printed on acid-free paper. ∞

press.princeton.edu

Printed in the United States of America

10  9  8  7  6  5  4  3  2  1

# Contents

# Figures

# Tables

# Preface

Neither of us have ever taught or worked in a K–12 school or school district. Therefore, one might reasonably ask, why should anyone want to read our book on how best to reform American education? There are three answers to this very sensible question.

First, both of us have been active and important participants for over twenty years in the debates, policy discussions, and litigation over how to improve education in America. We bring to the table a vast reservoir of knowledge, including intimate familiarity with the research and experts involved in these debates. As a college professor and researcher, one of us (Hanushek) sparked a national debate over the role of money and funding in bringing about improved student achievement, a debate taken as an expert witness to the most important school finance trials of the last four decades. The other (Lindseth), in his role as an attorney representing states as diverse as New York, Florida and North Dakota, has played a lead role in many of the most important school finance cases of the last twenty-five years, advising governors, elected officials, and state education leaders on topics related to school finance and reform.

Second, it is precisely because we are not part of the traditional educational establishment that we believe this book is valuable. We have not hesitated to challenge the present way of doing things, unlike powerful forces in the educational community deeply vested in the status quo who resist any significant changes in the operation and funding of schools, despite strong evidence that the system is not working well for millions of students.

Third, the major focus of our book is not about what educational theories or strategies work best in the classrooms, which the authors readily leave for decision to the educators. It is rather about creating an integrated education and funding system that encourages, promotes, and rewards good decision making by educators at all levels, leading to an objective few can disagree with: significantly improved achievement for all children. This is in contrast to the current system in most states, which treats school finance and policy decisions as separate, reinforcing incongruous and poor results.

In writing this book, we had several objectives.

We wanted to do more than describe the current structure and its successes and failures. Although a recounting of the past and present is necessary to a full understanding of the seriousness of the problems we face and what has already been tried in an effort to address them, we wanted the book also to deal with solutions. We have therefore set forth specific elements of an integrated solution that we believe will lead to real improvement. Our proposals are straightforward, they make sense, and the wherewithal and expertise necessary to implement them already exist in many states. The key issue is whether the nation has the political will to adopt them in light of likely opposition by powerful interest groups deeply tied to the present system.

We wanted the book to be appealing to the general public, and not simply to a limited audience of economists, lawyers, and policymakers. Although our arguments are well documented, we have relegated discussion of much of the complex scientific research supporting them to the endnotes in order to keep the main body of the work interesting and readable. For those interested in specific studies or a more detailed description of the scientific research supporting our positions, the endnotes and references sections of the book provide that information. This is not a book about multiple regression analysis, coefficients of variations, or abstruse legal arguments, but an understandable discussion of what is wrong with our education systems and what needs to be done to fix them.

We wanted the book to speak with a single voice. Although we come from different disciplines, we have each rewritten each other's contributions to the book so many times that we believe it is difficult to tell which one of us wrote what. Each of us has been accused of being a "wanna-be" in the other's profession, and we therefore did not hesitate to critique each other's work.

Finally, we wanted to be evenhanded with the evidence even as we presented our strongly held conclusions on the issues. This was perhaps the most difficult, since there are such sharp divisions of opinions about how best to reform education in America. Yet we have strived to cite all the evidence, and not just that favorable to our positions, so a reader interested in further pursuing the discussion will have references on all sides of the issues available.

We hope that you, after reading the book, will agree that we have met these objectives.

Many people have contributed over the years to our understanding of the nation's K–12 education problems and to our thoughts on how best to address them. They include not only people we have worked with, but also many who hold differing views on the issues, who pointed out weaknesses in some of our positions, and who helped us to better focus our arguments. Over the years we have learned much from all sides of the debate.

We wish to especially thank the following individuals and organizations for their support and input.

The Hoover Institution and the Sutherland Asbill & Brennan law firm, with which we have been proud to have been affiliated for so many years, and which have unwaveringly supported and encouraged us through the years as we wrote the book.

Our many friends and colleagues who offered their ideas and comments on the manuscript, as well as helped us with research, editing, and just plain logic. These included Rocco Testani, Josh Mayes, Molly Clarkson, and Jessica Wang at Sutherland who brought their legal experiences into the project, John Kain who was an early mentor and collaborator, and Cristina Sepe, Trey Miller, and Russell Roberts who provided detailed suggestions on various sections. Anne Himmelfarb substantially aided the effort with a skillful editing of a very rough manuscript.

The members of the Koret Task Force on K–12 Education of the Hoover Institution, who deserve special recognition. Discussions with this innovative group over several years honed the arguments that underlie our perspective and our solutions. Moreover, the task force's jointly written book (*Courting Failure: How School Finance Lawsuits Exploit Judges' Good Intentions and Harm Our*

*Children*) in which we both participated convinced us that we should undertake this book with a goal of producing a more comprehensive policy statement.

The Packard Humanities Institute, which has provided steady support and encouragement for our underlying research and policy endeavors.

Brian Steely, who helped turn our ideas into an informative book title and saw how it could be illustrated on the current cover.

Our publisher and editors at Princeton University Press, including Seth Ditchik, Terri O'Prey, and Joan Gieseke, who ensured a high-quality publication.

Finally, we want to thank our spouses, Carroll (Lindseth) and Macke (Raymond), who not only read one version of the manuscript after another and offered their helpful comments, but also endured many a lonely night as we worked on the book.

Schoolhouses,
Courthouses,
and Statehouses

# Introduction

American students are no longer competitive. For more than thirty years, student achievement has remained flat, even as education spending, adjusted for inflation, has almost quadrupled. Huge numbers of children cannot perform at basic levels in reading, math, and science, even by the time they reach the twelfth grade. This crisis is a national one, and the failure to find effective solutions threatens not only our individual well-being, but also our country's leadership in the world community. The principal solutions relied upon in the past have proven ineffective. Boosting student achievement will clearly require fundamental changes in the operation and financing of schools. No matter how much money we spend, we cannot hope to address this crisis simply by adhering to the practices of the past.

The importance of education in American life is difficult to overestimate. It is an article of faith, supported by fact, that is drummed into most children by their parents and repeated continuously by our leaders. It is the key for most people to experiencing the "American Dream," and for the better part of the twentieth century, the United States led the world in providing education for all of its citizens. Our country reaped huge benefits from a well-educated workforce, and as a result, we have enjoyed a standard of living that is the envy of the rest of the world. Yet, despite a financial commitment to K–12 education unmatched by any other country, in the last several decades, our education system has been failing us in important ways, particularly when it comes to our poorest and most vulnerable students.

The statistics are alarming. A quarter to half of twelfth graders enrolled in our public schools test below even the basic level in reading, math, and science skills. These statistics contrast dramatically with a 2003 national survey that found that nine out of ten parents of grade 6–12 students expected their child to continue education beyond high school and two-thirds believed they would finish college.[1]

These statistics mask an even larger problem among the nation's poor and minority students, whose performance levels are much worse. A huge achievement gap has proved stubbornly resistant to closure over the decades, and has not significantly narrowed for almost twenty years. The average black and Hispanic students are as many as three or four grade levels behind the average white student.

As a consequence, U.S. students no longer lead the world either in the number of years of school completed or in the skills learned while in school. Indeed, they are not even close, ranking below average among the world's developed countries, even though the United States outspends almost all other developed countries on education by a wide margin. The country seems to be stuck in a rut, and achievement levels have remained largely stagnant since the 1960s despite massive efforts to improve them.

National and state leaders have tried to address this distressing situation in a number of ways over the last three decades. Few policy areas are as complex or as hotly debated as educational reform. Ideology, economics, politics, science, common sense, personal circumstances and experience, and a variety of different self-interests all enter into forming the mosaic of education reform. The public discussion seldom separates these elements, and from the same facts, different people draw widely varying conclusions that reflect their personal views of the relative influences of this mixture of ingredients. One group, often identified as "conservatives," argues that current funding of schools would be sufficient if only the money were spent more efficiently, while another group, usually described as "liberals," argues that the country is spending too little on schools and that more money is necessary to fix the problem.

A number of different policies designed to improve education has grown out of these debates. First and perhaps most important, governments at all levels have dramatically increased the amount of money they spend on K–12 education. Between 1960 and 2005, spending per pupil rose dramatically; adjusting for inflation, per-pupil expenditures almost quadrupled.

Most states have also made serious efforts to improve equity in funding among students and school districts. Using funding formulas that compensate for local wealth differences, states have been able to reduce the disparity in funding between school districts that come from schools' reliance on local property taxes to raise revenues. Funding formulas in many states have also been changed to drive more state aid to school districts with large proportions of students deemed "at risk" of academic failure. Whereas in the past, school districts with predominantly poor and minority enrollments had below average funding, that pattern has been reversed, and school districts serving high percentages of at-risk children are now, on average, as well, or better, funded than others.

These fiscal efforts not only have improved the fairness of the system, but also have enabled school districts to lower class sizes, hire additional personnel, and offer an array of specialized programs never imagined in the 1960s. Unfortunately, these additional resources have not significantly altered the patterns of low student achievement observed over the last several decades. The puzzle of why dramatically increased funding for schools has not shown up in student outcomes has baffled many. It is so at odds with what we see in other sectors of the economy that some economists simply reject the observation out of hand, presuming that they must have missed something in the analysis.

Indeed, some state legislatures have begun looking for other ways to improve student achievement, including holding schools and school districts more accountable for outcomes, expanding the pool of qualified teachers, and supporting programs like charter schools, which provide parents with more choice and exert pressure on the public schools to improve. On the federal level, the No Child Left Behind Act embraces many of these approaches. Some evidence suggests that these policies are having a positive impact, but their long-term effect is uncertain.

Perhaps the most significant feature of the evolving politics of school finance has been the increasing involvement of the courts, initially focusing on an equitable allocation of educational resources between school districts and more recently turning to the level of appropriations for K–12 education in many states. Serious constitutional and practical problems are associated with having the judicial branch of government involved in making decisions related to educational policy and appropriations, historically considered the responsibility of the legislative and executive branches. Notwithstanding these concerns, state courts, deriving their authority from state constitutional provisions, have struck down the educational funding systems in over twenty states on the grounds that they do not provide sufficient funding for an "adequate" education and have ordered the state legislatures to make up the shortfall. Only in the last several years have the courts begun to take a more deferential attitude and to uphold appropriation levels set by state legislatures.

These "adequacy lawsuits," as they are called, reached their peak in New York in 2004, when a Manhattan trial judge ordered the state legislature to increase funding for the New York City public schools by $23 billion over the next five years. This included a $5.6 billion increase in annual expenditures, a 45 percent bump over then current expenditures. If implemented, it would have brought per-pupil spending in the city's public schools to more than twice the national average. The highest court in New York eventually reduced this judgment, ordering "only" a $1.9 billion annual increase, but it did not back away from the principle that courts may properly set minimum appropriations for K–12 education.

Two-thirds of the American public is confident that increased funding for schools would lead to higher student learning.[2] As a result, at least publicly, few people appear to disagree with the underlying premise of such litigation: that massive increases in spending on education will enable all children, regardless of their background, to achieve at high levels—and many courts, like the legislatures, have also called for significant increases in K–12 spending. However, though judges are generally deemed less susceptible to political pressures, they have largely sided with powerful vested interests in the educational community to preserve the status quo, albeit at a higher level of spending, and have made little effort to change how education funds are used or to explore other methods of school reform. Consequently, the impact of court-ordered or induced remedies on achievement has largely mirrored that of previous legislative efforts. Of the four states that have had the most significant judicial remedies in place the longest, only one—Massachusetts—has seen significant improvement by its students over the term of the court remedy. Even there, it is not clear whether achievement improved because of increased funding or because of other, more innovative remedial measures that the Massachusetts legislature found the political courage to pass. In the other three states— Kentucky, New Jersey and Wyoming—achievement patterns remain largely unchanged from what they were in the early 1990s when the remedies commenced; low performance and sizeable achievement gaps persist, despite huge increases in K–12 expenditures.

Both the judicial and legislative responses have been heavily influenced by the belief that science can provide the answers to the achievement dilemma. In many states, judges and legislators alike were convinced that so-called costing-out studies conducted by expert consultants could determine how much it should cost to provide an education resulting in high achievement for all students, regardless of their background. They were also convinced that certain programs and policies would lead to higher achievement if only the additional funds were available to implement them. But policymakers have not been well served by the scientific community, and costing-out studies are a prime example. The results of such studies vary wildly depending on the researcher and the methodology; they are often internally inconsistent, leading to sometimes ludicrous results; and, most important, they cannot be replicated in other studies, a failure that violates a basic tenet of science. Despite these fatal weaknesses, such studies have been cited and relied upon by many courts and legislatures in deciding the proper level of funding for education.

Other types of studies use more appropriate scientific methodologies, but still fail to produce consistent results. Classic examples are the studies on the effects of class size reduction. While the Project STAR (student/teacher achievement ratio) experiment in Tennessee found that reducing class size in the early grades (to between fifteen and seventeen students) significantly improved student performance, literally hundreds of other studies have reached less posi-

tive conclusions. And the results from implementing class size reduction policies have been commensurately disappointing. A good
example is found in the California class size reduction program, a
much emulated policy and one of the most expensive reform strategies ever undertaken in American education. That program, despite
its multi-billion-dollar price tag, has resulted in little or no improvement in the achievement of the state's poor and minority students even though the spending remains embedded in state policy.
Regrettably, this is not an isolated or unique example where policies, based on some scientific evidence, fail to lead to the promised
or expected gains in achievement when applied on a broad scale.

If scientific evaluations produced a list of programs that could
reliably be implemented on a systemwide basis, then the solutions
would be relatively straightforward: legislate the termination of the
ineffective programs and direct and fund implementation of the
programs that work. But experience has shown that such top-down
approaches are rarely effective. Schools differ, and programs that
work in some might be ill-suited and ineffective in others. Thus,
the formula for effective reform must be one that encourages districts and schools to seek out and implement those programs that
work for them and raise student achievement. The current system
in most states, however, is not suited to this approach, and in many
states may actually discourage such performance-oriented decision
making, preferring instead to specify policies and programs from
the state capital.

A major impediment to effective school reform is that financial
decisions have historically been separated from policy decisions
about how to improve student outcomes. What appear to be "pure
finance" decisions can and often do create barriers to improving
student outcomes. Our recommendation is for states to use financial and other incentives as a way of energizing and motivating
schools, school districts, board of education members, teachers,
principals, administrators, parents, and children to do their best.
Such incentives are currently absent from the system. It should not
be surprising that when there is little cost to failure and little reward for success, America's schools often fail and rarely succeed
in educating our children to the highest levels. It is time to recognize

that the finance system can be an important tool not only in paying for needed resources and programs (its present role) but also in motivating students, teachers, and school administrators to find more effective solutions.

With these principles in mind, we set forth in this book the parameters of an education policy and finance system that fully integrates school funding mechanisms with educational policy goals to promote higher achievement and more efficient use of funds. We call our proposal "performance-based funding" because each facet of it is designed to promote better performance by the stakeholders in the system, including schools, administrators, teachers, students, parents, and taxpayers. High uniform standards, strong accountability measures, performance-based compensation, increased management and spending control at the local level, dissemination of performance data (for schools and students), and other incentives all serve to encourage better performance. Other components of the proposal, such as value-added measurements—those that measure the contribution specifically made by schools to improve achievement—and the elimination of perverse disincentives that encourage "gaming" of the system, are also important. They ensure that incentives and other financing are based on data that truly reflect factors the school controls, and not outside influences, positive or negative. Still other components, such as giving parents some choice in determining where their children attend school and allowing districts to augment funding at the local level, engage parents and the community in encouraging schools to produce well-educated students—and in holding them accountable if they do not.

A performance-based funding system will undoubtedly step on some toes and meet with vigorous resistance from those interested in preserving the status quo. The politically powerful teachers' unions, in particular, are on record as opposing performance-based pay, modification of teacher tenure laws, and expanded choice options. In the past, they have been very good at convincing the public that what is good for the unions is also good for teachers and, most important, for children. But this trend is changing. More and more people are asking, for example, how it can possibly benefit children to retain unqualified teachers or to pay bad teachers the same amount as good teachers. (America's foreign competitors do neither of these things.) Many union supporters, aware that the public is beginning to recognize these truths, are starting to soften their stance on some of these issues.

Undoubtedly, some costs will be involved in changing from the current system to the system we propose; teachers and others with job security guarantees and other vested rights will not willingly give them up without recompense. However, such costs are likely to be substantially less than many of the education reform measures currently in vogue, such as class size reduction programs. Most important, by paying these transitional costs now, we ensure that future education monies will be productive. State legislatures will bear the brunt of the task, but courts that elect to undertake such cases can also play a more constructive role than they have in the past—for instance, by making clear that schools have problems other than money shortages, and by giving reform-minded legislatures more leverage in trying to bring about necessary changes.

In the chapters that follow, we develop in detail what has transpired in the past and what it will take to get America's schools back on the right track. But it is perhaps also important to stress here what this book does not attempt to do— either because, in our opinion, such quests may not be fruitful or because the solutions are better left to more qualified persons. First, we avoid debating what particular education programs and strategies will work best to raise student achievement. The fact is that some strategies may work well in some schools or school districts, but not in others. We leave those decisions to the people best qualified to make them: the educators on the ground in the local schools and districts. Under our proposal, it will be in their self-interest to use resources to improve student achievement, while under the present compensation and reward system, whether a teacher or program actually helps children is typically irrelevant.

Second, this book does not argue for decreasing financial and other support for public education, but for making more effective use of our education dollars at whatever level they might be set.

Finally, unlike the proponents of many education fads in the past, we make no claims that the measures we propose will eliminate the existing achievement gaps. So many factors, inside and outside the schools, influence student achievement that no one can credibly make such promises. Nor do we attempt to parse out the fault for this predicament. Rather, we choose to focus on what schools can do, with the help of incentives provided by the school finance system, to solve the problem of low achievement.

We do say, however, that a performance-based funding system is likely to significantly raise achievement for all students, once again making our students competitive on the international scene, and ensuring that the nation will not wake up again forty years from now with its students still performing at 1970 levels. We also believe that this program will dramatically improve the achievement of minorities and disadvantaged students who have yet to garner the full benefits of our schools.

These measures will not be easily accepted or implemented, given strong opposition to some elements of our proposal from a number of quarters. But in view of the record of the last several decades, it is imperative that we get started.

# 1 | Just How Important Is Education?

The importance of education to our way of life is self-evident. The $600 billion our country spends on K–12 education exceeds the national defense budget. The centerpiece of President George W. Bush's domestic legislative agenda was the No Child Left Behind Act. Endless policy statements, media stories, and public pronouncements begin and end with words like this: "We must ensure that our children have the skills necessary to compete in the twenty-first century."

The economic effects of education are especially compelling. Successful schools are important to us individually, to our society, and to America's leadership position in the world. The education level of the family breadwinner(s) largely determines a family's economic well-being, and this effect is multigenerational. If a mother and father are high school dropouts, their children are at dramatically increased risk of academic failure. But the quality of a person's education affects far more than his or her individual or family circumstances. It has an impact on the whole of society, affecting not only the standard of living enjoyed by our citizens, but also the fairness of our economic and social systems. A good education has always been the key to enabling even the poorest of our citizens to achieve the American Dream, and its role is even more important in today's high-tech, global economy. A major problem facing the nation is the significant achievement gap between middle-class and white children on the one hand and poor and minority children on the other.

Our country is blessed with rich material resources, clear property rights, and a well-developed market economy—the things that make for favorable economic outcomes. But our future will depend

**TABLE 1.1.**

Lifetime Earnings Estimates for Full-Time, Year-Round Workers, by Sex and Educational Attainment, 1997–99 (in millions of 2007 dollars)

|  | *Women* | *Men* |
|---|---|---|
| Less than high school | 0.9 | 1.4 |
| High school | 1.3 | 1.8 |
| Some college | 1.5 | 2.2 |
| Associate's degree | 1.7 | 2.3 |
| Bachelor's degree | 2.0 | 3.2 |
| Master's degree | 2.4 | 3.7 |
| Professional degree | 3.7 | 6.1 |
| Doctoral degreee | 3.2 | 4.8 |

*Source*: Day and Newburger (2002), adjusted to 2007 with consumer price index.

less on these, perhaps, than on the full development of our human capital, and that can occur only if our educational system is strong.

Our overall argument is simple. Just maintaining the status quo into the twenty-first century will not serve us well either as individuals or as a nation. Because this is the foundation of our argument for fundamental reform, we begin by reviewing the importance of education for our well-being. While nobody seriously doubts education's critical nature, few fully appreciate the true magnitude of its impact.

## Education and Financial Achievement

Most people realize that the longer you stay in school, the more money you will make. This commonsense perception is borne out by statistics compiled by the U.S. Bureau of the Census on the difference in average lifetime earnings that individuals with varying levels of school completion can expect. Table 1.1 shows these differences.

As the table demonstrates, average lifetime earnings rise rapidly with the number of years of school completed. The differences are dramatic for both men and women. A male worker who finishes high school can expect to earn almost 30 percent more over the course of his lifetime than a high school dropout. If the worker goes to college, even if he fails to graduate or earn a degree, he can expect to earn from 54 to 63 percent more than a high school dropout. If he obtains a college degree, he is likely to earn over 125 percent more. While women on average tend to earn less than men, their lifetime earnings resulting from additional schooling increase in proportion to those of male workers. The numbers in table 1.1, however, do not tell the whole story. They focus on the quantity of education a child receives and not necessarily its quality.

The revolution in the United States during the twentieth century was universal schooling through the secondary level, and much of the early empirical work on the importance of schooling to an individual's economic well-being rightly concentrated on the years of education completed.[1] The quantity of schooling is easily measured. But there is also a wide variation in earnings for those with the same amount of schooling, and many with less schooling earn more money—in some cases considerably more money—than those with more schooling. For example, over 35 percent of high school dropouts will actually earn more than the average high school graduate.[2]

Some of the differences in these earnings are due to luck. Others can be traced to more subjective character traits such as discipline and reliability. But a significant amount is due to the knowledge and skills an individual develops. These skill differences are in turn heavily influenced by the quality of education that an individual experiences, and not just the number of years he or she attends school. A growing body of evidence suggests that differences in skills learned may be as, or even more, important as predictors of future earnings than the number of years spent in school. To be sure, measuring skills or "quality" is difficult. In recent years, however, with increased demands for school accountability, studies have begun to identify cognitive skills, such as those used in reading and mathematics, as a central component of a good education. Moreover, important aspects of the relevant cognitive skills—analytical abilities, reasoning power, and information processing capacity mixed with specific knowledge—can be measured by the use of standardized tests. For the first time, comprehensive data linking cognitive skills to later-life economic outcomes are available.

Recent investigations show that "quality" of education, as generally measured by test scores, is strongly related to individual earnings, productivity, and economic growth, even when the "quantity," or the number of years of schooling completed, is held constant. Available analyses provide remarkably consistent evidence about the relationship between achievement and earnings.[3] These analyses emphasize different aspects of individual earnings, but each finds that earnings are strongly influenced by measured achievement after allowing for differences in the quantity of schooling, the experiences of workers, and other factors that might also influence earnings. For example, an individual moving from the fiftieth to the seventieth percentile of the achievement distribution can expect to earn 6 to 8 percent more per year over his or her entire work life.[4] To put this statistic into better perspective, this difference in achievement is roughly equivalent to the difference in scores on international tests between an average U.S. student and an average student in a higher-achieving European country.

School quality and quantity are, of course, related to one another. Students who do better in school, as measured either through grades or through scores on standardized achievement tests, tend to finish more years of school. A study by economist Steven Rivkin of Amherst College finds that variations in test scores capture a considerable proportion of the systematic variation in high school completion and college continuation rates. Under his analysis, the differences between black students' and white students' test scores fully explain black-white differences in high school graduation and initial college attendance rates.[5]

These findings are hardly surprising. Common sense tells us that someone who does well in school is more likely to remain in school, and that a student with a ninth grade education possessing basic verbal and math skills will probably earn more than a high school graduate without these skills. Moreover, there is evidence that the rewards for mastering different skills have been increasing over time. The U.S. economy has a voracious appetite for ever more skilled workers, and it is hardly news that those who learn more earn more.

This variation in achievement is measured by most state accountability tests, which seek to determine whether students have mastered or become proficient in an array of skills. The recognition that mastery of skills is more important than the mere number of years spent in school has prompted many states to require students to pass a graduation test before being awarded a high school diploma. Prospective employers want some assurance that a high school diploma implies skills and not merely that the graduate has occupied a seat in school for twelve years. For policymakers, the message seems clear. Efforts to improve education must ensure not only that students stay in school, but also that they develop and master certain basic cognitive skills before they graduate and move on to higher education or the workforce.

Thus far, we have focused on the relationship between the quality or quantity of a person's education and his or her economic well-being. The impact of education, however, does not stop with one's own generation. It reaches across the generational divide and can have devastating effects on children and grandchildren, not only while they are growing up, but also after they become adults. Extensive research into the determinants of achievement consistently points to parental income, education, and socioeconomic status as the strongest predictors of how well a child does in school.[6] This research (discussed more extensively later on with regard to school resources) has not focused on the precise family characteristics and practices that are important, but it makes the overwhelming case that parents' economic circumstances filter down to their children and thus have implications for the long term.[7] A person who drops out of high school or learns little in school may be consigning not only himself to a life of lower earnings or even poverty, but perhaps his children and grandchildren as well. Consequently, education is the paramount weapon in the fight to break the cycle of poverty that traps large numbers of poor and minority families.

## Education and Poverty

Improving our education system also has important implications for the fairness of our society and economic systems. Just as the United States has an achievement gap, it has an income gap. In 2006, over thirty-six million, or 12.3 percent of all American citizens, lived below the official poverty line.[8] Children fared worse: over 17 percent of those younger than age eighteen live in poverty. Twenty percent of U.S. households earn $20,000 or less per year, while a similar percentage earn $92,000 or more each year.

In the aggregate, the role of schooling in perpetuating—or breaking—the cycle of poverty is clear: 21 percent of adults with less than a high school education find themselves in poverty, compared to 4 percent of those with a college degree. The underlying hope of the War on Poverty was that investments in high-quality schools could overcome deficits originating in the home and enable students to build a better life for themselves and their families than their parents had. Indeed, the Elementary and Secondary Education Act of 1965 was one of the first pieces of legislation in President Lyndon Johnson's War on Poverty and established a significant federal role in the financing of compensatory education for poor children.[9]

Unfortunately, the goal of closing the income gap through improved education is far from being achieved. If anything, income disparities have become more pronounced in the last thirty years. Since the early 1970s, the bottom 60 percent of earners has seen income growth at half the rate for the top 20 percent and a quarter of the rate for the top 5 percent.[10] Increases in the rewards for more schooling are a part of this expansion, but earnings have also spread out within groups of people with the same schooling level.[11]

We have already alluded to studies finding that skill differences largely explain both differences in the earnings of blacks and whites, and the widening of differences in earnings among people with the same levels of schooling.[12] These analyses have emphasized the increasing rewards for skills and the implications of this trend for wage inequality. Owing to insufficient long-term data, this research has tended not to look directly at measured cognitive skills.[13] Nonetheless, the findings about individual earnings indicate that variations in cognitive skills also have an important and direct impact on racial and other variations in the distribution of incomes.[14]

Governments have historically employed a variety of direct income transfer programs to ameliorate the disparities across families, but such programs have undesirable effects. In particular, transfer programs generally reduce work incentives and thus have deleterious impacts on overall levels of income. This problem has led to a parallel emphasis on improving the human capital and skills of the poor, so that the natural operation of the economy will pull them out of poverty through higher returns from work. The recent evidence on the importance of cognitive skills suggests that the best way to close such gaps in earnings is to improve education for all students, especially for poor and minority students who make up a disproportionate share of those at risk of academic failure. In other words, closing achievement gaps is a critical first step in reducing and eliminating income gaps. Without the first being accomplished, the second is unlikely to occur.

### Education and the Nation's Economic Well-Being

Besides being crucial to the economic and social well-being of individuals and their families, an effective educational system is essential to maintaining our nation's strong economy. The impact of measured labor force quality on economic growth is perhaps even more important than the impact of education on individual productivity and incomes. Economic growth determines how much improvement will occur in our overall standard of living. A more educated society may lead to higher rates of invention, make everybody more productive with new and better production methods, and lead to more rapid introduction of new technologies. These "externalities"—influences of individual education outcomes on other people— provide extra reasons for being concerned about the quality of schooling.

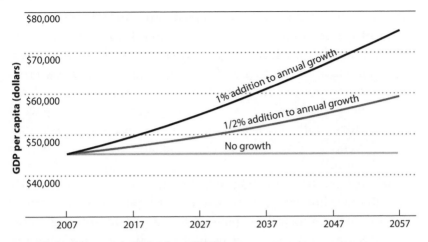

**1.1**  Effect of Economic Growth on U.S. Income

Throughout the twentieth century and into the twenty-first century, the strong and growing U.S. economy enabled its citizens to enjoy a standard of living envied by the rest of the world. The current economic position of the United States is largely the result of its strong and steady growth over the twentieth century.

The effect of differences in growth rates on economic well-being is easy to see. Figure 1.1 begins with the value of the nation's gross domestic product (GDP) per capita in the year 2007 and shows its value after fifty years under different growth rates. If GDP per capita grows at just one-half percent each year, this measure of U.S. income (or wealth) would increase from $46,000 to $59,000— or a 30 percent increase over the period. If it were to grow at a full one percent per year, such income would be almost two-thirds higher, reaching over $75,000 in 2057. In short, seemingly small differences in growth rates have huge ramifications for the income and wealth of a society.

A number of factors clearly contribute to a country's economic growth.[15] Almost certainly the most important factor sustaining the growth of the U.S. economy has been the openness and fluidity of its markets. The United States maintains generally freer labor and product markets than most countries in the world. Its trade unions are less extensive than those in many other countries, and

even more broadly, the U.S. government intrudes less into the operation of the economy, with less regulation, lower tax rates, and
fewer nationalized industries than elsewhere. These factors encourage capital investment, permit the rapid development of new products and activities by firms, and allow U.S. workers to take advantage of new opportunities. While identifying the precise impact of
these factors is difficult, a variety of analyses suggest that such market differences are very important explanations for differences in
growth rates.[16]

At the same time, our nation's educational system has clearly
been another important ingredient in our economic success. Over
the twentieth century, the expansion of the education system in the
United States outpaced the growth of schooling in other countries
around the world, as we pushed to open secondary schools to all
citizens and to expand higher education through land grant universities, the G.I. bill, and direct grants and loans to students. As a
result, in comparison to other nations, the United States labor force
has historically been better educated, explaining to a large extent
the relative strength of U.S. economic growth.

The empirical work supporting analyses of economic growth has
largely emphasized differences in the years of school completed
across countries. Again, this is natural because assessing quantity
of schooling is reasonably straightforward. The typical study finds
that quantity of schooling is highly related to economic growth
rates. But, again, quantity of schooling is a very crude measure of
people's knowledge and cognitive skills. An average sixth grader
in a rural hut in Bolivia probably does not learn as much over the
school year as an American sixth grader. Yet when empirical analyses focus exclusively on differences in average years of schooling
completed between countries, they assume the two experiences to
be equivalent.

Recent work on economic growth goes beyond such crude assumptions and delves into the role of cognitive skills, as measured
by standardized test scores. These analyses, which include information about international differences in mathematics and science
knowledge (information gained by testing over the past four decades), find that differences in school quality have a remarkable

impact on economic growth.[17] In technical terms, according to the existing evidence, each one standard deviation difference on test performance is related to a 1 percent difference in annual growth rates of per capita GDP. As shown in figure 1.1, the impact of even such small-sounding differences in growth rates is very large. In sum, systematic investigation across countries demonstrates a clear relationship between math and science skills on the one hand and productivity and growth on the other.[18]

To put this in better perspective, a one-half standard deviation improvement on the international tests is approximately what it would take in 2006 to get our math and science skills up to those of Canada. It is still, however, somewhat less than it would take to reach the very top rankings on international tests, occupied currently by Hong Kong, Taiwan, and Finland.[19] A reform program designed to move the United States to these top spots or even to Canada's level would require dramatic changes in U.S. schools but would yield a huge return. In figure 1.2, we compare aggregate gross domestic product as it might change if improved schooling elevated cognitive skills of students by one-half standard deviation, i.e., to the Canadian level. Figure 1.2 traces the growth dividend expected from such an educational improvement relative to the total annual education budget for the United States; it employs three alternative "reform packages," which are presumed to produce the same level of student performance—a one-half standard deviation improvement—but at varying speeds, i.e., over the course of ten, twenty, or thirty years. Educational expenditures for K–12 are calculated to grow at their historical rate of 3 percent annually (after inflation). We plot against this the growth dividends resulting from a one-half standard deviation improvement plan, assuming the three different time periods for implementing necessary reforms. This figure shows vividly that effective reform (i.e., reform that actually yields improvement in student performance) has a huge cumulative effect on the economy.

Assuming education spending continues to increase at historical rates, figure 1.2 indicates that a ten-year reform plan begun in 2005 that increased average student performance by just a half standard deviation could be expected to produce an annual reform dividend

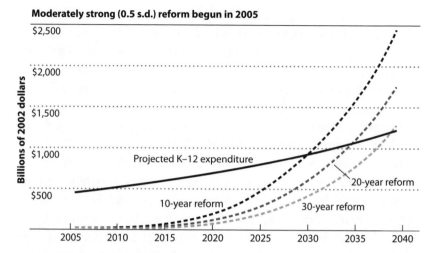

**Moderately strong (0.5 s.d.) reform begun in 2005**

**1.2** Equalling Canadian Achievement: U.S. Growth Dividend vs. K–12 Expenditure

by 2030 equal to the entire U.S. investment in K–12 education. Even if the reform program were spread out over twenty years, it would produce the same size dividend by 2035.

We can also put this into a historical U.S. perspective. In 1989, the governors of all of the states met to discuss the education of our students. One of the goals they established was for U.S. students to be first in the world in math and science performance by the turn of the twenty-first century. Had we met that goal, GDP would, according to historical patterns, have been $300 billion greater in 2008 than it actually was.

However, as we discuss in chapter 2, unfortunately no education reform effort ever tried has resulted in very much improvement, let alone the truly substantial improvements just posited. The key to reform is figuring out how to produce such improvements, a topic we take up in later chapters.

## Testing Student Skills

Testing to measure students' achievement remains controversial. On the one hand, the movement toward standards and account-ability has emphasized the need to measure students' performance and to use test scores in judging the performance of schools as well. On the other hand, a segment of the school policy community has argued against the testing—because it does not think testing measures important attributes, because it views test scores as invalid or unreliable, or because it considers test outcomes irrelevant.[20] The research we reviewed earlier, however, demonstrates at the very least that differences in performance on existing tests have significant implications for both individual success and the success of larger groups. Clearly, performance on standardized tests of math and science is directly related to individual productivity and earnings and to national economic growth.

None of this says that the existing tests cannot be improved, merely that these tests do indicate something real that has important ramifications for individuals and the economy.[21] Further, just because the skills we now test are important does not mean that other skills are not also important. Some research suggests that other types of skills also bear on future economic success,[22] and many people argue that schools should also be involved in developing these skills, rather than just reading, math, and science. If, for example, aggregate growth is partly fueled by a facility for invention, creativity should be fostered in schools. We do not disagree with this point of view, and, as a matter of fact, most schools do seek to develop skill sets extending well beyond math, science, and reading. However, to be useful, these other skills must be identified and measured, and we must learn how to actually teach them. Be that as it may, however, none of the arguments for also recognizing other skills diminish the importance of the cognitive skills that we now measure.[23]

## Quality of U.S. Colleges

The quality of U.S. colleges also affects the economy. Americans can be proud of their institutions of higher education. By most accounts, U.S. colleges and universities rank at the very top in the world, and there is plenty of evidence attesting to their high quality.[24] Few foreign students are tempted to emigrate to the United

States to attend elementary and secondary schools—except perhaps as a way of gaining entry into the country. They do, however, emigrate in large numbers to attend U.S. colleges and universities, even if this means paying full, unsubsidized tuition.

A number of economic models measuring economic growth emphasize the importance of scientists and engineers.[25] These models suggest that the technically trained college students who contribute to invention and to development of new products provide a special element to the growth equation. In both science and engineering, the United States appears to have the best programs. If this is so, the U.S. system of higher education may continue to provide a noticeable advantage over other countries.

But the principal raw material for U.S. colleges is the graduates of our elementary and secondary schools. Because so many of these students require extensive remedial education at the postsecondary level, our colleges and universities are less effective than they might be. The large number of underprepared American students also leads colleges to substitute foreign students, who have obtained their elementary and secondary school education abroad, for U.S. citizens.[26] Just as dependence on foreign sources of oil is not in our nation's best long-term interests, increasing dependence on other countries for our future engineers and scientists is problematic. If large numbers of these engineers and scientists begin returning to their home countries instead of staying in the United States, we may find ourselves facing a diminished supply of these talented and innovative people.[27]

Research confirms, then, what common sense has already told us: a well-educated and highly skilled workforce is critical to the success of our nation's future. In the next chapter, we examine just how well our schools are doing in producing that workforce.

# 2 | U.S. Education at a Crossroads

The pride of Americans in their educational system is fading. In the last century, the United States led the world in introducing broad-based schooling for its populace, giving American children from all walks of life educational opportunities unheard of in the rest of the world. The underlying belief was that increased years of schooling would promote individual and national development. Today, on the other hand, high dropout rates and low scores on state-administered academic tests call into question the effectiveness of our system. Even though most parents have favorable impressions of their own children's schools, they recognize that public schooling overall faces real problems.[1]

Instead of continuing to lead the world in educational attainment, we have fallen behind most other developed nations over the last thirty years, with consequences that will be felt over coming decades unless the situation can be reversed. The overview of the state of American education we provide here underscores the difficult task our policymakers face in once again making our education system competitive. We focus on two measures: the years of schooling completed and the skill levels achieved by students at different grade levels.

## Years of Schooling Completed

While policymakers and the public alike are concerned about school dropouts, the data on dropout rates are very limited, and it is difficult to find reliable information on the current situation and on the trends. A recent reconciliation of the data by Nobel Prize–winning economist James Heckman and his coauthor Paul LaFontaine, however, provides some eye-opening statistics.[2] According to

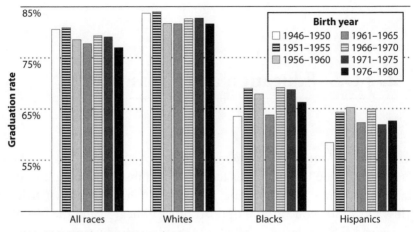

**2.1** U.S. Graduation Rates, by Race

their calculations, high school completion rates peaked at about 80 percent in the 1960s and have fallen by approximately four percentage points since then.[3] Among minorities, the statistics are even more dismal, with only about two-thirds of black and Hispanic students graduating from high school.

Figure 2.1 displays the overall pattern in graduation rates by race for cohorts of students born between 1946 and 1980. Such students would normally have graduated between roughly 1965 and 2000.[4] Tracing across the tops of the bars for each group shows the overall pattern in graduation rates, and the picture is not very encouraging. The generally low graduation rates and the lack of significant improvement—and this in spite of the greater economic rewards for those with diplomas—vividly demonstrates the challenge facing us. What is perhaps most disturbing about these patterns of student completion is that, despite concern on the part of the public and policymakers, they have not improved over the last several decades.

Figure 2.2 shows that the percentage of students completing high school and attending college increased rapidly following World War II, from about 37 percent prior to World War II to over 70 percent in the mid-1970s. But at this point, graduation rates for young adults ages twenty-five to twenty-nine—previously the prin-

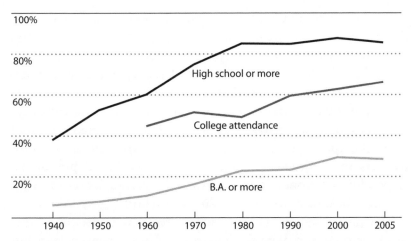

**2.2** High School/College Completion Rates and College Attendance Rates, Ages 25–29

cipal indicator of the power of U.S. schooling—stopped increasing.[5] These graduation rates have remained fairly stagnant for the last thirty years, and young people today are graduating from high school at about the same rate that they did in 1975.

The overall percentage of high school graduates in the country's labor force (adults of all ages) has continued to increase at a slow rate because younger people continue to graduate at higher rates than their fathers, mothers, grandfathers, and grandmothers did, thereby raising the overall average among all adults. However, this overall rate of completion for the entire adult population has also begun to level off. Moreover, although the gap between graduation rates for blacks and whites steadily narrowed during the postwar period, that trend has also come to a halt in more recent years.

It is possible to see the dropout problem as due more to students themselves, and their flawed decision making, than to the quality of schools or the educational opportunities they offer. But another perspective is also possible. What if the student is not learning enough to justify the time he or she spends in school? Perhaps it makes more sense to drop out of school and to enter the labor market. Thus, a key element to solving the dropout problem is to convince children that the time they spend in school is a worthwhile investment in their future. Our schools must ensure that students in every grade are learning enough to make staying in school the option that makes most economic sense to them.

While high school completion may have remained flat, the rate of college attendance (whether immediately after high school or following some interim period spent working or in the armed services) has increased, particularly since 1980. Yet as figure 2.2 indicates, the uptick in college attendance has not been entirely positive. As the college attendance rate has increased, presumably responding to economic incentives, college completion rates (attaining a B.A. or more) have begun to level off.

This phenomenon has been more noted than understood.[6] It is, however, consistent with the hypothesis that the new entrants into college are not as well prepared as their predecessors, and that a larger percentage of them therefore do not make it to graduation. This hypothesis is further bolstered by statistics showing the increasing prevalence of remediation courses in college, as more students begin college with not college-level courses, but classes designed to prepare them for college material.[7] States have recognized this trend and have mounted campaigns to ensure that all students are "college ready."[8]

Even with the relatively flat pattern of attainment, the overall stock of highly educated workers has continued to expand. The United States began its move toward an educated population before the beginning of the twentieth century, and each generation has obtained more schooling than the previous one. As a result, the average years of schooling completed by our population has continued to rise, and the United States still maintains its international superiority in terms of the education level of its entire workforce. But that advantage is rapidly slipping away. While the United States has seen flattening completion rates, countries around the world have been dramatically increasing the years of school completed by their students. Figure 2.3 shows secondary school completion rates for both developed countries (OECD) and a selection of other countries for youths graduating in 2003.[9] Although most Americans are convinced that the United States provides a far better education than other countries, these statistics show unmistak-

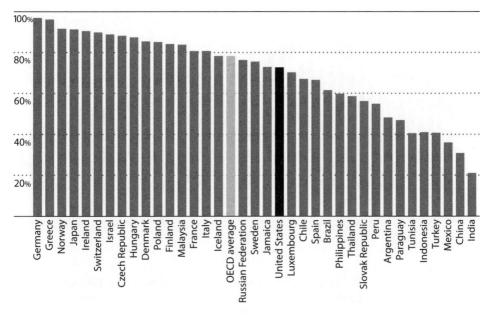

**2.3** Completion of Secondary School: World Rankings, 2003

ably that, at least in terms of the quantity of schooling, America no longer leads. The United States is not currently even near the top of world rankings in the percentage of its students who complete secondary school. As figure 2.3 demonstrates, U.S. completion rates are less than the average for the rest of the developed world. Countries like Jamaica, Poland, and Malaysia all have higher completion rates.

Rankings of countries by total years of schooling, including higher education, show the same trend. The colleges of the United States are the best regarded in the world, and the long tradition of broad college attendance does ensure a large pool of highly educated people. But, again, the United States does not currently rank anywhere near the top in expected total years of school attainment for today's young people. As figure 2.4 shows, the expected attainment of today's students is significantly below the average for developed countries. Other countries have jumped on the higher education bandwagon with a commitment that far exceeds America's. To be sure, these data refer only to current youth, and

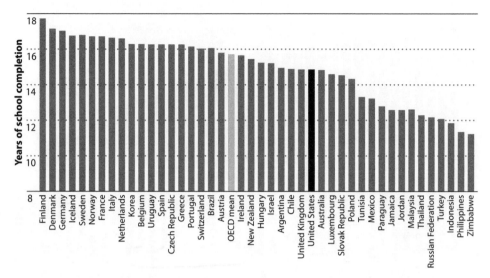

**2.4** Expected Total Years of School Completion, Including Higher Education:
World Rankings, 2003

other developed countries still have some distance to go before the
proportion of their entire adult population who have completed
secondary school equals or surpasses that of the United States.
Nevertheless, it is apparent that the United States is steadily losing
its advantage.

In sum, the leadership of the United States in school attainment
has turned around, whether measured in terms of high school or
college completion. By 1975, almost three-fourths of American students graduated from high school, far more than in most other
developed countries. That level, however, was reached three decades ago and has not significantly improved since then. The rest
of the developed world was late in investing in human capital and
universal schooling, but recently—largely due to the example set
by the United States—they have moved to expand the schooling
available in their countries. Today U.S. youth no longer lead world
rankings of high school completion or of expected total schooling.
The lesson is clear: we can no longer rest on our laurels. Given
current trends, a number of countries will have more educated
workforces than ours in the near future.

## Achievement Levels (or the Mastery of Cognitive Skills)

While the number of years students remain in school is important, equally critical are the knowledge and skills students gain while attending school. Policymakers and schools remain concerned about low high school graduation rates, but most of their efforts now focus on ensuring that children at each grade level learn certain skills, as measured by state-administered criterion-based tests. This concern that students master skills is perhaps most apparent in the provision of the federal No Child Left Behind Act (NCLB) that mandates full state accountability. It requires, in other words, that states measure performance of all of their students and that schools make acceptable yearly progress toward the goal of having all students reach the minimum proficiency levels in math, reading, and science by 2014.

NCLB is merely the most recent attention-getter regarding the quality of U.S. schools, even if it is the most widely recognized. The United States got its first wake-up call in 1957 following the Russian launch of *Sputnik* and Russia's early lead in space programs. This technological feat led many Americans to question the quality of their science instruction, and it dramatically reminded Americans that their world leadership in science and technology was not assured. These doubts soon blossomed into a much broader concern about the quality of American schools. Yet the country continues to struggle to bring students up to the desired level of proficiency, as both federal and state tests and assessments make clear.

We look primarily at the National Assessment of Educational Progress, or NAEP, a national standard performance measure that has been called the nation's report card, to see where our students stand today. We rely on NAEP scores for several reasons. The tests have been given on a consistent basis, so that scores in different years can validly be compared to determine if there has been any increase in the learning and mastery of cognitive skills. Scores are also available going back many years, so that long-term trends can be determined and evaluated. In contrast, the state tests not only

**TABLE 2.1**
Percentage of U.S. Public School Students Falling "Below Basic" in Reading, Math, and Science on NAEP Tests, 2005 and 2007

| Students | Reading Tests | | |
|---|---|---|---|
| | 4th Grade (2007) | 8th Grade (2007) | 12th Grade (2005) |
| All | 33 | 26 | 27 |
| White | 22 | 16 | 21 |
| Black | 54 | 45 | 46 |
| Hispanic | 50 | 42 | 40 |
| Students | Math Tests | | |
| | 4th Grade (2007) | 8th Grade (2007) | 12th Grade (2005) |
| All | 18 | 29 | 39 |
| White | 9 | 18 | 30 |
| Black | 36 | 53 | 70 |
| Hispanic | 30 | 45 | 60 |
| Students | Science Tests | | |
| | 4th Grade (2005) | 8th Grade (2005) | 12th Grade (2005) |
| All | 52 | 41 | 46 |
| White | 18 | 26 | 35 |
| Black | 62 | 72 | 81 |
| Hispanic | 55 | 65 | 70 |

vary from state to state, but have been given on a consistent basis in most states for only a relatively short period. Long-term assessments using the results of those tests would not only be impractical, given different standards and tests in the fifty states, but they would also be impossible in most instances because of the lack of consistent data over the long term even within states.

Unfortunately, the NAEP scores and trends paint a disturbing picture. Although the United States spends considerably more per pupil for K–12 education than almost any country in the world, large numbers of its students fall below even the "basic" level in reading, math, and science skills.[10]

As shown in table 2.1, over a quarter of twelfth grade students cannot read at the basic level, almost 40 percent have not learned

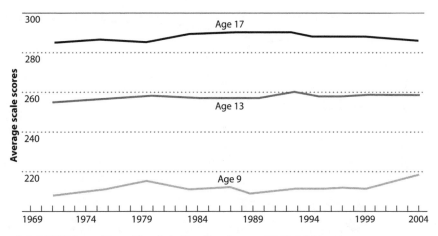

2.5 NAEP Long-Term Trends in Reading Scores, 1969–2004

basic math, and almost half fall short of basic skills in science. Black and Hispanic students do considerably worse. Almost half of twelfth grade African American students cannot read at the basic level, almost three-fourths cannot do basic math, and four out of five have not learned basic science. The failure pattern among Hispanic students is almost as bad. White students do significantly better, but even there the picture is distressing. For example, in math and science, approximately one-third of them fail to test at the basic level.

Worse yet is the lack of improvement over the past several decades (which we can trace because, since around 1970, the U.S. Department of Education has given the NAEP tests in mathematics, reading, and science to a random national sample of students at different ages).[11] The long-term trends in student achievement show that younger students have somewhat improved their skills in reading, math, and science since 1973, but these relatively higher levels of skills disappear by the time the students reach high school. While the trends for all three age groups are important, the trend for seventeen-year-olds is the most critical; whether they have struggled or been successful in earlier grades, children must have mastered skills by the time they leave school.

Figures 2.5, 2.6, and 2.7 show the NAEP long-term trends in average scale scores for nine-, thirteen-, and seventeen-year-old

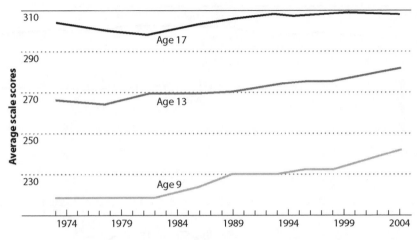

**2.6** NAEP Long-Term Trends in Math Scores, 1973–2004

students in reading, math, and science tests for roughly the last thirty years.[12]

As indicated, the youngest students, the nine-year-olds, fared the best, registering noticeable increases in reading and math, but only a slight increase in science. Thirteen-year-olds did not do quite as well, although they showed improvement in reading and math. Their science scores, on the other hand, remained stagnant over the thirty years.

The bad news is that by the time the nine- and thirteen-year-olds reached their third year of high school, most of the progress they had made in the earlier grades disappeared. The scores of the seventeen-year-old students were basically the same in 2004 as they were in 1973. Reading scale scores were exactly the same (285) in 2004 as they were 1973. Math scores increased from 304 in 1973 to 307 in 2004, a minor difference that is not statistically significant.[13] Science scores were the worst. NAEP reports long-term trends for science for the period 1969 through 1999, and during that period, the scores declined from 305 to 295, a statistically significant decrease. In short, the nation's students did not significantly improve over the thirty-year period on either reading or math, and they lost significant ground in science.

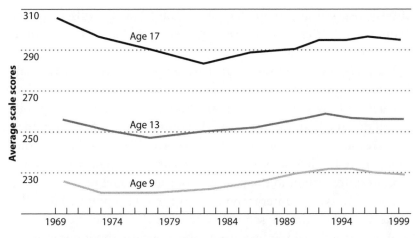

**2.7** NAEP Long-Term Trends in Science Scores, 1969–99

Discussions of achievement today tend to focus on the performance of students on state tests, a natural outgrowth of the NCLB legislation that sets all requirements in terms of each state's own tests. Under NCLB, individual states can decide what constitutes proficiency in their state—and they do so in quite varied ways, especially when it comes to the stringency of their standards.[14] Nevertheless, in almost every state, the proportion of students failing to meet state proficiency standards, particularly among poor and minority children, remains high, mirroring the results of the NAEP tests.[15]

There are two different perspectives on the trends in test scores. The first is simply that, regardless of the reasons for any changes over time, they reflect the skills of our labor force. Understood this way, the flat performance on the NAEP tests is of serious concern (particularly when matched against the poor performance on international tests). In 1970, the United States had a pool of approximately forty-six million public school students. In 2003, the pool was approximately forty-nine million. Representative samples of both groups took the NAEP tests, and students finishing high school in 2004 performed at roughly the same level as those students taking it almost thirty-five years earlier. Overall achievement had not improved, and young people entering the workforce in

2004 possessed approximately the same level of skills in math, reading, and science as those entering it in 1970. This finding seems incontrovertible.

The second way of looking at these scores is more controversial. This view notes that flat performance occurred despite the fact that our nation now spends more than three times as much per pupil, in real dollars, than we did in 1970. This matching of performance with resources strongly suggests—as we believe—that serious changes are needed because the schools are absorbing significantly more resources than in the past without improving results.

There are two counterarguments to these viewpoints. First, defenders of the current school system, such as the independent commentator Gerald Bracey, argue that concern about our schools is overstated, that achievement has actually improved, and that the flat trends are misleading. Specifically, they highlight the fact that the relative proportion of Hispanics in the student population has increased particularly dramatically over the period of observation of the NAEP long-term trends. Because Hispanics on average score below white students, their increased proportion can drag down the national average even if all scores stay the same or even increase a little.[16] However, this point, while mathematically true, has virtually nothing to do with the flatness of the overall trend in NAEP performance. Reweighting the NAEP scores of different ethnic groups so that the distribution of students is held constant yields virtually no change in the aggregate pattern of NAEP scores.[17]

A second counterargument, developed by former *New York Times* educational writer Richard Rothstein, is that the student population today is more disadvantaged than it was thirty years ago, meaning extra resources have been necessary to maintain the same achievement levels.[18] But the assertion that students are more disadvantaged is difficult to support. Table 2.2 identifies significant changes in the characteristics of families that have taken place over the last four decades—some commonly accepted as having negative implications for student achievement and some positive. On the negative side, the proportion of children living with both parents declined steadily from 85 percent in 1970 to 69 percent in 2000.

**TABLE 2.2**
Changes in Family Characteristics, 1970–2000

|  | 1970 | 1980 | 1990 | 2000 |
|---|---|---|---|---|
| Less favorable changes | | | | |
| Percentage of children under age 18 not living with both parents | 15 | 23 | 27 | 31 |
| Percentage of population ages 5–17 not speaking English at home | n.a. | 9 | 13 | 17 |
| Little Change | | | | |
| Percentage of children in poverty | 15 | 18 | 20 | 16 |
| More Favorable Changes | | | | |
| Percentage of population ages 25–29, high school graduate or more, | 74 | 85 | 86 | 88 |
| Percentage of families with three or more children | 36 | 23 | 20 | 15 |
| Preschool enrollment rate, 5-year-olds | 69 | 85 | 89 | 88 |
| Preschool enrollment rate, 4-year-olds | 28 | 46 | 56 | 65 |

*Source*: U.S. Bureau of the Census, Current Population Reports, various issues; U.S. Bureau of the Census (2007), table 223.

The percentage of children not speaking English at home also increased from 9 percent in 1980 to 17 percent in 2000, due mainly to an expanding Hispanic enrollment. But on the more positive side, poverty measures indicate little change in the proportion of economically disadvantaged students. From 1970 to 1990, the proportion of children living in poor families rose from 15 percent to 20 percent, although, by 2000, it had receded to 16 percent, not much different than in 1970. Family sizes have also fallen. In 1970, 36 percent of children lived in families with three or more children; by 2000, only 15 percent did. Parental education levels, regarded by many as the strongest predictor of student achievement, have also improved. Counting GED certificates, adults ages twenty-five to twenty-nine with a high school or greater level of schooling increased from 74 percent to 88 percent (up from 61 percent in 1960). Finally, enrollment in kindergarten and preschool programs increased dramatically over the period. By 2000, 88 percent of five-year-olds and 65 percent of four-year-olds were enrolled in kinder-garten and preschool programs, compared to 69 percent and 28 percent in 1970.

It is difficult to assess with any accuracy the impact of these op-posing family demographic trends. While extensive research, be-ginning with the famous Coleman Report (discussed in chapter 3) in 1966 and continuing through today, has demonstrated that dif-ferences in families' educational and economic circumstances are very important for student achievement,[19] most of these studies have not delved very far into the specific causal impacts on achieve-ment traceable to any particular set of family factors.[20] It remains unclear, therefore, whether the overall net effect of these trends has been to help or harm student achievement.

We can say, however, that no credible evidence exists showing that stagnant achievement over the last forty years is due in any significant respect to adverse changes in the demographics of the U.S. student population.[21]

## International Comparisons

If the level of quality indicated by state and national test scores is satisfactory, then it may not be too important that scores have remained flat for the last several decades. But are they satisfactory? To get some sense of how American students are doing relative to others, we can again turn to international comparisons. In 1963 and 1964, the International Association for the Evaluation of Edu-cation Achievement (IEA) administered the first of a series of math-ematics tests to a group of countries. These assessments faced a variety of problems: it was difficult to develop an equivalent test across countries with different school structures, curricula, and languages; difficult to select populations to be tested; and difficult to select the nations to participate. The undertaking did, however, prove the feasibility of such testing and set in motion a process to expand and improve it. Subsequent testing, sponsored both by IEA and more recently by the OECD, has included both math and sci-ence, as well as additional tests in reading, and has expanded the

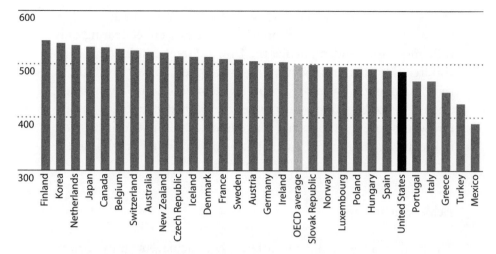

**2.8** Mathematics Average Scores, PISA, 2003

group of participating countries. The general model for both organizations has been to develop a common assessment instrument
for different age groups of students and to work at obtaining a
representative group of students to take the tests.

The international picture is not comforting for the United States.
OECD began to conduct its PISA tests (Programme for International Student Assessment) in 2000. These tests provide standard
assessments in math, science, and reading for fifteen-year-olds, and
are now administered on a three-year cycle. Figure 2.8 shows results for mathematics from the PISA tests administered in 2003.
The United States trails most developed countries, ranking twenty-
fifth out of the thirty participating countries. The United States
has done slightly better in the other subjects—placing twentieth in
science and sixteenth in reading—but still ranks in the bottom half
in all three subjects.[22]

These differences in performance are truly large. The average
American student would be at the twenty-seventh percentile of
math performance in Finland or Korea. Closer to home, our fifteen-
year-olds would be at just the thirty-first percentile of Canadian
fifteen-year-olds in 2003.

This performance picture has not changed much over time.[23]
From the earliest testing in the 1960s through today, the United

States has generally placed below average.[24] In the early years, it could be argued that many foreign countries were educating only their most able students while the United States educated all of its children, but that argument no longer applies; as described, today the United States has more dropouts before the completion of secondary schooling than most other developed countries. Importantly, the foreign experience has demonstrated that it is possible to greatly expand school participation and attainment while at the same time maintaining high achievement.

## Achievement Gaps

The final area we examine is differences in achievement by various racial and ethnic groups. The de jure segregated schools that survived until the *Brown* decision in 1954 (and after) have become less segregated; nevertheless, black students continue to perform at levels far below those of white children on virtually any measure of academic achievement.[25] This achievement gap has narrowed over time on some measures, but on others, it has remained virtually unchanged for over twenty-five years.

Until recently, data on graduation rates appeared to show some closing of the black-white gap. School completion data compiled by the U.S. Department of Education suggest that a 12.5 percentage point gap in high school graduation rates for black and white students in 1980 had shrunk to 7 percentage points by 2005.[26] However, that seemingly favorable trend may be more an artifact of the data than a reality. According to the careful study by Heckman and LaFontaine, much of the apparent narrowing of the gap results from treating recipients of GED certificates as high school graduates. The GED (General Educational Development) uses a test that high school dropouts can take to establish that they know what a typical graduate knows and thus qualify for an equivalency diploma. What is the difference, some might say, but the authors argue that receipt of a GED certificate is not the same as graduating from high school with a regular diploma. In the labor market, workers with a GED resemble high school dropouts much more

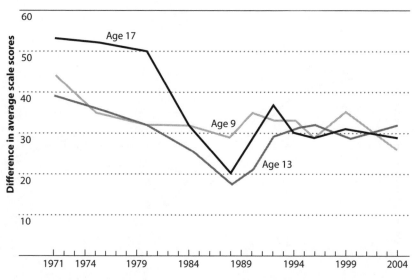

**2.9** White-Black Achievement Gap, Long-Term Trends in NAEP Reading Scores

than graduates, which is not particularly surprising since it is a short test that requires little preparation on average.[27] When GED recipients (who are disproportionately black) are eliminated from the calculations and several other problems with the data are corrected, Heckman and LaFontaine conclude that "there is little convergence in high school graduation rates between whites and minorities over the past 35 years."[28]

In any event, there is an even larger problem than the graduation trends. Since the beginning of NAEP testing, there have been large and persistent gaps in black-white achievement and mastery of cognitive skills, such as reading and mathematics.[29]

As shown by average scale scores (see figures 2.9 and 2.10) these gaps did shrink somewhat during the 1970s and early 1980s, but they have not significantly narrowed for the last two decades. For the critical seventeen-year-olds, the reading gap in the mid-1980s was about the same as it was in 2004. It had narrowed for a few years in the early 1980s, but progress stopped by 1990. In math, the same trends hold true. In 2004, the gap was 29 scale score points, only slightly smaller than the 1984 gap of 32 points. The

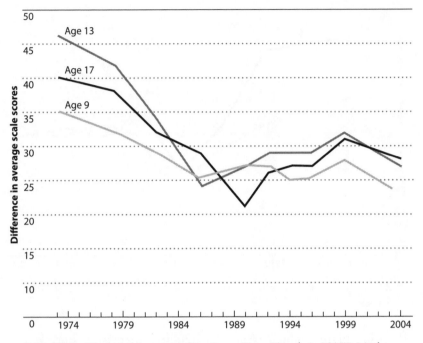

**2.10** White-Black Achievement Gap, Long-Term Trends in NAEP Math Scores

math gap also narrowed for a while in the mid-1980s, but has remained, with some variations, at much the same level since 1988.

We have shown the gap for seventeen-year-olds on all three tests by presenting average scale scores, but it can also be expressed in standard deviations. Using this measure results in the same trends, but enables us to describe the size of the gap in perhaps more understandable terms.

Figure 2.11 shows that black students score between three-quarters of a standard deviation and one standard deviation below white students on the NAEP reading and math tests. Statistically, this means that less than a quarter of black students perform above the average score for white students. Put another way, the average black student scores at a level similar to the bottom quartile of white students. On the math test, black students are about one standard deviation behind, meaning that the typical black student is achieving at a level equal to the sixteenth percentile of whites.

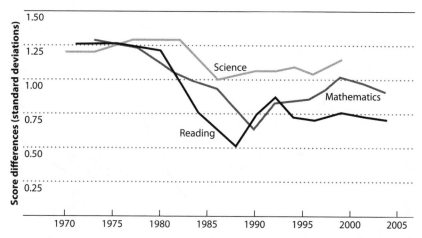

**2.11** Trends in White-Black Achievement Gap for Seventeen-Year-Olds (in standard deviations)

The magnitude of these gaps can also be expressed in yet another way. The NAEP tests are calibrated so that the performance on tests at different grades is designed to fall on the same continuous numerical scale. Using the same scale, student scores should get progressively better as they progress from grade to grade. For example, the average difference between a fourth grader and an eighth grader is roughly one standard deviation. Therefore, if the average black student is three-quarters of a standard deviation behind the average white student, that gap is equivalent to approximately three years of schooling. If the student is one standard deviation behind, then the difference is four years of schooling. These are truly huge differences.[30]

Similar achievement gaps exist between white students and other historically oppressed minority groups, as well as between poor children (as determined by eligibility for the federal free and reduced lunch program) and more affluent children. Figures 2.12 and 2.13 show the pattern of achievement gaps for Hispanic and white children. Both indicate very large gaps that have not tended to close over time. In reading, the size of the gap in 2004 is similar to what it was in 1980. While it narrowed for a few years, it has widened since 1990. In math, the story is much the same.

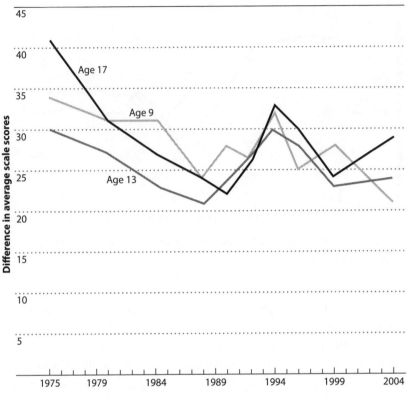

**2.12** White-Hispanic Achievement Gap, Long-Term Trends in NAEP Reading Scores

The issue of minority achievement is most pressing in the nation's largest school districts. Over 70 percent of students in the largest twenty-five districts are minorities.[31] Or, looked at from a different perspective, almost 30 percent of all black students and over a quarter of all Hispanics attend schools in one of the largest fifty districts of the nation. These large urban districts thus face disproportionate challenges, being charged with closing the significant achievement gaps of their mostly minority students.

As an overall summary, the nation has made little progress over the last thirty years in closing achievement gaps. And these gaps will likely have long-term consequences for the well-being of not only black and Hispanic families, but also the nation as a whole. Given the importance of cognitive skills for earnings, achievement

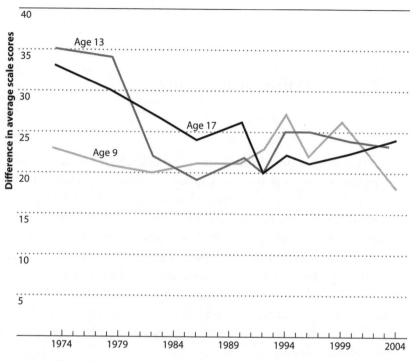

**2.13** White-Hispanic Achievement Gap, Long-Term Trends in NAEP Math Scores

gaps presage continuing problems with economic separation, and these differences are likely to persist into future generations as the offspring of poorly educated parents themselves have trouble achieving in school.

# 3 | The Political Responses

This chapter examines how the political branches of government—the executive branch and the legislature—have responded to the crisis in American schools; later chapters deal with the responses of the judicial branch.[1] Historically, school policy has been most influenced by the elective branches, because it is the governors and state legislatures that propose and pass the laws, regulate the delivery of educational services, set the educational standards for schools and students, and establish the necessary funding systems. Most important, it is within the parameters set by them, both fiscal and nonfiscal, that large-scale education reform is undertaken.

Policymakers and much of the public have been on notice that large numbers of U.S. students and schools have not been living up to most expectations for at least a quarter of a century. Although the launching of *Sputnik* in 1957 dramatically raised awareness among the American public that U.S. leadership in science was threatened, it was probably the publication of a 1983 government report entitled *A Nation at Risk* by the National Commission on Excellence in Education that sparked the period of public concern regarding education that continues unabated to this day.[2] The commission used strong language to describe its concerns, dramatically stating: "If an unfriendly foreign power had attempted to impose on America the mediocre educational performance that exists today, we might well have viewed it as an act of war. As it stands, we have allowed this to happen to ourselves."[3] It went on to place blame squarely on the schools: "We conclude that declines in educational performance are in large part the result of disturbing inadequacies in the way the educational process itself is often conducted."[4]

Although this report was longer on diagnosis of the problem than on solutions, it served as an important catalyst for significant reform efforts.[5] Unfortunately, as highlighted in the previous chapter, these reforms have not resulted in significant improvements in student outcomes—the central focus of A Nation at Risk.

State lawmakers have taken five principal approaches in addressing problems of low student achievement. First and foremost, states have passed measures and appropriation bills that dramatically increased spending for K–12 education. Second, they have adopted equalizing mechanisms to reduce disparities in funding for school districts. Third, beginning in the late 1980s, states began to adopt academic standards and to hold schools and school districts accountable for meeting them, a policy approach now embedded in both state and federal law by NCLB. Fourth, states have experimented with alternative ways to bring qualified teachers into schools, including changing the old certification rules and promoting alternative entry paths (beyond regular colleges of education) into the teaching profession. Finally, and most recently, states have begun to experiment with school choice programs, including charter schools and vouchers. We examine each of these approaches in detail next.

## Increased Spending and Resources for K–12 Education

Strongly influenced by a powerful education lobby but also bolstered by a pliant electorate, legislatures have first and foremost responded to the stagnant performance of American students by substantially increasing spending on schools. From 1960 to 2005, spending per pupil on K–12 education in the United States rose dramatically, from $375 to $9,305. Inflationary increases account for a large part of this growth. Adjusted to 2007 dollars, the spending growth would be from $2,606 in 1960 to $9,910 in 2005. But this still represents nearly a quadrupling of per-pupil expenditures during this period, giving school districts today almost four times the purchasing power they had in 1960.[6] Figure 3.1 shows the growth in real spending per pupil. While there have been a few periods of slower growth, such as the early 1990s,

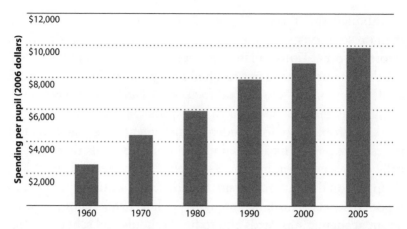

**3.1** Spending Per Pupil in United States, 1960–2005 (adjusted for inflation)

there is no doubt about the overall picture: sizeable increases in the resources for schools.

To put these amounts into a broader context, the United States spends more than most other countries in the world on the education of its children. As shown in figure 3.2, cumulative per-pupil expenditures on elementary and secondary school students in Fin-

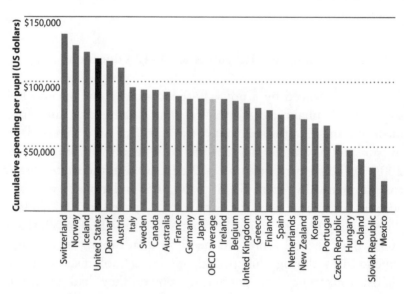

**3.2** Cumulative Per-Pupil Expenditures for K–12 Education in United States and Other Developed Countries, 2001

TABLE 3.1

Public School Resources in the United States, 1960 vs. 2000

|  | 1960 | 1980 | 2000 |
|---|---|---|---|
| Pupil–teacher ratio[a] | 25.8 | 18.7 | 16.0 |
| percentage of teachers with master's degree or more[b] | 23.5 | 49.6 | 56.8 |
| Median years of teaching experience[b] | 11 | 12 | 14 |
| Real expenditure/ADA[c] | $2,541 | $5,823 | $8,691 |

*Sources:*

[a] U.S. Department of Education (2007), table 61.

[b] National Education Association (2003). Note data refer to 1960–61, 1980–81, and 2000–2001 school years. See U.S. Department of Education (2007), table 66.

[c] U.S. Department of Education (2007), table 167. ADA is students in average daily attendance. All figures are put in constant 2005–6 dollars using the consumer price index adjusted to a school-year basis.

land, Korea, and Japan, whose scores on the PISA exams place them at the very top of the world rankings, are only 60–75 percent of what the United States spends per pupil across the primary and secondary years. Germany and France spend about three-quarters of what the United States does.[7] (With higher education spending, the relative spending disparities get even larger.)

This unprecedented commitment of financial resources to education has led to, among other things, smaller class sizes and a multiplicity of special personnel and programs. As shown in table 3.1, from 1960 to 2000, the number of teachers for every pupil increased by more than 60 percent, the percentage of teachers with a master's degree or higher more than doubled, and the median experience of teachers increased by almost 30 percent. Pressures on salaries from competing industries, a commonly noted element of spending increases in education, cannot explain these dramatic increases in personnel and the movement to teachers with more qualifications.[8]

These increases are remarkable, but it still can be difficult to understand where all the money has gone. A simple example focusing on a single school will illustrate the huge increase in educational resources that has taken place in the last forty or so years. In 1962, one of the authors graduated from a rural school in the upper Midwest with approximately 190 students in grades 1 through 12. As indicated in table 3.2, in 1962, its professional staff consisted of 9 full-time people—3 elementary school teachers and 6 secondary school teachers, 2 of whom doubled as the school district's superintendent and school principal. By 2007, total enrollment in the school, now K–12, had declined to 106 students. However, its licensed staff had increased to 14.6 full-time equivalents. Additionally, the size of the school's physical plant had been significantly expanded. In short, in 2007, the school's licensed staff had increased by over 60 percent, while its enrollment had declined to a little over half its 1962 level.

This school's experience is representative of the national picture. As shown in figure 3.3, the growth in instructional staff tracked the growth in students from 1920 through 1970. From 1970 to 1990, however, total enrollment fell, while instructional staff continued to grow, especially during the 1980s. When enrollment turned around and began growing again, instructional staff grew even faster. This growth in personnel—which is reinforced strongly by growth in noninstructional staff and spending—underlies much of the spending growth over this period.[9]

The problem, we stress, is not that education spending has significantly increased. The world is a more complex and technical place than it was forty years ago, and our students must be prepared to compete in a global economy in which our competitors grow stronger every year. We should be striving to improve our education and be willing to pay the necessary costs. The problem is that we are not getting much in return for our massive financial commitment. While adults in the system may have seen more and improved employment opportunities, children have not been obvious beneficiaries. During the same period that educational expenditures and school resources have been significantly increasing, student achievement in reading, math, and science has remained essentially flat. Sadly, our students are still performing at 1960 and 1970 levels, which is surely not what the nation bargained for in return for its huge investment.

To be sure, it is possible that the spending increases are not as large as they appear because so great a share of them has gone

**TABLE 3.2**
Staffing and Enrollment, Munich Public Schools, 1962 vs. 2007

| *1962* [a] | *2007* [b] |
|---|---|
| *Elementary* | *Elementary* |
| Grades 1–2 teacher | Kindergarten teacher |
| Grades 3–4 teacher | Grades 1–2 teacher |
| Grades 5–6 teacher | Grades 3–4 teacher |
| | Grades 5–6 teacher |
| | Music teacher |
| | Paraprofessional |
| | Teacher aide / physical education |
| *Secondary* | *Secondary* |
| Grades 7–8 teacher | Music teacher |
| Social science teacher / superintendent | Social science teacher |
| Math teacher / principal | Math / physical education teacher |
| Music teacher | Technology edncation teacher |
| Science teacher / coach | Science teacher |
| English / foreign language teacher | Family and consumer science teacher |
| | Math teacher / librarian |
| | Computer applications and business teacher |
| | *Administration* |
| | Superintendent |
| | Secondary principal and activities administrator |
| | Elementary principal |
| | *Part-Time* |
| | Title 1 teacher |
| | Learning disabilities teacher |
| | Counselor |
| | Speech disabilities teacher |
| | Social worker |
| | Regional technician |

[a] Enrollment: 190; total professional staff: 9 full-time.
[b] Enrollment: 106; total professional staff: 18 full-time, 6 part-time.

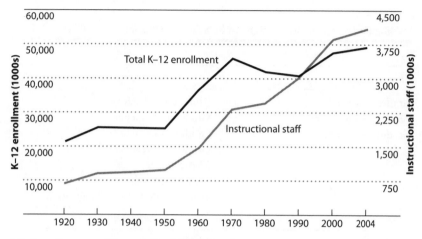

**3.3** Enrollment and Instructional Staff Trends, 1920–2004

into special education, where achievement gains are not as likely to be documented or reported. It is also possible that over the years, the pool of students has become more disadvantaged, making them more difficult (and expensive) to educate (though the previous chapter suggests that whether students are more disadvantaged is not clear). But while factors like this may partly explain stagnant performance, they do not alter the general conclusion that increased spending has yielded little in terms of improved student achievement.

### Increases in Special Education Costs

Let us further examine the claim that the large increase in education costs relates to special education programs and personnel for students with physical and mental disabilities. There is no question that resources devoted to special education have risen significantly since the mid-1970s. One would expect concomitant increases in the achievement of these students, but until recently, special education students tended either not to take standardized tests or not to have their results reported. Thus, even if special education programs have improved student achievement, we may simply not know about it.[10]

Concerns about the education of children with physical and mental disabilities were translated into federal law with the enactment of the Education for All Handicapped Children Act in 1975. This act prescribed a series of diagnostic requirements, counseling activities, and educational services for handicapped students. To implement this and subsequent laws and regulations, school systems expanded staff and programs and in many cases developed entirely new administrative structures to handle "special education." The general thrust of the educational services has been to provide regular classroom instruction where possible (to "mainstream"), as well as specialized instruction to deal with specific needs. The result has been significant growth in the number of students classified as requiring special education services. Between 1977 and 2006, the percentage of students classified as disabled increased from 8.3 percent to 13.8 percent.[11] The number of special education teachers increased at an even faster rate.

The magnitude of special education spending and its growth, however, are insufficient to explain the mismatch between spending and performance. Using a standard estimate of the cost differences between regular and special education reveals that the rise in the number of special education students between 1980 and 1990 (the period of most rapid growth in special education placements) explains less than 20 percent of the total growth in expenditures during that period.[12] Separate analyses for individual states show some variations in state spending, and at times suggest larger impacts on cost growth than seen nationally, but in no state is the magnitude sufficient to explain a significant portion of the overall spending growth during the period.[13] Thus, while special education programs have led to higher costs, they remain a relatively small portion of the total spending on schools and of the increase in educational expenditures since the 1960s.

Estimates of differential costs are not readily available for other programs added since 1960, such as language instruction for immigrants and nonacademic programs like sports, art, or music. No evidence suggests, however, that these are sufficiently large or costly to explain the magnitude of spending increases.

## *The Impact of Increased Spending on Student Achievement*

If a school superintendent had been asked in 1960 whether she could significantly improve student performance with four times her current funding, her answer undoubtedly would have been an emphatic yes. Yet the aggregate spending and achievement trends for the last forty years show that she would have been wrong. This may seem a surprising and counterintuitive result,[14] but the lack of any consistent relationship between more spending and better test scores has been documented time and time again, both in actual practice and in hundreds of scientific studies based on empirical data.

Perhaps the most dramatic test of whether spending more money leads to higher achievement occurred in the Kansas City, Missouri, school district (hereafter, KCMSD) from the mid-1980s to the mid-1990s. In 1986, a federal judge decided to do something about the abysmally low test scores of black children in the KCMSD on nationally normed standardized tests. Relying on his authority to "desegregate" the school district, Judge Russell Clark ordered KCMSD administrators to determine what it would take to raise student test scores to the national average and then ordered the state of Missouri to pay the lion's share of the necessary costs.[15] To further finance this undertaking, he ordered the KCMSD school board to double the property tax rate in the school district and declared invalid any state laws limiting the amount of such tax increases.[16] Under Judge Clark's orders, over $2 billion in additional state and local funds were made available to the school district of thirty-seven thousand students over the next twelve years.[17]

As a result of its extraordinary court-ordered funding, the KCMSD went from spending at the national average to spending more per pupil than any of the 280 largest school districts in the country.[18] Although student enrollment remained relatively constant, the district's annual budget ballooned from $125 million in fiscal year 1985 to $233 million in 1988 to $432 million by 1992.[19] While school districts in the rest of Missouri were spending $4,500 per student, the KCMSD was spending almost three times as much.[20]

Hundreds of millions of dollars were spent on state-of-the-art facilities, including fifteen new and fifty-four renovated schools, a 2,000-square-foot planetarium, a twenty-five-acre farm with an air-conditioned meeting room for 104 people, a model United Nations wired for simultaneous language translation, broadcast-capable radio and television studios, movie editing and screening rooms, a temperature-controlled art gallery, a 3,500-square-foot dust-free diesel mechanics room, a robotics lab, a 1,875-square-foot elementary school animal room for use in a zoo project, and a mock courtroom (complete with judge's chamber and jury deliberation room).[21] In addition to magnificent facilities, Judge Clark ordered large across-the-board raises for teachers, cafeteria workers, and janitors; the hiring of hundreds of additional teachers and staff; the purchase of thousands of computers; special programs for at-risk students; and before- and after-school programs. He also established pupil-to-teacher ratios of twelve or thirteen to one, the lowest of any major school district in the nation.[22] He made every school in the district a magnet school, and ensured they were appropriately equipped and staffed.[23] The district had so much money to spend it did not know what to do with it all. It bought hundreds of thousands of dollars worth of 286- and 386-generation computers, then let them sit on storeroom shelves until they became obsolete. Its administration had three to five times more employees than other districts of similar size.[24]

Despite having almost the equivalent of a blank check, the KCMSD failed to raise the scores of its students on nationally normed tests or otherwise improve achievement.[25] As Paul Ciotti summed up the Kansas City debacle: "The results were dismal. Test scores did not rise; the black-white gap did not diminish; and there was less, not greater, integration."[26] And this grim result occurred despite the fact that "Kansas City did all the things that educators had always said needed to be done to increase student achievement—it reduced class size, decreased teacher workload, increased teacher pay, and dramatically expanded spending per pupil—but none of it worked."[27]

Kansas City no doubt represents a sad example, but it is not as unique as one might hope. A range of other districts, including the

Abbott districts of New Jersey, discussed in a subsequent chapter, have also been given a license to dream. Unfortunately, the dreams have seldom helped the students.[28]

These results have also been confirmed by hundreds of different studies estimating the relationship between resources and achievement using accepted statistical approaches. Although they do not agree on every point, the majority of the studies have found that differences in either the absolute spending level or spending increases bear little or no consistent relationship to differences in student achievement.[29]

Perhaps the best-known study on this issue was *Equality of Educational Opportunity*, commonly called the "Coleman Report" after its lead author, University of Chicago professor James Coleman.[30] In 1964, Congress funded this massive study to assess why the black-white achievement gap persisted ten years after the *Brown* case had been decided. A finding that surprised many, including Coleman himself, was that variation in school resources had little or nothing to do with differences in student achievement, and that almost all the test score gap was attributable to the widely varying social and economic conditions of black and white citizens.[31]

The findings of the Coleman Report were extremely controversial, but since its publication in 1966, a vast literature on spending and related resources (such as class size, teacher experience, and teacher education) and on other effects on achievement has confirmed many of the report's original conclusions.

Begin with pupil–teacher ratios: almost three-quarters of all studies find that they bear no significant relationship to achievement. The studies that do find a statistically significant relationship disagree on whether a higher pupil–teacher ratio has a negative or a positive impact on achievement.[32] The now-famous STAR study from Tennessee, a random assignment experimental study conducted during the 1980s, found that reducing class size has a positive influence on student achievement, and it is repeatedly cited by advocates of smaller classes.[33] But in stark contrast to this study are not only hundreds of other studies reaching the opposite conclusion, but also the disappointing results of California's multi-billion-dollar effort to reduce class sizes in grades K–3, the largest such program by far in the country.[34] Moreover, programs to reduce class size are the most expensive type of school reform, involving as they do both additional operational and capital costs. Lost in the debate has been the fact that even the gains postulated by the supporters of class size reduction are truly modest and unlikely to be worth the tremendous expense of such programs.

The vast majority of available studies—over 90 percent—also find that the level of a teacher's education has no statistically significant positive effect on students' achievement. Teacher experience has historically been thought to influence performance more strongly, but recent studies have consistently found that the impact of experience is concentrated in the first year or two of teaching, and that additional experience results in few or no gains.[35] These studies on student achievement vary in quality, but once we adjust for the quality of the study, the lack of a systematic relationship between resources and achievement becomes even more evident.[36]

Teachers' salaries also appear to have no consistent influence on students' achievement, largely because the factors that determine teachers' pay—experience and education level—themselves have no consistent influence on achievement. A teacher who has been successful in improving her students' achievement is as likely to have a low salary as a high salary.[37] Further, since salaries make up the largest component of school district expenditures, it is not surprising that variations in instructional expenditures also have little consistent relationship with achievement.[38]

Another piece of evidence that education spending and achievement bear little relationship to each other is the lack of any significant correlation between what states spend on education and what their pupils achieve. States vary widely in what they spend on schooling. In 2004, per-pupil spending ranged from a low of $5,337 in Utah to a high of $14,263 in New Jersey.[39] Utah spends significantly less than the rest of the nation, but from Arizona and Oklahoma at the bottom through the top of the range, there is a reasonably steady and consistent increase in the distribution of expenditures by the states. And even though there is some movement over time in the relative rankings of the states, the overall variation across states was not very different in 2004 than it was in 1970.[40]

In part, these differences in spending clearly represent variations in the cost of living across states. But when the spending figures are adjusted to take these variations into account, spending still varies from $11,554 in adjusted dollars in Vermont to $4,756 in Utah.[41] Whether figures are adjusted or not, the story is still the startling variation that exists, with top spending states spending over twice as much per student as those at the bottom. If the level of spending were related to achievement, we would expect significantly higher achievement in states that spend more. What we see instead, when NAEP scores in reading and mathematics in each state are correlated with its per-pupil spending, is no significant relationship between performance and spending.[42] This finding remains true when regression analysis is employed to take other factors into account, such as the parents' education level, changes in spending between 1992 and 2002, and increases in test scores between the fourth and eighth grades. Moreover, differences in the proportion of school funding derived from local or state sources also appear to have no bearing on performance.[43]

In summary, whether one looks at increases in spending over a long period of time or variations in spending between school districts or states, there is little or no evidence that higher spending is related to better achievement. The lessons to be drawn from these patterns, or, more accurately, the lack of any patterns, seem inescapable. Simply spending more dollars has not resulted in significant improvements in achievement,[44] and it would be folly to continue along this track. We do not mean that legislatures ought to reduce their financial commitment to education, or call a halt to any further increases in education spending. But the United States already spends significantly more per child on education than other developed countries in the world, without comparable results. We must devise an education and finance system that results in wiser and more efficient use of the funds we already have, rather than simply continue to add more funds to the existing system each year. The proposal we outline later in this book shows how to use school funds to promote better decision making and higher achievement.

Many in the education community have belittled the conclusion that increased spending is not the answer to problems of poor student achievement; they cast it as the "money never matters" argument and raise it as a straw man to be beaten down in debates over education reform.[45] The research, of course, does not say that "money never matters." Nor does it say that "money cannot matter." It simply underscores the fact that decisions made in schools, within the existing system of constraints and incentives, have blunted any benefits of added funds, with the result that more spending on schools has not been translated into substantially better results.

Fortunately, there is mounting evidence that money, if spent appropriately, can have a significant effect. For example, one of the authors has found in his own research that the quality of a child's teacher is critical to his or her performance in school. This finding is confirmed by other analyses of student performance that show clear differences in learning gains for students with "good" teachers compared to those for other students with less effective teachers.[46] But this same research also reinforces the findings about resources already discussed, because it finds no consistent relationship between these "good" teachers and their level of education or years of experience, the usual means of evaluating the quality of a teaching staff (or certainly the factors determining their pay). Teacher quality—measured by gains in student achievement—simply is not consistently related to these characteristics of teachers (except for the effect of the first year of teaching experience). The challenge is to devise a system that uses money to ensure that there are effective teachers in the classroom, not teachers with qualities that bear little relationship to student achievement.

## Increased Equity in Funding for K–12 Education

A second major thrust of education finance reform over the last several decades, spurred on to a significant extent by the courts, has been to make funding systems more equitable—that is, to reduce disparities in the educational opportunities available to students within each state, most often measured in terms of the per-pupil expenditures in the school or school district.[47] Because variations in spending or increased spending have had little or no consistent impact on student achievement, there is no reason to conclude that policies designed to reduce such disparities are likely to raise student achievement. Nevertheless, since equity considerations have been at the heart of most changes to school funding formulas over the years, it is necessary to look closely at these reforms.

Historically, these efforts have concentrated on reducing disparities in education spending between districts with high property values—and more taxable wealth—and those with low property values—and less taxable wealth. In its simplest terms, the reform seeks to increase the "horizontal" equity—equal treatment of equals—in funding across the state's school districts. At the same time, states have made efforts to provide equal educational opportunities for all children by channeling greater resources to disadvantaged or at-risk children. This is often referred to as "vertical" equity—the underlying premise being that providing equal opportunities for at-risk children (those deemed more difficult and expensive to educate) requires greater and not merely equal funding.[48]

### Development of State Funding Formulas to Increase "Horizontal" Equity

The most significant changes to state education funding formulas and laws have addressed significant disparities in per-pupil spending between school districts that cannot be readily justified by higher local costs. School funding is derived almost entirely from a combination of state, local, and federal funding, with state and local funding usually making up at least 90 percent of the total and federal funding most of the rest. In 2002, three-quarters of the local school funds raised nationwide were from local property taxes.[49] It is the use of this tax that gives rise to significant spending disparities between districts in many states. School districts that enjoy significant property wealth can raise more tax revenues for their schools than school districts that are property-poor if they levy at the same tax rate, and sometimes even if they levy at a lower rate. The disparities that resulted were often striking, historically allowing some property-rich school districts to spend four times as much per pupil as "property-poor" districts.[50] As a result, beginning as early as the 1920s, and accelerating in the 1970s with the filing of "equity lawsuits" in state courts, most legislatures have modified their school funding formulas to reduce these disparities.

The popular rationale behind more recent attention to school funding and the local property tax is that the quality of a child's education should not depend on the wealth of his or her neighbors or of the district in which he or she resides. This principle was a significant part of the intellectual backdrop to the court cases involving equity, and was forcefully raised in the seminal work on equity in school finance, *Private Wealth and Public Education*, by John Coons, William Clune, and Stephen Sugarman.[51] These lawyer-scholars laid out the rationale and arguments for increased judicial involvement in determining school spending based on equity considerations.

Although court cases beginning in the 1970s brought significant media and other attention to these disparities, states had taken steps long before then to ameliorate these differences in their school funding formulas. In the 1920s, New York introduced the idea of a "foundation" funding formula, sometimes called a Strayer-Haig plan after the authors of the New York innovation.[52] Under the foundation formula, the state provides equalizing grants to local districts so that poor districts have more funds for schools than they would be able to raise based on their low property tax wealth. The state typically declares a foundation level, coupled with a base tax rate that it expects all districts to set. It then calculates state funding for each district to ensure that all districts have revenues equal to or greater than the foundation amount, assuming they levy at least the base tax rate (sometimes referred to as the "minimum tax effort").[53] For example, assume that a state sets a base tax rate of 2 percent and a foundation level of $5,000 per pupil. Any district with a property tax base of at least $250,000 per pupil would on its own be able to raise the $5,000 with a 2 percent tax. However, if a school district had a property tax base less than $250,000, the state equalization grant would make up the difference between $5,000 and what the local district could raise with a 2 percent tax. For example, a district with property wealth of $100,000 per pupil would be able to raise $2,000 with a 2 percent tax, and the state would then contribute $3,000 per pupil in an equalization grant to get the district's funding up to the foundation amount.

What if the district is wealthy and can raise more than the foundation level? In that case, the state might simply provide no aid to the wealthy district and allow it to raise whatever it could on its own for its schools. Or, less commonly, it could require the local district to send to the state some or all of the excess tax revenue above $5,000 per pupil for redistribution to less wealthy districts.[54] If a district wants to spend more than $5,000 per student, it is typically on its own. A low wealth district wanting to spend more than $5,000 per student could set its tax rate above 2 percent, and its spending would be the foundation amount of $5,000 plus its property tax base multiplied by how much its tax rate exceeds 2 percent. For example, the $100,000 per student district that set a tax rate of 3 percent would have revenues of $6,000 per student (the foundation amount of $5,000 plus 1 percent of $100,000). A wealthier district, i.e., the $250,000 one, would realize $7,500 (3 percent of $250,000).

Although foundation plans are the most common way of dealing with funding disparities, other plans have also been adopted by states to ensure some level of minimum funding for every school district or to ease disparities that result from differing taxes bases. The least complicated is a flat grant from the state, which provides the same amount to all districts; any local spending above the grant amount depends upon the individual district's property wealth and tax rate. A version of this plan adjusts the amount of the grant according to factors that result in higher costs in some districts than others, such as pupil handicaps, sparse population density, or grade level.

Another method of allocating funding between districts is through "district power equalization."[55] Under this approach, the state permits each district below some level of property tax wealth to obtain revenues as if it had the state guaranteed level of wealth, such as the property wealth of the district at the seventy-fifth percentile ranking in property wealth per pupil. Any district below this guaranteed level that levied at the same tax rate receives equalizing funds from the state to enable it to have the same revenue level per student as that which would be generated by multiplying the tax rate times the state guaranteed tax base, rather than the district's actual tax base. This plan is sometimes called "variable matching" because the state grant to the district depends directly on the district's choice of tax rate, whereas the state grant under a foundation plan does not depend on the particular tax rate that a district chooses. As in the foundation plan, a district with wealth at or above the seventy-fifth percentile would not receive a state grant and would have only the revenues generated from its own tax base. In a less common version, such as Texas' "Robin Hood" statute, the wealthy district might have to return to the state for distribution to property-poor districts any "excess revenues" above those that would accrue at the guaranteed tax base. In all of these types of formulas, except for the flat grants, the revenue available to the district relies on both the level of the guaranteed tax base and the choices of different communities as to what rate to tax their residents.

Finally, a substantial part of state funding may flow to districts in the form of "categorical" grants. These grants are distributed to particular districts for specific purposes, such as special education programs, pupil transportation, and programs for at-risk children. There is great variety in how these funds are distributed, and not all districts may receive them.[56]

As a result of the push for more equitable distribution of education funding, as well as states' own wishes to ensure for all school districts a minimum amount of funding they can rely on regardless of their own local tax base, the type of funding formulas preferred by the states has changed over time. In 1971–72, when equity lawsuits were first being filed, two states relied almost exclusively on a uniform flat grant (Arizona and Connecticut), and six states relied on a cost-varying flat grant (which varies by pupil or district characteristics). Most of the remaining states (thirty-three) used some form of equalized grants.[57] By 2005, forty-three states

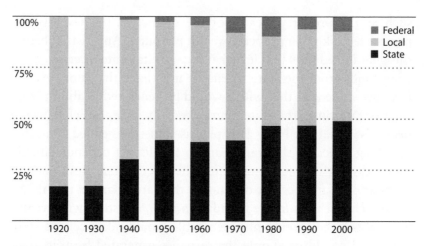

**3.4** Sources of Revenue for Schools, 1920–2000

were using a foundation plan, three provided full state funding (Hawaii, Vermont, and Washington), two used plans with variable matching of local funds (Delaware and Wisconsin), and only one continued to employ a flat grant (Delaware).[58] This shift in the type of financing formulas used by the states has had a significant equalizing effect.

Another trend that has helped reduce spending disparities between districts is the significant growth in the share of school revenues provided by the state. Until about 1930, over 80 percent of school funds were raised locally, with the rest coming from the state (see figure 3.4). During the 1930s, the states began to step forward in funding local schools and were providing about 40 percent of education funds. The state shares continued to grow, and by 1979 state revenues for schools exceeded local revenues. Although there has been some cyclical movement, the states appear to have settled in at providing roughly half of all school district funding.[59]

The federal government's share of funding has also increased across the century, although it still makes up only about 9 percent of total K–12 revenues. From the 1930s through World War II, federal funding accounted for about 1 to 2 percent of school spending. The passage of the Elementary and Secondary Education Act of 1965 increased federal funding to about 8 percent of the total funding. The federal role has been restricted to specialized programs, such as compensatory funds for disadvantaged students, vocational education programs, and later special education programs, and has never included general or base level funding.

These funding approaches, along with the trend toward states and the federal government assuming a greater share of school funding, have reduced disparities in funding between school districts in most states.[60] First, the different types of funding formulas guaranteed that some minimum amount would be available to every school district in the state, regardless of local property wealth. By raising the guaranteed spending levels, they lessened the disparities in funding arising from reliance on the property tax and in that sense had a positive effect on the equity of the funding system. Furthermore, state funds, too, can be distributed to avoid the inequities that arise from different local property tax bases. If anything, the distribution of state funds has favored property-poor districts. The same is true of federal funds, which are distributed largely on the basis of pupil need and in practice favor lower income districts, which tend to have more disadvantaged children. Therefore, any increase in either state or federal funds will naturally lead to a more even distribution of funds, or, at least, one that does not put poor communities at a disadvantage.

Despite these changes, however, disparities in spending between school districts remain. The principal reason is that, although the various funding formulas often increase spending at the lower end of the range, they do not necessarily affect the upper range of spending. If almost all local communities want to spend near the foundation level set by the state, these school funding formulas will lead to mostly even spending, even if there are substantial disparities in the local tax base. On the other hand, if the foundation level is considerably below what many communities would like to spend on their schools, some districts are likely to opt to tax at higher than the minimum rate assumed under the financing formula, and these districts will consequently be able to raise more money than other districts taxing at the base rate. Generally, a number of districts do opt to tax at higher rates, and thus disparities in spending, albeit smaller than before in most states, have persisted.[61] Thus, while modification of state funding formulas has undoubtedly lessened disparities in funding between school districts, it has not eliminated them.

These remaining disparities could be further reduced or perhaps even eliminated if there were legal limits on the additional money a local district could raise by increasing its tax rate beyond the base rate used in the state's funding formulas. And indeed, a few states have such limits (e.g., those imposed by the "Robin Hood" plan of Texas). However, important considerations have prevented most states from doing this. The question often boils down to how much choice local residents should have in determining the funding levels for their schools. One school of thought is that the rich, if allowed to, will always provide more funding for their children's schools than the poor, who cannot afford it, with the result that children of poor families will be disadvantaged, not only today but also across generations. The opposing argument is that families who have a strong preference for more or better education for their children should be allowed to express that preference by voting to provide more money for their community's schools. After all, local control of schools is one of the most deeply entrenched of American traditions, and communities are reluctant to give it up. Further, when families become invested in their schools through paying higher taxes to support them, they are likely to take a greater interest in the effectiveness of those schools. The option to pay more also tends to keep families in the public school system as opposed to seeking out private school alternatives.

On the first point—equal funding versus local control—well-meaning people may come to different conclusions. The next point, however, is less debatable: the degree of local involvement and funding for schools does appear to influence the public's support for its schools.

There is another reason, not much discussed but lying just beneath the surface, for not judging equity solely on the basis of a district's property wealth or its spending level, which relates to the value of housing and how the quality of the schools influences it. If a district becomes known for having good schools, more families will want to get their children into the district, thereby bidding up the value of housing.[62] The result is a higher tax base from which the schools can benefit. These districts, often considered wealthy, not only can spend more on education than poor districts, but also can do so at lower tax rates. However, to suggest that such families are getting a financial break is not entirely fair. If they are paying more for a house because of the good schools associated with it, they are, in effect, incurring a hidden cost not only directly attributable to the schools, but also potentially beneficial to the schools, through enhancement of the local tax base.[63] Allowing some of that expanded tax base to benefit local schools has other advantages. If good decisions by schools cause housing prices to go up, school officials have yet another incentive to improve their schools. People who are paying a premium for housing based on the quality of the local schools are likely to be considerably invested in the schools' continued success, not only because their children attend them, but also because the effect of letting them go downhill will cause the value of their home, the largest single asset of most families, to drop. Even people who have no children in the local schools have reason to support them, simply because better schools make their homes more valuable. Some effort to equalize school funding is clearly necessary to enable poor communities to finance their schools sufficiently; but any effort that eliminates incentives for local taxpayers to support their schools financially beyond minimum required tax rates also has serious downsides. Such policies are likely to result in less money for education, without necessarily benefiting the property-poor school districts.

The best example of what can happen when school funding is equalized by limiting a locality's ability to raise additional money for its schools has occurred in California. After a school equity suit in that state led to very limited local control over school budgets, the voters passed Proposition 13, which placed severe limits on the level of taxation and local spending for schools.[64] The result was a financial disaster for California's schools. In 1970, only nine states spent more than California on education. After the passage of Proposition 13 in 1978, California's spending per pupil relative to other states plummeted, and by 2005 it ranked thirtieth in the country. Indeed, when adjustments are made for regional costs, California drops to forty-sixth in 2005, with even perennially low spenders such as Alabama and Mississippi outspending it on education.[65]

### Development of Funding Formulas to Provide "Vertical" Equity

Seeking completely equal funding for schools might not be a good policy for other reasons as well. Some variation in spending may be warranted because districts serve different types of populations (disadvantaged, English language learners, etc.) or face other variations in cost, such as more or less expensive labor markets or more or less difficulty in realizing economies of scale.

Let us look at the argument that equitable considerations require more money to be spent on "at-risk students." The notion here is that some children, because of disadvantages stemming largely from neighborhood and family circumstances, are likely to cost more to educate than others, and that equal educational opportunities for them will require additional, specialized programs to overcome deficits upon entry into school.

The majority of federal support for schools is aimed at either economically disadvantaged students or special education students. There is substantial variation both across states and within states in the distribution of these federal monies, depending upon local needs. For example, while Chicago gets eighteen percent of its funding from the federal government, more affluent suburban districts tend to get 5 or 6 percent.[66]

To address the issue of different student needs, many states have further included some type of student weighting in their school funding formulas to ensure that more state funds are allocated to students deemed at risk of academic failure. These include students with disabilities, students who do not yet speak English,[67] and students from families living in poverty, frequently identified by their eligibility for the federal government's free or reduced-price lunch program. Under most of these formulas, a regular full-time student with none of these characteristics counts as one student, while a student with one or more of these characteristics effectively counts

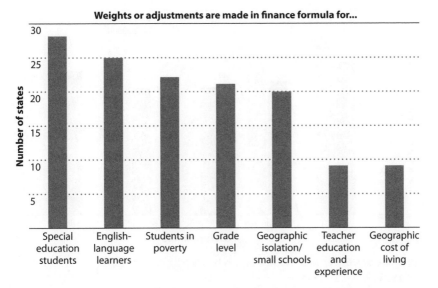

**Weights or adjustments are made in finance formula for...**

3.5 Use of Weights in School Finance Formulas, by State, 2004

as more than one student. For example, a student from a family living in poverty might be counted as 1.2 students, meaning that the school district would receive 20 percent more funding for him. A student with a disability might be counted as 2.1 students, meaning that the school district would receive over twice as much funding for her.

The use of such student weightings has become fairly common, as figure 3.5 shows. In 2004, a majority of states (twenty-eight) used weights for special education funding, with a lesser number using them for English language learners and students living in poverty. The other prevalent weightings take into account district characteristics such as regional costs or grade levels served. The size of the weightings varies considerably between the states that use them. Implicit poverty weights in 2001 were, for example, estimated to range between zero and 50 percent.[68]

The magnitude of these weightings, as we discuss in more detail in chapter 7, has little scientific basis. Weightings are more often than not based simply on what other states are doing rather than on any independent evidence or analysis showing that, for example, it costs 20 percent more to ensure that a poor child reaches the state

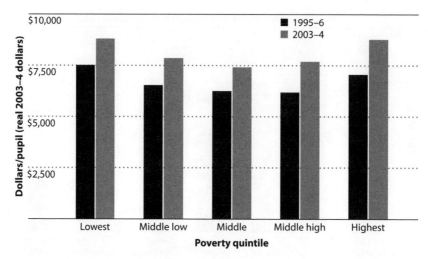

**3.6** Current Per-Pupil Expenditures by District Poverty Level, 1995–96 vs. 2003–4

proficiency level. Moreover, given the lack of any consistent relationship between the amount of money spent and achievement, there is no way to predict whether significantly increasing the weighting, e.g., from 1.2 to 1.4 for at-risk students, will result in a significant improvement in students' achievement, or none at all.[69]

Regardless of the effect of such student weighting formulas on achievement, it is clear that they drive more money to districts with high proportions of disadvantaged children. Nevertheless, it remains a common misperception that school districts with large numbers of poor children have significantly less money per pupil spent on them than other districts. While that may have been true at points in the past, for the last decade or more school districts serving the most disadvantaged populations, on average, have more to spend on each student than more economically advantaged districts.[70] As shown in figure 3.6, by 2004 the poorest districts—those in the highest 20 percent of the poverty distribution (by district)—spent as much on average as the wealthiest 20 percent of districts, and significantly more than those districts in the middle three quintiles.[71]

Part of this misconception may be due to the tendency to equate largely poor student enrollments with "property-poor" districts—

that is, those with low property tax bases. The public and legal sentiment for equitable fiscal systems invariably begins with a rightful concern about the treatment of poor and disadvantaged populations. Because housing values tend to be closely related to family incomes, it is often presumed that the wealth and income of a district can be discussed almost interchangeably. Images of Jersey City and Newark come to mind, where very poor populations are trapped in decaying cities with limited taxing ability.

However, the story is not quite so simple. Because of the high value of commercial and industrial property within their borders, many central city districts with large proportions of poor students are quite property wealthy. Manhattan and Atlanta are good examples. The public school populations of both cities are relatively poor—both because of where families choose to live and because so many wealthier residents send their children to private schools—but the taxable wealth of the districts is enormous.[72] Thus, although most of Atlanta's public school enrollment is poor and the district receives less state aid than the average school district in Georgia, it is nonetheless able to spend 50 percent more per pupil than the average school district in the state (approximately $12,000 versus $8,000).[73]

Of course, as we have stressed, spending lots of money does not guarantee good schools, and there is evidence that, despite high district funding, many large urban schools serving largely disadvantaged populations have difficulty retaining good teachers after a year or two, leaving them with disproportionately large numbers of new teachers. Because the new teachers in these schools are the lowest paid, the result is that, even though a district's funding is average or greater, some schools may enjoy considerably less funding than others.[74] In other words, the district may be distributing school funds in a way that favors some schools and neglects others, particularly those with less experienced staffs. Rigidities in the current system, including transfer provisions in union contracts and compensation systems that refuse to recognize the higher cost of attracting and retaining teachers in hard-to-staff, inner-city schools, contribute to this problem.

One current proposal that has received considerable attention would extend the concept of weighted student funding by distributing funds directly to each school based on the characteristics of its students, without routing the funds through the school district.[75] The system is based on the same principle as the student weighting formulas in current use, with one major difference. Under current school funding formulas, student weighting is used to calculate the amount of funding for the school district, which is then left to allocate the funds among its schools. Under the new proposal, the funds would be allocated directly to the schools based on the makeup of their enrollment.[76] This concept has a second objective in addition to more equitable funding: it seeks to change the underlying politics of districts by undercutting the effect of union-based and other teacher seniority and transfer rules that have built up over the years. And for that reason, such weighted-student funding is vigorously opposed in some quarters.[77] For example, when New York City's mayor Michael Bloomberg tried to push such a funding approach, he was met with fierce opposition from the teachers' union. The union argued that such a redistribution of funds would destabilize the city's good schools, which had the most senior teachers, at the expense of helping schools in poorer neighborhoods. In the end, the mayor was forced to drop his proposal.[78]

In summary, legislative changes have increased the fairness and equity with which funding is allocated between school districts and students, and that is certainly a worthy accomplishment in itself. At the same time, however, these efforts appear to have done little to improve student achievement. Until quite recently, it has been difficult to find any studies of the effects of school finance judgments, even though such cases have been around for over thirty years and have been the driving force behind many of the funding changes. There has been virtually no analysis or investigation of whether more equal spending leads to more equal achievement by students. The little evidence we have suggests that it does not.[79]

## The Standards and Accountability Movement

A third and more recent policy approach by states has been to adopt uniform academic standards for all schools, coupled with a variety of measures designed to hold schools and school districts accountable for their students' meeting them. Perhaps partially in reaction to the recognition that increased funding has failed to improve student achievement significantly, these changes, often referred to as the "standards-based reform movement," began in the late 1980s and early 1990s.[80]

An early expression of the standards movement was the first National Education Summit, a historic meeting between President George H. W. Bush and the nation's governors, held in Charlottesville, Virginia, in September 1989. The 1989 summit meeting led to the adoption of six national education goals, later expanded to eight by Congress. The goals were a series of lofty and ambitious generalizations. For example, the goals began with "All children will start school ready to learn," hardly a controversial goal as it stands. But they also included the goal that "U.S. students will be first in the world in mathematics and science achievement." To oversee movement toward the goals, the National Education Goals Panel was created and worked to develop measurable standards corresponding to the goals.[81]

The principles underlying the standards movement are both simple and sensible. The state should specify what students are expected to know at each grade and in each subject. These content standards should then be used to guide the instruction in the classroom and to establish testing regimes that measure whether children are meeting the standards. School authorities at all levels can then be held properly accountable for the success or failure of their schools.

Much attention has focused on the federal accountability statute, the No Child Left Behind Act of 2001, adopted in early 2002. As a condition for receiving federal funds, NCLB required that each state establish an accountability system and set guidelines for stu-

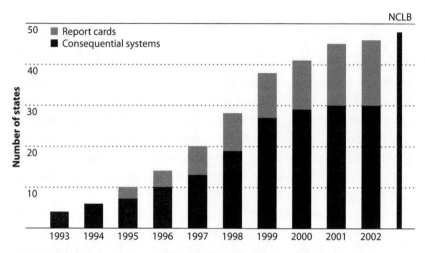

3.7  State Accountability Systems, 1993–2002

dents to meet proficiency (as defined by the separate state content standards). But even before passage of NCLB, virtually all states had introduced their own accountability systems. As shown in figure 3.7, beginning in the early 1990s, most states adopted some form of assessment and accountability system.

Some of these systems merely required the public reporting of test results for each school (the "report card" systems in figure 3.7). However, the majority also attached some consequences to performance, such as significant public recognition or monetary awards to schools and school personnel for gains in achievement. Florida, for example, adopted its "A+ plan" in 1999. The plan includes important accountability provisions: using data on student performance, it grades schools from A to F according to both overall achievement and growth in achievement. It also attaches both positive and negative consequences to school grades, including ultimately giving vouchers to students in failing schools so they could attend better schools. Schools that improved in their grade received extra funds that could be used for further school improvement or for staff bonuses. The accountability system also included a student component, such as requiring students to pass a state test in order to receive a high school diploma. Early evidence on this plan suggests that it has been associated with improved student achievement.[82]

NCLB expanded on the existing accountability plans in most states in several ways. It made the consequences uniform across the states; required the states to report student performance separately by race/ethnicity, economic disadvantage, and other student categories; and established time paths and deadlines for getting all students to proficiency by 2014. The details of the accountability systems adopted under NCLB differ from state to state, but NCLB itself is clearly an extension of a broad set of reform initiatives already under way in most states before its passage.[83]

An important question is, of course, whether such standards and accountability systems have improved student achievement. In fact, some evidence suggests that accountability systems have had positive impacts on student learning. The most straightforward demonstration of the power of accountability relates to improvements in NAEP scores after the introduction of state accountability systems. Controlling for parental education, school spending, and other policy differences of the states, states introducing accountability measures with real consequences have experienced more rapid learning gains than those states without such systems.[84]

The analysis of performance on state tests since the enactment of NCLB also suggests a general improvement in student achievement.[85] A majority of states have seen growth in student achievement since 2002, as well as some narrowing of achievement gaps over this period. The gains on state tests are more striking than those on NAEP tests, even though the aggregate NAEP trends also show some encouraging, if small, gains.[86]

It should be noted, however, that isolating the impact of state accountability policies is inherently difficult. Because accountability measures invariably are applied to the entire state at the same instant in time, variations across schools within a state cannot be employed to assess the impacts of the accountability provisions. Therefore, it is necessary to rely on state-level variation in student outcomes. Yet states themselves differ not only in their accountability policies but also in a variety of other ways involving both the characteristics of their school populations and other school policies. If these differences are not properly accounted for, they can contaminate the estimates of the impacts of states' accountability systems.[87]

Another issue that enters directly into school policy considerations—both in legislatures and in the courts—is how the content standards and goals should be set and interpreted. The content standards themselves are developed and ratified in a variety of ways across states. Typically, the state department of education will ask subject experts to devise a specific set of standards reflecting what students should learn in school. The process and the results differ across states; some set lofty goals and others minimum requirements. Further, in some states the department of education or state board of education alone is responsible for standards, while in others the legislature may need to approve the standards.

Each state then devises "criterion-referenced" tests to gauge how well the students have mastered the skills outlined in the content standards.[88] The state also establishes levels of "proficiency," which are simply the collective judgment of a panel of educators on what the desired level of achievement should be for every student.

Although NCLB increased the importance of these proficiency levels by declaring that all students should meet them by 2014, it left the task of defining "proficiency" up to the individual states. The result is different standards and testing regimes from state to state. Some states have adopted rigorous and demanding standards that define proficiency at a level considerably above that achieved by students in the past, while for others proficiency is quite similar to the performance level of students when the standards were adopted.[89] These differences in definitions of proficiency have led to a situation in which states with high proficiency standards have large numbers of "failing" schools under NCLB, while states with low standards have relatively few "failing" schools.

Figure 3.8 plots the percentage of students scoring at or above the state proficiency level on the fourth grade math test in 2005 and compares this with the NAEP score that would correspond to each state's proficiency cutoff level. The pattern is clear. Those states where the NAEP equivalent cutoff level is low (e.g., North Carolina and Mississippi) have much higher pass rates on their state tests, while states where the NAEP equivalent cutoff is high (e.g., Massachusetts) have the lowest passing rates on their state tests. In Mississippi, which has not been known historically for the

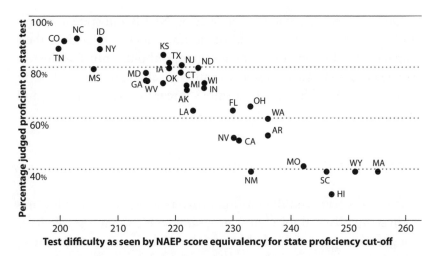

**3.8** Passing Rate on State Fourth Grade Math Tests, Compared with NAEP Scores Equivalent to State Proficiency Cutoff Score

quality of its schools, only 21 percent of students failed to meet math proficiency in fourth grade, yet the state's cutoff score was very low compared with the NAEP standard. In North Carolina, only 9 percent of students failed to meet proficiency standards in 2005, but these "good" scores, like those of Mississippi, result in large part from its having chosen a very low proficiency level. In contrast, Massachusetts shows over 60 percent of its students failing to meet fourth grade math standards, but this is largely a reflection of its choice to evaluate its students against a very high proficiency goal. Despite these low pass rates on the state tests, Massachusetts' students lead the nation on the NAEP tests. Mississippi, North Carolina, and four other states (Tennessee, Colorado, Idaho, and New York) have chosen cutoffs below the level NAEP would call "basic," while Massachusetts and Wyoming have chosen cutoffs well above what NAEP considers "proficient."[90] This pattern of proficiency on state tests and the equivalent level of NAEP scores also holds true for comparisons of fourth and eighth grade reading and eighth grade math, the other grades and subjects for which such comparisons are possible.[91] The result is a call in some quarters for uniform standards applicable to all states, but this is unlikely to come about for political reasons.

On balance, the principles underlying NCLB and state accountability systems are sound, and the initial evidence regarding their
impact on achievement is encouraging, although not conclusive.
We believe that such systems, with the changes we outline in
chapter 8, should be part of a state's integrated school policy and
finance system.

## Increased School Choice Options

The most recent, and the most controversial, education policy initiatives involve school choice programs, which many states have
sought to expand. The father of school choice is the economist
Milton Friedman.[92] Friedman acknowledged that government may
want to intervene in education for a variety of legitimate reasons,
but he argued that none of these reasons, including ensuring a minimal level of education for the population or enabling the children
of the poor to attend schools, requires governments to actually operate the schools. Friedman postulated that although schools may
require some sort of government financial mechanisms, there is no
reason why governments should be involved in running them.

Friedman proposed vouchers as the best means of balancing legitimate state interests and the natural interests of families. The
vouchers, essentially government checks to schools, would transfer
funding to the public or private schools that parents choose for
their children. Parents could use the school voucher to shop for the
best school without having to make residential location decisions—
without, that is, having to live within the district they chose.[93] Interestingly, the original book by Coons, Clune, and Sugarman that
was important in launching court involvement in school finance
also identifies vouchers and more choice as a clear remedy to the
inequities in local schools.[94] In fact, Coons and Sugarman went on
to write a separate book propounding the value of expanded choice
(while Clune turned toward adequacy arguments and further court
involvement).[95]

Choice advocates argue that the availability of vouchers benefits public school students by breaking the public school monopoly

and forcing public schools to improve in order to compete more effectively for students.[96] If public schools did not improve, they would appropriately lose their students in a more open school "marketplace."

Voucher plans, although implemented in a few places, have not caught on in most states. Major voucher programs have been implemented in Milwaukee, Cleveland, and Washington, DC, although even in those places the numbers of participants remain relatively small.[97] Florida adopted two different voucher programs in the late 1990s. The first allowed children in schools deemed "failing" by the state under its grading system to obtain an "opportunity scholarship," which they could use to transfer to other public and private schools, with state funding following them. In 2006, the Florida Supreme Court struck down this program based on its interpretation of the state constitution's education clause; the program never progressed far enough to involve more than a couple of hundred students.[98] The second program is limited to children with disabilities and allows them to transfer to private schools, with state funding following them, if their parents are dissatisfied with their children's public school. This program has flourished, with over sixteen thousand students taking advantage of it in the 2006 school year.[99] Other states are now also experimenting with voucher programs for disabled children.[100]

The research results on vouchers have been mixed, but generally suggest that (1) the expenditures in the voucher schools are almost always noticeably less than those in the competing public schools, (2) parents tend to be happier with the private schools they have chosen through the voucher programs than with the competing public schools,[101] and (3) the achievement of students receiving vouchers appears to be as high as or higher than that of students in comparable public schools. In addition, studies of the Florida Opportunity Scholarship program found that public schools concerned about losing their students to private schools under the voucher program made gains in student achievement.[102]

Charter schools represent another option for parents wanting more choice in which school their children will attend. "Public schools" in the sense that they are government funded, charter schools differ in fundamental ways from traditional public schools, notably in operating to varying degrees outside of the normal public school administrative structures. Because they are creatures of the separate states and operate in different ways according to state rules, there is no common model for them. They differ widely in the rules for their establishment, in the regulations that apply to them, in the public and other financing behind them, and in a host of other potentially important dimensions.[103] Some states, for example, impose a variety of requirements concerning teacher certification, curriculum, acceptance of special education students, and the like. These requirements, often cast as "leveling the playing field," in effect limit the ability of the charter schools to innovate and genuinely compete with the public schools — and may often be interpreted as political attempts to hobble charter schools and to limit their spread.[104] Other states, however, relieve charter schools of a substantial amount of regulation and truly solicit innovation and competition.[105] To the extent that they survive through their ability to attract sufficient numbers of students, they are indeed schools of choice.

The nation's first charter school legislation was passed in Minnesota in 1991. Many other states followed, and by 2005, some thirty-nine states and the District of Columbia (through Congress) had operating charter schools, ranging from only a few in several states to almost 500 in Arizona and in California.[106] In the nation as a whole, charter schools have increased from a handful in 1991 to 3,294 schools serving almost nine hundred thousand students, or approximately 1.8 percent of the public school population, in 2005.[107] In some places, charters serve a significant share of schoolchildren: 18.3 percent of students in the District of Columbia, 8.4 percent of students in Arizona, 4.7 percent of students in Michigan, and 2.8 percent of students in California attended charter schools during the 2004–5 school year.[108]

Charter schools seem to hold some promise for improving student achievement, but there also seem to be wide variations in the performance of charter schools, at least during their start-up phase. Research suggests that after this initial period, the average achievement gains in charter schools exceed those in the regular public schools.[109]

One other aspect of charter schools deserves mention. Schools selected by parents with their children's needs in mind have potential advantages for student achievement, because students are likely to do better in an environment that meets their own interests and needs. More open and competitive markets also enforce a discipline on the traditional public schools, which must seek to improve if they are to retain students. Analysis of charters needs to investigate not only whether students in charter schools do better than their public school counterparts, but also whether public school students benefit from the competition charters provide. Although it is still very early in the development of charters, research by Caroline Hoxby of Stanford University has found preliminary evidence that competition with charters does lead to improvements in the regular public schools.[110]

In addition to charter schools and vouchers, other avenues offering choice are expanding. A particularly popular version of public school choice involves an open-enrollment plan, under which students can apply to a different public school in their district rather than the one to which they are originally assigned. In a more expansive version, no initial assignment is made at all, and students apply to a ranked set of district schools, often including magnet schools that offer a specialized focus, such as college prep or the arts.[111] In 2001–2, 3 percent of all students attended magnet schools.[112] Nonetheless, as we discuss later, such within-district choice plans involve substantially different incentives for the schools, because a district faces no threat of losing students through the choices of school by parents.

Finally, there has been a surge in home schooling. A significant number of parents have withdrawn their children from the regular public schools and taken personal responsibility for their education. Some estimates put the number of home schoolers between 1.5 percent and 2 percent of all schoolchildren, although there is some uncertainty about the numbers.[113] In any event, little is known of the movement of children in and out of home school environments, or at what level they achieve.

Despite the expansion of charter and other schools of choice in recent years, the fact remains that most children in America attend traditional public schools. If significant progress is to be made in educating our children, it is those schools that must be improved, although giving parents more choice can be a means to the end of improving them.

## Teacher Certification

The legislative initiatives just described have not been the only ones tried in an effort to improve student achievement. For example, states have also tried the so-called 65 percent solution (directing school districts to ensure that a certain percentage of their budgets is actually spent in the classroom); various policies discouraging social promotions; a succession of reading, science, and math initiatives; and others. Few studies exist concerning their effect on achievement, however, so we leave their analysis for a time when more data become available. One effort, however, deserves special mention: the effort to ensure teacher quality, most notably through state certification.

States vary in their requirements for certification, though all set minimum requirements in an effort to ensure that no students are subjected to unqualified teachers. The evidence on the effects of certification on teacher quality is mixed.[114] While extensive research has been done on the importance of teacher certification and credentials, it has proved to be quite controversial. Much of the earlier work was based on unreliable statistical methods, although more recent studies have used more reliable techniques.[115] We remain confident that teacher quality is extremely important for improving student achievement, but we are less confident that the teacher certification requirements of most states actually ensure well-qualified teachers.

Most states require teachers to meet certification requirements either upon hiring or within a short period of time after hiring. The studies that investigate teacher certification rely upon observations of existing school systems, where the lack of a teaching certificate generally implies a special situation. For example, urban school systems with heavily disadvantaged populations frequently find it hard to attract sufficient numbers of fully certified teachers and thus resort to hiring noncertified teachers. Or they may hire teachers from specialized recruitment programs such as Teach for America, which recruits top graduates of some of the best colleges to teach in difficult-to-staff urban schools for a two-year period.[116] In this case, not having a teacher certificate is offset by having a degree from a high-quality college or university. These differences make studies of certification very difficult to conduct, and the generalizations that can be drawn from their findings are unclear.

Because teacher certification requirements can vary dramatically among states, simply identifying whether a teacher is certified can mean very different things. Even within a state, a teaching certificate may indicate different things depending on how the teacher entered the profession: some states award certificates to teachers who enter the profession through nontraditional paths, but these certificates rest on different criteria from those given to typically trained teachers.

While certification requirements undoubtedly screen out some unqualified teachers from the classroom, they may also exclude others who would be quite effective. Not only may potentially good teachers be unable to pass the necessary examinations, but also the sometimes extensive coursework and other requirements may discourage other well-qualified individuals from even attempting to enter the teaching profession.[117] The nature of this trade-off depends in large part on the objectives and skills of administrators who make teacher personnel decisions.

Alternatives to traditional certification requirements are being debated. One possibility is to stop focusing on screening out poor teachers (which can be done only with considerable error anyway since we do not fully understand what characteristics are associated with effective classroom teaching); instead, schools could apply some minimum entry standards and then evaluate actual classroom performance. A number of states no longer insist that prospective teachers have a degree from a traditional teacher preparation program, but allow entry from other educational programs including summer training institutes, instruction in pedagogy that is concurrent with teaching, and the like.[118]

Available evidence suggests that there are few consistent differences in teacher effectiveness between traditionally trained teachers and those who enter the profession through alternative entry programs.[119] Therefore, making entry into teaching more difficult by increasing the requirements for certification is probably not an effective way to find—and staff schools with—the teachers likely to raise student achievement.

## Conclusions

State governments have responded to problems of stagnant student performance by making education a legislative priority. Increases in K–12 appropriations have greatly outpaced inflation over the last forty years, and there are various initiatives to distribute education dollars more equitably. Unfortunately, in spite of spending enormous sums—and in spite of spending more on disadvantaged children than other children—we have seen little improvement in achievement or closure of the achievement gap. Essentially, the nation's children are still performing at the same level they did in 1970, when the country spent only less than half as much, in inflation-adjusted dollars, as it does now.[120]

In the last decade or so, states have adopted academic standards and started to hold schools and school districts accountable for meeting such standards. In 2002, the federal government endorsed and strengthened these measures through the enactment of NCLB. More recently, limited choice programs have been introduced in many states. These later initiatives show some promise and can play an important part in improving our public schools, but they alone are not the answer. More fundamental changes will have to be made if we are to expect performance to significantly improve.

Frustrated with this lack of progress, many proponents of better education have turned to courts for solutions, and we take up those efforts next.

# 4 | Court Interventions in School Finance

Until the 1950s, virtually all important decisions regarding elementary and secondary schools and their funding were made by elected officials of states and localities. The federal government was only marginally involved, and neither the federal nor state courts were involved in any meaningful way.[1]

The world of education is now very different. The federal government has become a major participant through, among other things, its funding of programs for disadvantaged students, its requirements for handling special needs students, and the state accountability systems mandated under NCLB. But an even more significant change has been the all-encompassing role assumed by the state and federal courts in matters of education policy and funding.[2]

The 1954 landmark decision of the United States Supreme Court in *Brown v. Board of Education* marked the turning point.[3] Relying on the equal protection clause of the Fourteenth Amendment of the federal Constitution, the Court struck down state-mandated racial segregation in the public schools. One year later, in *Brown II*, the Court instructed the federal district judges around the country to dismantle "with all deliberate speed" the racially segregated schools prevalent in the southern United States.[4] The courts have been an important institutional player in America's public schools and their financing ever since. Lawsuits were brought first in federal courts to enforce equal rights under the federal Constitution and then later in state courts to ensure the equitable distribution and adequacy of educational resources under state constitutions. Now, no serious discussion of education policy and finance can take place without a thorough consideration of the role of the courts.

In this chapter and the two that follow, we examine the history of court involvement in school finance, the different approaches taken by the courts to educational "adequacy," and the effects of court interventions. Neither the federal nor state constitutions vest the judiciary with any role in the creation, funding, or operation of the schools. The power of the courts to intervene is derived solely from their authority to enforce certain rights under both federal and state constitutions, such as the right to equal protection of the laws. Thus, we consider here the underlying constitutional aspects of court involvement in school policy, including not only its legal basis, but also the constitutional limits to it. Because the courts are not immune from the political and practical difficulties that have plagued the other branches of government in trying to improve education,[5] we also look in the next two chapters at the institutional capacity of the courts to bring about real school reform and at the effects of the courts' efforts.[6]

## Federal Desegregation Litigation and *Milliken II* Remedies

Court-ordered funding of school programs began in the federal courts. Following the *Brown* decision in 1954, the courts focused on dismantling the system of racially segregated schools, first in the Deep South and later in other parts of the country. Not much desegregation took place in the decade following *Brown* because of vigorous opposition from local and state officials. However, by the mid-1960s this resistance began to crumble, and by the late 1960s and early 1970s, court orders requiring local school officials to eliminate patterns of racial segregation in student assignments, faculty and staff assignments, extracurricular activities, student transportation, and facilities had become commonplace.[7] Initially, the court decrees were directed at reassigning students to eliminate one-race schools (including the controversial "busing orders"), integrating faculty and staff, and ensuring equal allocation of facilities and other resources. But beginning in the early 1970s, the federal courts also began to address funding issues and to order states and local school districts, as part of their desegrega-

tion plans, to improve the quality of education offered in predominantly black schools by providing extra funding for "educational
enhancements."

The courts justified these funding remedies on several grounds.
First, they would facilitate desegregation by preparing black children, who lagged behind white children academically, for the transition to newly integrated schools.[8] Second, additional programs
and funding would make the schools more attractive to nonminor-
ity students and aid in attracting and retaining a more diverse student body.[9] Third, increased spending would remedy reduced
achievement levels of black students caused by segregation.[10]

The first significant educational enhancements were ordered in
Detroit and have become known as "*Milliken II* remedies" after
the name of the Detroit school desegregation case.[11] The federal
judge overseeing the case focused on the predominantly black enrollment in city of Detroit schools, contrasted with the mostly
white enrollment of Detroit's adjoining suburban school districts,
and approved a cross-district busing remedy: white children from
the mostly white suburban school districts would be sent to schools
in the city, while black children from the city would attend schools
in the suburbs. This "interdistrict" remedy met with fierce opposition from the suburban districts, and in 1974, the Supreme Court
in *Milliken I* overturned the district court's order. *Milliken I* severely limited the power of the federal courts to impose cross-
district busing remedies without proof of complicity of the suburban districts in causing the segregated schools in the central city.[12]
No such proof was presented in the Detroit case, and therefore
the district judge could not draw on white students from Detroit's
suburbs to integrate the inner-city schools. The message was clear,
both for Detroit and for other cities facing the same difficulties: the
federal district courts had to look for other means to desegregate
predominantly black big city schools.

On remand, the district judge ordered the Detroit school district
to implement an array of education programs, including specialized reading and remedial programs, in-service teacher training
programs, testing programs, and additional counseling and career
guidance services.[13] The court reasoned that these programs were

necessary to remedy the pernicious effects of segregation.[14] Because it had previously found the state of Michigan partly liable for the segregation of Detroit's schools, it ordered the state to pay half the cost of such remedies. The state appealed, but the educational enhancement remedy, paid for partly by the state, was approved by the Supreme Court in its historic *Milliken II* decision.[15]

Similar remedies followed in other cities and states where predominantly black populations made racial integration in the schools impracticable. The most notable involved the Kansas City, Missouri, school district, described in chapter 3, and a case in St. Louis during the same time period where the federal courts required the state to pay approximately $1.5 billion for an extensive interdistrict transfer program as well as magnet schools, capital costs, and education programs in the city's predominantly black schools.[16] During the same general period, several other states were also ordered to pay for *Milliken II* programs. Arkansas was ordered to pay more than $250 million for magnet schools and remedial and compensatory programs in the Little Rock school district.[17] Ohio was held liable for half the cost of educational programs designed to improve black student achievement in the state's major cities, including Columbus, Dayton, and Cleveland.[18] Benton Harbor, a predominantly black school district in western Michigan, received approximately $50 million when the federal court ordered the state to implement the School Development Program (designed to boost student achievement through collaboration of schools, parents, and community) and other enhancements.[19] Following a federal court order, the state of New York paid approximately $527 million in extraordinary aid to the Yonkers school district of twenty-six thousand students over an eleven-year period.[20]

The federal courts' focus on specific programs and the funding to implement them was understandable, but it also had long-term ramifications. As educator witnesses testified about programs to improve student achievement, the courts took the logical step of ordering states and sometimes local school districts to pay for them, and over time judges became accustomed to making educational decisions from the bench. Further, the natural metric for tallying up the impact of these decisions became the amount of funding they required. Such money-oriented decisions had increasing influence on the pattern of future decisions, not only in the federal but also in the state courts.

Beginning in the mid-1990s, *Milliken II*–type cases began to grind to an end. The process began with an appeal by the state to the U.S. Supreme Court in the Kansas City desegregation case of a court order requiring the state to fund extraordinary salary increases to the KCMSD teachers and other staff. The lower courts had upheld the payment of such costs for two reasons. First, the higher salaries were necessary for hiring the qualified staff that would help make the KCMSD attractive to potential white transfer students from the suburbs—who were needed to integrate the predominantly black KCMSD schools.[21] Second, additional resources would help KCMSD black students, who lagged far behind white students on nationally normed standardized tests, raise their scores to the national average.[22] In a sweeping opinion known as *Jenkins III*, the Supreme Court rejected both justifications for the remedy. Relying on *Milliken I*, it ruled that the district court exceeded its authority in ordering the state to fund measures aimed at attracting white students from suburban school districts when these districts were not themselves responsible for segregation in the KCMSD.[23] The Court further held that measures designed to raise achievement of KCMSD students to the national average could not be sustained without proof that the previously segregated school system was responsible for the current poor achievement of the district's black students. Without proof of such a link, the U.S. Supreme Court concluded that the federal courts had no authority to order additional funding and programs to raise student achievement.[24]

*Jenkins III* effectively ended the practice by federal courts of ordering local and state authorities to increase K–12 education funding as a desegregation tool. During the next several years, cases against states previously ordered to provide *Milliken II* remedies were dismissed or phased out.[25] But by then the battle for increased funding for schools had shifted to the state courts, as school finance suits began to be filed under the auspices of state constitutional provisions.

## "Equity" Cases

The federal court rulings on desegregation within districts concentrated first and foremost on racial balance, in essence assuming that if both black and white students attended the same schools, equity would naturally follow. These racial balance guidelines were also extended to characteristics of the faculties and school resources and quality.[26] However, the federal court desegregation cases demanded equity only within school districts; they did not address significant funding disparities across districts. As a result, initially the federal courts and then the state courts began to pay more attention to disparities among school districts beginning in the late 1960s and early 1970s. Since no good measure of quality existed, the proxy for equity and equal educational opportunity became per-pupil expenditures (PPEs). The amount being spent on each student would indicate how fairly resources were distributed. As an equity measure, such data had logical merit, since they allowed inferences about what resources a school could afford and made comparisons across schools possible. But as we showed in chapter 3, equating the quality of a school or a school district with the amount of their funding involves a leap of faith and is not well supported by the evidence. Nonetheless, equity in funding, as opposed to school outcomes or other measures of success, became the primary focus of the courts' inquiries and remedies in the 1970s and 1980s, and intricate formulas were developed to assess the degree of "equity" in a state's funding system.[27]

Because differences in the tax base of school districts meant that property-rich districts could generally afford to spend more than property-poor districts, even after taking into consideration state equalization grants, large disparities in spending were widespread, and, beginning in the late 1960s, various groups began to file suits to force states to provide for more equalized spending per pupil across school districts. Similar to *Brown* and its progeny, these suits were also based on equal protection principles, either the Fourteenth Amendment of the federal Constitution or similar provisions in state constitutions. The effort began in the federal courts, although concurrent actions were also being taken in the state courts, including, most notably, California and New Jersey, during the same period.

## Initial Efforts in the Federal Courts

In Texas in the late 1960s, schools in low property wealth districts had significantly less to spend than schools in districts with high property wealth. The differences were striking at the extremes, with the wealthier districts in Texas spending four times as much per pupil as the property-poor districts.[28] In 1968, the Texas system of funding schools through local property taxes was challenged in federal court as discriminatory and in violation of the equal protection clause of the Fourteenth Amendment.

But plaintiffs were unsuccessful. In 1973, the United States Supreme Court rejected their claims in *Rodriguez v. San Antonio*. The Court ruled that education was a matter left to the states and was not a fundamental right under the federal Constitution, which does not mention education in its text.[29] It also ruled that classifications based on the wealth of the school districts were not "suspect" classes under the federal Constitution.[30] The net effect of these rulings was that Texas' system of funding education would not be strictly scrutinized by the Court, as suspect classifications based on student race were, but would instead be judged under the more lenient standard of whether it had a rational basis.[31] The Supreme Court ruled that the Texas system satisfied that test in permitting and encouraging local participation in and control of each district's schools.[32] Thus, it declared, the funding system did not violate the Fourteenth Amendment.[33]

The *Rodriguez* decision was a blow to the civil rights bar, and doomed any further efforts by them in the federal courts to equalize spending between school districts.[34] However, the battle for more equitable funding between school districts was far from over, as civil rights groups and property-poor school districts had already begun to pursue their equal protection claims in state courts under state constitutional provisions. There they would enjoy much more success.

### State Court Equity Cases

The claims pursued in the state courts argued that the education
funding "pie" should be divided more equally among state's school
districts and rested on the premise that the quality of a child's education should not depend upon his or her place of residence.[35] The
forerunner of these state court "equity" cases was *Serrano v. Priest*
in which plaintiffs challenged California's education funding system.[36] In California, as in Texas, the public schools were financed
largely through a combination of local property taxes and state
revenues. The lion's share of the funding came from local property
taxes, which varied greatly from school district to school district.
While the state employed a foundation formula to moderate disparities in property tax bases, the foundation amount was relatively low. It still left significant disparities in school district spending, with California's wealthiest districts spending roughly four
times as much per pupil as its poorest districts.[37]

The *Serrano* case, which had been filed in the late 1960s, was on
trial when *Rodriguez* was decided by the Supreme Court. Nevertheless, in 1974, the trial court ruled for plaintiffs, and two years
later, in its landmark opinion in *Serrano II*, the California Supreme
Court affirmed the decision. The court explained that while plaintiffs had no claim under the federal Constitution under the *Rodriguez* ruling, it did have a claim under the California Constitution
under which (1) education was a "fundamental interest" and (2)
classifications based on wealth in the distribution of education
funds were subject to strict scrutiny by the court. It rejected the
state's argument that its school funding system was justified in the
interest of maintaining local control of the schools, the basis employed in *Rodriguez* to justify such disparities, and ruled instead
that local control was actually inhibited by the finance scheme.
Some school districts, the court opined, received so little money
under the existing system that local control was "chimerical"; that
is, poor districts actually had very little control because they had
so little money.[38] The state system for financing K–12 education,
the court therefore ruled, was unconstitutional.[39]

Lawsuits in other states either were already moving along concurrently with *Serrano* or were encouraged by the court's decision. For example, in 1970, *Robinson v. Cahill* was filed in New Jersey; the case is especially noteworthy because it and its successor case, *Abbott v. Burke*, have yet to leave the courts almost forty years later.[40] By 2007, almost forty states had been the subject of "equity" lawsuits. As shown in table 4.1, plaintiffs were successful in a little less than half of these cases, as the state courts decided them under the particular wording—and their own interpretation—of individual state constitutions and the particular state funding formulas. But regardless of whether plaintiffs were victorious in court, or a suit was even filed, the legislatures in many states felt the pressure and responded by modifying their education funding formulas to provide further equalization.[41]

Supporters of equity suits were not entirely explicit in their expectations, but most seemed to assume that equalization would be achieved by "leveling up." In other words, disparities in funding levels across districts would be evened out by increasing expenditures in low-wealth districts to the level of spending in the wealthier districts, such as those districts having a tax base per pupil at the seventy-fifth percentile. But as the litigation progressed and state financing systems evolved, "leveling up" was not consistently occurring. While these suits might have reduced funding disparities between school districts, they did not always lead to overall increases in the total level of spending, with the experiences varying across states.[42]

The states also varied in the degree of equalization that came after reform of their finance systems, whether the reform was court-ordered or self-initiated. In all cases, local variation remained. No state, whether in response to its courts or of its own volition, opted for simple equalization of funding per student. The reformed systems, then, represented political decisions about the balance of equal spending goals, cost differences, local control options, tax equalization, and more.[43]

Despite meeting with success in many states, equity suits lost steam in the 1990s and began to be replaced by "adequacy" lawsuits. These new suits sought not only to reallocate the education

**TABLE 4.1**
Results of Educational "Equity" Lawsuits, August 2008

| Rulings Favoring Plaintiffs | Rulings Favoring States |
| --- | --- |
| Alaska | Colorado |
| Alabama | Georgia |
| Arizona | Illinois |
| Arkansas | Idaho |
| California | Minnesota |
| Connecticut | Maryland |
| Iowa* | Michigan |
| Kansas | Maine |
| Montana | North Dakota |
| Missouri | Nebraska |
| New Jersey | New York |
| New Mexico* | North Carolina |
| Tennessee | Oregon |
| Texas | Oklahoma |
| Vermont | Pennsylvania |
| Wyoming | Rhode Island |
| | South Carolina |
| | South Dakota |
| | Virginia |
| | Wisconsin |

\* Settlement favoring plaintiffs.

"pie" but also to avoid the possibility of "leveling down" by expanding funding for all districts.[44] There were several reasons for this change in focus. First, equity lawsuits were not always successful. As indicated in table 4.1, plaintiffs lost equity cases in more states than they won; consequently, they needed a new approach if they were to force state legislatures to adopt more equitable funding formulas.[45] The best example of this was in New York, where in 1982 the Court of Appeals (the highest court in New York) rejected equal protection and equity claims under both the state and federal constitutions, ruling that "primary responsibility for the provision of fair and equitable educational opportunity within the financial capability of our state's taxpayers unquestionably rests with that branch [legislative] of your government."[46] A decade later, plaintiffs found another, more successful way to return funding issues to the courts in New York when CFE—the Campaign for Fiscal Equity—asserted that the New York City schools were not adequate under the state constitution. (We discuss this case in more detail later in this chapter.)

A number of the losses highlighted problematic features of equity cases for the courts. Equalizing spending was not as simple as it sounded, and often conflicted with other important and legitimate state goals and policies. For one thing, equity suits threatened the local control cherished in American education. As the Supreme Court stated in *Milliken I*: "No single tradition in public education is more deeply rooted than local control over the operation of schools; local autonomy has long been thought essential both to the maintenance of community concern and support for public schools and to quality of the educational process."[47] The source of most funding disparities was not the state, but a subset of districts raising more money to support their local schools. A court decree limiting their ability to do so might reduce overall funding for education without helping the poor districts,[48] while a decree compelling them to share funds might persuade them not to levy higher taxes at all—and the funds needed to achieve equity would not be forthcoming.[49] Thus, the courts had to walk a fine line between competing policies of equality between school districts and local control and taxpayer incentives to support the schools. The result, even where plaintiffs were successful in court, was that spending was rarely completely equalized between school districts, although as previously pointed out, disparities in funding were significantly reduced.

Second, even in equity cases where plaintiffs were successful, the remedy did not always turn out to be the panacea envisioned by them. California is the classic example. Following the *Serrano* decision, the California legislature revised its school financing system to produce almost perfect equity, but an unfortunate and unintended effect was to eliminate much of the incentive that localities had to tax themselves to support education. Under the new financing scheme, any additional revenues would likely benefit other school districts. Seeing no connection between the high taxes they were paying and the funding of their local schools, the taxpayers revolted and, in 1978, passed Proposition 13, which severely limited the amount of property taxes collected in the state and put severe restrictions on the ability of localities to raise funds.[50] As described in chapter 3, the result was dramatic: in a little over one generation, the state went from the top to being a middle to low spender on K–12 education.

Third, not all parties were satisfied with "equal funding" of school districts. They argued that equal funding was not sufficient for districts with large numbers of "at-risk" children—whom most educators consider more costly to educate—and that such districts required not equal, but greater, funding to ensure "equal educational opportunities."[51] Even where plaintiffs preferred equity that was closer to equal, that did not mean that all these parties would benefit from a court's decision to promote equity. The *Levittown* case is instructive. It was brought by a group of low spending and low-wealth districts, but New York City, with relatively high property wealth, entered as a plaintiff-intervener, realizing that an equalization decision for the original plaintiffs might harm it.[52] Such divergent interests are hard to satisfy simultaneously, at least without an infusion of new funds.

Since equity suits do not require an expansion of the education pie, some school districts face the possibility that their share of school funding might be reduced to drive more money to the lower wealth districts. Consequently, such suits are not uniformly popular among school districts; some of them may stand to lose money. In contrast, every school district in an adequacy case stands to nominally win as the funding pie is expanded.[53] As author Peter Shrag points out: "Advocates of the adequacy idea argue, quite correctly, that unlike equity, adequacy can be a winner for all schools. It does not require redistribution."[54] For that reason, adequacy suits are popular among powerful segments of the community, including the public school educational establishment, union leaders, many parents, and even local taxpayers. Witness New York City, where the Republican administrations of both Mayor

Rudy Giuliani and Mayor Bloomberg supported the *CFE* decree because it promised a flood of state aid to New York City—and hence the potential to lower local taxes. There is, of course, one catch to this argument. The funds have to come from someplace. Thus, while all schools might come out ahead in funding, the citizens of all school districts clearly will not.

## "Adequacy" Cases

As a result of all these factors, equity cases have become secondary in recent years to state court "adequacy" lawsuits. These suits are fundamentally different from either the federal court "desegregation" cases or the state court "equity" cases that followed them. They have their genesis not in the equal protection clause, but in the so-called education clause of state constitutions.[55] Virtually every state constitution requires that the state or its legislature provide some form of free public education for the children of the state. This requirement is normally couched in very general terms, such as the requirement that the state or legislature provide a system of "free common schools" (New York),[56] "cherish the interests of literature and the sciences" (Massachusetts),[57] "make suitable provision for finance of the educational interests of the state" (Kansas),[58] or establish "a complete and uniform"[59] and "a thorough and efficient system" of public schools (Wyoming).[60]

As necessary components of their decisions in adequacy suits, the courts must decide what level of education is required under the vaguely worded state constitutions, whether the state provides such an education, and, if not, what needs to be done to remedy the situation. Often courts also decide whether the state appropriations for K–12 education are sufficient to pay for an "adequate" system, and, if not, how much more funding is needed. Since the additional money must come from somewhere, such decisions have enormous implications when it comes to increasing taxes and/or curtailing other governmental services. Although courts are quick to say these decisions are beyond their responsibility, adequacy cases by their very nature move courts into the policy arena and require them to decide questions that have historically been the domain of the executive branch and legislature. Indeed, most state constitutions specifically vest authority over appropriations in the legislature. Since the typical state spends about one-third of its budget on K–12 education, spending decisions are not minor, and the involvement of courts can result in a sizeable shift of power from one branch of government to another.[61] Not surprisingly, this situation has led to serious confrontations among the courts, the legislature, and the executive branch in a number of states.

A constitutional debate lies at the heart of most adequacy cases. On one side, a significant number of state courts—some nine thus far—have concluded that decisions regarding the content, quality, level, and appropriate funding of K–12 education are ones of educational policy and appropriations, which properly belong to the legislative and executive branches. Since few state constitutions contain explicit standards that would enable the courts to determine whether the legislature is in violation of the constitution, these courts have ruled that adequacy lawsuits present "political questions" inappropriate for them to consider under the separation of powers doctrine. Accordingly, they have dismissed the lawsuits at the outset,[62] without deciding whether the education being offered was "adequate." [63]

The majority of courts faced with adequacy claims, however, have elected to consider them, reasoning that the constitutional right to a free public education is empty unless the courts are willing to enforce it when legislatures fail to fulfill their constitutional duty. Courts in these states have rejected separation of powers arguments and embarked upon further proceedings to determine if, in fact, the education being offered meets the requirements of the state constitution as they interpret them. Even in these cases, however, the courts must be mindful of the limits on their authority in deciding how deferential to be toward the other branches of government.

Because the doctrine of separation of powers is so important to adequacy litigation, we will take it up first. We then discuss cases in which the courts have decided to exercise their authority and heard evidence on the plaintiffs' allegations.

## Cases Dismissed under the Separation of Powers Doctrine

Division of responsibility and allocation of authority among the three branches of government is part of almost every state constitution. This separation of powers holds that the branches ought not to interfere with one another as each carries out the duties assigned it under the constitution. Thus, a court should not assume for itself a power or function vested in another branch of government.[64] For some advocates and beneficiaries of increased spending on education, whether the legislature or the courts make these decisions amounts to little more than a "turf war" among politicians. To others, however, it is a far more significant issue and goes to the very heart of our constitutional form of government.

In 1787, when the delegates from the thirteen colonies drafted the constitution of what became the United States of America, their greatest concern was how to structure a government that would protect the people from tyranny in any form, whether an autocratic central government or ruler, or big states lording it over little states. There were no democracies in the world for them to study and emulate, so they devised their own ingenious compromise: a tripartite system of government which included checks and balances to prevent any person or branch from gaining ascendancy over another. The executive, legislative, and judicial branches of government each had defined powers and responsibility, as Alexander Hamilton stated, in one of the most famous of the Federalist Papers:

> The Executive not only dispenses the honors, but holds the sword of the community. The legislature not only commands the purse, but prescribes the rules by which the duties and rights of every citizen are to be regulated. The judiciary, on the contrary, has no influence over either the sword or the purse.[65]

If the people of a democracy, acting through their elected representatives, decide to allocate more of the public treasury to schools, they have that authority. It is another matter entirely, however, if a judge, accountable to few, decides that in his or her opinion, a higher quality of education should be furnished, or that the education budget should be increased (and other budgets accordingly diminished), or that taxes should be raised to fund additional education programs. Legislatures are, of course, fundamentally different from courts. The legislature is a "political" branch. Its members are elected by popular vote and represent the public at large. Normally, judges are not elected. In New York, for example, the seven members of the Court of Appeals, the state's highest court, are appointed by the governor for fourteen-year terms, which is akin to a lifetime appointment for many of them.[66] Other than voting for governor, the general public has no say in who is appointed. In Kansas, the justices of the supreme court are appointed by the governor from a list of three candidates submitted by a judicial nominating commission, whose members are also appointed by the governor.[67]

Because many state judges enjoy what are in effect lifetime appointments, they come much closer to resembling the autocrats our ancestors were so concerned about when they came up with our tripartite system. It is difficult to hold them accountable for their decisions, even if they turn out to be political and educational failures, e.g., Judge Clark's "license to dream" in Kansas City. The court process also makes it very difficult to change remedial measures once the court has decided upon a course of action. While the decisions of trial judges are subject to appeal, they can generally be reversed only for "clearly erroneous" factual findings and mistakes in applying the law. Justices of a state's highest courts are especially invulnerable as they literally have the last word; there is no appeal from their decisions even if they are dead wrong. In contrast, legislators in most states are up for reelection every two years. If the public thinks they are appropriating too little or too much money for K–12 education, it can vote them out of office. Even where judges are elected, election rules make it extremely difficult to unseat a sitting judge.[68] During campaigns for reelection, most state bar association rules prevent candidates from discussing cases before them or likely to come before them[69]—meaning that the public might never have a chance to learn the judges' views on adequacy, much less make sitting judges justify to the electorate unwarranted, extravagant, or downright foolish decisions.

The difference between elected officials, who represent the people and make laws, and judges, who interpret the laws, is fundamental to our constitutional system of government. It was, after all, "taxation without representation" that sowed the seeds of the American Revolution; the colonists revolted over a tax on stamps and tea, which now seems trivial. In comparison, the New York State court's decision in the *CFE* case, had it been upheld, would have cost every household in New York over $1,000 per year.[70]

Virtually every state constitution is modeled after our federal Constitution and creates a similar tripartite system of state government. Generally speaking, the legislature is endowed with the responsibility to make the laws, the executive is to enforce them, and the judiciary is to interpret them. Admittedly, there is often a fine line between "making" the law and interpreting the law. Judges can in effect make the law when they interpret the language of vaguely worded statutes or constitutions to mean something far different from what may have been envisioned at the time of their enactment. For example, New York's constitution requires the legislature to provide "free common schools." But do those words cede to the courts the power to decide what quality of education must be provided in the state's public schools and what amount of money the legislature must appropriate each year to support them? To answer yes to either of these questions may, as a practical effect, empower the courts to make the laws in New York State regarding K–12 education, or, at the very least, give them significant influence and perhaps even a judicial veto over education policy and appropriation decisions made by the legislature.

If the legislature or executive branch exceeds its authority as specified in the constitution, the courts have the power to enjoin the operation of such laws to prevent "tyranny." But, if the court abuses its power and intrudes in areas reserved to the other branches, there is no "check" within the constitution itself to bring the courts back into the fold. Once the highest court of the state rules, the only way to overturn or reverse the ruling is by amending the constitution, a very difficult and cumbersome process in most states. Therefore, the potential of judicial "tyranny" from adequacy suits is very real, as was demonstrated by controversial court decrees in New Jersey and Kansas that came very close to enjoining any further funding for the public schools. Only when the legislatures acceded to the will of the courts and provided a level of funding meeting their demands did the courts withdraw their threat.[71]

In every state constitution, the power to establish and fund an educational system and its components is vested in the legislature. Most state constitutions also endow the legislature with the exclusive power to tax and appropriate money to support not only education, but also other state and local operations of government.[72] These powers are granted to the legislature for good reason. The decisions that go into establishing and funding an education system are political and not legal in nature. They include such policy questions as what level and quality of education should be offered in the state's public schools; how much of the state treasury should be appropriated for public education, as opposed to other governmental operations and services; how much the public should be taxed to support public education; how the tax burden should be allocated between local and state government; what types of education reforms will best serve the state's children; how control and support of schools should be allocated between state and local government; and so on. At a time of national debate over how to improve the achievement of at-risk students, the courts have no special wisdom about which reforms to pursue. There are many schools of thought about the best way to reform education in America. Should efforts be directed, for example, at increasing school funding as opposed to promoting more competition and choice? Should accountability systems play a more important role? Should the state concentrate on reducing class sizes, which is extremely costly, or look for more cost-effective programs that offer the same, if not greater, odds of success? Or should reforms be a combination of such approaches, and, if so, what should the mix be?[73]

Ironically, it was the New York Court of Appeals, the same court that later issued the final *CFE* opinions, that perhaps best explained why courts should not be making these policy and funding decisions. In 1983, the New York Court of Appeals denied relief to plaintiffs in *Levittown*, a school equity case mentioned earlier. In refusing to intervene in the state's method of allocating education funding between school districts, the court reasoned that the "determination of the amounts, sources, and objectives of expenditures of public moneys for educational purposes . . . appropriately is largely left to the interplay of the interests and forces directly involved and indirectly affected, in the arenas of legislative and executive activity." Further, the court stated "[t]his . . . is the very essence of our governmental and political policy," and it would therefore "normally be inappropriate for the courts to intrude upon such decision-making."[74]

In distinguishing the questions they can legitimately tackle from those deemed "political questions" beyond their jurisdiction, most state courts follow the rationale of the United States Supreme Court in *Baker v. Carr*, a voting rights case.[75] In that case, the Court set forth six criteria for determining whether a case involved a political question, which should properly be handled by the other branches. Two of these criteria come into play in virtually every educational adequacy case. They are (1) whether there is a "textually demonstrable commitment" of the issue in the constitution to another political branch, such as the legislature, and (2) whether there is "a lack of judicially discoverable and manageable standards" for resolving the case.[76] In other words, courts should not get involved if (1) the constitution specifically vests another branch with responsibility for the matter in issue, or (2) the constitutional language does not set forth workable criteria a court can apply in deciding the case. Either implies the case involves a political question and should thus be dismissed. As we have already indicated, at least nine courts that have applied the *Baker* principles to adequacy cases have concluded that they involved "political questions" outside their jurisdiction.

Perhaps the most informative of these cases arose in Illinois. Although its state constitution required, among other things, "high quality public educational institutions and services,"[77] the Illinois Supreme Court decided that the constitution did not contain "judicially discoverable and manageable standards" and that whatever the justices did would emanate not from the constitution but from their own notion of what constituted a "high quality" education.

The court held that "it would be a transparent conceit to suggest that whatever standards of quality courts might develop would actually be derived from the constitution in any meaningful sense" and that "the question of educational quality is inherently one of policy involving philosophical and practical considerations that call for the exercise of legislative and administrative discretion."[78]

Plaintiffs in adequacy cases often argue that they seek only a declaration from the court on whether the statutory framework making up the state funding system for education is constitutional—and not a court order requiring the legislature to take any specific actions or appropriate any specific amounts. This argument has been successful in a number of cases; however, it ignores what often happens in adequacy cases after an initial liability order. Once the plaintiffs obtain a declaration that the funding system is unconstitutional, and the legislature fails to meet often huge monetary expectations, their next move is to seek a court order requiring the legislature to increase funding to an amount deemed adequate. The Florida Supreme Court had no problem anticipating this result, holding:

> While plaintiffs assert that they do not ask the Court to compel the Legislature to appropriate any specific sum, but merely to declare that the present funding level is constitutionally inadequate, what they seek would nevertheless require the Court to pass upon those legislative value judgments which translate into appropriations decisions. And, if the Court were to declare present funding levels "inadequate," presumably the Plaintiffs would expect the Court to evaluate, and either affirm or set aside, future appropriations decisions.[79]

And just as the Florida court predicted, court orders in states like Wyoming, New Jersey, New York, Arkansas, and Kansas made it plain that legislatures would have to come up with funds in the amount specified by the court in order to avoid further penalties.[80] Court orders of this sort bring the courts into direct conflict with the legislature, which in almost every state has the exclusive power to appropriate funds for public purposes.

The separation of powers doctrine remains a powerful obstacle to court intervention in many states. Yet the majority of state courts faced with this threshold question have decided they do have the power to hear such cases.

## Cases Heard on the Merits

Adequacy plaintiffs have convinced the majority of state courts to exercise jurisdiction and address the evidentiary questions raised in adequacy lawsuits: is the education being provided "adequate" under the state constitution and, if not, why not? Their argument is simple and straightforward. Judges are sworn to uphold constitutional rights. If the state constitution guarantees a free public education, and the education provided cannot reasonably be termed an "education" in today's world, the courts have no choice but to enforce the constitutional right to an "education." Indeed, many judges would deem failure to intervene to protect the constitutional rights of the state's children an abdication of their oath of office. Thus, in the Arkansas adequacy case, the court held that "[t]his court's refusal to review school funding under our state constitution would be a complete abrogation of our judicial responsibility and would work a severe disservice to the people of this state. We refuse to close our eyes or turn a deaf ear to claims of a dereliction of duty in the field of education."[81] Other courts have reached a similar conclusion.[82] The result is that many state courts have elected to exercise authority over this traditional legislative area and to strike down the legislature's work as being insufficient under the state's education clause.[83]

We believe the courts' decisions to intervene in educational policy and funding have been heavily influenced by several factors. First and probably most important, America does face an educational crisis—one outlined in the first two chapters—and advocates have convinced the courts that its cause is lack of educational opportunities, that the state legislatures are not doing their job, and that, unless the courts intervene, another generation of children will be denied an adequate education. Well-intentioned judges have been persuaded to help solve one of the most important—and vexing—problems the nation faces, aided in large part by plausible-sounding solutions put forth by plaintiffs and their supporters.

Another influence on judges is the moral legacy of *Brown v. Board of Education*. Although *Brown* rested on different legal principles, it is commonly invoked by plaintiffs in adequacy cases, who argue that such cases represent the next step in ensuring equal rights for all students.[84] *Brown* is perhaps the most shining example in our nation's history of the societal good courts can accomplish, and its effect on state court judges is clear.[85]

For judges sympathetic to extending *Brown* but troubled by the vagueness of the education clauses, the standards-based reform movement in education has served as the missing link to judicial intervention. Adequacy plaintiffs have argued that state standards provide an objective description of what the constitution considers an adequate education and that this objectivity gives the courts the "judicially discoverable and management standards" they need to decide what would otherwise be a "political question."[86]

The results of statewide tests are widely available now and are cited to prove that current education spending is insufficient: if substantial numbers of students are not scoring at the proficient level or above, the argument goes, the cause must be inadequate funding. This argument is reinforced by the catchphrases used by many state education departments, such as "all children can learn, given sufficient resources."[87]

The passage of the federal No Child Left Behind Act in 2001 has also bolstered plaintiffs' cause. As a condition to receiving federal funds, NCLB requires every state to adopt academic outcome standards and to ensure that all students, with a few narrow exceptions, meet such proficiency standards by the year 2014. During the years leading up to 2014, all schools must make "adequate yearly progress" (AYP) toward meeting such standards. Moreover, under NCLB a school district can no longer mask the poor performance of certain subgroups of poor and minority pupils by reporting their academic performance as part of a larger group. Districts must report the performance of different subgroups of pupils, such as those eligible for the federal free and reduced-price lunch program and members of minority groups. This makes it possible to assess the school's performance in educating subgroups who have historically not performed well.[88]

Although no court has yet based its decision in an adequacy case solely on the failure to meet AYP requirements, courts have relied on costing-out consultants—hired to determine what additional funding is needed to ensure an adequate education for all students—who are increasingly incorporating NCLB and the state standards they require into the definition of an "adequate" education (see chapter 7).[89] Perhaps most importantly, NCLB adds credibility to the claims commonly asserted in adequacy lawsuits that schools alone, if provided sufficient resources, can raise all children to proficiency levels.[90]

As a result of such influences, the "golden age of adequacy suits" for plaintiff groups ran through the 1990s and into the twenty-first century. Plaintiffs were able to convince the majority of state courts with adequacy cases before them to deny motions to dismiss on the grounds that they involved political questions and to allow the cases to go to trial. They were then able to win their cases at trial, and even more importantly, uphold their trial victories on appeal. As described in more detail in the next chapter, these court decisions shared several common elements: (1) judges' direct or implicit belief that high standards for achievement necessitate a higher level of resources, (2) the tendency to disregard reasons other than lack of funding for educational shortcomings found by the courts, (3) little deference for legislative choices, and (4) a preference for remedies focused on increasing funding for K–12 schools. The combination of these elements in effect imposed strict liability on the state once plaintiffs were able to show substantial numbers of children had failed to meet state academic or other achievement standards. Since this threshold can be met in virtually every state, plaintiffs prevailed in almost every adequacy case that survived a motion to dismiss and went to trial during this period, including cases in New York, New Jersey, Kentucky, Arkansas, Connecticut, Vermont, New Hampshire, Kansas, and Montana.[91]

However, beginning in 2005, a decade and a half of plaintiff victories came to a fairly abrupt end, starting with decisions upholding the existing state systems of education by the highest courts in Texas and Massachusetts,[92] and continuing with a string of defense successes in other states. These decisions have been characterized by their increasing deference to legislative choices, as long as such choices appear to be rational. Since 2005, courts in Oklahoma, Kentucky, Colorado, and Oregon have granted defendants' motions to dismiss on separation of powers grounds, and dismissed the cases without a trial.[93] In Arizona, the appellate courts concluded that the state had no liability for achievement disparities it had not caused and dismissed the case prior to trial.[94] Plaintiffs have not fared much better in cases that survived a motion to dismiss. In 2008, the Wyoming Supreme Court finally dismissed that state's long-running adequacy suit following a trial court decision mostly in favor of the state.[95] In Alaska and Missouri, plaintiffs lost after lengthy trials on the merits.[96] In South Carolina, the case was tried and decided in favor of the plaintiffs, but the trial court granted relief relating only to preschool education.[97] Perhaps the biggest disappointment for plaintiffs came in New York, where the state's appellate court, showing far more deference to the legislature than it had in prior rulings, scaled back the annual increase in operating aid to New York City's public schools from \$5.6 to \$1.9 billion, the minimal amount proposed by the state itself. In rejecting the other cost calculations, the court, echoing the Texas ruling, held: "The role of the courts is as [the lower court] assumed, not to determine the best way to calculate the cost of a sound basic education in New York City schools, but to determine whether the state's proposed calculation of that cost is rational."[98]

As of the end of 2007, there had been final decisions in adequacy cases by the highest courts in twenty-eight states and lower court rulings in another three. Their results are briefly summarized in table 4.2.

Next we consider the most illustrative cases that went to trial: Kentucky, where the adequacy movement began; New Jersey, where the state has been in court over its school finance system for well over thirty years; New York where the movement peaked and then ebbed; and Texas where the courts began to question some of the basic tenets underlying plaintiffs' arguments and to give increasing deference to the legislature.

**TABLE 4.2**
Results of Educational "Adequacy" Lawsuits, as of July 2008

| Dismissed on Separation of Powers Grounds | Rulings Favoring Plaintiffs | Rulings Favoring Defense |
|---|---|---|
| RI (1995) | Ky. I (1989) | Mass. II (2005) |
| Ill. (1996) | Mass. I (1993) | Tex. (2005) |
| Fla. (1996) | Ariz. (Facilities) (1994) | S.C. (2005)* |
| Pa. (1979) | Wyo. (1995) | Ariz. (Operations) (2006) |
| Neb. (2007) | N.H. (1997) | Mo. (2007)* |
| Okla. (2007) | N.J. (2002) | Alaska (2007)* |
| Ore. (2006)* | N.Y. (2003) | |
| Ky. II (2007) | Kans. (2005) | |
| Colo. (2006)* | Ark. (2002) | |
| Ala. (2003) | Mont. (2005) | |
| Ohio (2003) | N.C. (2004) | |
| | Wash. (1978) | |
| | W.Va. (1979) | |
| | Vt. (1997) | |

* On appeal.

## KENTUCKY: THE ROSE CASE

It can be said that the adequacy movement started in Kentucky.[99] In 1984, a former employee of the Kentucky Department of Education named Arnold Guess began to talk to school superintendents around the state about using the courts to reform schools. With the help of Bert Combs, the former governor of Kentucky and head of one of the state's major law firms, he formed the Council for Better Education, an association of sixty-six school districts. In 1985 the council filed suit against the governor and other state leaders, contending that the legislature had failed to provide the "efficient system of common schools" required under the Kentucky Constitution.[100] A sympathetic trial court concluded that an "efficient" school system must "provide sufficient physical facilities, teachers, support personnel, and instructional materials to enhance the educational process," and that the "General Assembly has all the power necessary to guarantee that the resources provided by Kentucky taxpayers for schools are spent wisely."[101] The court found the legislature's efforts to increase funding wanting, and declared Kentucky's system of financing public schools unconstitutional. The court left it up to the legislature to revise the system, but expressly held that "'substantial additional monies' would have to be raised to provide this constitutional school system."[102] In reaching its decision, the court relied mainly on national and regional comparisons showing that Kentucky lagged behind most states, including states in its own region, in education spending and resources, as well as on evidence of low achievement in property-poor districts.[103]

The state appealed the decision, but in 1989, the Kentucky Supreme Court upheld it. In words that were to become the touchstone of adequacy cases all over the country, it set forth its definition of an "adequate" or "thorough and efficient" education as one providing "each and every child" with the following capacities:

> (i) sufficient oral and written communication skills to enable the student to function in a complex and rapidly changing civilization; (ii) sufficient knowledge of economic, social, and political systems to enable the student to make informed choices; (iii) sufficient understanding of governmental processes to enable the student to understand the issues that affect his or her community, state, and nation; (iv) sufficient self-knowledge and knowledge of his or her mental and physical wellness; (v) sufficient grounding in the arts to enable each student to appreciate his or her cultural and historical heritage; (vi) sufficient training or preparation for advanced training in either academic or vocational fields so as to enable each child to choose and pursue life work intelligently; and (vii) sufficient levels of academic or vocational skills to enable public school students to compete favorably with their counterparts in surrounding states, in academics or in the job market.[104]

These seven competencies move beyond the "thorough and efficient" education specified in the Kentucky Constitution, and, while few would argue that children ought not to develop these competencies, they hardly constitute operational definitions that are easily judged or applied. Nevertheless, they have been repeatedly cited by other state courts to add a qualitative component to vaguely worded constitutional provisions couched in the most general terms.[105]

A movement to reform Kentucky's schools was already under way when the Kentucky Supreme Court's decision was rendered, and the court order provided the additional pressure and cover for the legislature to finally enact such reforms—and the tax increases related to them. Besides making it clear that more money was needed, the court held that the legislature had to "carefully supervise it [the education system], so that there is no waste, no duplication, no mismanagement, at any level."[106] Within a year after the court handed down its decision, the Kentucky legislature enacted several school reform bills and approved a $1.3 billion tax increase in the state's corporate income tax and sales tax to fund significant increases in K–12 education appropriations.[107] With Kentucky as the necessary precedent related to the broad scope of potential court actions, reformers began to pursue adequacy cases more aggressively in other states.[108]

## NEW JERSEY: THE *ABBOTT* CASE

If the Kansas City case is the poster child of federal desegregation remedies gone awry, New Jersey deserves that dubious honor in adequacy cases. Such was its notoriety that the New York Court of Appeals justices involved in one of the first *CFE* appeals were openly concerned about avoiding the seemingly endless litigation that had occurred in their neighboring state. Their concern was understandable: New Jersey has been in continuous litigation over its school finance system for over thirty-five years, with no end in sight. Filed originally in 1970 as an equity case (*Robinson v. Cahill*), the suit's main goal was more equitable funding for a number of property-poor school districts. Because of low property tax revenues, these districts spent significantly less than the state average, despite having a student population at high risk of academic failure. Relying on language in the New Jersey Constitution that required a "thorough and efficient" education, plaintiffs obtained a series of court orders significantly increasing revenues and spending for New Jersey's thirty-one poorest and mostly minority school districts (known as the "Abbott districts" after the name of the current lawsuit).[109] In its own version of equity, the New Jersey Supreme Court ordered the Abbott districts funded to ensure "parity-plus." First, they were to be funded not at the state average, but on a par with the state's highest spending districts. Second, they were to receive additional state payments for special programs enabling these students to overcome disadvantages associated with poverty.[110] "Equitable" funding had, at least in New Jersey, become synonymous with the highest funding in the state.

In 1998, any pretense that New Jersey was an equity case vanished, as the courts focused on whether student performance in the Abbott districts was adequate and ordered a series of expensive programs for all of them. These included whole school reform programs in each school, half-day preschool programs for three- and four-year-olds, technology, alternative schools, school-to-work and college transition programs, a variety of supplemental programs, and extensive building and renovation of facilities.[111] The court orders have pushed spending in the Abbott districts to record levels. As of the 2005–6 school year, their per-pupil *regular* education budgets were the highest in the state, at $12,928, far exceeding the $10,072 spent by the middle-wealth districts and even the $12,018 spent by the "high wealth" districts.[112] In addition, the Abbott districts receive a disproportionate share of state aid for at-risk children, pushing their total spending even higher. For example, in 2004, the Abbott districts spent a total of $16,889 per pupil, almost $5,000 more per student than similarly situated other poor districts in the state.[113] As a result, in 2005–6, the Abbott districts received approximately 57 percent of all state aid for K–12 education in New Jersey, even though they only enroll about 20 percent of the state's pupils.[114]

Despite such unprecedented spending, the case is far from over. After more than a dozen trips back and forth between the legislature and courts, the parties are still in court, as plaintiffs seek additional funding for, among other things, more "reading tutors, school nurses, social workers, guidance counselors and summer programs."[115]

## NEW YORK: THE *CAMPAIGN FOR FISCAL EQUITY* CASE

The *CFE* case in New York is notable not only because it involved the nation's largest school district with over twelve hundred schools and a million students, but also because it received so much attention, in large part because of the stupendous amounts of money at stake.[116] The litigation effort was spearheaded by Michael Rebell, the executive director of the Campaign for Fiscal Equity (CFE), an umbrella organization consisting of several of New York City's worst-performing community school districts and a number of education advocacy organizations. A self-described "child of the sixties," Rebell had already sued the New York City schools for problems in its special education programs. In a major coup, he enlisted Simpson Thacher & Bartlett, one of New York City's most powerful law firms, to assist him on a pro bono basis in the adequacy litigation. In 1993, CFE, with the Simpson Thacher law firm and Rebell leading the way, filed suit.[117] The New York attorney general's office initially handled the defense of the case, but when a trial became imminent, it retained Sutherland Asbill & Brennan, an Atlanta-Washington, DC, firm with significant prior experience in representing state entities in school finance litigation, to represent the state at trial.[118]

The ground rules for the trial were set in 1995 by the Court of Appeals, New York's highest court, in a ruling reversing the initial dismissal of the case on separation of powers grounds.[119] In its *CFE I* opinion, the court interpreted the New York Constitution, which simply calls for "free common schools," as requiring a relatively low level of education. The legislature, the court held, had to establish a system of schools that would provide a "sound basic education" for each child, consisting of "minimally adequate" facilities, teaching, and curriculum. These minimal resources must be sufficient to import "basic literary, calculating and verbal skills" necessary to enable children to "eventually function productively as civic participants capable of voting and serving on a jury."[120] Only a basic level of education requiring minimal resources was required to meet the constitutional mandate, or so it seemed when the ruling was made.

The case was tried from October 1999 to May 2000 in one of the longest trials in New York history before Justice Leland De-Grasse, a Manhattan trial judge. Plaintiffs' argument was fourfold, and was typical of arguments made in other adequacy cases: (1) New York City public school students performed poorly, as illustrated particularly by their scores on state academic tests and by low graduation rates; (2) the schools lacked sufficient resources, demonstrated by overcrowding in some schools, large class sizes, and unqualified teachers, as shown mainly by comparison of the credentials of New York City teachers with teachers in the rest of the state; (3) expert testimony promised that achievement could be significantly improved if the school district had sufficient money to provide additional programs and resources; and (4) a "broken" political process had failed to provide sufficient funding for New York City's schools.

The state countered with evidence that (1) the city's schools were providing at least the basic level of education set as the constitutional threshold by the court in *CFE I*, as evidenced by systematic formal evaluations rating over 99 percent of its teachers as qualified and its schools on average as meeting high standards; (2) its schoolchildren were scoring at the national average on standardized tests, despite having a larger at-risk population than most big cities, a strong indication the schools were doing an adequate job; (3) to the extent that some schools did not have sufficient resources, the reason was not a lack of state funding but waste and mismanagement by the district, illustrated perhaps most dramatically by the erroneous assignment of over 135,000 students to expensive special education programs; and (4) the district, with an annual operating budget at the time exceeding $10,400 per pupil, had sufficient funds to provide the basic education required.[121]

Justice DeGrasse ruled in the plaintiffs' favor, citing, among other things, low teacher quality, large class sizes, substandard libraries and computer technology, low test scores on state performance tests, and high dropout rates. Seemingly contradicting the "minimally adequate" standard espoused in *CFE I*, he held that the quality of education required under the constitution was one that would produce an "engaged, capable voter" with the "intellectual tools to evaluate complex issues, such as campaign finance reform, tax policy and global warming."[122] Largely disregarding evidence of mismanagement and waste at the local level, as well as conditions outside the schools influencing achievement, he concluded that such problems were caused by a lack of sufficient funding of the schools, even though New York City was at the time the highest spending of the fifteen largest school districts in the country.[123]

The case next took a tortuous route through appeals, which produced, among other things, a startling statement by the appellate division (the intermediate level of New York courts) implying that only an eighth grade education was required under the constitution. After the original judgment was affirmed by the New York Court of Appeals, it returned the case to Judge DeGrasse to determine how much more money was required to provide a "sound basic education" in New York City.[124] With advice from three judicial referees, DeGrasse approved the amount sought by the plaintiffs, an additional $5.63 billion per year, plus another $9.2 billion for capital needs over the next five years.[125] These increases were over and above the $12.6 billion already being spent each year on the New York City public schools, and if implemented would have brought the city schools' annual operating budget to $18.2 billion a year at the time, or approximately $17,200 per pupil—an amount over twice the national average.[126]

Under Justice DeGrasse's phase-in schedule, the state was ordered to pay a total of $23 billion in additional operational and capital funding to the New York City public schools over the next five years.[127] At the conclusion of the five-year period, he ordered further cost studies every five years designed and supervised by the board of regents and state education department to determine future costs, thereby setting in place a mechanism for indefinite court supervision.[128]

In 2006, New York's highest court finally deferred to the significantly lower amount advanced by the state—a $1.93 billion increase over 2004 expenditures.[129] This order effectively ended the litigation. However, the biggest twist came several months later, when newly elected Democratic governor Eliot Spitzer (and the New York attorney general at the time of the trial and subsequent hearings of the referees on funding requirements) brokered a political deal with several Long Island Republican representatives to increase revenues for the New York City school district by approximately $5.4 billion ($3.2 billion from the state and the remainder from the city) over a four-year period, even though the court order required an increase of just $1.93 billion, approximately one-third of that amount. The case had come full circle: unable after years of litigation to win the enormous increases in education spending they sought in court, plaintiffs finally got what they wanted through the political processes they had so diligently attacked in court as broken.[130]

### TEXAS: THE *WEST ORANGE-COVE* CASE

The 2005 decision of the Texas Supreme Court stands in stark contrast to almost fifteen years of adequacy decisions favoring plaintiffs and marks the beginning of a different approach in the courts' treatment of such cases. The *West Orange-Cove* case began in 1989 not as an adequacy case but as a state court equity lawsuit.[131] A number of property-poor Texas school districts contended that wide disparities in spending by Texas districts—a result of their over-reliance on local property taxes—violated the equal protection clause of the state constitution. The courts agreed and struck down the school financing system. In response, the Texas legislature passed what became known as the "Robin Hood" law, in which a minimum foundation amount to fund each school district was financed by taking a portion of local property taxes from about ninety "property-rich" districts and redistributing these funds to "property-poor" districts. At the same time, a cap on local property tax rates was enacted. In the following years, these ninety districts all raised their property tax rates to or close to the cap. The rising costs of education, they claimed, required them to tax at the maximum level and effectively eliminated any discretion of the local taxing authorities to tax at a lower rate. Thus, they argued, local property taxes had become a de facto "state property tax" with the tax rate set by the state. In 2001, the property-rich districts filed suit to strike down the "Robin Hood" tax system as an illegal "state property tax" barred by the state constitution.[132]

After the suit was filed, two groups encompassing about 282 mainly property-poor school districts educating about one-fourth of the state's students moved to intervene so they could assert both adequacy and equity claims.[133] Their motion to intervene was granted, and when the case over the illegality of the alleged "state property tax" was tried in the summer of 2004, so were the associated adequacy and equity claims. Leaving little doubt where he stood, the trial judge issued a 120-page opinion striking down the Texas school finance laws on the grounds that they (1) were an illegal "statewide property tax" and (2) did not provide sufficient funding for an adequate education in either the plaintiff or intervener districts.[134] Although the Texas Constitution required nothing more than "a general diffusion of knowledge," he concluded that the Texas system did not meet that standard, and in support cited NCLB and state statutes encouraging higher standards; an increasing influx of poor students into the state who often struggled with the English language; the "uncontrollable" costs of dealing with such students; an impending shortage of teachers; insufficient library facilities and books; and a host of facility shortcomings.[135] The system, he decided, was underfunded to the tune of $1.6 to $6.2 billion per year based on cost studies introduced by plaintiffs.[136]

The state appealed the decision to the Texas Supreme Court, which agreed that the financing scheme involved an unconstitutional "state property tax," but reversed the trial court's ruling on the adequacy claims. Demonstrating at the outset a different mind-set than courts in other states, the court began by stating that "we must decide only whether public education is achieving the general diffusion of knowledge the Constitution requires" and not whether it is "achieving all it should—that is, whether public education is a sufficient and fitting preparation of Texas children for the future." These larger questions, it held, involved "political and policy considerations properly directed to the Legislature,"[137] which under the constitution had "much latitude in choosing among any number of alternatives that can reasonably be considered adequate, efficient, and suitable." It explained that "[i]f the legislature's choices are informed by guiding rules and principles properly related to public education," and "the choices are not arbitrary," then the system does not violate the constitutional provision.[138] In short, the courts "must not substitute their policy choices for the Legislature's."[139] Finding that the actions of the legislature had not been "arbitrary," the court rejected the plaintiffs-interveners' adequacy claims.[140]

In reaching its decision, the court examined the components of the education system created in Texas—a state curriculum, standardized testing, accreditation standards, and consequences for failing to meet these standards—and concluded that this system met the requirements of the Texas Constitution.[141] The court acknowledged "wide gaps in performance" between disadvantaged students and other students, high dropout and noncompletion rates, and a low rate of college preparedness. However, it refused to condemn Texas' K–12 education system, holding that low performance outcomes "cannot be used to fault a public education system that is working to meet their stated goals merely because it has not yet succeeded in doing so."[142] Instead, the court accentuated the positive: student scores had improved on Texas' standardized tests, even as the tests themselves were being made more difficult, and NAEP scores in Texas had improved relative to other states.[143] The court recognized that the "end-product of a public education and resources" are related, but insisted that "the relationship is neither simple nor direct."[144] It explicitly asserted that "more money does not guarantee better schools or more educated students."[145] With regard to the adequacy of funding, the court noted that "almost all schools are meeting accreditation standards with current funding," and it pointedly disregarded evidence of costing-out studies offered by both plaintiffs and defendants opining that between $236 million and $6.17 billion would be required in order to provide an "adequate" education."[146]

This account of the evolution of school finance lawsuits and their constitutional underpinnings, beginning with the famous 1954 *Brown* decision, shows the extent to which courts asserted their authority in adequacy lawsuits after desegregation and equity lawsuits had wound down. Judge Clark's orders in Kansas City ($2.1 billion over ten years) was not in the same league as Justice DeGrasse's order that spending be increased for the New York City public schools by $23 billion over five years. In some states, courts became the final decision makers regarding not only the quality and programmatic components of K–12 education, but also the share of the state's treasury to be appropriated for improving schools. It is difficult to predict the future, as the course of school finance lawsuits has continued to shift. In the last several years, as the courts have grown more deferential to the legislature, their attitude toward adequacy suits has changed. Whether the courts will continue this minimal intervention approach or once again decide to assert themselves aggressively in the school finance arena remains to be seen.

# 5 | Practical Issues with Educational Adequacy

The constitutional basis of adequacy suits is not the only hurdle faced by the courts. When courts try to translate broad constitutional principles into workable solutions, certain practical difficulties make the task especially challenging. These difficulties surface both during the liability phase of the litigation (when the court is engaged in determining whether the state's system of education complies with the constitution) and during the remedy phase (when the court is trying to ensure an appropriate remedy is implemented). In this chapter, we discuss first the practical difficulties of dealing with the issues at the center of most adequacy cases: defining an "adequate" education, establishing causation, and formulating an effective remedy. We then analyze several characteristics of courts and the trial process that are not well suited to adequacy lawsuits and that limit the ability of the courts to fashion effective judgments.

## Defining an "Adequate" Education

"Adequacy" is both a legal and a factual concept, and one that has been difficult for courts, litigants, educators, legislators, and the public to grasp. Hardly anyone disagrees with the notion that children should have an adequate education, but, as the Supreme Court said in the *Rodriguez* case, "[W]hat constitutes an appropriate education is not likely to be divined for all time by the scholars who now so earnestly debate the issue."[1]

State constitutions typically use words like "general," "thorough," "efficient," "uniform, "general diffusion of knowledge," "suitable," "adequate," and "free common schools" in connection with the education they require.[2] But every state already supports, through a combination of state and local funding, public schools, including at least one-half day of kindergarten and grades 1–12. Therefore, the question before the courts is never whether a state is providing schools and instruction; it is whether the quality of such schools and instruction is high enough to satisfy the constitutional language. The vagueness of the constitutional language, however, forces the courts, through their powers of "interpretation," to formulate a more definitive standard to be used by the litigants and lawmakers. Yet, in most cases, the definition developed by the court also consists of generalities. As one commentator has pointed out, "[D]efining a generality with more generalities does not make a generality more precise."[3]

Nor does the reference to standards bring much clarity and specificity to discussions of adequacy. A large part of the confusion is that education is a field rife with standards of one sort or another. In virtually every state, a range of different standards coexist. Even though the various standards have different purposes and different provenance, several invariably will be introduced into court proceedings without much discussion of their purposes or import.

A typical state has a set of aspirational outcome standards related to the levels of achievement that it hopes its students will reach, even without being confident that the standards are attainable by all or even most students. Often couched in lofty language, these standards are frequently linked with specific content standards, which provide further detail about desired achievement in each grade and subject. But states also have so-called input standards (that govern matters like class size and the ratio of administrators or guidance counselors to students). These input standards again come in different varieties: some are truly aimed at minimal conditions, while others—frequently labeled "opportunity to learn" standards—are themselves more aspirational. Then there are standards for certifying teachers, administrators, guidance counselors, and so on, as well as standards for school accreditation. Finally, some states have statutory or constitutional standards guiding spending on education.[4]

The appeal of standards is that they are invariably linked to some quantitative measures and are thus specific and objective—and therefore seem to offer a firm and observable foundation for vague constitutional requirements. We ought to recognize, however, that constitutional obligations *virtually never* enter into the formulation of any of these standards. Instead, they are derived from the rules and procedures of schools, and from policy discussions within state boards of education, state education departments, legislative bodies and committees, and special commissions, to name a few. Some of these are elected bodies, others appointed.

Moreover, the standards adopted rely on different theories of educational reform and improvement. Some states, such as Massachusetts, believe improvement comes from setting very challenging goals for the state's students. Others, such as Texas, believe that it is best achieved by beginning with more modest but attainable goals and then ratcheting them up over time. Both Massachusetts and Texas have enjoyed success relative to other states, but neither reform approach has been tested in any real sense, and different approaches may well depend on the circumstances of different states. The range of strategies can, however, be inferred from the distribution of state outcomes related to NCLB cutoff scores shown in figure 3.8.

The import of this messy array of standards and goals is that courts have a menu of choices, each with greater or lesser state authority behind them, but each also with tenuous linkage to the requirements of state constitutions. More importantly, the various state standards frequently imply very different ways of judging the schools and are not, in general, very consistent from one state to another. Standards also make assumptions about the relationship between educational resources (for example, class size) and achievement (such as improved test scores). Yet there is often little empirical evidence suggesting that the inputs required actually bear much, if any, relationship to the desired outcomes.

The courts do not help matters much in their often convoluted and conflicting discussions of the appropriate standard. A court, for example, may initially speak of requiring a "minimally adequate" or "basic" education, suggesting that once that floor is exceeded, the court's role ends.[5] But often these words are ignored, particularly when it comes to specifying the amount of funding deemed necessary for such an education in any remedy phase of a trial. Instead, citing cost studies that rely on aspirational state academic standards (adopted without regard to the state constitutional language) and other ambitious goals, courts order appropriation increases intended to support much more than a minimum or basic education.

Consider what happened during the course of the CFE litigation in New York. The courts initially defined adequacy as a "sound basic education" requiring "minimally adequate" resources, but what did this standard mean in practice?[6] The court went back and forth on this absolutely critical question. Part of the *CFE I* decision understood adequacy as requiring only a basic education, one that imparts "basic literacy, calculating and verbal skills."[7] In a subsequent opinion, however, Justice DeGrasse understood it to require an education that would enable students to understand "DNA evidence, statistical analysis and convoluted financial fraud," clearly a much higher standard.[8] In *CFE II*, the court further explained that a "sound basic education" must include a "meaningful high school education."[9] New York City schools were obviously already offering a high school education, so the operative word in the court's definition was "meaningful." But what does it take for a high school education to be "meaningful"? After three decisions from the Court of Appeals, two from the appellate division and two from the trial court, it is still difficult for someone reading the court's various opinions to decide whether New York's constitution requires a basic education, a world-class education, or something in between.

The New York courts' formulations of "adequacy" provided so little useful guidance that they were ignored in the so-called costing-out process, during which interested parties attempted to put a price tag on an "adequate" education in New York City. Instead, the cost consultants relied on varying mixes of the state academic standards for the outcomes that they and their sponsors deemed adequate for New York's students, even though the standard used by most of them, the Regents' Learning Standards, had been expressly rejected by the court as the standard of adequacy.[10]

If the courts cannot answer even these basic questions about what level of achievement constitutes adequacy, then literally hundreds of other operational questions that enter into the evaluation of evidence and the crafting of a remedy become even more difficult to address. How small do class sizes have to be in order to offer an adequate education? What qualifications must a teacher possess in order to be deemed "adequate"? What courses need to be offered for the curriculum to be "adequate"? What kinds of special programs need to be provided for at-risk students in order to make their education "adequate?" The answer to each question presumably requires the court to have a detailed understanding of the educational process and the effectiveness of different programs and policies, something that, as we argue in chapter 7, even experts in the field, much less the courts, do not have. Such educational questions are just the tip of the iceberg when it comes to actually implementing ambiguous court pronouncements on what constitutes the education required by a state constitution.

As we discuss in more detail later, policies that work through setting and regulating inputs have proved ineffective and even, in some cases, damaging to schools.[11] Simply put, requirements for employing certain levels of inputs—hours of instruction, for example—have in the past proved expensive and have not led to significantly higher achievement. Moreover, these choices, no matter how commonsensical they seem, can harm schools when they require changes that are not reliably translated into student performance. For example, California has detailed regulations on how many guidance counselors must be hired by each district. Guidance counselors may well be valuable, but is it good policy to dictate how many (and what their training must be) from the state capital without regard to district size, district circumstances, or alternative uses of funds? And, if the requirements are not met, is it a constitutional violation?[12] Moreover, with complicated regulations, conflicts arise. For example, a New York teachers' union official, representing the physical education teachers, testified in the state assembly that the legislature should work to enforce the physical education regulations, noting members' comments that they were " 'totally disheartened' by how many of their schools have eliminated or reduced physical education instruction to allow more time in the day for academic intervention services—all for the sake of raising test scores."[13] Is the court prepared to make judgments on such trade-offs? And does the failure to provide the physical education time found in the regulations constitute evidence of a constitutional violation?

The courts have in the end resorted to various heuristics to determine whether the existing system of education is "adequate" under the constitution. On the resource side, they have used equity-type evidence to judge what is sufficient and what is not, comparing the resources available in certain districts to those in other districts in the state or even outside the state.[14] The New Jersey case is a classic example of how judges use such comparisons; the court insisted first on parity for the Abbott districts with the highest spending districts, and later on "parity plus"—in effect defining adequacy as something achieved only by exceeding the highest spending in the state. Similarly, in reaching his decision that New York City class sizes were too large and its teachers not qualified, Justice De-Grasse relied heavily on comparisons between the city and the surrounding wealthy suburbs. The Arkansas courts compared resources and student performance in Arkansas with national averages.[15] However, such equity-type evidence often begs the question, since existing resources, although less than those of other districts in or outside the state, may in fact still be "adequate," particularly if the education required is only a "basic" one. For example, Westchester County and other suburban school districts surrounding New York City are among the highest spending school districts in the world, and attract well-qualified teachers with some of the highest salaries in the country. The mere fact that New York City does not spend as much as Westchester County, or have teachers as qualified, says little about the adequacy of either the city's schools or its teachers.

One obvious source of objective "input" standards are accreditation standards adopted by the state itself or by accrediting agencies approved by the state. These standards often specify in detail the maximum class sizes, pupil–teacher ratios, administrative personnel, and other resources a school needs in order to be accredited.

Oddly, many courts have been reluctant to rely on such evidence, preferring instead the testimony of expert witnesses and school superintendents.[16] Or they rely on state policies and standards not related to accreditation, which have the effect of raising the constitutional standard and lowering the burden of proof at trial for plaintiffs. Many courts use aspirational state academic standards to judge whether the outcomes of the education system are "adequate." The effect of such rulings has been to raise the constitutional floor almost to the ceiling, since such standards may be difficult for any state to meet. Adequacy cases in Wyoming and Kansas illustrate this development, the former involving high input standards and the latter high output standards.

In Wyoming the court set the constitutional standard so high that, if literally applied, it could never be attained. The Wyoming Constitution requires the legislature to "provide for the maintenance of a complete and uniform system of public instruction" and to provide sufficient revenues to "create and maintain a thorough and efficient system of public schools, adequate to the proper instruction of all youth of the state, between the ages of six and twenty-one years."[17] In a 1995 decision, the Wyoming Supreme Court "interpreted" this language to require that a Wyoming education "be the best that we can do." The court also informed the legislature that a "lack of financial resources will not be an acceptable reason for failure to provide the best education."[18] In other words, under the court order, Wyoming's legislature had to provide and pay for the "best" education no matter how much it cost. In case anyone failed to get its point the first time around, the Wyoming Supreme Court revisited the case in 2001 and confirmed that when it said "best," it meant the "best"—that is, "of a quality that is both visionary and unsurpassed."[19]

The Wyoming court's ruling, if maintained, would thus ensure indefinite court control over education policy and funding. No matter how much money is spent on education, there will always be "visionary" education programs and services that Wyoming has not yet tried, and superintendents ready to make the case for them.[20] Indeed, between 1996 and 2007, Wyoming climbed from spending just over the national average to one of the highest, if not the highest, spending states in the country.[21] Finally, in 2008, thirteen years after its decision that education in Wyoming had to be the "best," the Wyoming Supreme Court perhaps recognized that this standard is impracticable, and it ruled that the legislature was furnishing the "thorough and efficient" education mandated by the state constitution. In dismissing the case, the court hardly mentions the impossibly high standard it had set earlier or whether the legislature was indeed funding the "best" education for Wyoming's children.[22]

On the output side, Kansas shows the result when courts require an outcome standard so high that no state satisfies it. In December 2003, a trial judge held that Kansas' system of financing K–12 education was unconstitutional because it failed to provide sufficient funding for the "suitable education" required under the Kansas Constitution. Kansas students are among the highest performing in the country, but the state, like every other, has an achievement gap. Under the judge's order, the new funding plan had to provide "resources necessary to close the 'achievement gap' " and to comply with "state accreditation standards, No Child Left Behind, and all other relevant statutory and rule requirements."[23] Although these are all worthy goals, not one of the fifty states has even come close to meeting them. A large achievement gap has existed in this country since test scores were first collected, and has persisted in every state, despite the end to legal segregation and the billions of dollars spent on remedial programs for poor and minority children.[24] Nevertheless, in 2005, the Kansas Supreme Court affirmed the trial court's ruling and ordered the Kansas legislature increase annual K–12 funding by over $850 million deemed necessary under a costing-out study to close achievement gaps that had thus far proved intractable.[25] No one would deny that schools should seek to narrow achievement gaps and educate all children so that they learn at acceptable levels regardless of their individual circumstances. But encouraging all children to meet high goals is far different from saying that until these goals are met, a state's educational funding system is unconstitutional and should remain under court supervision. If that were the case, the courts would be running the school systems in all fifty states.[26]

Many people, including judges, have a difficult time distinguishing between legislatively or administratively set standards and constitutional standards, but the difference is a critical one. Only the violation of the latter confers any authority on the courts to intervene. Yet the line between the two becomes blurred in many adequacy cases, with the courts ordering states to ensure not the minimum education referred to in the constitution, which would give the legislature significant discretion in what changes to make and how to pay for them, but the "high minimum" education required by state academic standards, which leaves little legislative discretion.

Adequacy plaintiffs point to the federal No Child Left Behind Act, which requires that all students be "proficient" or better as measured by state tests by 2014. However, having Congress set an admirable goal many years in the future is quite different from judging adequacy under the language of individual state constitutions. As we have said, there is no evidence that when NCLB was adopted and states were setting academic standards, either Congress or state legislators were attempting to interpret the constitutions of any of the fifty states. And surely most states would object to the view that federal law superseded the specific elements of the educational clauses in state constitutions. On a practical level, NCLB is also a law subject to change and modification, and 2014 is far in the future. We can only speculate about what the target or standard will be by 2014, or what the tests that measure compliance with those standards will contain.[27] Indeed, according to Michael Rebell, who initiated the CFE lawsuit in New York, most educators consider NCLB's goal of universal proficiency by 2014 to be "grossly unrealistic."[28]

We say again: there is nothing wrong with setting high standards for all children. Indeed, we endorse standards that challenge students to do their best. As Robert Costrell of the Department of Education Reform at the University of Arkansas has explained: "One approach to standard-setting is to set an ambitious goal with the aim of stimulating progress toward that goal, even if that goal may never be fully achieved." NCLB's goal of 100 percent proficiency by 2014, he reminds us, is an "obvious example."[29] But linking a state's financial liability to a legal requirement that will be difficult or impossible to meet—all children must meet high state academic standards—"risks transforming a race to the top to a race to the bottom" in setting standards.[30] A state should be able to encourage its students to meet high academic standards without the catch-22 implication that, if it sets them too high, it will be held financially liable for billions of dollars. As Costrell points out: "Under adequacy doctrine, states would, in effect, be barred or at least discouraged from setting high standards strategically as a means toward obtaining educational progress."[31]

This is no idle concern. A number of states have slashed their proficiency standards precisely because of the potential sanctions built into NCLB.[32] Even a proponent of adequacy litigation like Michael Rebell acknowledges as much in a recent article.[33] The threat to high standards posed by constitutionally based adequacy suits is potentially much more significant than that posed by NCLB sanctions, and it would not be surprising to see other states lower their standards as the financial impact of adequacy decrees hits home and as legislators realize the role that high state academic standards play in judges' decision making. Although no state has yet to lower its standards in direct response to an adequacy suit, several have considered the possibility.[34]

The difficulty of translating vague constitutional guidelines on education into workable definitions has made it almost impossible to discern any pattern in adequacy court decisions across the country. The states with the highest spending end up with court orders requiring even higher levels of spending, while those states with the lowest spending often avoid liability completely. In 2004, the highest-spending states, on a per-pupil basis, were New Jersey, New York, Vermont, Massachusetts, and Connecticut. All have been held liable in adequacy lawsuits and have been ordered to increase spending. The lowest spenders were Arizona, Nevada, Idaho, Mississippi, and Utah. None have been ordered by the courts to increase their spending on K–12 education.[35]

These anomalies cannot be explained by reference to the strength of the constitutional provisions in the various states. Even adequacy litigation proponents find little relationship between the court decisions and the constitutional language.[36] Scholars and some courts have used a four-category system to rate the strength of the duty imposed upon state legislatures by their state's education clauses. Under this system, a Category I clause is the weakest and merely requires "free public schools." New York's education clause requiring "free common schools" is an example of a Category I clause. A Category II clause includes some minimal standard of quality. Kansas falls into this category with its requirement that a "suitable education" be provided. Category III requires "stronger and more specific education mandates and purpose preambles." Wyoming, with its requirement of a "thorough and efficient" education falls into this category. The strongest are Category IV clauses, which impose a maximum duty on the legislature. Illinois, and Florida's clauses, which require the legislature to provide and pay for "high quality" schools, are Category IV clauses.[37] The result is that New York, a very high spender with the weakest constitutional language in the country, has been ordered to provide an education second to none, while Illinois and Florida, relatively low spenders with the strongest constitutional language in the country, have never been held liable in an adequacy case.[38] For such reason, constitutional scholars Joshua Dunn and Martha Derthick described the trial court's decision in the *CFE* case as follows: "The judge had become completely unmoored from the text [of the New York Constitution] and was sailing in purely policy waters."[39]

Judges who make use of state standards in interpreting the state constitution do so with some risk. An apparently straightforward choice of standards for adequacy can have profound effects for state educational policy and the dynamics of student performance. It may be that judges have begun to recognize this fact, because in more recent decisions, they have drawn back from asking whether children are meeting state academic standards, and have instead considered whether they are making progress toward meeting them. This was true in both Texas and Massachusetts, where the high courts upheld the constitutionality of the state education systems, despite significant shortcomings in the area of student performance. The courts reasoned instead that the states had succeeded in raising student performance, even though, as the Massachusetts court stated, "much work remains."[40]

## The Element of Causation

Perhaps the clearest finding of research on student achievement is that a wide range of influences enter into determining what a student knows. Although the Coleman Report may have overstated the case, this early investigation of student performance demonstrated vividly that family background and school peers had a powerful impact on outcomes.[41] Such findings have been reproduced in broad terms in virtually all subsequent studies. Recent analyses have emphasized the importance of the preparation and knowledge that students bring with them to schools.[42] Some researchers even suggest that the role of schools in affecting student outcomes is limited, if not negligible.[43]

It is easy to overstate this case, but it does raise an important issue. We may as a matter of social policy want schools to compensate for student deficits arising elsewhere. Indeed, the faith in schools to level the playing field for children was behind U.S. efforts to bring about universal public schooling, as well as a variety of compensatory programs and income-based higher education admission and aid programs. But, at the same time, no one can seriously claim that the magnitude of existing achievement gaps has been caused by the schools.

The issue of the causative link between existing achievement levels and achievement gaps on the one hand and the education provided by the schools on the other enters into court discussions in a variety of ways. First, establishing causation is a required element of virtually every legal cause of action. Second, causation is a crucially important issue, not only in "assessing blame" but also in devising effective remedies. Yet, it is also a contentious area of research, opening the courts up to scientific disagreements that are not readily resolved in trials. Third, if a court relies on student achievement in finding that the constitution has been violated, then its remedy, in order to be effective, cannot ignore issues of causation and the multiple influences on achievement.

Proof of causation is critical in almost every court case. To be liable for breach of contract, one must have caused the breach. Tort liability depends on proof that the defendant's negligence was the proximate cause of the plaintiff's injury. In prior federal court school desegregation litigation, both states and school districts were held liable for and ordered to correct only those deficiencies that they had caused and had the power to correct. Thus, in *Freeman v. Pitts*, the Supreme Court declined to hold school districts liable for one-race schools caused by demographic forces.[44] In the desegregation case of *Milliken v. Bradley*, the Court refused to extend its remedy to suburban school districts unless it could be shown that such school districts had played a role in causing segregation in the city schools.[45] In *Jenkins III*, the Court held that the state of Missouri and the Kansas City school district could not be held liable for the low achievement of black children, except for the incremental effect caused by prior illegal or de jure segregation.[46] In the state court "equity" cases, the states had it within their power, and their power alone, to correct inequities in their school funding laws.

The language of most adequacy decisions also appears to require proof of causation before plaintiffs are entitled to relief. But this language is often ignored by the courts in reaching a final decision. This fundamental rule of law, and its violation in adequacy cases, is again best exemplified by the New York case. Prior to the trial, New York's Court of Appeals in *CFE I* ruled that plaintiffs had the burden to prove both that (1) there had been a failure to provide a "sound basic education" in the New York City public schools and (2) such failure had been "caused" by the state financing system. Recognizing the difficulties inherent in reliance on outcome measures, the Court of Appeals instructed the trial court to use caution in relying on outcome measures such as standardized tests, because such outcomes were caused by a "myriad of factors" other than the state funding system.[47] Yet, because of the difficulty in parceling out responsibility for low student performance among so many different factors, the trial court largely ignored this advice, and relied heavily on subpar outcome measures without really addressing the causation issues.

Just as happened in New York, other courts have tended to duck the issue of causality and responsibility altogether. Instead, they have taken the easy way out, finding implicitly or explicitly that it is the responsibility of the state to correct problems from virtually any source—state policy, local practices and policy, and even adverse home and neighborhood environments. Because school districts are political subdivisions of the state, the courts are able to hold the state vicariously liable for waste, inefficiency, and mismanagement at the local level.

This approach has enormous consequences, at both the liability and the remedy stages of an adequacy lawsuit. It virtually guarantees that a state will be held strictly liable for poor student performance, regardless of the level of funding it provides. Because the court disregards significant causes of low achievement, other than a lack of funding, during the liability stage, it tends to overlook them during the remedy phase, when the focus is on solving the problem highlighted by the court: insufficient funding. Reluctant to "blame the victim," the courts have largely bypassed in their decisions the factors outside the schools that influence student achievement, such as poverty, crime, drugs, and home and neighborhood problems. The assumption is that schools, given sufficient funding, can overcome such problems. If they do not, they must not have enough money and resources.[48]

No empirical evidence indicates that our current schools, even those with ample resources, are able to systematically turn students at risk of academic failure into high achievers. Although a few individual schools may have succeeded in reaching this goal, no district has come close to achieving and sustaining it on a systemwide basis.[49] Ironically, the states and school districts that seem to have the most success suggest that resources are not the key. For example, in the 1990s, North Carolina and Texas were generally recognized as having had the most success in educating their poor and minority populations, yet neither state even approached the national average in their per-pupil expenditures on K–12 education.[50]

We believe that skirting around the admittedly sensitive issue of what causes poor achievement, as the courts have largely done, ends up hurting both teachers and children, and that the issue must be tackled before any serious headway can be made in the fight for improved schools. First, as we will discuss in chapter 6, the courts' remedies—based on the premise that more educational resources are the key to solving the problem—have not obviously helped children. The premise itself is, of course, open to serious question. Convincing research shows the very significant role that home and community play in a child's education. If legislators continue to believe that spending on the schools can overcome the harmful influences of the home or community, then potentially effective ways of addressing the problem, such as programs that promote stronger families and better jobs, may be relegated to the back burner.

Holding schools solely responsible for student achievement also suggests that educators working in low-scoring schools are incompetent. If all students can learn, and they do not, it must be the schools' and teachers' fault; insufficient resources can be blamed only up to a point. The truth is that a teacher in a high-poverty school may be doing a good job if only 70 percent of her students meet state standards, while a teacher in a wealthier community may be doing a poor job even though 90 percent of her students meet state standards. Yet it is the schools in high-poverty communities that tend to be designated as "failing." These schools already have a difficult time attracting qualified teachers,[51] and their disadvantaged students are more difficult to teach. The schools are often located in less desirable neighborhoods. If on top of all this, the system places the blame for students' low achievement on the teachers and administrators—who may in fact be doing a good job—it becomes even tougher for such schools to attract good teachers. Richard Rothstein perhaps puts it best in his book, *Class and Schools*, when he suggests the harm that may be done by policies based on the view that all children can learn given sufficient resources. These policies

de-legitimize good and great teachers who dedicate themselves to raising minority achievement in realistic increments. They drive out of the teaching profession decent teachers who feel inadequate to the task of reaching utopian goals, or who resent the cynicism of politicians and administrators who demand that such goals be attained. If this disconnect continues between what is realistically possible and the goals we establish for educators, the nation risks abandoning public education only to those willing to pander to political fashion by promising to achieve in schools what they know, in their hearts, is not possible.[52]

Properly assigning responsibility for societal and individual problems external to the schools remains problematic, and illustrates how difficult it is to define "adequacy." But there is some hope that new "value-added" measures of student achievement, discussed in chapter 9, will make it feasible to separate out the impacts of schools and teachers from other influences so that the true causes of low achievement can be first determined and then addressed.

Determining causation also involves the issue of efficiency—specifically, how efficiently local districts use funds. Although the constitutions of twelve states use the word "efficient" in describing the required attributes of their education systems, courts rarely try to determine whether inefficient spending—paying for unproductive programs, wasting resources, negotiating costly and onerous union contracts—explains why a district lacks necessary funds. While courts are not hesitant to order cost studies, no court has yet ordered a management audit to ensure that local monies are being efficiently utilized and to identify savings that could be put to more productive uses. Even though Wyoming's constitution requires, among other things, an "efficient" system of education, the court's opinions are almost silent on the efficient or cost-effective use of funds. Indeed, as previously discussed, the court's order to provide the "best education," an education "visionary and unsurpassed," indicates that "efficiency" was the furthest thing from the court's mind in reaching its decision.[53] One of the many court decisions in the New Jersey adequacy litigation discusses the need for efficient expenditure of funds, but makes it clear that it is looking to the state, and not the local districts, to ensure efficiency.[54] Courts in Kansas and North Carolina used the same rationale to avoid addressing local waste and mismanagement.[55]

But while making the state responsible for solving local problems may seem like a simple solution, it is anything but—particularly when the court makes no effort to identify or quantify the effects of waste and inefficiency arising from purely local decisions and actions. A whole host of practical, legal, and political factors combine to inhibit the legislature from interfering with the local running of the schools. For example, the North Carolina court made the state responsible even for the supervision of principals and teachers, a task totally impractical in the real world. Moreover, the legislatures, left mostly with orders requiring more money but with virtually nothing specifying the degree or nature of local shortcomings, are under very little pressure to adopt the sweeping reforms measures needed to address local waste and mismanagement. These reforms, therefore, have very little chance of being adopted. As we will suggest in chapter 9, court decisions could be worded to encourage the legislatures to enact such reforms, but to date, judges have preferred simply to make the state responsible in a general way for solving such problems.

These local problems are not minor; indeed, they will pervade our discussion about funding systems aimed at improving school outcomes. Examples from the New York City trial provide some indication of the scope of the issue, as witnesses for plaintiffs and defendants alike discussed in stark terms the waste and inefficiency in school operations. School officials and plaintiffs' experts used words like "ineffective and inefficient," "inhumane," and "dysfunctional and cumbersome" to describe the district's recruiting practices.[56] The system for removing incompetent teachers was just as bad. Chancellor Harold Levy called it "broken" and the administration itself "oblivious to the serious consequences of its institutionalized indolence."[57] The districts involved in the New York litigation rated over 99 percent of their teachers as "satisfactory" on the evaluation form developed in conjunction with the teachers' union.[58] However, at trial, the superintendents testified that the rating forms meant little and that "unsatisfactory" ratings were reserved only for the "worst of the worst" or those teachers "actively endangering children."[59] The 204-page collective bargaining agreement itself contained a variety of workplace rules that inhibit efforts to operate the schools more efficiently. The work rules extended to the whole range of school operations. Among other things, they prohibited secondary school teachers from teaching more than three hours and forty-five minutes a day.[60] Thus, classes in New York City schools had four to six more students than classes in the rest of the state, even though pupil–teacher ratios were almost the same.[61] It was these rules that in 2006 forced the New York City public schools to keep forty-four unneeded assistant principals, at an annual cost of roughly $5 million; their jobs were protected by the union contract.[62]

There was ample other evidence of waste and mismanagement. In 1998, a commission, which included the chancellor of the New York City schools, unanimously concluded that the school system, relying on referrals and overly restrictive guidelines, was placing "tens of thousands" of students who were not disabled into special education programs, greatly increasing their cost.[63] Fraud and corruption were rampant in the school system: investigators found corruption in community school board elections, patronage and nepotism in local school boards, social promotions, fiscal mismanagement and irresponsibility, payments for no work, and fraudulent inflation of funding levels.[64]

Astonishingly, nowhere in their several opinions do the New York courts find that such gross local mismanagement and even wrongdoing had a significant causal effect on performance or on the availability of sufficient funds. But this is not atypical of the courts' hands-off approach to assessing the adverse effects of local waste or other factors. The evidence, of course, may be difficult for courts to grapple with, particularly when elements of the problem, such as existing contract provisions, are common across schools. But both the immediate and long-run implications are evident. When, for example, the parties in CFE tried to settle the case later, the city of New York, which also funds the city schools, refused to contribute anything, as Mayor Bloomberg was able to rely on court orders that laid the blame on the state and were largely silent about local waste and mismanagement.[65]

Although the issue of causation is central to proving legal liability, courts hearing school finance cases have attempted to avoid it. Instead of acknowledging that local problems might be a cause of poor student achievement, most courts hold simply that the state created the local districts and thus is responsible for their performance. Legal principles aside, there is some appeal to putting the onus on the state to improve the achievement of low-performing students, regardless of cause. It seems like an "easy fix" that avoids getting the court entangled in the affairs of the local school districts. The problem, however, is that the causes of achievement shortcomings are critically important when it comes to crafting an effective remedy.

## Problems Relating to Remedy

After liability is determined, the next step is determining a remedy. In many adequacy cases, this has been increased funding of education. Minimally, the directive of the court has been to return the case to the legislature, usually with some direction to determine how much more funding is required (e.g., conduct a cost study) and then to take steps to provide such funding.[66] This has been the procedure followed by the courts in New York, Arkansas, Montana, Kansas, New Jersey, Wyoming, and a number of other states.[67]

Courts have sought financial remedies for several reasons. First, until recently, plaintiffs and their experts, supported by state policy pronouncements like "all children can achieve at high levels, given sufficient resources," have been able to convince the courts of two important premises. The first is that low achievement can be overcome with more money and resources, and the second is that a rational and scientific means exists to determine how much more money is needed. At the same time, courts have been wary, and in some cases downright scornful, of testimony that suggests that more money is not the solution to low achievement.[68] Many find the notion counterintuitive, despite hundreds of studies and real-life examples showing that there is little relationship between student achievement and spending, at least as school districts have traditionally spent their budgets. Perhaps if fundamental changes were made in the way the money was spent, such remedies might be more effective, but that is rarely, if ever, a part of any court-ordered remedy. Indeed, plaintiffs almost always oppose significant changes in the way education funds are spent, thus almost guaranteeing no improvement in student achievement. Nor do the cost studies often relied on by the courts or legislatures recommend any changes in the status quo. In fact, they affirmatively state that decisions on how to spend additional funds are to be left to the school authorities.[69]

This promise of an easy and effective solution is an alluring one, but it has proved illusory. Additional spending has not solved the problem. Nor can costing-out studies tell the courts or legislatures how much an education designed to produce acceptable student performance should cost.

A second reason courts turn to financial remedies is that they save the court from involvement in the day-to-day operation of local and state school systems. In that sense, they are consistent with the goal of minimizing judicial interference by leaving the resolution of local waste and mismanagement problems to the legislature. Given the practical problems it would entail, many—but not all—courts properly infer that involvement in the affairs of local school districts and state education authorities would be a nightmare.[70] The way out of the dilemma is painfully obvious: most courts simply opt to avoid the issue. But if local district management, waste, and inefficiency are significant problems, it is wrong for courts to ignore them or try to mask their symptoms with more money. Nor should it be suggested that with enough money, problems of inefficiency and mismanagement can be overcome; this is unfair to the taxpaying public. The biggest reason that courts should not simply ignore local mismanagement is that doing so sends a strong signal to the local school districts that more money will be forthcoming regardless of how the district is managed. (We show later in this book how courts can take a much more active stance in identifying these problems for the legislature without making themselves into a super–school board, hopelessly entangled in running the schools.)

Take the court's opinion in *CFE II*, which concludes that insufficient funding was at fault based on evidence that some of the shortcomings plaintiffs alleged, e.g., large class sizes, could be resolved if the state provided the New York City school district more money. Obviously, more money can buy more things, but this line of reasoning ignores the possibility that the district might have had the necessary funds but wasted them. Under this rationale, the board of education could have been wasting half of its entire $10 billion–plus budget, and the plaintiffs could still have established the necessary causal link by showing that more money from the state would have covered up the shortages (caused by waste) and enabled the school district to purchase educational resources its schools were lacking (as a result of waste).[71]

Finally and perhaps most important, remedies requiring increased funding are far easier for the courts to order, monitor, and enforce. The application of simple mathematics will enable the court and parties to determine whether the state is in compliance with the court's order. And the remedies can be enforced through injunctive relief (the state must comply, or the court will enjoin the operation of the present school funding laws and close down the schools).

In summary, courts have tended toward such spending remedies because they believe they will work and because they are the easiest to monitor and enforce. The problem, of course, is that these remedies have not worked, as we show in detail in the next chapter. Nor do they give the legislature the tools it needs to address many of the underlying problems of poor student achievement. Finally, by intervening in appropriations—the power most clearly delegated by most state constitutions to the legislative branches, and certainly most zealously guarded by legislatures—such remedies raise important issues of separation of powers. The strain in the relationships between the different branches of government can be enormous. George Will, the well-known conservative columnist, was so outraged by the court order in the New York school litigation that he had this advice for the state legislature: "New York's Supreme Court can neither tax nor spend. The state legislature is not a party to the suit, so it cannot be held in contempt. Perhaps it should just ignore the court's ruling as noise not relevant to the rule of law. Which happens to be the case."[72]

The idea that the achievement problems can be solved simply with more resources has obviously already been considered by state legislatures. One needs only look at the spending record described in chapter 3. Is it possible that the effect of added resources has not shown up yet because we have yet to reach some minimum level? This seems unlikely, since U.S. school spending leads most of the world by a considerable margin, while U.S. achievement does not. Or is it that the legislatures have not just given more resources but have also encumbered them with spending directives, regulations, and the like that have muted their effectiveness? If that is true, the courts should deal with the specific issues of causation, i.e., the constraints inhibiting the effectiveness of added resources. In most cases, they have not, wrongly concluding that increased resources will solve the problem.

## Problems Inherent in the Makeup and Processes of the Courts

Neither the courts nor the process of litigation is designed to address the types of complex policy issues that typically arise in adequacy cases, and that makes an effective outcome even more unlikely.[73] To start with, courts are not policymaking bodies, and neither their makeup nor the processes they follow lend themselves to the task of making policy. Judges have no particular expertise when it comes to education or finance matters. They are generalists, handling all manner of cases. They also do not have staff members with educational expertise at their disposal, in contrast to legislative bodies, which through their various senate and house committees and their permanent staffs, can draw upon a wide range of experience and expertise in complex education policy and finance issues.

Courts also are limited in their access to information. In a trial, only the views of the particular advocacy organizations bringing the lawsuit and the views of the "state" get aired before the court. Although the "state" has a seat in the courtroom, its contribution may be severely limited, depending on who directs the defense of the case. The judge is legally forbidden to consider the opinions of anyone who is not a party to the suit. The only evidence that matters is that presented by witnesses, who in most cases are members of the educational establishment who stand to benefit from the case and are unlikely to challenge the status quo. Legislatures, on the other hand, have access to a wide range of information from many different sources with different points of view.

Nor is the litigation process conducive to formulating policy. Judges rely on the direct examination of witnesses followed by cross-examination by the other side to elicit the information on which they will make their decision. This technique is designed to ferret out the truth or to determine which witnesses are the most credible. It is not intended for the development of nuanced policies to address problems of poor student performance.

Other aspects of the litigation process, which work fine in typical lawsuits, fail in adequacy suits mainly because of the parties involved. In normal litigation, collusion among the litigants might be grounds for sanctions and dismissal of the lawsuit, but not so in many adequacy lawsuits.[74] The judicial process is not designed for suits in which half or more of the defendants are in league with plaintiffs.[75] Plaintiffs in adequacy cases include public school districts seeking higher funding, advocacy groups eager to channel more resources into education, and the teachers' unions. All are committed to the existing system of education in this country.[76] The defendants are the state, its governor, and the state educational authorities (board of education, department of education, and superintendent of education). Often one or more of these defendants are aligned with the plaintiffs and their supporters to obtain substantial increases in appropriations for K–12 education. As a result, they either sympathize with or are ambivalent about opposing plaintiffs' claims. This is particularly true of the state education authorities, who often line up with plaintiffs.

As a result, the usual adversarial nature of litigation is lost or weakened. In a typical lawsuit, the plaintiff's claims for more money are tempered by the other parties to the suit; in an adequacy suit, more money for the plaintiffs may also be the goal of some of the defendants. The litigation process is based on the premise that all the real parties in interest are before the court and that each party is represented by an attorney who will be a "zealous" advocate for his or her client. Unfortunately, this predicate to a fair and impartial decision-making process is absent in many an adequacy case, where the lawyers charged with defending the state's system of education find themselves representing one or more defendants acting in concert with the plaintiffs.

The reasons for this collusion are not difficult to fathom. State education authorities belong to the public school establishment, and part of their job is to lobby for higher appropriations for education. Adequacy suits hold out the promise of more money for education; with more money comes greater state control, which most state departments of education would like to have. Increased appropriations for education, top priority in funding over other state programs and sectors, more state education personnel, greater control over local districts— what is not to like for state education officials? Moreover, it is not their responsibility to worry about where the money is going to come from; that is the job of the governor and legislature.

Consider what happened in New York. The state board of regents, state education department (SED), and state commissioner of education, all initially named as defendants in the *CFE* lawsuit, were all solidly behind plaintiffs during the trial of the *CFE* case. It turned out that the SED had a "study group" that had been working for over a decade to accumulate evidence that a plaintiff could use to sue the state for more money for education. The Equity Study Group was formed to support the board of regents' adoption of the New Compact for Learning in 1999, which sought, among other things, to eliminate the link between socioeconomic status and performance.[77] At the initial meeting of the study group, then state commissioner of education Tom Sobol made it clear that one of its main purposes was to pave the way for litigation against the state: a "purpose of this task force is to establish a body of work that others who may be so inclined can use to challenge in court the equity of the current system."[78] Five members of the study group later appeared as expert witnesses for the plaintiff at trial.[79]

The New York situation is not an isolated instance. When North Dakota was sued in an adequacy case, the commissioner of education demanded that the Department of Public Instruction (DPI), one of the defendants, be assigned its own lawyer so it could join the lawsuit with plaintiffs.[80] During the course of the litigation, a high-ranking DPI official attended meetings with plaintiffs' attorney sponsored by the National Access Network, a plaintiffs' organization that encourages adequacy litigation around the country.[81] Kansas provides yet another example. In adjudging whether legislation enacted in 2005 brought the state's education funding system into compliance with the state's education clause, each of the state defendants, including the "State," its governor, the state board of education, and the commissioner of education, took different positions.[82]

As an additional complication, the real parties in interest, those persons and governmental bodies that do have an incentive to defend the case (i.e., the legislature or its leaders), are not parties at all; even if initially named in the suit, they seek to be dismissed at an early stage. No politician wants to be sued in any circumstances, and legislators do not want to be seen as "anti-education" or "anti-children." They choose to put off the day of reckoning until they are out of office and seek to get out of the case at the earliest moment, often with the cooperation of the plaintiffs who sued them in the first place. The result is that many of the state officials who remain parties to the suit align themselves with plaintiffs, while the state officials who are the real parties in interest rarely participate in the defense of the case. At some point, the legislators may find themselves back in the fray, as they are handed the bill, but to a legislator in this era of term limits, two years is like a thousand years. By then, the problem will be someone else's to solve.

It is also very difficult for state defendants to argue for reform measures that have not gone through the "give and take" of the political process. The legislature is not normally a party to the case, and even if it were, it would be difficult to convince legislative leaders to advocate particular remedies that may not yet have been debated and adopted through the legislative process. The "state" is often unable, for essentially political reasons, to put its best foot forward at the trial. How can it decide upon the remedies to pursue in court before they are fully "vetted" and adopted by the legislature? With the state thus handicapped and unable to propose alternative solutions, the result is vigorous support for higher spending from plaintiffs and their powerful supporters.

The root of the problem is that the defense is forced to make political choices as part of the judicial process, and this is virtually impossible to do. Two particularly important issues are in play. First, because the governor and legislature have programs in existence, the defense must generally base its case on these—even if the policies are in transition or are intermediate programs. Second, witnesses for the defense are not encouraged to provide nuanced positions, because any judgment is likely not to be nuanced: the choices are often either no additional funding or the generally large and political unviable sums demanded by plaintiffs. These circumstances, as well as the fact that the state education authorities may differ among themselves about proper remedies, tie the state's hands, especially during the remedial stage of an adequacy case.

Moreover, organizations seeking to offer alternatives to plaintiffs' quest for greater appropriations are not allowed to participate in the trial. In an adequacy case brought against the state of Arizona by six local school districts whose students were performing far below standard, a pro-voucher group tried to intervene. Instead of ordering that more money be provided to the districts that had failed for years to properly educate their pupils, they argued that the court should order the state to provide funds directly to the students, who could then use them to immediately obtain an adequate education at another school. The motion to intervene was summarily denied by the court.[83] Similar motions to intervene by voucher advocates have also been denied in both New York and Georgia.[84] A recent New Jersey lower court decision also dismissed a case seeking more choice for students being ill-served by the existing system.[85] Once a state is held liable, usually with a court order directing or strongly suggesting more money as the remedy, alternative views of how to improve education get even less attention, as legislators focus on how to come up with the money to satisfy the court order and not on specific reforms.

The broader issue is that education is not the public's only concern or the only item on the legislative agenda. While the legislative process is sometimes derided because it devotes time and resources to a range of issues and not just education problems, its role is to weigh and balance the many demands facing it. Many educational advocates quite naturally prefer the courts because the discussion there is confined to a single issue: education. There are no competing demands, and advocates for other programs or taxpayers are excluded.[86] Those who favor more funding for schools may consider litigation a useful pragmatic device, but it violates the political processes that have been built into the federal and state constitutions. And even these advocates might start to question the wisdom of this approach if other interest groups, such as voucher proponents, find ways to introduce their agenda into court deliberations over appropriate remedies.

All these practical matters we have discussed—difficulties in defining adequacy, the reluctance of courts to address causation, their preference for monetary remedies, and the unsuitability of courts and the litigation process for adequacy cases—have combined to favor liability findings against the state and to encourage decisions that trace any inadequacies in the educational system to a lack of money. Other obstacles to improving student achievement have been lost in the legal shuffle and ignored in the remedy phase of the case. The result in many states has been to maximize judicial intervention in an area specifically relegated to the legislative branch by most state constitutions: the power to appropriate funds from the public treasury. In the last several years, a few courts have adopted a more deferential stance, but only the future will tell whether the courts continue in that direction.

# 6 | The Effectiveness of Judicial Remedies

There is one most curious aspect to the involvement of state courts in school finance. In the four decades during which these cases have touched on over forty states, it has become commonplace for the plaintiffs to cite the number of cases in which the plaintiffs have prevailed, and to oftentimes describe the nature and magnitude of the judgments in other states. On the other hand, plaintiffs rarely, if ever, introduce evidence that relates a court's ruling requiring more equitable or increased funding to better performance of students on state achievement tests or other performance measures.

In this chapter, we take up this critical, but often omitted, issue. Have court interventions helped children? If they have, then perhaps the strain on our democratic institutions and tripartite system of government is worth it, and we might be able to justify disregarding troubling questions court interventions raise about judicial authority and decision making. If, on the other hand, judicial interventions have not led to better achievement, then one would be hard-pressed to justify their continuation. The ultimate objective of an adequacy remedy is to help children, who are the focus of the case because either their schools lack resources or their achievement is unacceptable. The resources themselves—and any collateral benefit to the adults in the system in the form of higher salaries, more job opportunities, or the demand for more services—are a means to an end: providing better education for children. If schools are spending a lot more money without seeing significant improvement in student achievement, only those with a financial stake in the particular programs would judge the remedy a success.

To answer this all-encompassing question, we examine whether judicial remedies have in fact helped children by looking at the experiences of Kentucky, New Jersey, Wyoming, and Massachu-

setts, the four states that have had significant court-ordered or induced remedies in place the longest. Unfortunately, the billions of
dollars in increased spending generated by adequacy lawsuits do
not appear to have substantially improved student performance.

Virtually no peer-reviewed or other credible articles or studies
claim to have found significant, positive effects on student achievement in states that have implemented adequacy remedies.[1] While
reports on the benefits of adequacy litigation readily emphasize the
prekindergarten programs, smaller classes, or new buildings made
possible by expenditures increased under the court order, they are
mostly silent on whether the additional resources have actually improved student performance.[2] Given the support adequacy litigation enjoys among professors in the nation's colleges of education,
the absence of articles documenting test scores rising in response
to more funding is striking.[3] If there were good news to report,
adequacy proponents would doubtless be singing the praises of
court-ordered remedies in every academic journal of note, and a
news media already favorably disposed toward adequacy lawsuits
would be publicizing the findings. The harsh reality is that in those
states where a court-ordered remedy has been in effect long enough
for a fair evaluation, patterns of student failure, especially for poor
and minority students, have not significantly changed.

The four states we consider in this chapter have had substantial
adequacy remedies in place over a long period of time. Each has
implemented massive spending increases for K–12 education
amounting to many billions of dollars, which have resulted in new
and improved facilities in many school districts, more up-to-date
textbooks, additional technology, increased numbers of personnel,
and expanded programs. Positive effects on student achievement,
however, have proved elusive.

Our analysis relies mainly on NAEP scores, instead of scores
on state-administered tests, for several reasons.[4] Most importantly,
NAEP test results are available for all four states over the entire
period of the remedy, whereas in several of the states the state academic tests have been changed during the course of the remedy,
making it difficult or impossible to compare scores pre- and post-
remedy. NAEP results also allow the academic performance of a
state's students to be compared with the performance of students

in other states over the period of the remedy. Since the remedies in three of the states we examine are statewide and affect all students, the only available comparisons are performance over time compared to what happened in other states. Finally, NAEP results are not susceptible to manipulation by state departments of education and school districts under pressure to look good. Although the states we evaluate did not participate in the NAEP testing program every year, we are fortunate to have test scores available for most of them on three tests—grade 4 reading and math and grade 8 math—both prior to the commencement of their respective remedies and at the present time. These measures allow us to compare student performance at two points in time: one before the remedy and one after the remedy had been in place long enough to have produced positive results.

During the period we examine (1992 to 2007 for most of the analyses), NAEP scores increased in almost every state, regardless of whether they received increased funding following an adequacy suit; therefore, the fact that NAEP scores in Wyoming, for example, increased over the course of the remedy tells us very little about the impact of the adequacy remedy in that state.[5] Given the extraordinary funding increases in the four states we examine, however, we would expect them to significantly outperform other states that did not enjoy the same financial commitment. For this reason, we assess how well our target states have performed relative to the rest of the nation. Moreover, since high overall test scores can mask the low performance of many poor and minority children, we rely on the test scores for those groups that have historically performed worst and who are the principal target of these remedial dollars.[6] If the remedy does not help these children, the result will be an even wider achievement gap, and the remedy could hardly be viewed as a success.

## Kentucky

We begin with Kentucky because adequacy proponents consider it a model of what an adequacy lawsuit can accomplish.[7] But the plaudits heaped on the Kentucky remedy have focused principally on structural reforms made following the *Rose* decision, and with good reason. There is little evidence that student performance has significantly improved since the enactment of the Kentucky Education Reform Act of 1990 (KERA), the legislative response to the *Rose* decision. Rather, the evidence is largely disappointing, particularly for Kentucky's black students, its largest minority group.

The Kentucky remedy has been in place since the early 1990s. While the entire reform package was complicated, the impact on state spending was clear. Between 1990 and 2005, spending per pupil in the United States rose by 24 percent (after adjusting for inflation). Spending in Kentucky rose by close to 40 percent, the tenth largest growth among the states. It is natural to question whether this boost in state spending led to improvements relative to the rest of the country.

In an early assessment of impacts, John Poggio, a professor of educational psychology and research at the University of Kansas, analyzed state test scores under the Kentucky Instructional Results Information System (KIRIS), and concluded that students had made some progress from 1992 to 1998.[8] However, he also acknowledged that Kentucky's scores on national assessments, such as NAEP and ACT, had not made the same progress as the KIRIS scores.[9] Further analysis of the state test scores after 1998 is not possible because the state stopped using the KIRIS tests that year, and replaced them with a new test called the Commonwealth Accountability Testing System (CATS). The CATS tests are sufficiently different from the KIRIS that no valid comparisons can be made.[10] However, Kentucky students have participated in the NAEP testing program for many years, and their scores can be compared from 1992 to 2007 to determine whether any significant improvement has occurred over that fifteen-year period.

Educational funding was significantly increased following the *Rose* decision beginning in the 1991–92 school year. NAEP scores should reflect any positive effects of this increase. We first investigated the test scores of Kentucky's black children, who constitute about 11 percent of the state's public school enrollment. It is these students who have perennially scored the lowest on both the NAEP tests and Kentucky's own tests. Their scores are available on three

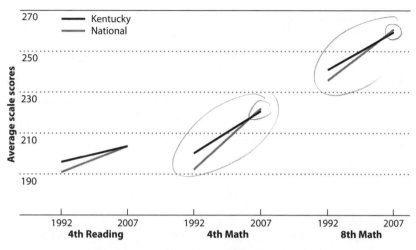

**6.1** Kentucky and National NAEP Trends for Black Students, 1992–2007

tests for several years beginning with 1992, when the remedy began, to the present (2007): fourth grade reading, fourth grade math, and eighth grade math. Figure 6.1 compares the NAEP scale scores for both Kentucky's black students and black students nationwide from 1992 to 2007 on these three tests.[11]

In fourth grade reading, black student scale scores in Kentucky increased 7 points from 1992 through 2007, from a score of 196 to 203. However, black students nationwide did better with a 12-point increase, from 191 to 203. Kentucky's black students had been 5 points above the national average for blacks in 1992 when the remedy commenced, but by 2007 they had fallen to the national average.

The trend was even worse for Kentucky's black fourth graders on the math test. From 1992 to 2007, their scores increased by 19 points, from 200 to 219. Nationwide, however, black students' scores increased by 30 points, from 192 to 222. In 1992, the state's fourth grade black students scored 8 points above the national average; by 2007, they had dropped to 3 points below it. The story was much the same for Kentucky's eighth grade black students. From 1992 to 2007, their math scores increased by 16 points, from 241 to 257, but nationwide, black student test scores rose by 23 points, from 236 to 259. In 1992, Kentucky's eighth grade black

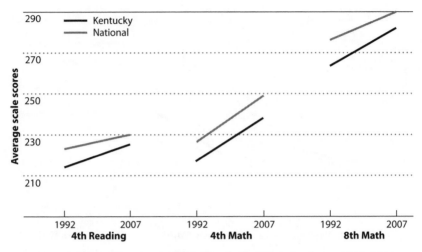

**6.2** Kentucky and National NAEP Trends for White Students, 1992–2007

students scored 5 points above the national average; by 2007, they were 2 points below it. In short, despite massive increases in spending and other reforms, Kentucky's black fourth and eighth graders have clearly lost ground to the rest of the nation on all three NAEP tests for which valid comparisons are available since implementation of the *Rose* remedy.

Kentucky's white students, 86 percent of the state's public school enrollment, fared better over the same period, although on all three tests their scores remained well below the national average for whites. As shown in figure 6.2, in fourth grade reading, Kentucky's white student scores increased by 11 points, from 214 to 225, compared to a national increase of 7 points from 223 to 230. In fourth grade math, Kentucky's white student scores increased by 21 points (from 217 to 238), matching the increase for white students nationwide (from 227 to 248). Eighth grade math scores rose 18 points (264 to 282), while the national average increased 14 points (276 to 290).

A recent analysis claims that the Kentucky remedy had some success in raising NAEP scores relative to the nation since 1998 on reading and since 2000 on math using the NAEP scores of all students, economically disadvantaged students, and black students.[12] However, the study suffers from major flaws, not the least of which is that its beginning scores are from 1998 and 2000, almost a decade after the remedy was commenced. Even allowing for that late date, however, the study itself indicates that on fourth and eighth grade math and reading tests, the same NAEP tests we use in our evaluation, Kentucky's gains for all three groups of children were significantly below the national gains on six measures, about the same on five measures and above the national gains on only one measure.[13]

These results are not very encouraging for Kentucky's much-celebrated adequacy remedy. Despite fifteen years of remediation, its white students still score well below the national average for whites on all three tests, while black students score under the national average for blacks in two of the three tests and at the national average in one (fourth grade reading). The state's white students have made some very limited progress relative to other states, but its black students have regressed over the fifteen-year course of the remedy when compared to the rest of the country on all three tests.[14]

## Wyoming

Even when compared to adequacy remedies in other states, the funding increases ordered in Wyoming have been extraordinary. Consistent with the *Campbell County* court decrees that education in Wyoming should be the "best" and "visionary and unsurpassed," and that the state should fund whatever such an education costs, the Wyoming legislature has responded with unprecedented hikes in its appropriations for K–12 education. Following the 1995 *Campbell County* decision, Wyoming's per-pupil expenditures rapidly escalated. Before 1996, Wyoming ranked slightly above the national average (4 percent) in its per-pupil expenditures; by 2005, its nominal expenditures were 12 percent above the national average, and it had climbed to thirteenth in the nation. But, it is more informative to look at spending adjusted for regional cost differences. On this measure, Wyoming climbed from the tenth highest spending state in 1997 to second in the nation (behind Vermont) in spending per child in 2005.[15] The cost model that the legislature (and the court) relied upon to determine funding "needs" was recalibrated in 2005, calling for substantial additional spending growth.[16] As a result, per-pupil expenditures increased another 27 percent between 2005 and 2007![17] This led the superintendent of public instruction, Jim McBride, to say that he "believes Wyoming will be the top state in public education in the next four or five years."[18]

The court remedy with the legislative responses has been in place for over a decade, and, in light of these dramatic spending increases, we might reasonably expect Wyoming's children to have already outperformed the rest of the nation, to say nothing of Wyoming's significantly lower-spending neighboring states. Unfortunately, that has not been the case.

By some measures, Wyoming's students appear to be doing well on the NAEP tests. According to the 2007 NAEP scores, Wyoming fourth graders ranked twelfth in both math and reading among the fifty states, and its eighth graders ranked eleventh and tenth in the same subjects. The 2000 NAEP scores in science place Wyoming seventh on the fourth grade test and ninth on the eighth grade test.[19] Its at-risk enrollment, defined as those students eligible for the federal free and reduced-price lunch program, did even better relative to comparable students elsewhere, ranking fourth and fifth in the nation in fourth grade math and reading, respectively.

Other, more relevant comparisons, however, tell a different story about achievement by Wyoming students. Using NAEP scores, we can assess the progress of Wyoming's students in the fourth and eighth grade on the same three tests to compare their performance with that of the rest of the nation during the course of the remedy.

The first thing that becomes apparent from a more detailed investigation is that Wyoming students are relatively advantaged compared to the rest of the nation. Because it has a homogeneous population with 89 percent white students and because incomes are relatively high, one expects the average scores of students to look favorable in comparison to other states.

We begin with Hispanic students, who constituted about 6 percent of the public school enrollment in 2005 and are the state's largest minority group. Their scores have been considerably

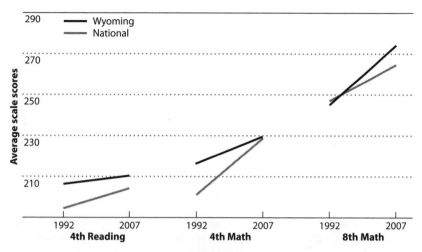

**6.3** Wyoming and National NAEP Trends for Hispanic Students, 1992–2007

lower than those of the white majority; therefore, for the remedy
to be a success, it must address this achievement gap. From 1992
to 2007, fourth grade reading scores of Hispanic children increased
by 4 points, compared to a 10-point increase for Hispanics nationally.[20] On fourth grade math, their scores increased by 13 points,
compared to a 26-point increase nationally. On the eighth grade
math test, Hispanic scores increased 29 points, compared to an
increase nationally of 19 points. Thus, in the fourth grade, Wyoming's gains on the reading and math tests for Hispanic children
lagged behind those of other states, while on eighth grade math its
increases were higher than those of the nation as a whole. On a
brighter note, despite losing ground to the nation in two of the
tests, Hispanic students in Wyoming were above the national average for their ethnic group in 1992 and remained so in 2007 (see
figure 6.3).

Because the remedy is statewide and benefits all students, we also
examined the scores of Wyoming's white students, who make up
about 89 percent of its student population. On grade 4 reading
tests, their scores increased 3 points, compared to a 7-point increase across the nation for whites. On grade 4 math, Wyoming's
white students increased their scores by 19 points, compared to a
21-point increase nationally. On grade 8 math, their scores in-

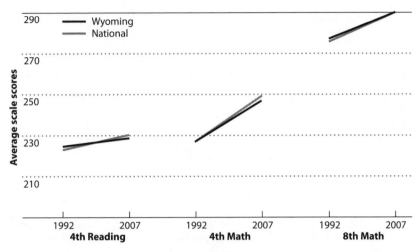

**6.4** Wyoming and National NAEP Trends for White Students, 1992–2007

creased 13 points, while nationally white students' scores rose 14 points. Besides falling short of the national increases on all three tests, the scores of Wyoming's white children did not exceed the national average on any of the three tests. Indeed, in fourth grade reading, Wyoming started out 2 points over the national average for white children in 1992 and finished 2 points under it in 2007 (see figure 6.4).

The dramatic increases in expenditures resulting from the court decision appear to have had little impact. The test score increases for both white and Hispanic students failed to keep pace with increases for these groups nationally on both fourth grade math and reading tests. For white children, the same was true for their scores on the eighth grade math test. The only positive result was for Hispanic children on the eighth grade math test, where they improved significantly more than Hispanic students across the country. On balance, Wyoming's students appeared to be performing no better—and on most measures were performing worse—in 2007 relative to the nation than they were in 1992.

Perhaps even more revealing is a comparison between Wyoming and its three neighboring states—North Dakota, South Dakota, and Montana. All four states are mostly rural with no large urban centers. They are in the same section of the country. Most im-

**TABLE 6.1**
Student Demographic Comparison for North Central Comparison States

| Demographic Profile | Montana | North Dakota | South Dakota | Wyoming |
|---|---|---|---|---|
| Median household income (2004–6) ($) | 38,629 | 42,162 | 44,624 | 47,227 |
| Children in poverty (2006) (%) | 15.2 | 11.4 | 13.3 | 12.0 |
| High school graduates pop > 25 (2000) (%) | 87.2 | 83.9 | 84.6 | 87.9 |
| College graduates pop > 25 (2000) (%) | 24.4 | 22 | 21.5 | 21.9 |
| Racial/ethnic distribution (2005) (%) | | | | |
| White | 84.3 | 87.2 | 85.0 | 84.9 |
| Black | 0.9 | 1.5 | 1.6 | 1.5 |
| Hispanic | 2.4 | 1.7 | 2.0 | 9.0 |
| Asian | 1.1 | 0.9 | 1.0 | 1.1 |
| American Indian | 11.3 | 8.6 | 10.5 | 3.5 |

*Source*: U.S. Department of Education (2008), tables 12, 20, and 40.

portant for a valid comparison is that the student populations of all four states are almost identical, being predominantly white with small minority populations and similar percentages of students from families in poverty (see table 6.1).[21] Household incomes are noticeably higher in Wyoming.

The four states are very dissimilar in one respect, however, and that is the amount they spend on K–12 education. As indicated in figure 6.5, North Dakota, South Dakota, and Montana spend below the national average.[22] The influence of the court-ordered increases in education appropriations for Wyoming is apparent, as its spending per pupil has moved not only significantly higher than the national average but also over $2,000 more than its highest spending neighbor, Montana.

Despite Wyoming's huge spending advantage, the other three states significantly outperform it on almost every measure. As shown in table 6.2, Wyoming students rank favorably in the fourth grade, but by the time they are in the eighth grade with four more

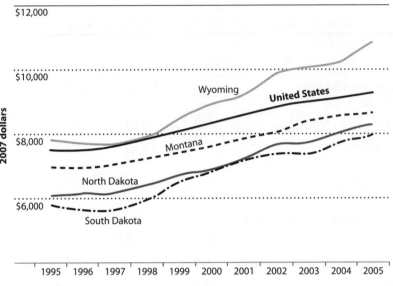

**6.5** Spending Per Student in North Central States, 1995–2005

years of schooling under their belts, they lag significantly behind the other three states on every NAEP test. For example, South Dakota students start behind in fourth grade (twenty-fourth in reading and twenty-second in math) but improve to seventh in the nation on both tests in the eighth grade. Wyoming students start at twelfth on both tests in the fourth grade, improving slightly to eleventh in math by the eighth grade but falling to eighteenth in reading by eighth grade. Each of the other (low-spending) comparison states in the north central region shows improvement in national rankings between the fourth and eighth grades, quite a different story from that in Wyoming.

Nor does Wyoming compare well on other outcome measures, finishing fourth out of the four states on all but one measure of school completion (it ranks third of the four states on college continuation rates). As shown in table 6.3, in 2005, North Dakota had the third highest graduation rate in the country; Wyoming ranked nineteenth. On college-going rates, North Dakota ranked first in the nation, South Dakota was sixth, while Wyoming was twentieth.[23]

**TABLE 6.2**
Rankings among Fifty States on 2007 NAEP Tests for North Central
Comparison States

|  | *Math* |  | *Reading* |  |
| --- | --- | --- | --- | --- |
|  | *Grade 4* | *Grade 8* | *Grade 4* | *Grade 8* |
| Montana | 13 | 10 | 7 | 3 |
| North Dakota | 7 | 3 | 9 | 9 |
| South Dakota | 24 | 7 | 22 | 7 |
| Wyoming | 12 | 11 | 12 | 18 |

*Source*: National Center for Education Statistics, http://nces.ed.gov/nationsreportcard.

Wyoming's relatively poor performance has been documented, but not remarked upon, by other commentators. In its Quality Counts (2007) issue, *Education Week* ranked all fifty states on their success in improving achievement over time relative to the rest of the country, relying on fifteen different factors, including reading and math performance, graduation rates, and participation in advanced placement courses. Wyoming ranked twenty-eighth among the fifty states. North Dakota, South Dakota, and Montana ranked sixth, seventh, and ninth, despite Wyoming's huge edge in spending.[24]

To summarize, the significant increases in funding for Wyoming's schools have not been translated into better achievement for the state's children, particularly in comparison to their much lower-funded neighbors, none of which has enjoyed court-ordered or other spending increases approaching the magnitude of those in Wyoming.[25] It does not appear that the state's dramatically increased spending on education has had much, if any, positive effect on student performance.[26]

## New Jersey

New Jersey has been in the throes of school finance litigation for something approaching forty years, longer than any other state. A remedy providing significant additional financial resources to the thirty-one Abbott districts was implemented beginning in 1991–

**TABLE 6.3**

Performance and Ranking among Fifty States of School Attainment for North Central Comparison States

| Performance Measure (year) | Montana | North Dakota | South Dakota | Wyoming |
|---|---|---|---|---|
| 9th graders' chance for college by age 19[a] (2002) (%) | 42.5 (12) | 61.8(1) | 48.1 (6) | 40.4 (20) |
| College continuation rate of high school graduates[b] (2004)(%) | 57.8 (24) | 67.6 (3) | 68.8 (1) | 59.0 (19) |
| Public high school graduation rate[c] (2005) (%) | 79.0 (12) | 84.8 (3) | 80.8 (10) | 75.5 (19) |

Source:
[a] NCHEMS Information Center:
http://www.higheredinfo.org/dbrowser/index.php?submeasure=62&year=2002&level=nation&mode=graph&state=0
[b] NCHEMS Information Center:
http://www.higheredinfo.org/dbrowser/index.php?submeasure=63&year=2004&level=nation&mode=graph&state=0
[c] NCHEMS Information Center:
http://www.higheredinfo.org/dbrowser/index.php?submeasure=36&year=2005&level=nation&mode=graph&state=0

92 with approximately $200 million in court-ordered additional funding that year. Since then, the annual amount of court-ordered funding for the thirty-one Abbott districts has steadily increased. In the 2005–6 school year, it reached $1.5 billion.[27] On average, New Jersey spends more per pupil on K–12 education than any other state, roughly twice the national average, but the Abbott districts spend even more.[28] As shown in figure 6.6 in 2005–6, the regular education budget in the Abbott districts was almost a thousand dollars a student higher than even the wealthiest school districts in the state and a whopping $3,600 more (or an additional $72,000 for a classroom of twenty students) than the other low-wealth districts.[29]

Moreover, these figures are for regular education only and do not include the disproportionate share of state funding that the Abbott districts receive because they have so many at-risk students. When those amounts are factored in, the gap between the Abbott districts and the state's other districts, both wealthy and poor, be-

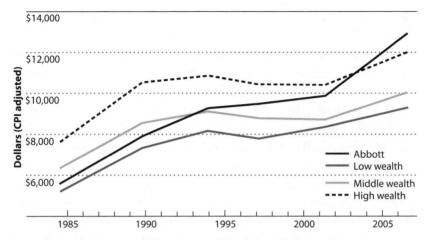

**6.6** Regular Education Budget Per Pupil in Abbott Districts and Other Categories of New Jersey School Districts

comes even wider.[30] The level of resources made possible in the Abbott districts by this additional spending is staggering. For example, in 2004–5, Newark, the largest of the Abbott districts, spent $21,978 per pupil, its pupil–teacher ratio was twelve to one, and the average teacher salary was $77,000.[31]

We would expect these substantial court-ordered increases in funding, all aimed at selected, low-performing school districts, to have raised student achievement significantly over the decade or more the increased funds have flowed. But certainly until 2003, there was little to indicate that the expenditure of approximately $3 billion in court-ordered increases was helping to improve student achievement in the Abbott districts.[32] One of the most comprehensive early studies was conducted by two economics professors from Rutgers University, who found "no evidence of a positive effect of expenditures in New Jersey public high schools in urban school districts with smaller per capita tax bases [the Abbott districts]."[33]

Pro-remedy advocates in New Jersey sometimes claim that there were "no effective mechanisms for assessing student performance [in New Jersey] until 2003" and are dismissive of studies showing no gains during the initial years of the remedy.[34] However, NAEP test scores are available for 1992, the year the Abbott districts began to receive significantly more money than other school districts in New Jersey (see figure 6.6). NAEP does not separately report the scores of the thirty-one Abbott districts; however, given the monumental effort directed selectively at New Jersey's poorest and most heavily minority school districts, any significant improvement in student achievement in those districts should be reflected in the NAEP scores in several ways. First, since the Abbott districts educate about half of the black and Hispanic children in the state,[35] and since the court-ordered state aid has gone exclusively to these districts, we would expect to see the test scores of black and Hispanic children improving at a rate significantly higher than in states that have not made nearly the effort New Jersey has. Second, since the aid is being poured into only these thirty-one predominantly minority districts, with predominantly white districts getting no additional aid, we would also expect the achievement gap between white and minority children in the state to shrink significantly. Since the enrollment of the Abbott districts is almost equally divided between black and Hispanic students, we analyzed achievement trends for both races. We begin with its black students.

Although New Jersey did not participate in the NAEP testing program from 1995 to 2003, it did in 1992 and 1994, as well as later, in 2003, 2005, and 2007. Therefore, we can compare the test scores of black children in 1992, when the court-ordered funds first began to be paid, to the scores in 2007. Comparable test results are available for these periods on three tests: reading and math in grade 4 and math in grade 8. The trends between 1992 and 2007 are shown in figure 6.7.

The scores of New Jersey's black fourth graders increased by 14 points on the reading test, while nationally they increased by 12 points. On fourth grade reading, New Jersey's black children did slightly better than other black children in the country for that period; however, almost the entire increase for New Jersey's black students in fourth grade reading tests has occurred in the last two years, as shown in figure 6.8. From 2005 to 2007, New Jersey's reading scores increased dramatically by 13 points, a higher increase than black students in any other state. In contrast, over the first thirteen years of the remedy, black scores in New

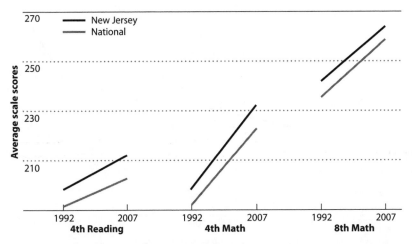

**6.7** New Jersey and National NAEP Trends for Black Students, 1992–2007

Jersey increased by only 1 point, while nationally, they increased by 8 points.

The fourth grade math scores paint a similar picture, albeit not as dramatic. As shown in figure 6.7, from 1992 to 2007, New Jersey's fourth grade math scale scores for black students increased 34 points, from 198 to 232, compared to a national increase for black students of 30 points, from 192 to 222. However, New Jersey's success in beating the national average over this period was also the result of significant increases in the last two years of the remedy. From 1992 to 2005, New Jersey's increases were below the national average.

Since the gains rest heavily on the scores for one year, 2007, there is a serious issue as to whether they are simply an anomaly. On the other hand, if the remedy is truly starting to bear fruit,[36] then the state might have finally stumbled upon the right formulation.

While New Jersey's black children may have showed some minimal growth in achievement relative to black children nationally in the fourth grade since 1992, assuming the 2007 scores are not an anomaly, that was not true for its eighth graders. From 1992 to 2007, black students' math test scores in New Jersey increased by 22 points, from 242 to 264. Nationally, they rose 23 points during the same period. Unlike the fourth graders, eighth grade math

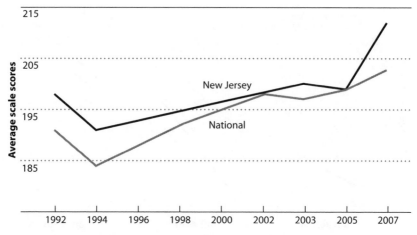

**6.8** New Jersey and National NAEP Grade Four Reading Trends for Black Students, Including Interim Years, 1992–2007

scores did not spike in 2007, and whether one looks at the period 1992 through 2005 or 1992 through 2007 does not make a significant difference.

In summary, the NAEP results for black students in New Jersey are mixed. From 1992 through 2005, its black students fell significantly behind the rest of the nation, despite enormous spending increases directed only at selected districts with over half of the state's black students. In 2007, the state's black fourth graders showed significant gains, especially in reading. But, over the entire fifteen-year period of the remedy, New Jersey's fourth grade black students improved only slightly more than black students in the rest of the nation, while its black eighth graders did slightly worse.

When we employ the same analysis for Hispanic students, the results are more heartening (see figure 6.9). Hispanic scale scores on the fourth grade reading test increased by 19 points from 1992 to 2007, compared to a 10-point increase nationally for Hispanic students. The results were not as good for math, but still New Jersey's fourth grade Hispanic students gained 30 points versus a gain of 26 points nationally. Its eighth graders also outpaced the nation in math, with a 26-point increase compared to a 17-point increase nationally. Moreover, these trends are not the result of extraordi-

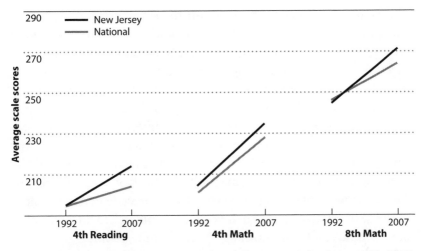

**6.9** New Jersey and National NAEP Trends for Hispanic Students, 1992–2007

nary increases in 2007. The scores show some progress for Hispanic students relative to the nation as a whole.[37]

Margaret Goertz, an education policy professor at the University of Pennsylvania, and one of her colleagues reached two important conclusions from their review of the state test scores from 1999 to 2005: (1) that the Abbott districts showed demonstrable improvement from 2001 to 2005 on the fourth grade math and reading tests, with the result that "the Abbott to non-Abbott achievement gap seems to be closing in the 4th grade," and (2) that there had been "relatively limited closure" of the achievement gap on the eighth grade reading and math tests.[38]

While Goertz's eighth grade results are consistent with our NAEP-based findings, her fourth grade conclusions are not. The state test results for reading clearly conflict with the NAEP results for the same period, leading to questions that are difficult to resolve with available evidence about which results are more valid. Moreover, the gap reduction in fourth grade reading scores during that period was as much the consequence of declining test scores in the non-Abbott districts as of increasing scores in the Abbott districts. While this may technically "narrow" the gap, it is a remedy few would advocate. On math, however, the NAEP scores were more consistent with Goertz's findings on the state tests. While fourth grade math scores increased in all categories of school districts in New Jersey, the increase was noticeably larger in the Abbott districts. As a result, the gap did narrow, although the test scores of students in the Abbott districts remained the lowest in the state.

In sum, even if we fully credit the extraordinary uptick in fourth grade scores from 2005 to 2007 to the Abbott remedy, black student performance in New Jersey is not materially different now from what it was in 1992, when the remedy commenced. In the eighth grade, student performance falls short of what the rest of the nation was able to do. In view of the unprecedented investment in the Abbott districts—an investment unmatched in any other state—these results are nothing to write home about.

Nor has New Jersey's adequacy remedy done much to improve achievement of Abbott district high school students. Available data show that of the over nineteen thousand high school seniors in the Abbott districts taking the 2003 eleventh grade test required for graduation in New Jersey, just 43 percent passed both the language and math sections.[39] In all other New Jersey districts, the passing rate was 80 percent. Moreover, in 2006, one in three high school seniors in the Abbott districts who graduated failed the mandatory examinations in reading, writing and math skills, but were allowed to graduate after completing a "Special Review Assessment" (SRA) evaluating basic skills. This compares to just 3 percent of graduates in affluent districts, 8 percent in middle-income districts, and 15 percent in other poor districts who took advantage of the SRA alternative.[40] This process has come under increasing criticism as a means to avoid the tougher graduation tests. Michael Cohen, the president of the respected bipartisan educational advocacy organization Achieve, Inc., describes the SRA process as offering "a loophole you can drive a truck through to earn a high school diploma."[41]

By most calculations, New Jersey was in 2007 at or near the top of state rankings on statewide high school graduation rates,[42] and some cite this as evidence of the success of the remedy.[43] These rankings are difficult to interpret, however, because the graduation rates employed in them are for the entire state, and not just the

Abbott districts. Equally as important, the graduation rates reported by the state have been severely criticized. As mentioned,
significant proportions of students who fail the graduation test,
particularly in the Abbott districts, nevertheless have been allowed
to graduate using the SRA procedure. In addition, New Jersey includes in its graduation reports students who failed to earn a high
school diploma, but later obtained a GED certificate, thereby pushing their reported graduation rates even higher.[44]

While not directly related to student outcomes, it is clear that
the remedy has also led to extreme inequities among the state's
taxpayers. As stated previously, in 2004, the Abbott districts spent
almost $5,000 more per child each year than other similarly low-
income school districts in New Jersey, even though their local tax
rates are far lower than those of other school districts in the state.
Since the state funds the lion's share of their budgets, the Abbott
districts have little incentive to tax their local community to financially support education, and they have dramatically lowered their
property taxes during the course of the remedy. Specifically, over
the past twenty years they have cut their local property tax rates
in half, while other school districts in the state have had to maintain
or even raise their rates (see figure 6.10).

Thus, while other low-wealth school districts in New Jersey provide over one-third of their own funding and tax their citizens at
an average rate of 1.64, the Abbott districts provide less than 20
percent of their funding, while taxing their citizens at less than half
that rate: 0.74. This, not unexpectedly, has led to a near revolt over
property taxes among New Jersey's citizens.[45]

*Abbott* and its predecessor, *Robinson v. Cahill*, may be the nation's longest-running school finance litigation, and is perhaps
the most famous (or infamous depending on your point of view).
But notwithstanding the 2007 spike in fourth grade reading
and math scores, even its most adamant supporters would be
hard-pressed to claim that it has been very successful in improving
student achievement. The proponents of the Abbott remedy are
generally eager to jump on any positive evidence. Yet, even if
the 2007 improvements in fourth grade NAEP scores are fully attributed to the court remedy, New Jersey students are still in

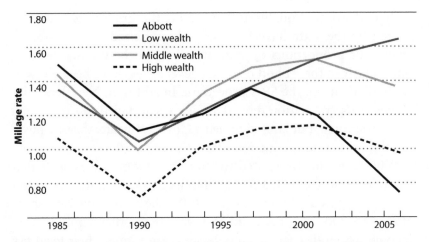

**6.10** Property Tax Rate Trends in Abbott Districts and Other Categories of School Districts in New Jersey, 1985–2006

roughly the same position as an earlier generation of students in 1992. If they were to continue for some period at the pace of the extraordinary hike in test scores in 2007, it would be encouraging, but there is yet little reason to predict huge success in the future based on that single data point. After forty years of searching for a solution, it is inconceivable that any judgment on the court's success would rest on whether a single data point is a new trend or just an anomaly.

## Massachusetts

Undoubtedly, Massachusetts is the brightest spot among the states that have implemented substantial adequacy remedies. NAEP scores of both white children, who constitute almost 80 percent of the state's public school enrollment, and Hispanic children, who are its largest minority group with 13 percent of the state's enrollment, have improved at a rate significantly faster than the nation as a whole. Although its other large minority group, black students, has not fared as well, black students nevertheless perform at levels above the national average for that group.

Massachusetts responded to having its finance system declared unconstitutional in *McDuffy* (1993) with what Robert Costrell,

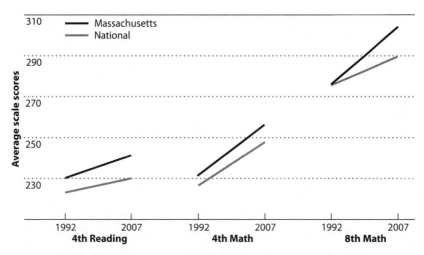

**6.11** Massachusetts and National NAEP Trends for White Students, 1992–2007

former chief economist of the state of Massachusetts, described as "unusually vigorous educational reforms."[46] These included large infusions of money into property-poor districts along with the introduction of rigorous standards, graduation exams, and overall accountability. The growth in per capita spending in Massachusetts was faster than the U.S. average with the tenth largest growth rate over the period 1994–2007.

Using the same three tests that we looked at for New Jersey, Wyoming, and Kentucky, we compared Massachusetts' NAEP scores in 1992, which roughly corresponds with the beginning of the remedy, with those in 2007, after the remedy had been in place for almost fifteen years.

As shown in figure 6.11, test score increases for the state's white students outstripped the national average for whites on all three tests by a considerable margin. Especially noteworthy were the eighth grade math scores. The scores for the state's white students increased 28 points, compared to only a 16-point increase nationally. When the remedy began, the state's scores were 1 point above the national average; in 2007 they were 15 points above it.[47]

Hispanic students in Massachusetts also made significant strides during this period, significantly outpacing Hispanics nationwide

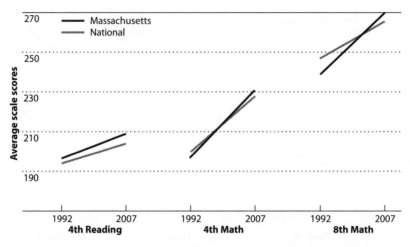

**6.12** Massachusetts and National NAEP Trends for Hispanic Students, 1992–2007

on all three tests. This was particularly true on the math tests for both the fourth and eighth grades. Significantly below the national average when the remedy began in 1992, the test scores of Massachusetts' Hispanic students were significantly higher than the national average by 2007 (see figure 6.12).

The news, unfortunately, was not as good for black students. As reflected in figure 6.13, the scores of the state's black students increased by 7 points on the fourth grade reading test from 1992 to 2007, compared to a 12-point gain for blacks nationally. In math, the results were a little better. The scores of black fourth graders in Massachusetts were higher than those nationally, but for eighth graders, the opposite was true.

As a result, on both fourth grade reading and eighth grade math, the black-white achievement gap increased over this period. Especially alarming was the gap in eighth grade math. In 1992, Massachusetts' black-white gap was 34 points, compared to a nationwide gap of 40 points. By 2007, the situation had reversed: Massachusetts' gap significantly increased to 41 points, while the national gap went down to 31 points.

Part of the widening of the achievement gap on all three tests is due to the significantly higher test scores for white students in Massachusetts compared to the nation, but a good part is also due to the failure of black students in Massachusetts to improve relative

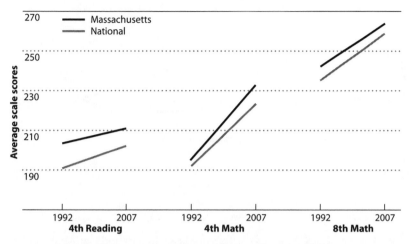

**6.13** Massachusetts and National NAEP Trends for Black Students, 1992–2007

to the nation as a whole. On a more positive note, however, the scores of Massachusetts' black students remain above the average for black students across the nation, as they did prior to the commencement of the remedy.

Our analysis indicates that both white and Hispanic students in Massachusetts have made impressive gains in their performance since the McDuffy decision. This progress in student achievement has been documented by others[48] and was cited prominently in the 2005 *Hancock* decision finding the system of education in the state to be adequate under the state constitution.[49] That there have been significant gains seems clear; what is less certain is whether such gains are attributable to increased spending or the other substantial reforms that Massachusetts implemented at the same time. These reform efforts began in 1993 immediately following the *McDuffy* decision declaring the state's system of K–12 education unconstitutional. Since then, spending on K–12 education has more than tripled, from approximately $3 billion to over $10 billion. But the remedial steps passed by the legislature also included a vigorous regime of academic standards, a high-stakes graduation test, and strict accountability measures of a kind that have run into resistance in other states, particularly from the teachers' unions.[50] The teachers' unions in Massachusetts resisted the nonfinancial mea-

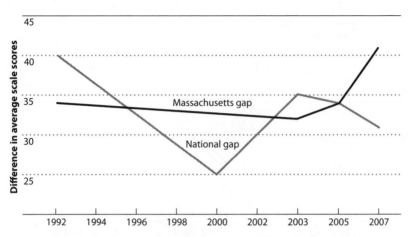

**6.14** White-Black Achievement Gap in Massachusetts and Nationally on Eighth Grade Math (NAEP)

sures, but using the window of opportunity opened by the *McDuffy* decision, the legislature found the political will to enact them.[51]

In conclusion, the results in three out of four states in which the courts' intervention has been substantial and of long duration have been disappointing. In Wyoming and Kentucky, there has been little or no positive effect on student achievement. Although the picture is more ambiguous in New Jersey, principally because of a dramatic increase in fourth grade test scores in 2007, the results in that state, especially at the higher grade levels, have also been largely disappointing. Only in Massachusetts have there been significant gains, although even there the benefit to the state's black students is unclear. K–12 spending has increased in these states by billions of dollars, but only in Massachusetts, where the legislature focused on structural reforms in addition to increases in funding, is there evidence of significant improvement in achievement. We can only conclude then, that, while court-ordered dollars have bought a host of services and facilities for schools—programs for at-risk students and preschoolers, smaller class sizes, additional support staff and other personnel, better school buildings, extended day programs, and full-day kindergarten, to name only some—these appear not to have generally bought the improved student performance so long sought and so urgently needed.[52]

# 7 | Science and School Finance Decision Making

Courts and legislatures alike find themselves looking for scientific research and evaluation to help in making decisions about education policy and appropriations. Unfortunately, while there are plenty of consultants, researchers, academicians, advocates, vendors, and others ready to help answer the key questions, the information they tend to provide is frequently flawed, one-sided, or misleading—pushing decision makers in costly and ineffective directions.

The twin questions policymakers and courts continuously grapple with are these: "What should money be spent on in order to achieve the desired results?" and "How much should an adequate education cost?" If science answers the difficult factual questions about what different programs accomplish and their cost, then courts or legislatures can concentrate on setting appropriate outcome goals and finding revenue sources.[1]

Unfortunately, answering these questions is not so simple. While science is potentially a source of reliable, objective information about programs and their expense, applying scientific methods to complex educational and funding decisions is fraught with problems. Necessary data may be unavailable; or they may be unreliable; or they may be subjected to unreliable analysis that fails to yield the desired information—and judges and legislators may not appreciate the importance of these issues. Particularly when presented with conflicting analyses, they might simply conclude that scientists frequently disagree, and thus they are free to choose whichever evidence matches their preconceptions or meets their purposes. But this conclusion can lead to very bad decisions—ones that are ineffective and expensive.

We begin with a simple summary: much of the information entered into educational debates does not pass muster as reliable and acceptable scientific evidence. We illustrate this by considering standard analyses introduced to answer the "how much" question and then turn to illustrative analyses of "how" to spend resources.

## A Simple Decision Model

With a fixed amount of money to spend, devoting more money to one item means that less money is available for another. This simple truth leads to a general rule about how to allocate funds across different resources or policies in order to get the highest achievement: spend additional funds on whatever yields the highest added achievement.

For example, suppose that by spending an additional $1,000 per pupil, a school could attract a high-quality teacher and improve student achievement by five points, or it could spend an extra $1,000 per pupil to reduce class size and improve achievement by one point. Obviously, spending the money to improve teacher quality is the better choice (assuming that these are the only two choices). We can calculate that improving teacher quality costs $200 for each point of increased achievement, while reducing class size costs $1,000 for each point of increased achievement.

What happens if we do not choose the most productive use of funds? If we put the $1,000 a student into class size reductions instead of teacher quality, that spending yields only one point of achievement. But would we still say that a point of achievement "costs" $1,000? Of course not, because we know we can buy an additional point for just $200 if we spend the additional funding on teacher quality instead of reducing class sizes.

Now translate these ideas to the situation at hand. States and local districts must choose among a variety of educational resources or policies. The added dollars should be spent where they have the biggest payoff—i.e., the "biggest bang for the buck." Moreover, the "correct answer" may change as more money becomes available to the district. For example, for a low-spending district, buying new textbooks might initially yield the largest improvements in achievement, but after everybody has their own new textbook, added spending on textbooks might do nothing for achievement, and something else will yield a more productive use of funds.[2]

What if the added funds were spent on hiring more teachers with master's degrees, a choice that, experience shows, is unlikely to have any significant effect on student achievement? Under this scenario, no matter how much was spent on master's degrees, a five-point gain in achievement would be unlikely.

This discussion illustrates two common errors that have been made over and over again in estimating what an "adequate" education should cost. First, the determination of true "cost" cannot be separated from the efficient use of funds. In estimating costs, we cannot ignore more economical or efficient ways of obtaining the desired achievement gains. Second, determining the funds that would be required to obtain some achievement goals depends upon accurately assessing the impact on achievement that each input or policy might have. This frequently proves difficult, particularly since the available research is often insufficient for projecting the impacts of varying programs on student achievement.[3] With this background in mind, we move to a discussion of various approaches to answering the fundamental question raised inevitably in consideration of school funding: how much will an adequate education cost?

## How Much Is Enough?

Both legislatures and courts have sought to ensure that schools have enough money to enable students to reach desired performance levels. In court, plaintiffs present "costing-out" studies as the scientific means of determining appropriate levels of funding; the implication, sometimes baldly stated, is that the process relied on by legislative bodies is both irrational and arbitrary. Costing-out studies have been conducted or are in progress in a majority of the states, and the demand for new ones has continued to rise as adequacy lawsuits proliferate.[4] Plaintiffs have discovered that there is great value in submitting a specific dollar amount for total required state spending—an amount, they argue, that should be treated as both necessary and sufficient for an "adequate" education.[5] Courts have clearly been influenced by this strategy, as judges have been willing to incorporate the results of such costing-out studies into their remedies or to order that such studies be conducted to guide the legislature in setting appropriation levels.[6] Indeed, during the liability phase of adequacy cases it has become commonplace for plaintiffs to disavow having any views on remedies and instead to ask simply that a costing-out study be commissioned so that everybody can proceed with knowledge of exactly what an adequate education would cost.

Legislatures also commission such studies to guide their appropriations, particularly when they are under pressure from the courts. They also sometimes request such studies on their own, thinking perhaps that outside experts can provide them with objective and scientific recommendations. In some cases, studies are commissioned with the hope that by going through the seemingly rational process of "costing out" an adequate education, the state can protect itself against a threatened adequacy lawsuit. This strategy, however, backfires more often than not. Such studies almost always call for sizeable increases in spending, which politically the legislatures are not ready to approve. However, once the legislature has commissioned its own study, these cost estimates often become exhibit A to the plaintiffs' lawsuit. Moreover, any estimates from these studies gain a higher profile by virtue of having been sponsored and sometimes endorsed by the legislature or state educational authorities themselves. Indeed, in the Kansas adequacy case, the court held that the results of a study by an outside consultant were conclusive against the state, even though the legislature itself had never endorsed them.[7]

Calculating what an adequate education should cost sounds like a straightforward undertaking, but it is anything but. While educators may have an idea of which programs and measures will result in better test scores (although as we have argued throughout much of this book, the evidence is, at best, mixed), there is no consensus in the scientific community on what it would cost to overcome the adverse effects of poverty and other social ills that now keep many children from achieving at levels comparable to middle-class children. The overarching problem —facing courts, legislatures, and the consultants hired by them—is the nonexistence of empirical evidence on which to base estimates of the costs of attaining desired levels of student proficiency, particularly for the most disadvantaged students—the central focus of most court cases. And there is no evidence because the outcome sought—high achievement for all or most students in a district—has not been achieved before, except in isolated instances.[8]

Calculating the cost of an adequate education would be simple if scholars could consistently show something like the following: an additional expenditure of $1,000 per pupil appropriately spent will translate, on average, into a five-point gain in student proficiency. Unfortunately, decades of research have not been able to show a clear causal relationship between the amount that schools spend and student achievement; certainly our analysis in the previous chapter showed none.[9] After hundreds of studies, it is now generally recognized that *how* money is spent is much more important than *how much* is spent. If schools do not spend additional money effectively, that spending is unlikely to have any effect on achievement. It remains difficult, if not impossible, to infer from current spending patterns what it would really cost to change achievement, even assuming efficient use of funds (or for that matter, continued inefficient use of funds).[10] This finding is particularly important in considering judicially ordered changes in school finances, because such orders seldom require or even suggest that money be spent differently from how it has been spent in the past.

It is, of course, possible to wonder why determining the amount of money needed to offer a sound education is so different from other appropriation decisions. After all, government officials repeatedly estimate how much it will cost, for instance, to build roads. But roads and schools really are different. We not only know the outcome we want—a new highway—but we can also identify with reasonable certainty the resources needed to achieve that outcome—so much asphalt, so many hours of labor, and so on. That is, we know the technology, and we can fairly accurately specify the recipe for a new road. We also know from experience what those resources will cost.

Little of this reasoning applies to the goal of providing an adequate education—largely because no coherent description of what it would take to meet the goal currently exists. Partly it reflects the fact that the process is so dependent on the skill and actions of the primary actors—teachers, principals, and of course the students.[11] Because it is difficult to measure or specify differences among these primary inputs, it is not feasible to identify just what would be required from schools to reach any level of achievement. Additionally, a multitude of factors outside the school's control affects performance. The child's ability, the education of the child's parents, their involvement in their child's education, the resources in the home, how much the child studies, how much TV the child watches, the child's motivation, the child's health, and a host of other circumstances beyond the control of the school authorities all enter into the equation. In building the road, of course, a variety of outside factors such as terrain, soil type, and weather conditions also affects construction costs, but these factors are not as dependent upon actions of direct participants in the project, and, again, the technology for dealing with them is better understood than with education.

Providing an adequate education, like building a road, also depends on the efficiency with which resources are used. But in public education, this efficiency factor plays a much more central role in thinking about costs than it does either in the private sector or in other governmental sectors.[12] The road contractor not only must competitively bid for the contract, but also must go on to build the road for his contract price if he expects to make a profit; therefore he has a strong motive to make the most efficient use of his money. (Note that when there is just one bidder, we tend to be more skeptical about whether the bid truly reflects the minimum cost of the project.) Public schools face much different constraints. They are a governmental monopoly, and parents, especially the poor, typically have few options except the local public school. Furthermore, both traditional behavior and union constraints may operate to inhibit efficient hiring and placement. An obvious example we return to later is that teachers are paid on the basis of years of experience and education degree, regardless of their performance or their results in the classroom. A principal desiring to pay teachers based on merit cannot do so in most states and districts. Nor is the pay for many principals based on student outcomes.

While in some districts vigilant parents and taxpayers may demand that school funds be well spent, the "right" answer is not well understood by school personnel, let alone parents. Moreover, school decisions are frequently designed to be insulated from outside pressure, implying that only the most aggressive and persistent parents and taxpayers can hope to have any influence. In many other districts, the concerns of school district constituents may be quite different. For example, in many poor communities, parents may, rightfully or wrongfully, believe they can have little impact on decisions. Further, the school district may be the biggest employer, and the pressure to provide and protect jobs may trump any considerations of efficiency.

The absence of a systematic positive relationship between spending and achievement presents a real challenge to the consultants who purport to describe the spending necessary to achieve adequate levels of student achievement. This dilemma is best exemplified in a candid statement from Augenblick & Myers (2002), a consulting firm that has conducted more costing-out studies than anyone else. In most of their studies, they readily acknowledge that

> resource allocation tends to reflect current practice and there is only
> an assumption, *with little evidence*, that the provision of money
> at the designated level will produce the anticipated outcomes.[13]
> (emphasis added)

Here you have the whole problem in a nutshell. There is "little evidence" that "provision of money at the designated level will produce the anticipated outcomes." Quite obviously, this is not simply a "disadvantage" of the study; it undercuts the entire study and its recommendations for additional spending.

We look now at four approaches used by consultants, each of which attempts to deal with the dilemma just pointed out in a different way. As might be guessed, these approaches all fall far short of standards for scientific validity, although they demonstrate some considerable ingenuity in crafting arguments with surface plausibility. They give the illusion of providing valid, useful, and reliable information, but it remains that—an illusion.

### Professional Judgment Approach

Perhaps the most commonly applied approach is the "professional judgment" method.[14] With a few nuances, the approach involves asking a chosen panel of educators—teachers, principals, superintendents, and others—to develop an educational program that would, in their collective opinion, produce certain specified achievement outcomes. Their efforts typically produce "model schools," defined in terms of class size, guidance and support personnel, and various programs that they deem necessary. The consultant in charge of the study then provides the missing elements (for example, costs for central administration or for computers and materials) and employs externally derived cost factors (for example, average teacher or principal salaries) to determine the total funds needed for the model schools.[15] The panel may or may not provide guidance on extra resources needed for disadvantaged children, special education, or the like. The end result is a cost figure based on a "basket of resources" that the panel members believe are necessary to meet the desired goals, which supporters of the methodology like because it is easy to understand and explain to legislators.

Professional judgment panels generally are instructed not to consider where the revenues will come from to pay for their model schools, or any other possible constraints on spending. They are allowed to "dream big," unfettered by any sense of reality or thought of trade-offs. Typically, they will be instructed as follows:

> You should not be concerned about where revenues will come from to pay for the program you design. Don't worry about federal or

state requirements that may be associated with some kinds of funding. You should not think about whatever revenues might be available in the school or district in which you work or about any of the revenue constraints that might exist on those revenues.[16]

With no incentive to be mindful of costs in coming up with their model school, panel members tend to go on a shopping spree and order everything their hearts desire, not the minimums actually needed to provide an adequate education.

This feature of costing-out studies is very attractive to those inclined to pursue additional funding through the courts, which are also single-issue-oriented and often ignore revenue constraints.[17] A 2003 study by Augenblick Palaich & Associates illustrates not only the extent to which professional judgment panels are urged to forget real-life spending constraints but also the kind of interplay that occurs between consultants and professional judgment panels (this time in North Dakota). In their final report, the consultants state: "We worked hard to push people to identify resources they thought were needed to help students meet state and federal standards in spite of their natural tendency to exclude items because local voters might not approve of them or schools could 'get by' without them."[18]

In fact, these admonitions to professional judgment panels to "dream big" amount to a fundamental redefinition of the term *cost*. The term *cost* is usually understood to mean the *minimum* expenditure necessary to achieve a given outcome, whether one is purchasing a car or seeking to raise student performance.[19] The idea is to establish the desired level of quality and determine the least amount of money required to obtain it. But that is not the way a professional judgment panel works. The panel is first told to put aside cost considerations in imagining an outcome—a high-quality education—and then asked what that high-quality education "requires," ignoring all other less costly options.[20]

Consider a father wanting to buy his teenage son a car. He asks his son to find out the cost of a good, safe, dependable car that he can drive to and from school. A different father tells his son, "I want you to find a car to drive to school, and money is no object."

In the first case, the son might price out a Honda Civic, an economical but very serviceable car. In the other, he might bring home a Hummer, an outrageously expensive model with all kinds of unnecessary bells and whistles. Both cars could do the job, but one is many times more expensive than the other. Professional judgment panels are like the second son; they operate without constraints of any kind on spending—except that the panels cannot even be assured that their Hummer will do the job.

Another major problem with this method is the inherent conflict of interest for panel members who may stand to personally benefit from the higher spending recommended by them. If the state wanted to determine what it should spend to build a two-mile stretch of highway, it would not convene a panel of road contractors likely to be given the contract, tell them not to worry about where the money to pay for the project is going to come from, and ask them to come up with a price. Yet this is exactly the way a professional judgment panel costing-out study works. Educators who benefit financially and otherwise from higher spending on education are told that money is no object, and then asked to tell the legislature how much they think should be spent on education in the state. Their evident self-interest in the outcome makes such studies little more than "wish lists," as one court described them.[21]

Some consultants try to ameliorate the conflict of interest by using educators from outside the state as panel members, since they will not themselves financially benefit from the results of the study. However, this tactic is commonly criticized by other consultants, who contend that out-of-state teachers and principals do not know enough about the particular state to make the necessary judgments. In a more outrageous example of bias and self-interest, the interest groups who commission the studies select the panelists themselves. In Missouri, the plaintiff not only sponsored and paid for the costing-out study it relied on in its adequacy suit; along with its supporters, including the state teachers' union, it handpicked the panel members.[22] In Massachusetts, where four plaintiff school districts were involved, teachers and principals from those districts, who had a direct financial interest in the outcome of the study and lawsuit, were allowed to sit on the panels. Amazingly, the mother of the named plaintiff in the original adequacy suit filed in Massachusetts was a member of one of the panels.[23] No wonder that even the special master who otherwise sided with plaintiffs in that case did not give any credence to the study.[24]

Professional judgment panels are effectively encouraged to maximize expenditures in the hope that the resulting amount will be enough to produce proficient students. A 2004 New York study conducted by a consortium of researchers from two groups—the American Institutes for Research and Management Analysis and Planning, Inc. (AIR/MAP)—even used a two-stage process in which subpanels first estimated the desirability of various educational components, and a super-panel then aggregated the results, input by input, from each of the subpanels. This design effectively maximized expenditure estimates by ensuring that any trade-offs between programs and resources made by the individual subpanels were ignored.

Courts relying on professional judgment studies to mandate spending levels assume that the panelists' model school will produce the desired results just because that was the panel's objective. But none of the reports ever test that assumption or evaluate the possibility of such achievement levels being reached. In fact, just the opposite holds. Reports generally include a disclaimer, citing other possible reasons why students may not actually achieve at these levels, despite the provision of the recommended additional funding. Take, for example, the statement in the New York City study sponsored by plaintiff CFE. After recommending an increase in annual spending for the New York City public schools of $5.63 billion, it added:

> It must be recognized that the success of schools also depends on other individuals and institutions to provide the health, intellectual stimulus, and family support upon which public school systems can build. Schools cannot and do not perform their role in a vacuum, and this is an important qualification of conclusions reached in any study of adequacy in education. Also, success of schools depends on effective allocation of resources and implementation of programs in school districts.[25]

Incredibly, the very experts who tell courts how much money will produce the desired student success admit in the same report that this money may do nothing of the kind.

Such studies do not rely on any empirical evidence. Even worse, they often ignore empirical evidence that directly contradicts the results of the studies. Consider a 2003 study by Augenblick Palaich & Associates, which used a professional judgment analysis to determine the spending level necessary for each of North Dakota's school districts to attain desired outcome goals in 2002.[26] It also specified the additional amount of aid each district would need to attain these outcomes or, in about twenty-five school districts, the amount by which spending already exceeded its recommended levels. Because information is available on the actual performance of North Dakota students for 2002, we were able to calculate the relationship between their performance and the fiscal deficits and surpluses determined by the Augenblick study. (Here, spending less than the study found necessary is termed a "PJ [professional judgment] deficit"; spending more is termed a "PJ surplus.") We would expect that student performance in districts with PJ surpluses would exceed, or at least meet, the panel's achievement goals, and that districts with larger PJ deficits would be further from achieving their goals than those with smaller PJ fiscal deficits. These expectations are appropriate, since the methodology already takes into account differing needs that arise from variation in school size, the concentration within a district of a disadvantaged population, and the like.

Yet the results of the PJ study were exactly the opposite of what one might reasonably expect. On the average, student achievement in districts with funding greater than the panel recommended, or a PJ surplus, was significantly worse than that found in districts with lower than recommended spending, or a PJ deficit (see figure 7.1).

Using a more sophisticated analysis, a regression of reading and math proficiency percentages of North Dakota districts, indicates a *positive* relationship between a PJ deficit and student achievement. In other words, the larger the PJ deficit, the higher the students' performance. This positive relationship between deficits and

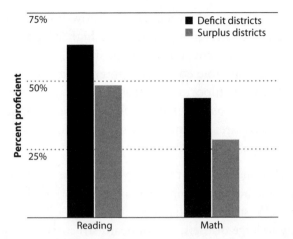

**7.1** Student Achievement vs. Adequacy of Funding, North Dakota

achievement levels holds true even after eliminating all surpluses and deficits greater than $2,000 to ensure that the analysis is not distorted by outliers. In short, the information provided by the PJ study was worse than no information. Its results would have dictated less, not more, spending for districts whose students were struggling the most to meet the state's academic standards, even though spending overall would substantially increase.

Such obviously silly results are far from unique. In another costing-out study by Augenblick's firm in Missouri, the results were similar. That study concluded that an average increase in funding of $4,874 per student was needed in Missouri's top twenty-five performing school districts, compared to only $2,551 in its twenty-five lowest-performing districts—again, the opposite of what one would expect.[27] These anomalous results pervade the professional judgment approach, which never tries to calibrate results to known achievement patterns.

In sum, it should surprise nobody that the professional judgment approach yields biased and unreliable recommendations, albeit ones that tend to be very useful to people interested in expanding educational spending. Panel members generally lack expertise in designing programs to meet objectives that are outside of their experience. While they may have experience making trade-offs within current school or school district budgets, they rarely have the research skills or personal experience to know how resource needs will change if they design a program for higher student outcomes or for different student body compositions. We have already pointed out the palpable conflicts of interest endemic to such panels. But their most important flaw is the failure to even consider other reforms, such as vouchers or charter schools or stronger accountability measures. As stated in the consultant's report on the New York study:

> PJPs [professional judgment panels] were not asked to reform other, often quite important, components of New York's education system. School district consolidation, charter schools, devolution of authority in large districts, school board structural reform, and a long list of other possible changes might well be in order. However, they were not the focus of PJP deliberations.[28]

The panels were given only one choice: spend money. At the hearing before the judicial referees in the *CFE* case, when one of the parties asked the referees to include charter schools in their recommendations to the legislature, the response denying the request was simple and to the point: "This is about money."[29]

## State-of-the-Art or Evidence-Based Approach

An alternative to the professional judgment approach is one that relies on the judgments of the consultants themselves. This approach has been immodestly called "state-of-the-art" by the major consulting firms using it.[30] Seeking to give their studies enhanced scientific cachet, they also refer to it in more recent applications as the "evidence-based" method. Generally, the method works as follows: The consultants review available research and select specific studies that relate to the typical programs and services considered necessary for a model school, such as small class sizes, and so on. They then develop a set of model schools based on the programs and services they select and price out their cost. They then use the costs of these model schools to determine statewide costs.

The most recent versions of the model are very precise: they quantify the effectiveness of *each* program or service included in their model schools by actually showing the impact on achievement that would result from implementing it for a single year (grade) for each student.[31] Perhaps they have supplied too much information. Their results, whether evaluated for each separate component or for the combined package, are simply not credible.

Let us take their claims at face value by looking at a recently conducted cost study using the evidence-based approach in Washington State conducted by Allan Odden and Lawrence Picus, the consultants who are the chief proponents of this methodology.[32] As is typical, the consultants designed a school around a series of programs that have surface plausibility: smaller class size, full-day kindergarten, expanded summer school, more professional development for teachers, and the like. They then reported what they believed to be the best evidence about how much improvement each component would bring about, and recommended including all of the components, regardless of their respective cost or effect. Figure 7.2 summarizes the consultants' evaluation of the achievement impacts of each component, garnered from the best research they could find, if Washington accepted their recommendations.[33] Thus, for example, they report that, according to their review of the best scientific literature, class size reduction would move the average Washington student (who starts at the fifty-seventh percentile of the national achievement distribution) up to the seventieth percentile.[34]

The consultants do not typically show the combined effect of the components they specify, but it is easy to calculate their projected combined impact. We have added to the chart our computation of the combined impact of implementing all nine components, which is found by simply summing the impacts of the separate programs. Such a calculation illustrates, perhaps better than anything, the unreliability and bias of the studies upon which they rely. As figure 7.2 shows, under their interpretation of the research, implementation of their recommendations would turn the *average* student in Washington, now performing at the fifty-seventh percentile, into the best-performing student in the country, scoring above the ninety-ninth percentile.[35] Indeed, by their reckoning, introducing only one of the nine components—classroom coaches—would in a

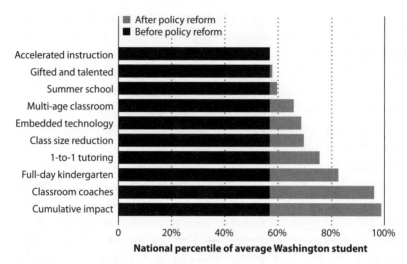

7.2 Picus-Odden Estimates of One-Year Impact of Specific Reforms on Average Student Performance in Washington State

single year skyrocket the average student in the state of Washington from the fifty-seventh percentile in the nation to the ninety-sixth percentile. Such results are simply not credible.

Past experience makes it is obvious that the consultants' programs—which are nothing more than repackaged versions of various existing programs—will not have any such results. Either the program evaluations are deeply flawed or the consultants have selected a particularly biased set of program evaluations.

This methodology has other serious problems. It specifically eschews attempts to calculate the minimum costs of achieving any level of achievement. In fact, it appears that the consultants seek instead to maximize expenditures. The programs they repeatedly recommend in state after state vary widely in their predicted effectiveness and cost, according to the consultants' themselves. Yet instead of concentrating on programs that yield high achievement per dollar invested, the consultants typically recommend doing everything, even though some of their programs would purportedly produce ten times the achievement of others for each dollar spent. For example, if instituting classroom coaches will raise achievement to the ninety-sixth percentile, does it really make economic sense to implement eight other programs, thereby doubling or tripling the cost, to move to the ninety-ninth percentile?[36] Rational government decision making would never make programmatic decisions in this manner (unless cost efficiency were really deemed irrelevant).

The only empirical bases for state-of-the-art analyses come from a small number of selected research studies that do not necessarily apply to particular states. And, most important, because those studies have been selected from the research base to suit the consultants' own purposes, there is no reason to believe that they provide an unbiased estimate of the more general empirical reality. Indeed, studies of the same programs that show little or no impact on student achievement are routinely disregarded in favor of those showing the highest impact. The usual response to such objections is simply to say that "while the evidence may not be perfect, it is the best we have." If it is that bad, however, it should not be used for policymaking.

While the concerns just cited are serious, another problem renders the entire process meaningless, even if these other concerns did not exist. For the evidence-based method to work (to actually improve achievement), the states and school districts must necessarily spend their money on the approaches they recommend and on which their cost estimates are based. Yet in Wyoming, where the legislature has relied upon cost figures generated by Picus and Odden using the "evidence-based" approach, the consultants' own studies show that nothing of the sort is taking place.[37] The consultants recommended smaller core classes, more professional development, and extending the school day. But Wyoming school authorities continue to spend money much as they did in the past, while ignoring the consultants' recommendations. They paid significantly higher salaries to existing teachers, dramatically increased the use of aides, and introduced more elective classes rather than concentrating attention on core classes.[38] Thus, although Odden and Picus have set forth a theoretical cost for an adequate education, the cost figures are unrelated to any potential outcomes, because the specific programs underlying them are being wholly ignored. Whether Wyoming's actual spending choices lead to the level of achievement posited by the two consultants will be totally happenstance, having nothing whatsoever to do with their "scientific" study and its calculation of the cost of an adequate education. Put another way, there is an infinite number of potential programs that could be costed out and subsequently ignored in practice. It is easy to invent imaginary schools that are either more expensive or less expensive than their choice. What makes the choices of these consultants any better than others in the set of imaginary schools?[39]

## Successful Schools Approach

Historically, the other method most commonly used to calculate the cost of an adequate education has been the "successful schools" approach. It begins by identifying schools—or districts—in a state that have been most effective at meeting some set of educational goals. Efforts to identify successful schools typically concentrate on student achievement, normally with no adjustments based on student background.[40] Spending on special programs, e.g., remedial education or special education, is stripped out of budgets in order to obtain a "base cost" figure for educating regular students in each successful district. Exceptionally high- or low-spending schools are often excluded, and the base costs for the remaining schools are averaged to arrive at a level of base spending that can reasonably be expected to yield high performance. (The high-spending districts are presumably eliminated because they are spending inefficiently, i.e., spending more than the minimum to achieve the observed outcomes. The rationale for eliminating low-spending districts is less clear).

The assumption underlying this method, and articulated by Ron Edmunds, the founder of the Effective Schools Movement, is that, if some schools in the state meet the required performance standard and spend in the range of, say, $8,000 per pupil, similarly situated school districts should also be able to meet the standard on similar amounts.[41] Thus far, the methodology makes a lot of sense. It is based on empirical evidence about spending by those schools that have been most successful.[42]

unless there's a school max match

However, this is not the end of the process. It is necessary some-how to generalize from these selected schools in two ways. The selected schools may differ from others in the state in terms of the backgrounds of students. And, building on the accountability and adequacy issues surrounding the analysis, it is often necessary to consider the implications for performing at a higher level than *any* of the schools currently observed in the state.

The method typically selects the highest-performing schools in the state, defined by student test scores and other educational out-comes, as the gauge for spending levels. These schools are almost always predominantly white and middle-class, meaning that the base cost excludes many of the nonschool factors that affect stu-dent performance in many less successful schools, such as family background, peer relationships, and previous schooling experi-ences. There is no reliable evidence that similar funding will yield similar achievement in two schools with student bodies from very different backgrounds; indeed, there is powerful evidence to the contrary. Therefore, the base costs have to be adjusted to take into account the requirements of special needs and other at-risk chil-dren. In most studies, the consultants simply add a weighting that increases funding for special needs students. (For example, a stu-dent qualifying for the free and reduced-price lunch program may be treated as 1.5 students, and a student qualifying for special edu-cation services may be treated as 2 students.) The consultant is then able to calculate the cost of being "successful" for schools with varying mixes of at-risk student populations. From those figures, they calculate total statewide costs of providing an "adequate" ed-ucation, i.e., one akin to that offered in the successful schools se-lected by them.

As previously mentioned, the problem is that no one knows what the proper weightings should be. Does it cost 1.2 times or 1.6 times the cost of an average regular pupil to educate an at-risk pupil, typically defined as one eligible for the free and reduced-price lunch program? Does spending 20 percent more, rather than 60 percent more, on such children significantly increase the odds that they will perform better? Past spending programs, such as the federal Title 1 program for disadvantaged students, have a very poor performance record, implying again that there is not sufficient experience with success to predict how spending on disadvantaged students relates to outcomes. Plaintiffs and cost consultants routinely rely on very high weightings, but in truth there is no consensus in the education or research community about what the weightings should be, or whether increasing them leads to higher achievement. In 2004, over half of the states had no multiplier for poor children. For those states that did, the weightings in 2002 varied from 1.02 to 1.59.[43] Other programs—those for English learners and for special education—also vary widely in form and in amount across the states, and also have little empirical basis. Ultimately, the successful schools approach seems to depend on guesswork as much as the professional judgment method.[44]

The adjustments for different types of students can also lead to anomalous results. For example, Augenblick & Myers performed a successful schools analysis on behalf of the Massachusetts teachers' union and other supporters of the plaintiffs in connection with that state's renewed adequacy case in 2004. The court found that two-thirds of the seventy-five schools that they had identified as "successful" under the current funding levels did not have as much money as his methodology declared necessary for success. According to the results of his study, spending would have to be increased in those districts in order for them to be "successful" or, by definition, adequate, even though under his definition of adequacy, they were in fact already meeting his standards of "success."[45]

Quite apart from such considerations, the successful schools approach faces the second basic methodological problem: there are limited (or no) data available that enable making accurate predictions about the cost of improved student performance. Consultants project the levels of student proficiency that would occur in the future if spending were increased, basing their projections on a school's current operations and current performance levels. They can say something about meeting the performance goals established under NCLB *only if* some subset of schools is currently achieving at the level that NCLB requires. However, essentially no district has yet reached the NCLB standards. Because the approach relies on observations about a set of schools with a given level of success, it has no way to project those observations to any higher performance level. For example, if 70 to 80 percent of students perform at the proficiency level in the schools identified as successful, there is no reliable way to extrapolate those results to a 95 percent level.

The inability to extrapolate to different performance levels seriously compromises the ability of this technique to consider alternative policy goals. Moreover, because it never identifies any set of policies, personnel decisions, or the like that contribute to the successful schools (but are absent from unsuccessful ones), the approach provides no real policy guidance to schools that want to do better.

## Cost Function Approach

The "cost function" approach, sometimes referred to as the "econometric" approach, relies on current spending and achievement patterns across all schools in a state to predict optimum spending solutions.[46] The most popular forms use statistical methods to describe how spending across a given state varies with achievement and with characteristics of the districts and their students.[47] They then use the results of their statistical analysis to derive appropriate spending levels for each district depending on its particular pupil mix and other measured characteristics.

Cost functions have entered into the adequacy debates largely as an alternative to the prior methods. The prior three approaches to judging adequacy have the appeal of being easily understood and of having surface plausibility. In contrast, early participants in developing costing-out methods, James Guthrie and Richard Rothstein, commented a decade ago, "At the most practical level, because of its technical complexity, there is little chance that statistical modeling can be proposed in any state as the primary means of calculating the cost of an adequate education or as the primary way of estimating how the costs of education may vary from place to place or from student to student."[48] But, as the flaws of the prior methods have become obvious, their usefulness and impact have diminished in both courts and legislatures. The econometric approaches have now gained almost the opposite appeal of the other methods: they are complicated and difficult to understand, so they must provide the scientific foundation for reliable costing-out of adequacy.

The technical complexity of these studies presents a challenge to us also, because understanding the nature of the studies, and why they fail to provide reliable answers to the "how much" question, requires more technical discussion than needed for the others. Nevertheless, given their growing use, it is important to lay out the fundamental issues, even if it requires dipping into statistical modeling issues.

For all their scientific pretensions, cost function studies also cannot come to grips with the lack of any significant causal relationship between student performance and spending.[49] As we have noted, there is a large body of statistical research examining how various levels of funding in schools influence student achievement, after taking into account differences in a range of background characteristics. This research, often called "production function" analysis and reviewed previously in chapter 3, has found little consistent relationship between spending and student outcomes. Even those studies showing that more money does improve student performance typically find only a very small effect of spending on student outcomes.[50] Given these small, if any, spending effects, these analyses imply that, absent other reforms to make the education system more efficient or responsive, it would take extremely large and unrealistic spending increases to make any meaningful progress in raising achievement.

Consultants doing "cost function" analysis take a slightly different approach and purport to have found a way to predict how spending must vary in order to obtain a given level of achievement. Instead of asking how much achievement would rise if a school were given an extra $1,000 per student (as the prior work has asked), they consider how much spending would increase if achievement went up by five points.[51] To a nonspecialist, these questions sound almost the same, and the nonspecialist would be right. Both methods rely on exactly the same data, and one would expect similar answers regardless of the method used. However, for mathematical reasons having to do with the drawing of the regression line in each approach, the results not only differ, but differ so much that it renders the results downright silly.

Let us look at what happened from parallel studies in California. As part of a broad set of studies of California's public schools, a number of costing-out studies were conducted to determine how much would have to be spent to allow the state's students to meet certain academic standards.[52] Jennifer Imazeki, a well-known expert in the area, applied both statistical approaches to the same data, but got such strikingly different results that it was obvious that the results of both studies should be disregarded. Using cost function analysis, she estimated that annual education spending in California would need to be increased by $1.7 billion a year to be adequate (on a base of approximately $50 billion).[53] Using production function analysis, based on the same data, she estimated spending would need to be raised by $1.5 *trillion per year—almost a thousand times greater.* Put into a slightly different perspective, this latter figure is thirty times the total amount California currently spends on its schools and three times larger than the spending on K–12 education for the entire United States.

The use of the same techniques in other states has also resulted in widely disparate results. For example, in recent studies conducted in Missouri, the use of one method indicated an increase of $367 per student would be required to meet academic targets, while the other estimated a $22,000 increase per pupil would be needed. Similar studies introduced in the Texas adequacy case also reached widely differing results.[54]

Importantly, the higher numbers obtained by the consultants come from the approach most accepted in the research literature (understanding how much achievement would change with additional resources), and their magnitude reflects the common finding that spending variations are not significantly associated with student achievement. Thus, it takes vast amounts of money to get any achievement change if schools stick to the current way of doing things. As these studies show, and as Imazeki acknowledges, the relationship between dollars and student achievement is so uncer-

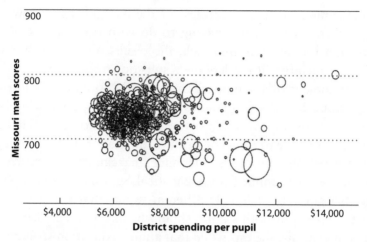

7.3  Missouri District Average Eighth Grade Math Scores vs. District Spending

tain that such results should not be used to gauge the potential effect of resources on student outcomes.[55] One can readily see this lack of any meaningful relationship by plotting achievement scores against per-pupil spending for the different school districts in a state. For example, figure 7.3 portrays the 2006 scores for each Missouri school district on the Missouri Assessment of Performance for eighth grade math.[56] The cloud of points, each representing the average test score of a Missouri school district, shows vividly the lack of any relationship between spending and achievement.

It is possible that the lower-scoring districts have disadvantaged student populations that are more difficult to educate and that therefore figure 7.3 does not accurately reflect whether higher spending is having a beneficial effect. However, using regression analysis, we can adjust for that possibility. We have done exactly that in figures 7.4 and 7.5, allowing for differences among districts in the racial composition of their student bodies, the percentage of students in poverty, as indicated by their participation in the federal government's free and reduced-price lunch program, and total enrollment. Figure 7.4 shows the relationship between achievement and spending, after controlling for these differences using the standard achievement-spending or production function approach,

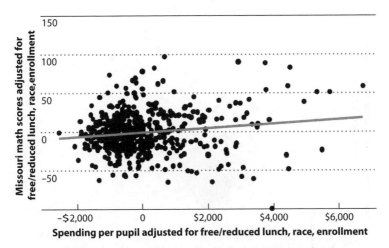

**7.4** Achievement–Spending Relationship: Production Function Results, after Controlling for Poverty, Race, and Enrollment

while figure 7.5 reflects the results using cost function analysis. Again, the central feature of both graphs is the "cloud" of points, each representing a Missouri school district, indicating little relationship between spending and achievement. The regression lines on each figure slope slightly upward, indicating that for lots of money some slight achievement gains might be realized. However, as pointed out earlier, the amounts are so large as to render the methods useless in trying to determine the amount of spending it would actually take to reach such achievement levels. For example, in the cost study presented by plaintiffs in the Missouri court case, the target for performance in Missouri called for increasing achievement in mathematics by sixty-seven points over their 2006 level. The slope of the line in figure 7.4 indicates that this would require additional spending per pupil of over $22,000, i.e., the regression line would have to be extended a very long way to the right before it was high enough on the y axis to reach sixty-seven added points. Put in context, this would require a quadrupling of K–12 education spending in the state, clearly something that for political and practical reasons is not going to occur. Indeed, any public official, including judges, who even suggested such an increase would be laughed out of office.

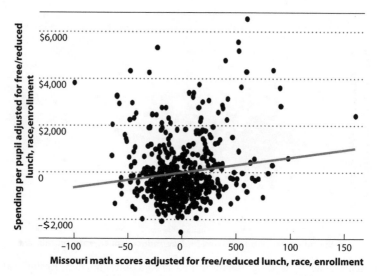

**7.5** Achievement–Spending Relationship: Cost Function Results, after Controlling for Poverty, Race, and Enrollment

The key part of the cost function approach, found in figure 7.5, is that the "no relationship" clearly seen in the figure takes on a different meaning. Now it appears that one can travel a long way in student achievement (on the horizontal axis) while only rising a little bit in terms of spending (the vertical axis). In sum, the cost function approach simply tries to capitalize on a different way of expressing the lack of relationship of spending and performance, a different way that appears more plausible than the outlandish interpretation of no relationship in figure 7.4.

These average spending relationships—whether estimated in the way of the "production functions" or in the way of "cost functions"—signify nothing more than the pattern of spending in a state. In order to interpret either of these relationships as describing the "cost" of changing achievement, one would have to presume that any inefficient spending is eliminated from the analysis. The trouble is that there is no budget item labeled inefficiency that can be factored into the statistical analysis. Inefficiency differences across districts are impossible to remove from the observed spending–achievement relationship in a state, resulting in the patterns we have observed: many high-achieving districts with low spending and vice versa.

Inefficiency can be buried deeply in the operations of districts in a thousand different ways: as salaries for teachers that are unrelated to the teacher's performance or quality, as programs that have no effect on student outcomes, or as the purchase of very costly inputs such as class size reduction instead of more cost-effective means of raising student achievement. Cost and production function studies do not consider any of these factors. Instead they typically include ad hoc measures of district characteristics in the statistical analyses and claim that they are related to efficiency. For example, in an attempt to provide some orderly pattern, the cost consultants in Missouri included characteristics of the district such as the amount of state aid per pupil, the percentage of the population aged sixty-five or older, and voter turnout in elections,[57] though how these factors are associated with more or less efficiency in a district is hard to fathom. The statistical analyses themselves show that these measures are only slightly related to spending differences across districts and could not possibly explain the wide disparities in spending for districts achieving at the same levels— i.e., the cloud of points in either figure 7.4 or 7.5.

Given the fundamental problems discussed, it adds little to go into detail about how current observations must be extrapolated. Obviously, if one projects to higher achievement—such as 100 percent proficiency in 2014 according to NCLB—it is necessary to go outside of the current observations.[58] Additionally, since much of the legal and policy focus is on low achievers, it is generally necessary to assume that high socioeconomic status (SES) districts directly show what low SES districts can do in terms of achievement.[59] If the other concerns about cost functions were appropriately addressed, these issues alone would be showstoppers. Nonetheless, one seldom gets to this point with cost functions.

### Comparing Approaches and Studies

But it is not just the two different cost function studies that produce wildly different results; the results of the four different approaches consultants use to estimate how much an adequate education should cost vary considerably as well— and fundamentally call into

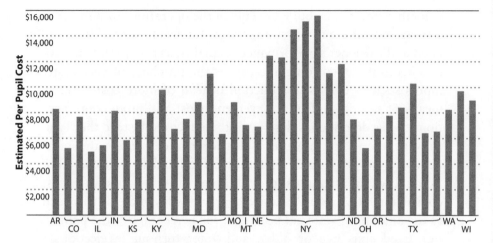

**7.6** Costing-Out Results in Eighteen States (adjusted for regional cost variations and expressed in 2004 dollars)

question their reliability. Even though the standard of adequacy may differ somewhat from state to state, it should presumably cost more or less the same to provide an "adequate" education in New York as in Illinois, assuming the cost numbers are adjusted to reflect different costs of living. However, the truth is that the cost study results not only vary from state to state, they are not even close.

Look at the results found by Bruce Baker, a supporter of costing-out studies and a consultant working in various school finance court cases, when he compared the results of thirty-six "costing-out studies" from seventeen different states. The results were striking, in several ways. As shown in figure 7.6, the "base" costs, with no monies added for special student needs, varied all over the map, from $5,210 in Illinois to $17,647 in one of the New York studies, when expressed in 2004 dollars.[60] When adjusted for regional cost of living differences, the wide disparities still remained, with some concluding it would cost about $5,000 per student and others concluding that over $15,000 per student would be required. Nor were those numbers outliers. The cost figures were arrayed all along the spectrum, as figure 7.6 demonstrates.[61]

One might try to account for such differences by arguing that different states have different quality requirements for an adequate education. But in Illinois, where the costing-out study concluded that $5,000 per student was sufficient, the state constitution contains the highest standard of the fifty states, requiring the state to provide its students with a "high quality" education. In contrast, New York, where costing-out studies concluded that more than three times as much money was necessary to satisfy the constitution, has one of the lowest constitutional standards of the fifty states. It simply requires "free common schools" and does not specify their quality.

Even within the same states, the cost studies result in vastly different cost figures depending on which of the four methods consultants used. On average, studies using the successful schools method conclude that the cost of providing an adequate education is about $2,000 a student less than the studies relying on the professional judgment model, even when such studies are of the same state education funding system. The Missouri costing-out study by Augenblick & Myers on behalf of the members of the Missouri Education Association used both these models and got two dramatically different results. The professional judgment model indicated that it would cost $7,832 per student in Missouri to provide an adequate education; under the successful schools model, the cost was $5,664, which was not only roughly the amount the schools were already spending, but also over $2,000 less per pupil than indicated by their professional judgment study.[62] The results of the successful schools study indicated no additional money was needed; the results of the professional judgment model indicated that almost a billion dollars more was required. It is difficult to take seriously the results of any of these studies, or consider any of the four methods generally reliable, when the same consultant studying the same schools can produce two such different results.

An analysis of costing-out studies by Augenblick & Myers in four separate states, undertaken by *Education Week* in 2005, found that the successful schools method resulted in significantly lower costs, varying from $735 per pupil lower in Maryland to $2,461 lower in Missouri.[63] This fact has not been lost on plaintiffs or state government officials who want higher spending on education, and consequently they have insisted that the professional judgment approach be used in most studies conducted in recent years.[64]

In summary, there are many analytical problems with costing-out studies, and there is little reason to believe that they can accurately determine the amount of funding necessary to provide an "adequate" education. Even some of the school finance consultants who have been paid hundreds of thousands of dollars to conduct these studies are no longer willing to vouch for them. James Guthrie, who is generally given credit for pioneering the professional judgment model in Wyoming and whose company MAP, in conjunction with AIR, conducted the costing-out study relied upon by CFE and the trial court in the *CFE* case in New York, has become thoroughly disillusioned with the manner in which such studies are being conducted and used, concluding that the claims made in them are "unsubstantiated" and "unreasonable."[65]

It is impossible even in retrospect to assess the accuracy of such studies, that is, to see after several years if they have accomplished what their purveyors claim. The amounts recommended in the studies conducted thus far have been so unrealistically high that it is doubtful that any state legislature will ever fund them at the recommended levels.[66] Therefore, if performance goals are not reached in two, three, or ten years, study advocates will always be able to argue underfunding as the reason for failure. Even if such levels of funding were actually provided and children still failed to meet the state standards, advocates of such studies could point to their disclaimers that money alone cannot ensure success[67] or plead failures in implementing the recommended programs.[68]

Most damaging, however, is the implication of such costing-out studies that our country's education problems, particularly those related to the low achievement of at-risk students, can be solved by increased spending alone. By their very nature, such studies ignore other more effective steps a state or school district might take to increase achievement, and focus solely on increasing spending.

## How Should the Money Be Spent?

Costing-out studies are not the only "scientific" evidence appealed to in courtrooms and legislative chambers. Research on the effectiveness of particular programs and educational strategies also plays a role in discussions of educational policy because it helps to answer the all-important question: how should education funds be spent?

It makes some sense, as a matter of principle, to justify particular policy decisions—regulatory frameworks or the use of state funding for particular programs—by citing scientific evidence that the program works. If science says that the program will raise student achievement, then the state may want to insist that all districts follow it. Legislatures can write such a policy into law, or state departments of education can require districts to pursue it, or funding can be structured to supply money if it is used. Or courts seeking remedies in adequacy suits may order that districts implement the program.

Whether the program, once implemented, bears the fruit suggested by the research depends on a variety of factors. First and foremost, the underlying scientific research clearly must be highly reliable and widely applicable. This proves to be a tough test, because many plausible-sounding policies linked to research prove ineffectual in application. Second, the implementation must be faithful to the underlying design if the research is to be a good predictor of the policy's impact. Policies that prove effective in some circumstances do not always travel well; small differences in implementation or local variations can produce quite different results. Third, policy initiatives aimed at a specific program can lead to unanticipated and sometimes harmful consequences as local decision makers react in unexpected and unintended ways to the incentives that are created. Finally, of course, the policy has to be a good one in the economic sense; that is, its educational returns must be sufficient to justify the expense of the program, as well as any related impacts on other programs.

It would, of course, be impossible to consider here all the existing scientific research on education, and how well scientifically based programs have fared once implemented by specific schools and districts. But we can illustrate some of the problems that have arisen in applying scientific research by looking at two popular policies: class size reduction and preschool education.

Debates over these two policy ideas have become central to many legislative and judicial deliberations in the last decade.[69] In other years, different programs might have made the top of the list. For example, in the 1990s, the central focus of many educational policy discussions was whole school reform.[70] This idea even produced a public–private partnership called the New American Schools with a design competition and federal start-up money.[71] Yet, after much hoopla and high hopes, implementation problems and the lack of obvious achievement gains led to its gradual demise.[72] Prior to that, the Office of Economic Opportunity experimented with "performance contracting"—hiring private firms to provide education and paying them based on results. But here the inexperience in writing contracts doomed the effort.[73] Other efforts in other years were likewise trumpeted, and likewise faded.

As the following discussion will make clear, the application of science to difficult questions of education policy has not been very effective. We believe that science could potentially be enormously helpful in finding solutions to education problems, but only if it is based on reliable and appropriate conclusions. Certainly, some research was unsuccessful because of flaws in the research itself, but more often, we believe, the problem has been the lack of appropriate data and the failure to properly evaluate policies before putting them in place. In the last section of this chapter, we address how better use could be made of science in education decision making, and why features of performance-based funding are critical to achieving those benefits.

### Class Size Reduction

The impact of class size on student outcomes is perhaps the most studied policy issue in education. By the early 1990s, most studies looking at this issue found only limited evidence that reductions in class size were associated with improved student achievement. While teacher–pupil ratios fell steadily after the 1960s, these reductions were seldom a primary policy choice.[74] In 1996 this situation changed when Governor Pete Wilson of California, looking for a way to put more money into schools without devoting all of it to higher teacher salaries, hit upon the idea of reducing class sizes across the state. Wilson's political popularity consequently shot up, inducing a majority of other governors and the federal government to very quickly announce their own programs to reduce class sizes.

The policy proposal is aided considerably by a surface plausibility. Smaller classes permit a teacher to individualize instruction and to spend more time with each student. As a result, they must by popular consensus lead to improved achievement.[75] Unfortunately, the issue is vastly more complicated.

The result of the rush to smaller classes was a search for evidence supporting the initiative, and the proponents of the policy—including parents, teachers' unions, and school personnel—seized upon a random assignment experiment in Tennessee that previously had been largely overlooked. Project STAR was a legislatively mandated evaluation of an experimental reduction in class size from the then standard of twenty-two to twenty-five students per class to thirteen to seventeen students per class.[76] Beginning with a set of seventy-nine schools that volunteered for the experiment and that had at least three sections of classes in each grade from K to 3, kindergarten students in 1985 were randomly placed in either small or large classes. Students were to stay in small or large classes for the entire four years of the experiment (K–3), and each spring the students would be tested in reading and math to gauge achievement growth in the different-sized classes.

The random assignment experiment is widely regarded as one of the most valid ways of separating the causal effect of a policy from other factors that might be influential.[77] Other analytical designs, including those most frequently applied to study class sizes before the STAR experiment, are more prone to questions about the influences of other factors, even though efforts are made to control statistically for such factors through regression analysis.

In the STAR experiment, student performance in the small classes averaged about one-quarter of a standard deviation higher than that in the larger-sized classes. An impact of this magnitude implies that a student at the center of the distribution would move up to the sixtieth percentile. Based on these estimates, findings from

this experimental program were immediately cited as support
for reductions (even as all other evidence was disregarded). Across
the country, teacher–pupil ratios declined rapidly. Indeed, the two
costing-out methods described earlier that rely on professional or
analyst judgments always include a significant class size reduction
component based largely on Project STAR. Similarly, most trial
presentations in adequacy cases include evidence from Project
STAR in order to justify increased funding of schools.

By the standards of random assignment experiments, Project
STAR was not a very high-quality experiment.[78] Over half of the
initial students dropped out of the experiment and were replaced
before the conclusion of the four-year evaluation; a sizeable portion of the students transferred from the large to the small classes
between kindergarten and the third grade; and a large percentage
of students (larger in the small class groups) did not take all of the
examinations. Perhaps most importantly, because the inferences
from the analysis depend upon no systematic assignment of teachers to classes of different sizes, there is no evidence about the allocation of teachers to the different treatment groups in the experiment—raising questions about the validity of the experiment.

Strikingly, although the experiment has received enormous attention and its design is very straightforward, no efforts have been
made to replicate it in the two decades since its completion. Thus,
any questions about its validity and its relationship to the vast
amount of other evidence about class size remain subject to continuing, often heated, debate.[79]

A central issue, something often disregarded in the policy discussions, is what generalizations can be made from such evidence. Ignoring the shortcomings in the study just summarized, it remains
the case that the experimental evidence refers just to a particular—
and particularly large—reduction, from twenty-four to fifteen students per class. The experiment does not provide information
about the achievement effects of reducing from, say, twenty-six to
twenty-one students or twenty-nine to twenty-five. Nor does it provide any information about grades other than K to 3. Further, since
*all* of the impact of moving to smaller classes actually was observed
in the first year, the experiment itself says nothing about the effects

of smaller changes in class sizes, class size reductions in later grades, or what have you. The evidence, it appears, cannot be the basis for broad generalizations.

In this case, we can observe the effects of trying to replicate the results of a small, controlled experiment with the blind implementation of such a program on a statewide basis. The problems, some unforeseen, that can arise during implementation are huge, and are best illustrated by what happened in California's well-publicized (and often-praised) program. That state's program was designed to provide extra funding to school districts to enable them to reduce class sizes in grades K–3 to twenty students or less.[80] However, the sudden reduction in class sizes across the state resulted in a commensurately sudden and sharp increase in the demand for teachers. In response, many school districts set out to attract and hire existing teachers from other districts. In the end, districts serving disadvantaged populations disproportionately lost their most qualified teachers, potentially harming the most important target group. Whatever positive effect reducing class size had in those districts was offset by the effect of losing many of their best teachers, and the net result was little or no improvement in achievement in such districts.[81]

Another unintended consequence of class size reduction programs in California has been to actually increase some class sizes. Since the additional funding in California is for reductions in grades K–3, school districts under financial pressure may seek to cut costs by hiring fewer teachers—and thus increasing the class sizes—in later grades. Therefore, classes of twenty students in K–3 are frequently followed by much larger classes in grades 4–6. The average class size in the state for grades 1–3 in 2006 was less than twenty, while that for grades 4–5 was twenty-nine.[82] No evidence suggests that this is an optimal strategy.

Our point is not that small classes have no positive attributes. It is undoubtedly the case that small classes can be very beneficial in certain circumstances—with certain teachers, with certain students, in certain subjects, and in certain grades. But the existing research does little to pinpoint those circumstances, even as it demonstrates that across-the-board class size reductions are, at best, a mixed bag. One important difficulty with such research is that in applying it, little effort is made to tailor the program to the specific circumstances of a school or district. It is this inflexibility, finally, that casts most doubt on the appropriateness of the policy. Class size reduction is the most expensive broad policy that is commonly contemplated by either courts or legislatures. Because of the increased need for teachers, even a small reduction from twenty-six to twenty-three students raises operating expenses by 10 percent,[83] to say nothing of the sometimes huge capital cost of constructing additional classrooms.

Debates frequently fail to ask whether spending an equal amount on some other policy, such as higher teacher quality, would not produce even greater achievement gains than those anticipated from class size reductions.[84] But because class size reductions garner large increases in funding for schools while involving essentially no changes in schools' structure or system of incentives, parents and teachers alike support them. For these reasons, programs to reduce class size have been very popular, whether for general policy purposes or for achieving adequacy.

As the projected benefits of class size reduction have failed to accrue, the policy push behind the initiative has diminished. Yet many states are left with expensive class size reduction programs in place—California currently pours $2 billion per year into its K–3 program—that are very difficult to modify because of continuing public and school support. Because the program is so widespread, it is impossible to assess precisely what its real value for student achievement may be. In the end, the mixed scientific evidence on the merits of general class size reduction programs and the experience in California and elsewhere make clear the risks of relying on limited, selective studies to approve hugely expensive programs.[85]

## Preschool Education

A second focus of current policy discussions with large ramifications for school finance is preschool education. In whatever version (e.g., universal or means tested), preschool education is frequently mentioned as the next "obvious" fix for the current schooling problems.

Support for preschool education is based on three different and plausible arguments.

First, preschool would address the problems of disadvantaged students who come to school far behind their middle-class peers. If language and other deficits, which have lasting effects on student outcomes, were lessened for these children by preschool attendance, the result might be smaller achievement gaps in the future.

A second argument for preschool rests on a variety of conceptual arguments for early investments in human capital—most notably articulated by Nobel laureate James Heckman. Heckman has argued that early investments in education are critical, since, in his words, "learning begets learning."[86] Investments made early in life enhance learning later in school and even into careers, making such investments economically attractive.

Third, key studies with strong research designs based on random assignment of students to programs have supported the efficacy of preschool education for aiding the school readiness of disadvantaged youth. The most well-known is the Perry Preschool Program, but others, such as the Abecedarian Program and the Early Training Program, also provide important evidence in favor of early childhood education.[87] A set of benefit-cost analyses of the Perry Preschool Program shows that this program appears to have been effective, conferring social benefits in excess of expenditures.[88]

Support for expanding preschool programs is currently very strong; courts in South Carolina and New Jersey, for instance, have found preschool education to be an essential element of an adequate education.[89] Yet serious questions remain about the reliability of the studies affirming the benefits of preschool, and about how generally applicable their results are. The evaluation of the Perry Preschool, Abecedarian, and Early Training programs relied upon a random assignment methodology that followed subjects over extended periods of time. But the numbers of children taking part in the experiments were relatively small. The Perry Preschool treatment group consisted of just fifty-eight children, the Abecedarian Program just fifty-seven children,[90] and the Early Training Program just forty-four children. Quite clearly, samples of this size raise the concern about whether the evaluation results can be generalized to much larger programs, especially when, upon reanalysis, many of the originally reported findings have turned out to be fragile.[91]

The experimental evidence has been supplemented by observational studies in other locations. Perhaps the most commonly cited study is the Chicago Child-Parent Center program, a program currently operating in the Chicago public schools.[92] This program is lower in cost than Perry or Abecedarian, although the benefits are also considerably less certain. More recently, studies of Tulsa— meant to provide evidence on a universal program in Oklahoma— have provided another interesting, albeit limited, evaluation of the results of broader programs.[93]

The beneficial results that have been identified are quite varied. First, as Michael Anderson demonstrates, girls experienced virtually all of the programs' benefits; boys were likely to experience no benefit or worse.[94] Second, a substantial part of the benefit fell outside of schools and the development of cognitive skills; the benefits found for girls related to reduced criminal behavior.[95] Thus, even if the programs are valuable for society, they do not appear to be a panacea for school achievement problems. Third, the results for varying preteen, teen, and adult outcomes differed across programs, so that it is not enough to simply recommend "preschool," but is rather necessary to identify the precise kind of preschool.

Probably most important, these programs are not your typical community or school-based program found in most states. The Perry Preschool Program, estimated to cost over $15,000 per child (in 2000 dollars), involved intensive treatment by teachers with master's degrees in child development, student–teacher ratios of 6:1, and regular home visits—but they ran just from October to May.[96] The Abecedarian Program is full day, five days per week, fifty weeks per year for five years beginning at birth, and includes medical care and home visits.[97] Over the five years of program services, it is estimated to cost $75,000 per child (in 2002 dollars).[98] Clearly, these programs are not within the range that would be considered on a broad scale in most states, but the experiments provide no information about which components are most valuable or what a more modest version (with significant benefits) might look like.

All this evidence indicates that there may well be benefits for society to instituting expanded preschool programs for disadvantaged students, but there are also potentially huge costs associated with doing it right—if in fact we even understand what "doing it right" would be. The rationale for preschool is that it is easier to remediate earlier rather than later, and that school will supplement what children experience at home to foster stronger educational development in the future.[99] At the same time, the educational benefits of existing programs that have been evaluated, except perhaps the most intensive and expensive, have been small and short-lived. The limited number of models that has been evaluated provides uncertain guidance about design of effective programs, particularly those that reach boys.

We believe the existing evidence supports a more extensive set of experiments and evaluations into the efficacy of different approaches to providing early education. In the words of preschool proponent William Gormley, "Preliminary results from a growing body of pre-K programs are encouraging, but not entirely convincing."[100] This is just the situation where strategic experimentation offers the most promise. But the evidence does not support instituting broad, full-scale programs—particularly when doing so would make evaluating and learning from the experiences very difficult. Implementing preschool programs on a statewide basis would be much like introducing the class size reduction programs in California, where universal coverage eliminated any appropriate comparison group and thus made any reliable evaluation impossible.

One other aspect of program design is also important. Any proposals of governmental support for preschool must consider which groups should receive programmatic help, how the programs should be organized, and how they should be financed.[101] The existing evidence on preschools is limited largely to their impact on disadvantaged students. There is no evidence about positive impacts for middle- and upper-income students.[102] Many who support expanded preschool appear to assume that the programs will be universal and will simply extend the current public schools back to earlier grades. But the scientific evidence for preschool provides support, albeit limited, for programs targeted only to disadvantaged students.

Finally, we add this important reminder. None of the rigorously evaluated experiments just discussed has been a public school program, and none of them suggests that the public schools would be any more effective at providing preschool programs than they have been at the K–12 level. [103]

Indeed, the disappointing results of Head Start indicate otherwise. Many people tend to forget that we in fact have a large public preschool program, introduced with the programs on the War on Poverty in 1965. Over nine hundred thousand three- and four-year-olds from families in poverty are currently enrolled in Head Start programs around the country. The federal Head Start program is considerably different from the Perry and Abecedarian programs. In 2005, just 35 percent of its teachers had a bachelor's degree, and the programs varied considerably in length and intensity. [104] The cost of Head Start is usually reported as slightly over $7,000 per pupil per year (in 2003–4 dollars), derived by dividing total program costs by the number of participants. As welfare specialist Douglas Besharov and his colleagues point out, however, this mixes together a variety of different programs; if run on a full-time, full-year basis, the program costs would be over $20,000 per year. [105] Against these expenditures, there is considerable uncertainty about the benefits. Many studies find no lasting impact, while others find a modest initial impact but one that tended to fade over time. [106]

Some states are moving to universal pre-K programs, including Oklahoma, Georgia, and Florida. The evaluation of these programs is difficult, because of their universal nature. And there is disagreement about the impacts on achievement. Those studies that show improvements in short-run achievement are matched by those more skeptical. [107] As with the previously described preschool programs, some reason for optimism about the potential for disadvantaged students survives, but the uncertainties also point to a need for gathering more systematic evidence before starting full-scale universal programs.

Finally, we bring the evidence back to the education policy context. The existing evidence suggests that the achievement gains from current and past preschool programs are relatively small and may fade out altogether as the student progresses in school. Thus, even the most optimistic view of the evidence does not suggest that preschool is likely to close the existing achievement gaps by itself.[108]

## Using Science More Effectively

Our position on science and the development of public policy should not be misunderstood. It is emphatically not meant to indicate that scientific evidence is inappropriate or that science should be avoided in developing educational policies—quite the contrary. We believe that better use of empirical evidence is the *only* way that policies will improve. A key element of our performance-based funding plan, described in the next chapter, is a scientific improvement process.

What we object to is the misapplication of scientific methods and the misinterpretation of scientific conclusions. Costing-out studies are simply bad science—political approaches masquerading as studies following scientific principles. On the other hand, other studies are pushed beyond their limits. For example, the science is just too uncertain on the impacts of class size reduction and preschool education to be applied as some would wish and without the appropriate caveats about the unreliability of available evidence.

Our concerns focus on the potential for misuse of the available evidence. Generalizing from small, specific studies to universal application of a legislated policy is, at the very least, a risky strategy and most likely an expensive and ineffective approach to improving schooling. Even where programmatic evidence is reliable and valid, applying the same program to heterogeneous districts of a state is unlikely to be successful. Consider what state educational systems look like. Nine states have over five hundred separate school districts.[109] California, the most populous state, has more than a thousand districts, including Los Angeles Unified with over 700,000 students and twelve others having enrollment exceeding

49,000.[110] At the same time, over half of the state's districts are K–8 districts. An effective common program that is legislated from Sacramento to cover the variety of activities in the state is, as the data have shown, impossible.[111] Yet, most discussions of class size reduction, preschool, and the like tend to assume that a specific program could be faithfully and universally implemented across an entire state.

There is actually little evidence that *any* policy extracted from the scientific evaluation literature has ever been successfully implemented across the heterogeneous districts of states. The available science does not support effective regulatory and implementation policies that reliably replicate evaluation results on a broad basis. The overall lack of relationship between spending, which is frequently related to programs that are justified by reference to scientific evidence and outcomes, provides evidence for this conclusion. One interpretation of the oft-mentioned difficulties of "going to scale" with a program is that it is rarely faithfully implemented across districts.[112] But the implementation issues remain, nonetheless, a central part of school policy, because different districts with different needs and capacities will tend to modify virtually any policy mandated (or voluntarily selected). Indeed, in places where funds have increased in accord with evidence-based costing-out studies (e.g., Arkansas or Wyoming), school districts have not used the extra funds in anything like the ways the costing-out studies prescribed.[113]

We object also to the tendency for advocates on different sides of an issue to rely on science selectively—that is, to choose just the studies that support a particular point of view.[114] A variety of commentators see the political use of research to be a very natural state of affairs.[115] Natural or not, it obviously compromises the value of scientific evidence, since choosing studies on the basis of results, rather than the quality of the study, is both an invalid scientific approach and one likely to lead to unsatisfactory outcomes. Certainly, science itself is not immune to bias, but the continuing dialog within disciplines, the scientific peer review system, and the mores of science work militate against such problems; whereas the political, or, for that matter, the judicial process, lacks such scientific checks and balances.

This concern about the selective (i.e., result-dependent) use of studies pervades the policy process, but it is most acute in the courtroom and legal setting. The adversarial system encourages testimony that is biased toward one or the other positions and that discourages nuance. Differing rules of evidence in the courtroom and in science compound the problem. Hearsay rules, while lessened with expert witnesses, work against broad development of scientific evidence in the courtroom. Additionally, the complexity of statistical analyses and the difficulty that nonspecialists have in penetrating complicated methodologies and the testing of hypotheses mean that scientific opinions and evidence are evaluated only in the crudest way in courtrooms.

The answer is to recognize the role that science can and cannot play in understanding and formulating educational policy.[116] Scientific evaluation, properly applied, can assess whether an already implemented policy is likely to be effective and is worth the expenditure. This is extraordinarily important.

In order to facilitate scientific comparisons of alternative programs, the Institute of Education Sciences (the research branch of the U.S. Department of Education) has developed a fledgling program to compile evidence on programmatic effectiveness, to evaluate the scientific reliability of the evidence, and to compare costs and effectiveness of alternatives where possible. This activity, the What Works Clearinghouse (WWC), currently addresses a limited number of areas of study, and each has a limited number of studies evaluated as being high quality—reflecting the recentness of emphasis in education research on scientific validity.[117] Nonetheless, an example is instructive. In March 2008, the WWC could provide comparative evaluations of ten separate programs to aid reading comprehension of English language learners. From this, one could readily discover that one program (Instructional Conversations and Literature Logs) had "potentially positive effects," while another (Read Naturally) showed "no discernible effects."[118] The interested person can quickly get a summary but can also dig deeper into the evidence and the potential for generalizing the results. Topics that are covered are largely driven by the availability of suitable scientific evidence, but the potential can be seen from available reviews ranging from elementary math programs to dropout prevention and character education interventions.

On the other hand, existing evaluations seldom provide much assurance that a mandated policy will have any given outcome. Indeed, under current operations, mandated programs are seldom evaluated at all. And the available evidence on educational programs cannot supplant the legislative process by providing a scientific answer to the question "How much should we spend on education?"

In the next chapter, we discuss in more detail the components of a performance-based funding system, which we believe can make science a more important and productive part of educational policymaking. A key component of these ideas is recognition that a single best solution that can be applied universally simply does not exist. There are some underlying general policies that might be developed through improved research and evaluation. But their applicability and specific use are likely to vary considerably across districts with different student demands and different district capacities. Both states and districts have to think in terms of a continuous improvement process—one that modifies basic policies over time to retain the good parts and drop the bad parts. The process clearly should rely heavily on scientific evaluation methods to disentangle the causal effect of policies on student outcomes, i.e., to go beyond mere associations that are observed across schools and districts and to pinpoint what can be expected if a given policy is instituted.

Unfortunately, scientific research and evaluation analyses got off to a slow start in education. Too little effort went into identifying the true effect of various policies and resources on student achievement, mainly because of the lack of appropriate data. Until recently, it was difficult to trace the impacts of teachers, schools, and policies on student achievement. This shortcoming has gone a long way toward being remedied with the development of accountability systems in all states (even if a number of states have resisted assembling these data into useful databases that permit such evaluation). And the tide appears to be turning. The No Child Left Behind Act mentions "research" over two hundred times as it calls for a closer linkage of evidence and policy.[119]

But the policy process has itself hindered the ability to judge the effectiveness of policies. All scientific evaluations are based upon having appropriate control groups to indicate what happens without any intervention. Simply put, it is very difficult to understand the impact of a policy without having a good idea of what would have happened without the policy. Yet programs are often implemented universally across districts or states—perhaps because of ignorance of the uncertainty surrounding a program, perhaps because of a sense that the problem is urgent and must be dealt with immediately, perhaps because legislators and governors do not want to admit that they are proposing policies that are uncertain, or perhaps because they are reluctant to deprive any children of the assumed benefit of the policy. But when applied universally, programs can seldom be evaluated with any reliability owing to the lack of any possibility to observe outcomes in situations where the policy was not implemented.

We propose making scientific research and evaluation a more fundamental part of the educational policy process. Doing so will require a variety of changes in the normal way of doing educational business, including the following:

- More comprehensive and relevant databases and assessment techniques, including value-added measures
- Evaluation components as part of the implementation of any new education policies or strategies
- Dedicated funding for independent evaluations
- Pilot programs to road test policies before they are implemented on a broad scale
- Enhanced roles for state departments of education in evaluating and identifying effective strategies and in providing information on them to local districts
- Increased flexibility for local districts so they can adopt and implement promising programs that fill their particular needs

Such changes will ensure that scientists have the necessary data and funding to conduct focused research on what works and what does not work under a variety of situations, that programs and strategies are appropriately and periodically evaluated after implementation, that the research is more credible, and that large-scale programs are not implemented until they have been tested in controlled pilot programs. They will strengthen the science behind education policy and ultimately strengthen our schools. They will not, however, eliminate the need for policymakers to make important judgments in evaluating and relying upon scientific evidence.

# 8 | A Performance-Based Funding System

In this chapter, we lay out the elements of a performance-based funding system—a system that we believe will lead to significantly better student achievement and at the same time make more effective use of valuable and limited education dollars.

Despite massive increases in funding for K–12 education, performance has not significantly improved, creating a puzzle for many observers of schools. Researchers, legislators, courts, and others have at the same time been reluctant to acknowledge that increased resources may not be the answer, but even that is beginning to change. Witness the recent report on schools in California, financed by a consortium of liberal-leaning foundations, which concluded: "It is clear . . . that solely directing more money into the current system will not dramatically improve student achievement and will meet neither expectations nor needs. What matters most are the ways in which the available resources are used."[1] Relying on these findings, the committee appointed by Governor Schwarzenegger to advise him on reforming California schools did not focus on resources but instead concentrated on structural reforms to the delivery of education.[2]

Even as we search for ways to improve student achievement, in part due to the pressure of NCLB and state accountability measures, the school finance system itself has rarely been used in this effort. Instead, school finance continues to be seen in most states solely as the way to get necessary funding to districts in order to implement a variety of educational strategies independently decided upon by educators and policymakers. Decisions relating to finance are largely separated from decisions on education policy; the only overlap involves calculating the amount of money necessary to implement the particular educational programs and strategies. The idea seems to be that the level of spending and its distribution across students, schools, and districts is one decision, and the educational policies and regulations another.

Not only does this separation frequently lead to bad policy outcomes, it also leaves on the sidelines a powerful weapon in the battle to improve student performance and to increase the efficiency of our schools: the financial incentives a well-designed school funding system can provide for teachers and school leaders to do a better job.

We begin with the principles upon which such a system should rest and conclude with a more specific description of essential components and application to state policy.

## Guiding Principles: Back to Basics

The performance-based funding system we propose rests on the following principles:

- If the objective is improving outcomes, the system should focus on outcomes. Accountability for performance should be substituted for restrictions on local decision making.
- The system should reward those who contribute to success, i.e., those who bring about high achievement.
- Rewards should be based on each person's contribution to success to the maximum amount feasible.
- School funding formulas should minimize unproductive "gaming" by avoiding rewards for things that are easily manipulated by school personnel.
- School funding policies must recognize the underlying heterogeneity of students and their educational challenges and ensure that all schools have the means to succeed.
- School authorities must gather relevant programmatic and performance data and use them to refine and improve performance.
- New policies or programs should be introduced in a manner that enables direct evaluation of their results.

In short, focus funding and policy decisions on student outcomes, provide incentives and funding to achieve outcome goals, and evaluate whether what is being done is consistent with improving student outcomes.

We offer this list with some humility. The proverbial Martian landing on Earth and presented this list might say, "And you had to write a book about this?" Our answer: "Unfortunately, yes." In fact, the more detailed answer would go on to acknowledge that we not only have to write this prescription but also have to anticipate a considerable struggle to see these elements incorporated into state and local policy. Indeed, many, if not most, elements have been discussed in one form or another. It is simply that the historic response has been, "Yes, we see the logic in the arguments, but it really is hard." Thus, it has been much easier to keep the general structure of current policy and finance and concentrate efforts on deepening and reinforcing existing incentives and operations. Easier, but mostly ineffective.

## A Performance-Based Funding System

We describe next a set of policies and funding mechanisms based on these guiding principles. A key element, which will become apparent, is their interlocking nature—and thus the necessity of considering them as an integrated system as opposed to a menu of components that can be ordered à la carte. We call it "performance-based funding" because it is an integrated set of policies and funding mechanisms, all designed to drive and reward better performance. While some of these notions play a role in the current systems of education in some states, none of the fifty states has adopted the integrated system we recommend.

### 1. Standards, Assessment, and Accountability

Perhaps the most important single change in K–12 education of the last two decades is the attention given to student outcomes—as opposed to the more traditional focus on the resources or programs of schools. The idea of focusing on student achievement is now deeply embedded in the structure of schooling, not the least because of the federal mandates of NCLB. At one level, little needs to be said about the necessity to retain this focus. Yet, because of controversies about the details of NCLB and because of efforts by some to turn back the clock to a prior era, we review key elements of standards, assessment, and accountability.

## WELL-DEFINED OUTCOME OBJECTIVES WITH STRONG ASSESSMENT

Education policy should begin with an explicit statement of the learning goals of schools—detailed by subject and grade. Local school leaders can then ensure that instruction is oriented toward meeting these goals, and that measurement and accountability are based on reaching them. These "output" standards—the learning levels expected and desired of all students—should be uniform for all districts and defined by the state. (The idea of uniform standards set by the state is not new, and, urged on by NCLB, all fifty states have already adopted, in one form or another, learning or content standards that apply to different subjects and grades.) The standards should be challenging ones that will enable our students to compete with students from around the world.[3]

## IMPLEMENTATION OF VALUE-ADDED ASSESSMENT

Any school incentive plan of the type we are proposing must reward results that are clearly due to the efforts of the schools, teachers, and other individuals. But a student's performance reflects a complicated mixture of current and past school factors, family influences, and influences of friends and neighbors. Rewarding an individual for a student's level of achievement would not be appropriate, since it may actually have little to do with the student's current school or teachers. In fact, doing so would be counterproductive, because it encourages schools and teachers to seek out high-performing students while avoiding low-performing students.

The solution is for the state and school districts to track individual students and their performance over time and across districts to assess the "value added" by individual teachers and schools—that is, their specific contribution to students' gains. Technology has become available to make reasonable assessments of the impact of schools as distinct from other influences, and these could in turn be used not only in court, but also by states and school districts in determining deficient performance properly attributable to the schools themselves, and not other causes. These models have been developed specifically for evaluating the effectiveness of teachers[4] and have also had a role in discussions of accountability systems for schools.[5] By linking teachers and schools with the academic records of individual students, it is statistically possible to provide direct information on the achievement gains attributable to current teachers and schools.[6] While absolute test scores that measure the ultimate objective might also play a role in any accountability and reward system, performance measures used as part of the incentive system should be primarily based on these value-added assessments.

The concept of value-added assessments is rapidly gaining ground, both nationally and in many states. Early criticism of NCLB was that it focused just on "proficiency" and did not pay sufficient attention to learning gains by students. NCLB has now authorized all states to participate in the U.S. Department of Education's experiment in using "growth models" for evaluating progress toward student proficiency.[7] These growth models, similar in concept and operation to value-added assessments, rest on the idea that looking at gains in student learning over time gives a more accurate picture of a school's or district's progress toward achieving universal proficiency than simply looking at the percentage of students proficient in any year. Considering the learning gains of students gives schools credit for promoting higher achievement even if some students have yet to reach the "proficiency" level. It also gives credit to promoting higher achievement for students who have already met basic proficiency. While overly narrow because it still focuses on just the proficiency cutoff, schools in the states participating in the NCLB experiment can meet AYP (adequate yearly progress) goals based upon projections of student learning gains. Information on growth also provides feedback that individual schools and districts can use to improve their educational programs.

The heart of any such assessment system is timely, accurate, and complete data about student performance over time and across districts, along with the ability to link such data to schools, programs, and personnel. This ability—the subject of further discussion later on in this chapter—obviously requires a reliable identification system for schools, teachers, and programs, as well as a comprehensive student-level database. Once it is possible to link student performance across grades, programs, and teachers, it becomes possible to isolate the impacts of various policies, policies, and personnel. Moreover, once students can be followed across schools and districts, they are far less likely to be "lost" simply because of high mobility rates among disadvantaged populations.

## A STRONG ACCOUNTABILITY SYSTEM

A strong accountability system is a critical aspect of our proposal.[8] Such a system should collect and analyze information concerning the schools' success in improving student achievement, provide understandable information to the schools and public on the performance of the schools, and put in place a mechanism for either improving the school or, failing any improvement, to ensure that the children attending the failing school have other options.

*Transparency*    Perhaps the most important aspect of accountability is providing the public, particularly parents, with timely, easy to understand information about the performance of the schools. Parents, more than anyone else, can put pressure on their children's school to improve, but to do that, they need accurate and appropriate information. NCLB requires reporting of student proficiency for schools and subgroups of students in each school, and in many states, annual report cards containing often voluminous information are issued for each school.[9] However, this information, while helpful, often omits the bottom line: is this school adding value or not? This information, as discussed, is a much more realistic indicator of a school's performance than the annual yearly progress reports required under NCLB.[10] Parents should know not only whether schools are adding value, but also about how they are financed (in actual revenue flows to the school from the district), and what curriculums and programs are in place. Florida, for example, assigns a letter grade of A, B, C, D, or F to each school based on a calculation that takes into account both gains in achievement and actual test scores.[11]

*Failing Schools*   When the state's evaluation process identifies a school as failing, the state can pursue a variety of approaches to help the school to improve, ranging from offering outside consultation to state takeover or reconstitution of the school or even school district. Or, as we discuss later, it can help students transfer to a better-functioning school or district. Unfortunately, past experience does not provide clear guidance on which state interventions are the most effective. Part of this problem stems from difficulties in accurately distinguishing schools that are not doing a good job from those that have a very disadvantaged enrollment. In each case students might be failing to meet standards, but the remedy, or even the need for it, might widely differ. Many states have neither had the necessary information nor the analytical capacity to distinguish between the radically different situations. That is another reason why developing and implementing value-added measures to properly assess school performance are vitally important.

Another problem, we believe, is the reluctance of state authorities, for political or other reasons, to take stronger action against schools and school districts that are demonstrably failing their students. If the current staff is unable to raise student achievement and the school district has failed to correct the problem, it is incumbent upon the state to get the school back on the right track. We endorse more local control and flexibility, but for that to be effective, the state must be prepared to act if the local district, after a reasonable time, is clearly not getting the job done.

Moreover, if the district is already failing, simply adding funds is unlikely to solve the problem. In fact, sending more money to failing schools (and taking it away if they succeed) may only exacerbate the problem, because schools then face a penalty for success—loss of funds and personnel. The Abbott districts of New Jersey are perhaps the most visible example of improper incentives. Abbott districts were chosen from among a large set of districts where parents had limited education and low income, but the twenty-eight (subsequently expanded to thirty-one) chosen also demonstrated chronic failure of their students.[12] Because they were doing a particularly bad job, they were given almost unlimited access to resources and programs—while similarly situated other districts were not because they had been able to do a better job with their students. Extra funds may be part of the remedy, but they must be provided in conjunction with other remedial steps that promote genuine solutions and truly hold the district accountable rather than rewarding it with more money. For example, if the Abbott districts were to significantly improve the achievement of their students, they might lose their special status and the money that goes with it, an outcome that they clearly would not like. Thus, they must walk a tightrope between showing some progress, but not enough to justify dropping the lawsuit. The perverse incentives are obvious.

*Transfer Options*   It takes time to improve a failing school. However, one group does not have the luxury of unlimited time: the current students of the school. Something must be done immediately, because these students do not have time to wait for a general fix. Students in failing schools— defined, say, as those that receive a bottom ranking on the state report cards for two years out of three—should be given scholarships (vouchers) that can be used to obtain admission to another public or private school. Any private school accepting scholarship students should agree to take the scholarship, set at the district average spending on schools, as full tuition for attendance. They should agree to provide test information on students so that the students' performance can continue to be tracked.

NCLB requires a transfer option, although only to other public schools. It relies, in our view, on a poor measure of school performance and does not become operative until the fourth year of failure. Nor has it consistently produced meaningful transfer options for affected students. If there are no high-performing schools in the district, there is no place to move. Moreover, if there are some good schools, they are invariably oversubscribed as other parents, including those without transfer options, seek to get their children into them. For this policy to have a significant impact, the state must ensure that the right to transfer to a nonfailing school is a meaningful one, even if that means the right to transfer to a school in another school district or nonpublic school if there are no viable options in the child's own school district. Note, however, that within-district transfers also weaken any incentives for good performance on the part of the district, because the funding related to the transferring students remains under the control of the district.

There is, as discussed, considerable opposition to vouchers that can be used to transfer to private schools. Much of this opposition is based on the perceived harm that vouchers will have on the public schools. We think this major concern is unfounded. Studies have shown that the availability and threat of vouchers are more likely to have a positive impact on the public schools.[13] Some legal and other concerns, however, are not so easily dismissed. For example, under the Blaine amendments of some states, using public monies for transfers to religiously affiliated schools may be barred by the state constitution.[14] Others worry about using public monies to finance schools that teach radical philosophies, such as the fundamentalist Islamic schools. These are legitimate concerns that will vary from state to state and will have to be taken into account by state planners in designing transfer options. Nevertheless, viable transfer options, whether they are charter schools, transfers to other school districts, or vouchers for use at private schools, are an important element of holding school authorities properly accountable. They also provide immediate relief for disadvantaged students who otherwise lack choice options.

## 2. Empower Local Decision Making

A performance-based funding system must give local school administrators flexibility over how they spend their budgets and how they run their schools, as long as they meet the outcome objectives set by the state. It must also bring parents and other local citizens into the equation.

## INCREASED DECISION-MAKING AUTHORITY BY LOCAL DISTRICTS

Historically, states have developed a variety of policies and regulations designed to guide and direct the actions of local districts. Many regulations have the character of attempting to put a floor on possible bad behavior, often motivated by a distrust at the state level of local authorities. But whether regulation of the educational process from the top can produce general improvements in student learning is open to question.

All policies involve a mixture of state, district, school, and classroom decisions and actions, but the implementation at the local level is most crucial to their outcomes. If the best policy from the state never has an impact on what takes place in districts, schools, and classrooms, there will be little or no impact on students. Moreover, if the local circumstances call for a different approach, a uniform statewide policy may be ineffective or even harmful in some districts. At the very least, it will be wasteful.

While the state is well equipped to define the desired outcomes, it is not well situated to direct classroom and other strategies designed to meet them. It may reasonably expect sixth graders to have mastered certain math skills, for instance, but how to teach these skills to a particular set of sixth graders is best understood by the teachers and schools themselves. The heterogeneity among districts in their capacity and needs makes it difficult to specify a single best approach to obtaining any given outcomes.

Let us take California as an example. Its six million students are taught by three hundred thousand teachers spread across a thousand districts and almost ten thousand schools. It not only has the second largest district in the nation with over seven hundred thousand students, but also has significant numbers of both elementary and unified districts with less than one hundred students. Now imagine developing a set of regulations that control the organization and teaching in all of these districts simultaneously. It is possible to look at virtually any part of the California Education Code and see the difficulties.[15] For example, section 41400–41409 indicates maximum ratios of administrative employees to teachers across different kinds of districts and how state support is reduced for having excess administrative employees. Section 44681–44689 "recognizes that the principal plays a pivotal role in the life of a school" and goes on to describe how districts should set up training for principals, when during the day and year training should be provided, and which topics should be covered. Clearly these (and the hundreds of other topics detailed in the education code) are important, but should they be dictated from the state capital? And, if districts follow the entire code on how to run their programs, who is responsible if the students do not meet their outcome targets—the local personnel or the state?

Wherever practical, decision making on how to meet state outcome goals should be local.[16] The state should clearly identify the outcome objectives, but it should also encourage local districts and schools to develop specific approaches for achieving them.[17] With the new accountability movement across the states, strengthened by NCLB, many states have followed exactly this course—specifying and holding districts responsible for meeting standards while loosening up the underlying regulations about how to achieve them.

But even the states taking this approach have not effectively used their finance systems to reinforce and encourage the necessary behavior to accomplish these goals. Most states, for example, continue to use categorical grants, which inhibit local decision making because they constrain the use of funds in very specific ways. For example, California distributes 30 percent of its education funding through over one hundred categorical programs, each requiring separate reporting and accounting.[18] They cover such things as class size reduction in grades K–3, oral health assessment, civic education, principal training, tenth grade progress reviews, middle school counseling, and a host of other "good" things. The most outlandish is a categorical grant program for districts that are deemed not to have sufficient other categorical funding.[19] Such a financing approach assumes—for reasons seldom stated—that local districts and schools will not make appropriate decisions. Perhaps state leaders believe that local leaders are poorly prepared or that they lack sufficient motivation. Perhaps they want to keep certain funds out of the equation when teacher and other union contracts are being negotiated. Or they may be driven by political considerations to seek credit for specific actions designed to improve schools.

The general failure of spending remedies has also contributed to states' unwillingness to cede control to local districts. Most legislators are aware of the research showing a tenuous link between money and achievement and the failure of past spending increases to produce higher student outcomes. Therefore, in legislating even higher spending, they do not want to appear to be "throwing good money after bad." They place restrictions on how the additional monies can be used to prevent money from being "wasted" by local school officials on their pet projects. The result is an array of categorical programs and special appropriations that come with a set of rules and limitations specifying, often in great detail, exactly how such monies must be used. This "top-down" direction has rarely been successful and further prevents local schoolteachers and administrators from taking actions that might be more effective in their particular schools or school districts.

A more positive rationale for categorical grants is that different districts have varying educational needs, some of which may cost more than others. Districts with, for example, large English language learner (ELL) populations may need specific funds to meet additional educational costs. Categorical funds in these cases represent an attempt to match resources with needs. But even this more reasonable-sounding justification may end up creating perverse incentives, when, for example, the school district stands to gain state aid the longer it can keep students in an ELL program. Thus, categorical programs can also encourage districts to do just the opposite of what might be desired.

This concern about the impact of central regulations and policies is the underlying motivation for the performance-based approach. This approach requires school districts to make appropriate educational decisions, including hiring personnel and organizing instructional programs, to accomplish the objectives set by the state. But to accomplish this goal, process regulations and constraints on local decision making about how to organize instruction, including the substantial use of categorical funding that pervades many current school codes, must be eliminated or the hands of well-intentioned and capable school leaders will be tied.

Local school leaders are constrained by more than just the finance system and state regulation. These other limitations—most notably, rules on assigning and terminating teachers—must also be addressed as part of any comprehensive reform effort. In many school districts, the obstacles to firing an unqualified teacher are so difficult and time-consuming that most principals reserve their time and effort for only the "worst of the worst."[20] In a typical big city school system, it takes two years to fire a tenured teacher.[21] The elaborate steps a principal must take to get rid of an incompetent teacher border on the ridiculous, as the due process rights of the teacher trump any rights of the students to learn. In New York City, for example, hundreds of teachers relieved of classroom duties remain on the payroll for months or even years before the district finally jumps through all the hoops demanded under union contracts and state law and is able to terminate them.[22]

Tenure and termination laws and rules must be revised to enable principals to remove teachers who are not doing their jobs. In New York, state law provides for tenure after five years, but New York City union contracts effectively reduce this to three years—and they make it nearly impossible for school districts to terminate a teacher. In California, teachers get tenure after only two years. But when Governor Schwarzenegger sought to increase this to five years in Proposition 74, the California Teachers Association (CTA), an affiliate of the National Education Association (NEA), assessed extra dues on each of its 335,000 members and raised over $50 million to fight it. Demonstrating the political power packed by teachers' unions, the proposition was voted down in November 2005.[23] Certainly due process and fairness to the teacher can be ensured without the innumerable obstacles that now protect all but the "worst of the worst." Unless state laws and the even more restrictive union contracts are changed, school districts and their students will continue to be plagued by teachers who are doing a lousy job.

Union contracts and related work rules also hamstring principals' ability to effectively manage their schools. For example, the collective bargaining agreement between the board of education and the New York City teachers' union has over two hundred pages of fine print, specifying in minute detail not only a teacher's rights and duties, but also hundreds of workplace rules that principals must contend with in trying to reform their schools and run them more efficiently. The union work rules permeate every aspect of the operation of the school. They govern teacher hiring, firing, and promotion, as well as evaluations and how they can be used. There are rules regarding student discipline, homework, class size, class schedules, school calendars, bulletin boards, seating arrangements, and duration of lessons, to mention only some. They specify the length of a teacher's workday, and the time he or she can actually spend in the classroom teaching students during that day.[24] Reform advocate Peter Schrag summed it up nicely, stating that the union work rules in New York City "made it nearly impossible to get rid of bad teachers or, under seniority rules, assign good ones to the schools that needed them most."[25] As Schrag concluded, between these endless work rules and the layers of bureaucracy in place to enforce them, the ability of principals to organize and operate their schools in an efficient manner is grossly limited.

A study of California governance reached a similar conclusion. Surveys of principals and superintendents contained in the Getting Down to Facts studies designed to investigate the poor performance of California schools found that "[t]he one factor that emerged most consistently across studies as inhibiting local leadership was the difficulty in dismissing ineffective teachers."[26]

It does not take a scientific study to tell us that; common sense is enough. As political scientist Terry Moe has said:

> How can it be socially beneficial that schools can't get rid of bad teachers? Or that teachers can't be tested for competence? Or that teachers can't be evaluated on the basis of how much their students learn? Or that principals are so heavily constrained that they can't exercise leadership of their own schools?[27]

In summary, decision makers—principals, superintendents, and others—must be held accountable for students' success, but they must also have the authority to run their schools.

We add a note of caution, however. The linkages between components of our plan, while present throughout, become very obvious here. If local decision making is not linked to outcome accountability, then it is probably going to result in worse, not better, student achievement. In other words, simply focusing on the distribution mechanism for basic funds and of decision making, as is done with early site-based management, without also making sure that schools are held accountable for student achievement and given some decision-making authority, is a recipe for a bad outcome. Why? The current accountability system does not identify or reward student value added to any significant degree, leading to potential misdirection of energies. Moreover, much of the current leadership was not trained or chosen in terms of their ability to make effective resource allocations and choices that improve student achievement. While they may grow into the job, the short-term disruptions and failures could be very large. Therefore, movement toward more decentralized decision making requires both effective leadership development and the implementation of the other components of this plan. Simply turning local decision makers loose without holding them accountable for results would be a recipe for disaster.

## INVOLVING PARENTS AND CITIZENS IN THE IMPROVEMENT OF THEIR SCHOOLS

A good educational system must involve the citizens and taxpayers of the local community and must provide incentives and options to them that ultimately accrue to the benefit of the students. On the finance side, a sound system of financing should give local districts the opportunity to supplement state funding on an equalized basis. There is considerable evidence that involving citizens directly in funding decisions for schools has important benefits for citizens and schools alike. First, it allows parents who are most intensely interested in schooling to actively influence the operation and funding of their schools. Second, it brings an added amount of accountability, because schools that do not use funds wisely will not tend to be supported by the voters. Third, all local citizens, not just

*charter school support*

parents, see the benefits of efficient and effective schools, because—
as any real estate agent will attest—the quality of schools directly
affects the value of homes and property in the district.[28]

At the same time, as dramatically pointed out by the *Serrano v.
Priest* case and its many successors, low tax bases in some districts
have led to wide disparities in the ability of districts to raise funds.
Therefore, any local funding (perhaps within some overall bounds)
should be based on equalized property values, with some sort of
state matching funds, so that the fiscal advantages of wealthy districts are neutralized.[29]

The system should also encourage local districts to open other
educational options to parents and their children, such as charter
schools. These schools should receive funding and rewards under
the same terms as regular public schools. By competing with them,
charter schools exert salutary pressure on public schools to perform well and keep the accountability system meaningful.[30]

Not everyone sees this competition as healthy. Indeed, in the private economy, no firm sees competition as good. Walmart would
like to crush its opposition and be the only general purpose retailer
in a region, even as it sees competition among its suppliers to be
good. And existing retailers try to make it difficult for Walmart
to enter an area, citing traffic congestion problems, environmental
concerns, or simply how difficult they would find it to compete
with Walmart.

So it is with public schools. Charter schools are under increasing
attack, particularly as they become the main choice for many public school families who view them to be very much like vouchers.
The result has been a variety of regulations and restrictions in many
states to control their growth (even though there is virtually no
opposition to charters among either the general public or school
employees).[31] Complicating matters is the mixed evidence on their
performance. This is partly because many evaluations observed
charter schools in their infancy. It also reflects the fact that some
charter schools do remarkably well, while others do quite badly,
resulting at least initially in little or no overall "net" gains.[32] Anti-
charter forces use the evidence that some are doing badly to suggest
that all charter schools should be terminated, when the logical re-

sponse is that bad charters—just like bad regular public schools—should be shut down, but good ones emulated and encouraged.

In most school districts, there is simply not enough information about charter schools to infer much about their performance. This is a problem for parents, who need this information to make informed choices about their children's schooling, and for the state, which needs it to evaluate whether individual charters are meeting their promises and expectations. Districts have trouble gathering information about charters, because it is difficult to separate the performance of the schools from the needs and capacities of students choosing them. Since charter schools are heavily used by disadvantaged students seeking a better alternative to their regular public school, the overall performance level of charter schools tends to be below the state average. But to properly assess the performance of charters, value-added assessments are needed. This will, again, require the development of longitudinal data and analytical capacity not currently available in many school districts.

The public has been much more receptive to charters than to vouchers, especially when vouchers can be used to transfer to a private school.[33] The concept of vouchers, introduced by Milton Friedman a half century ago, is anathema to most public school personnel.[34] Their opposition has led to easy slogans that have public traction: "We should fix our public schools, not harm or destroy them." The primary harm seen is that, if students leave a district, federal and state funding goes with them, leaving the district with fewer resources. Often omitted is the fact that they will also have fewer students to educate, and hence should require less funding. Never mentioned is the hope that public schools might also use this as an opportunity to reconsider how they can use their resources more effectively. The only legitimate issue is whether the public schools can readily adjust their spending to reflect the loss of students in light of certain fixed costs—such as central office staff, facility maintenance, and the like—that they might not be able to promptly reduce. This should, however, be a short-term transition problem, and existing data and analysis suggest it should not be an especially important issue over the long run.[35]

The power of the anti-voucher message has, nonetheless, been demonstrated whenever ballot proposals put vouchers to the test.[36] We are a nation of public school attendees who believe deeply in the importance and value of public schools for both the individual and the nation. Opponents of vouchers have mobilized strong support for the institution of common public schooling in virtually every public discussion of vouchers. During the 1990s, opponents of vouchers uniformly emphasized the importance of preserving *public* schools as a strategy to defeat vouchers that would permit attendance at private schools.

In the long run, expanded choice options will provide the most benefit to students in the public schools, as their schools respond to competitive pressures to reform. This is the real payoff of choice programs because, like it or not, most children in America will continue to be educated in the traditional public schools.[37]

Some have argued that choice may happen naturally as new technologies come on-line to serve populations traditionally not well served. Drawing on experiences from other industries, business analyst and Harvard professor Clayton Christensen sees advances in technology leading to very different kinds of choice in schools: "No one knows for sure what the education world will look like in the future. But if the path we are on continues, ten years from now we are likely to have a completely different discussion about the impact computers have on schooling and on learning."[38]

Political scientists Terry Moe and John Chubb go further to suggest that technology may also significantly alter the politics of schools. Specifically, the power of teachers' unions to block school reforms will, by their projections into the future, be reduced by the radical decentralization of education that is a result of new learning technologies.[39]

In both the immediate term and the long run, however, greater choice also empowers low-income families to enjoy some of the educational options and opportunities that middle- and upper-income families have long possessed by virtue of their ability to choose residential locations with good schools or to send their children to private schools. The new choice opportunities for low-income and minorities families undoubtedly lead to their greater utilization of charter schools. Families with more options are already exercising their choices.

## 3. Direct Rewards and Incentives

The school finance system should be an integral part of motivating schools, teachers, and administrators to do a better job at raising the achievement of their students. Teachers who succeed in significantly improving the achievement of their students should receive higher pay or bonuses along with other career awards. Administrators in schools where student achievement improves should also be rewarded. The schools themselves should receive increased funding that can be used for the benefit of all their students, perhaps in ways that directly motivate students to do better on state tests, such as additional field trips to places that children would find exciting.[40] The exact form of these rewards would be determined by individual districts within state guidelines that require objective measures and would use, to a significant extent, data on individual student achievement. The dollar incentives must be sizeable enough to have an impact, and the state should provide a "bonus pool" that districts could access to pay approved performance bonuses.

To some, this proposal reflects a radical change. They ask whether the state should be providing more funding and rewards to schools that have the most successful students, as opposed to those in which students continue to struggle. But those concerns are precisely why absolute measures of student achievement are insufficient and why value-added measures so important. It would indeed be unfair and counterproductive to base rewards on factors not under the control of the teacher and school, such as family influences on performance. Using value-added measures makes it possible to reward gains in achievement, which are perhaps more likely to occur at schools currently at the bottom of the achievement scale than at schools serving mostly high achievers, since the potential for significant improvement is greater at low-achieving schools.

The ultimate goal of direct rewards and incentives is to ensure that classrooms are stocked with highly effective teachers. This task is particularly difficult today, because rewards are not closely related, if at all, to teachers' effectiveness. Moreover, decisions to enter teaching or to remain in teaching are almost entirely made by the teachers themselves, affected by the rewards that can be expected by individual teachers but influenced very little by any active management decisions reflecting their performance. A personnel system designed to improve student achievement must clearly alter this incentive and management structure in significant ways.

## PERFORMANCE-BASED PAY FOR TEACHERS

The most important part of this system of rewards and incentives involves teacher compensation and career progression.[41] The consensus among academicians and educators is that the single most important school factor influencing student achievement is the effectiveness of the student's teacher.[42] Therefore, any serious attempt to improve achievement has to start with placing and keeping better teachers in the classroom.

The current manner in which teachers are compensated not only fails to meet this goal, but actually works against it. With a few minor exceptions, teachers across the country receive automatic pay raises with every year of added experience and every additional college degree, despite the fact that research shows little or no relationship between teacher experience and education on the one hand and student achievement on the other.[43] This system, which bars any differential pay, provides no incentives or rewards for good teachers, prevents principals from paying more to fill slots where there are state and nationwide shortages, and does not allow school districts to pay higher salaries or bonuses to persuade good teachers to work in hard-to-staff schools.

Under most current systems of teacher compensation, teachers' actual performance in the classroom—their ability to turn out students who achieve at acceptable levels—is irrelevant unless their performance sinks to a level so low it gets them fired, a very rare event. As long as teachers can maintain their jobs, even if just barely, they are paid the same as every other teacher in the system with the same number of years teaching under their belts and the same college degrees. Tracey Bailey, a national Teacher of the Year, blamed a variety of problems on the teacher's unions, which he believed were protecting "a system that too often rewards mediocrity and incompetence" and led him to join and support a non-union professional association for teachers.[44] However, this is not solely a union-inspired problem, and these same issues arise in states that do not have collective bargaining.

In most other businesses and professions, the compensation and promotion system is an integral part of attracting and retaining the best employees, but not so in public education. The lockstep system used in almost every school district provides little incentive for good teachers to remain in teaching, while at the same time encouraging poor teachers to continue in the classroom. Where else in America can one do a poor job yet be paid the same as one's most successful colleague—and get a pay raise each year to boot?

This method of setting teacher compensation desperately needs to be changed if the quality of the teaching force is to be improved. First, compensation for teachers must be performance based so that it rewards those teachers who do the best job teaching students. The effects of this change on teacher quality should be obvious. Armed with a pay schedule that rewards hard work and excellent performance, school districts will be able to hire and retain more effective teachers. They will also attract a more qualified pool of teacher candidates, as ambitious and bright college students realize they can both teach and enjoy economic reward if they do a good job. Research into teacher labor markets indicates that the "compression of salaries" is a more serious deterrent to entry into the profession than the relative level of salaries (compared to alternative professions).[45] Moreover, districts will not be forced to reward unsuccessful teachers with undeserved pay raises, inducing them to leave teaching sooner than they would under the current system.

There is growing research to show that rewarding successful teachers is one of the most important steps a school district can take to improve achievement. A bipartisan group called the Teaching Commission, headed by Lewis Gerstner, the former chairman of IBM, found that "our current compensation system fails our teachers and our children. It does nothing to reward excellence because all teachers, regardless of effort or performance, get the same automatic pay increases." It concluded with this warning: "Until teachers are rewarded and given responsibility for what really matters—their impact on student achievement—we cannot expect to see a marked change for the better in student performance."[46] There it is, pure and simple: pay teachers based on their performance, as we do virtually all other professionals, or forget about improving student performance.

The method of evaluating teachers for performance pay is, of course, important. The statistical approaches to estimating the value added by teachers is one component.[47] Nonetheless, a variety of issues related to the uncertainty and reliability of estimates impact these statistical measures, and they should be supplemented with direct evaluations by principals, supervisors, and/or peers.[48] Unfortunately, today we do not appear to devote much effort to evaluating teachers, although this may simply reflect the fact that such evaluations mean little for the individual or for the operation of the schools under the current system.[49] Developing better evaluation systems and skills is one obvious place where capacity must be expanded.

Second, schools and districts must have the flexibility to offer financial incentives to qualified teachers willing to work in hard-to-staff schools. In city after city, the most inexperienced teachers are assigned to the lowest-performing schools, which typically also have the highest percentages of the city's at-risk pupils.[50] This is a pattern repeated throughout the country because most teachers prefer to work in schools in less troubled neighborhoods and with fewer children who are at risk. Consequently, they either do not apply for such jobs or transfer to other jobs as soon as they are able to under the seniority provisions of the contract between district and union. If we are ever to persuade our best teachers to work in such schools, where they are most needed, financial incentives are a must. If they are paid at the same rate as their counterparts in less troubled schools, most teachers are going to opt for the more pleasant, less demanding work environment.

Under the salary schedules now used in most school districts, "combat pay," as it is often called, is forbidden. Moreover, the teachers' unions adamantly oppose any differential pay, even though surveys show that a majority of the teachers themselves are in favor of extra pay for serving in schools that are difficult to teach in.[51] When New York City wanted to encourage more qualified teachers to transfer voluntarily to troubled schools by offering higher pay, the union opposed it. It was willing to accept the proposal only when it was revised to require such teachers to work longer hours for their "extra" pay.[52] Even then the proposal was limited to only forty schools.[53] Unions, of course, recognize that some schools are more difficult to staff than others, but they find it convenient to argue that what is needed is to raise everybody's pay, even though such a policy would leave the difficult-to-staff schools in almost exactly the same position.

But even here, we must keep focused on student outcomes. We do not want to keep every teacher or administrator in hard-to-staff schools. We want to keep the *effective* ones there. Turnover is desirable when it results from the departure of ineffective teachers. In fact, at least some analysis shows that it is not just the best teachers leaving schools with significant populations of disadvantaged students, but also even larger numbers of the less effective ones.[54]

Third, school districts and schools must be able to pay more for teachers in shortage areas, such as math and science. This would do more than anything else to erase such "shortages," as college students would be encouraged by the prospect of higher pay to concentrate in those areas. This idea is not a new one—and its history gives some sense of the difficulty in making rational policy within schools. In response to the science crisis highlighted by the launch of the Russian satellite *Sputnik*, two leading economists of the day suggested in a 1962 book that the shortages of qualified science teachers were directly related to the demands for people with science skills in the rest of the economy, and they recommended that schools adjust salaries to meet the competition for specific skills.[55] Even though this suggestion largely preceded the development of teachers' unions and collective bargaining, the economists' sound advice was disregarded.

As Chester Finn, noted Washington educational gadfly, has said, rewarding some teachers more than others is a matter of common sense:

> Common sense argues that teachers of subjects in short supply should be paid more than those in overstocked fields, that teachers working in hard-to-staff schools should earn more than those in schools with hundreds of applicants, and that outstanding teachers should be paid more than mediocre ones.[56]

The major teachers' unions, however, continue to insist upon across-the-board pay raises for all teachers, with no differentiation based on performance or scarcity.[57] The unions argue that if pay is raised for all teachers, better-quality candidates will be enticed into teaching, resulting in an improvement in the overall quality of the teaching force. But even assuming this argument to be valid, it would take decades for poor and mediocre teachers currently in the system to retire and leave only the truly qualified teachers in our classrooms.[58] Moreover, if that were really the purpose of such pay raises, then the unions' focus would be on increasing beginning salaries.[59] However, step increases under negotiated union contracts are normally back-ended—that is, they reward older teachers and union members with large increases, while keeping raises for new teachers who are not union members to a minimum.[60]

For example, a common complaint expressed throughout the trial of the *CFE* case was that New York City did not pay beginning teachers enough to be competitive with the affluent suburbs, yet when the teachers' union contract was renegotiated in 2005, nothing was done to remedy the situation. Instead, the new contract disproportionately rewarded senior teachers, who are least likely to leave for the suburbs, and who, not coincidentally, are more likely to be in positions of power within the union. These senior teachers received raises in the 11 to 12 percent range, while pay for beginning teachers increased at only half that rate.[61]

Kansas City further demonstrated the shortcomings of this approach. The teachers' union there steadfastly opposed any kind of merit pay for teachers; therefore, the massive court-ordered pay increases were distributed across the board. This resulted in a 40 percent pay hike for every teacher in the district, although even plaintiffs' attorney acknowledged that 20 percent of teachers were "totally incompetent."[62] The across-the-board increases, together with the increased retirement benefits linked to higher pay, likely induced these admittedly ineffective teachers to stay even longer.[63] The outcome was that, even after spending billions, Kansas City was unable to upgrade its teaching staff, and pupil performance continued to stagnate.

Despite such vigorous opposition to performance-based compensation plans, a number of states have begun to experiment with them.[64] The Teacher Advancement Program (TAP), operating with the support of teachers in the regular public schools of 13 states across almost 200 schools in 2007, establishes teachers' pay based in part on their students' performance.[65] In 2006, Florida began the STAR (Special Teachers Are Rewarded) program when it put $147 million into a bonus pool for any district that developed a performance pay plan fitting within state guidelines (this morphed into the Merit Award Program).[66] That same year, Governor Rick Perry of Texas established the Governor's Educator Excellence Awards program that would fund teacher awards for improving student achievement by up to $330 million by 2008–9.[67] In both Florida and Texas, plans have to be locally based and receive approval of the state department of education, but the awards depend upon overall improvement in school achievement. Other states and locations—Denver, Minnesota, and others—are also well into experiments with different versions of performance pay plans. The U.S. Department of Education established the Teacher Incentive Fund with an initial $99 million to support localities that establish reward systems based on increases in student performance. Added in are a variety of smaller individual plans such as the Benwood Initiative in Chattanooga.[68] Even in New York City, the story may be changing as the school district has begun developing a performance pay system (at the elementary school level), relying on private contributions for support.[69]

Most large-scale performance pay programs plans are relatively new, and both their usage and nature are in constant flux. They tend to change quickly over time, as districts experiment with how best to design them and as the unions continue their attack on them even after they are introduced. Nonetheless, the concept is so obvious and so ubiquitous in virtually every professional field. As Michael Podgursky and Matthew Springer, two specialists in the operation of teacher labor markets, state: "While the literature is not sufficiently robust to prescribe how systems should be designed— for example, optimal size of bonuses, mix of individual versus group incentives—it is sufficiently positive to suggest that further experiments and pilot programs by districts and states are very much in order."[70] From the current array of experiments that are ongoing, the refinement and use of such plans can only increase as we go forward.

## PERFORMANCE-BASED PAY FOR ADMINISTRATORS

Many discussions of performance pay stop with teachers, presumably reflecting the research that identifies teacher effectiveness as the key to higher achievement. It is important, however, that performance pay be extended to other school personnel. First, many accounts of high-performing schools identify the central role of an effective principal. If in fact school leaders have a central role, they should be rewarded for their value added to the operation of the schools.

Second, and perhaps more important, the managers have a direct influence over the effectiveness of the teachers. And logically, they should share the rewards that go to successful teachers.

Having school administrators who face incentives that are different from those of the teachers is a huge mistake. Absent would be the assurance that school administrators make decisions that maximize student outcomes. Indeed, one of the common concerns expressed by teachers is a worry that principals involved in making pay and hiring/retention decisions might make them largely for political reasons. They fear that these decisions may be influenced by friendships, personal animosities, the greater subservience of some teachers who may have agendas with which the principal might disagree, or what have you.

However, these problems are lessened—and may disappear completely—if the principals and administrators are rewarded based on the same criteria that teachers are. In that case, principals who make arbitrary decisions or ones that do not enhance student outcomes would be directly affecting their own compensation. Thus, the incentives of principals and teachers become aligned by a common goal—increasing student achievement.

Rewards for performance in schools are often compared to rewards in business and industry. What is the lesson here? It is not that businesses always make the right decisions or that they always get pay and personnel decisions absolutely correct. Clearly, politics can and do enter into decisions of private businesses. The lesson, however, is that these decisions tend to be self-correcting. Managers making the wrong decisions find that their divisions do not do as well as might be expected, and they tend to get fewer rewards and find that their own jobs are in jeopardy. Firms that make wrong decisions on a larger scale tend not to be competitive.

## SCHOOLWIDE REWARDS

One of the continuing debates whenever the subject of performance rewards comes up is whether they should go to individuals, as described earlier, or should be group rewards. Several competing considerations come into play. First, the performance of some people in schools cannot be easily related to student outcomes. This situation applies, for example, to teachers in nontested subjects—say, physical education teachers or history teachers in most districts. Even further, it is difficult to develop value-added measures of performance in many subjects. The high school biology teacher's student outcomes cannot be readily compared to the student's knowledge coming into the course.[71]

Second, there are valid concerns about destructive competition among teachers. If one teacher thought she was competing directly with others in the school, she might not cooperate with other teachers in developing lessons, in evaluating student programs, and so forth.

Third, the functioning of a school as a whole involves the interactions of all of the teachers and other personnel. If the school is to be highly effective, it must encourage the cooperative behavior of all.

These arguments raise legitimate concerns and indicate why private firms typically have a combination of group and individual rewards. But while a mixture of individual and group rewards may be appropriate, the use of group rewards alone would not be good policy. In a school context, the excellent teacher must have incentives for teaching at currently poorly performing schools. If there are only group rewards, the good teacher would not take on tough tasks in schools where the other teachers or the administrators were not also effective. Failing schools and schools with concentrated disadvantaged populations would find turnaround difficult if all performance rewards were group rewards.

We have little current experience on which to base calculations of the right balance between individual and group rewards. And the right balance may well vary across districts. This balance question is simply another where there is no known "right" answer and where it is necessary to embark upon further experimentation and evaluation to come up with the best solution.

### SELECTION AND RETENTION DECISIONS

Performance pay operates by offering rewards that are directly related to effectiveness in raising achievement—by classroom teachers, by administrators, and by other school personnel. Nonetheless, there are concerns about paying different amounts to people doing the same ostensible job.

An alternative, or complementary, policy is to make more active decisions about retention of teachers, based on classroom effectiveness and on contribution to the mission of raising student achievement. In a rough sense, paying more to highly effective teachers and less to ineffective teachers is similar to making decisions about retaining a teacher and then paying those with demonstrated effectiveness the same as others with similar experience who have also proven effectiveness. In such a system, teachers who are retained could be paid more than teachers under the current system because they are more effective in leading students to higher levels of achievement.

Even a relative few ineffective teachers can do substantial damage. Consider the impact of low-quality, or ineffective, teachers on student achievement. One study based on current estimates of differences in teaching effectiveness finds that the students of the bottom 5 percent of teachers gain at best two-thirds of a grade-level-equivalent year (as opposed to the normal gain of one grade level for each school year).[72] Some differences are much more dramatic. The bottom 1 percent of teachers get no more than one-half of a grade level equivalent in annual gains from their students. Using these estimates, if we could eliminate the bottom 6 to 10 percent of teachers (in terms of classroom effectiveness), we could improve achievement of the average U.S. student to something approaching that of Canadian students or the better European students.[73] In a typical school with thirty teachers, this would entail removing the worst two to three teachers and replacing them with teachers of the same quality as the remaining ones.

This kind of policy is consistent with a McKinsey & Company study of international performance led by the architect of British school improvement, Sir Michael Barber. Barber found that the best school systems in the world do not allow ineffective teachers to remain in the classroom for long. [74]

Making active decisions on retention and tenure are, of course, quite alien to the current school system. A number of states currently have laws and regulations that lead to tenure decisions as early as two years, with the mode being just three years.[75] Moreover, the typical teacher evaluation process is very cursory.[76] Few teachers are involuntarily separated from teaching, particularly after the probationary period. Indeed, some of the nation's worst-performing states—California and the District of Columbia—require decisions on tenure at the end of just a two-year probationary period, making it very difficult to evaluate teachers even if school administrators had the will to do so.

More serious consideration of retention decisions clearly would have to be linked with pay policies. In simplest terms, teachers could and should be paid more if they are more effective on average. This higher pay would compensate for the increased risk teachers would face because of the lack of assurance of being able to stay in their teaching jobs.[77] But the higher salaries would attract new people into the profession—those who would be willing to be judged on their own merits, much like most other professionals in society. For example, in most private schools, retention decisions play an important role in maintaining a high-quality teaching force.[78]

Emphasizing the importance of selection into teaching—whether by teachers' self-selection or by school administrators—also underscores a different perspective from that found in prior discussions of merit pay in schools. Merit pay has actually been used quite broadly, although generally in forms very different from the performance pay currently being considered. The typical merit pay system of the past was small and generally in the form of an annual add-on to salary.

Evaluations of these limited merit pay systems have typically paid little attention to their impact on teacher selection and retention. Instead, they have tended to focus on changes in the performance of existing teachers, i.e, whether the implementation of a merit pay plan has succeeded in motivating teachers in ways that raise the achievement of their students. From this perspective, researchers have not found merit pay to be very effective as a device for improving student achievement.[79] Part of the reason is that such plans typically have a short shelf life. But another, perhaps more important, reason is that these assessments assume that the most significant impact of merit pay will be that individual teachers will be motivated to work harder and that this extra effort will result in higher student achievement.

We think this evaluation approach misses the main benefits of the performance-based pay system we envision. Most teachers already work hard; the problem is that some of them are not very effective, and promises of extra pay, even if they induce additional effort, are unlikely to change that. Our point is that the impact of performance pay is more likely to be seen through its impact on the overall quality of the teaching force. That is, success would depend on whether the incentives lead better teachers to enter and stay and poorer teachers, especially those at the very bottom, to leave. The end result will be a more highly qualified teaching force made up of good teachers with a demonstrated track record at raising student achievement. Equally important, many of those teachers who have not been effective will have left the teaching force to pursue other lines of work.

The bottom line is that developing a system that more regularly ensures a high-quality teacher in every classroom is very important. Accomplishing this goal means aligning the entire pay and personnel system with its impact on student achievement.

## 4. Information, Evaluation, and Continuous Improvement

The first priority in implementing performance-based funding is to improve methods of collecting, linking, and analyzing data. An integral plan to our entire program is developing the data systems and the evaluation capacity necessary to put schools on a continuous improvement path. The standard of educational policy in the past has been to begin by declaring the answer, often arguing that it is both obvious and supported by research. With the answer in hand, the task is simply mobilizing the resources and developing the will to put the answer into place.

We now have extensive evidence that "the answer" is not sitting in front of us. Indeed, there is every reason to believe that there is no single answer. There are some common themes—such as getting the incentives right for students and personnel in the schools—but the application of such ideas is likely to vary widely. This notion lies behind the change in focus from a centrally regulated system of schools to one with local decision making and rewards based on outcomes (rather than how it was done in the past).

The performance-based funding system we describe rests on being able to track student results. Although many states have been working on assigning unique student identifiers that would allow tracking of students from year to year, school to school, and school district to school district, most are still incapable of following student performance over time or from district to district. Therefore, this capacity needs to be developed. We do not underestimate the difficulty of this task. The Data Quality Campaign, a national collaborative effort to improve state data quality, has found clear shortcomings in student data across the entire nation.[80]

On the more positive side, one of the most significant immediate outcomes of NCLB is that schools everywhere now assess student performance on an annual basis across a significant number of subjects and grades. Districts and states are expanding on the minimum requirements, adding assessments of skills in the earliest grades and end-of-course and consequential graduation examinations at the later grades. What has frequently been lacking is the will to develop appropriate statewide databases that link students over time and to their schooling experiences. Part of this may reflect myopia in some states about the central importance of developing the information needed both to design teaching at the school and classroom level and to provide the overall management tools to improve the schools. Part may also reflect nervousness or antipathy on the part of some to linking performance to value added of student achievement.

In order to understand whether a program will help children do better in school, we need to be able to distinguish the influence of the program from the influence of a variety of other factors, i.e., sorting out the value added of a program. The difficulty is that schools are dynamic places where many things frequently happen simultaneously. Thus, it is often hard to tell whether programs are effective. Ideally, we would have information about how well students would have done without the program, but these data are generally unavailable. It is precisely the same issue as discussed previously with respect to teachers.

This point at a programmatic level can be most easily understood by recalling California's class size reduction program discussed in the previous chapter. Because this program was implemented in all districts at precisely the same time, state-level performance could be observed before and after the program was introduced, but no one could say what performance levels would have been in the absence of the program. Dramatic changes taking place simultaneously with the program—most notably, staffing changes brought on by the class size reductions themselves—made it hard to know what result could be attributed to what influence. Even districts that decided to forgo state funding and postpone the introduction of class size reductions for a year would probably not have been an appropriate control group, since they undoubtedly had other difficulties that precluded their ability to capitalize on the class size reduction program.[81] Since no evaluation design was included in the California class size reduction legislation, there has been no credible evaluation of the effectiveness of this extremely expensive program—currently costing some $2 billion per year.[82] While studies can tell us whether performance has increased or decreased in districts that implemented the class size reductions, no one can tell us whether these changes are due to the reductions in class size or other factors, such as changes in the makeup of the districts' faculties.

The lesson is that any legislation funding new programs should stipulate and pay for timely evaluations of the effectiveness of the programs. Moreover, major new programs should be evaluated on a trial basis before they are introduced across the state. Alternatively, a staggered introduction of new programs could, if done correctly, provide for reliable evaluations of effectiveness.[83]

California's mistakes are repeated on a smaller scale in many, if not most, school districts where programs are continued year after year without any credible evidence that they are effective. It is a rare school district that practices "zero-based budgeting"—that is, reexamining and justifying each budget item from year to year. Once a program is funded, most districts continue to fund it every year, even as more new programs are being added. Yet everything we know about improving schools suggests that progress will depend in part on regularly assessing and evaluating policies and programs. Those that are effective can be retained and expanded. Those that are not should be dropped.

This approach is currently beyond the capacity of most states and school districts. Most states lack the necessary data for such an approach, a strategy for acquiring the necessary data, and the analytical capacity to evaluate programs effectively and regularly. States must work to build up the knowledge base about program effectiveness, including the design and impact of performance incentives. It is critical that these states have the needed data and the ability to analyze that data, along with the means to share information about scientifically supported programs and policies with districts and schools across the state. States should also be more aggressive about figuring out what makes an effective teacher and school administrator, although such research should be independent and not consigned to the states' colleges of education, which have a vested financial interest in maintaining the status quo.

State departments of education should be responsible for making analytical and evaluation services available to the schools and districts. In general, the state has advantages over individual districts in calculating and disseminating information about program outcomes. Not only is it more cost effective to centralize these functions at the state level, but the state is also less likely to be swayed by local politics and relationships in its evaluation of programs. Moreover, the state is not operating in a vacuum and can use information gained from other districts in its evaluation. It is also in a better position to share information about the effectiveness of programs in one district with other districts for which the program might be appropriate.

Any good finance and policy system should be thought of as an evolutionary, or continuous improvement, one. Experiences with current programs should guide modifications over time. Today, new policies are introduced not so much because schools recognize that past ones were not working but because they are drawn to faddish ideas. Without an active evaluation and research program to guide policy decisions, systematic improvement over time is unlikely.

## 5. Rational and Equitable Funding

Our performance-based funding actually has two distinct components: the incentive component described to encourage high achievement and a base funding, described here, that deals with differential district and student needs. The finance system should ensure that schools have an appropriate amount of funding to provide basic educational services. The system must also address special circumstances faced by individual districts because of their location, special needs population, or other factors justifying differential funding.

## A BASE FUNDING SYSTEM TO ENSURE THAT EACH
## SCHOOL HAS APPROPRIATE RESOURCES

The finance system, including local, state, and federal funding, must provide aggregate funding that reflects the specific demands and challenges facing specific schools. The easiest way to do this is to link funding to individual students, with extra funding provided based on environmental factors such as expectations of special education needs, district cost differences, transportation allotments, disadvantaged needs, language needs, and so on. The amount of funding should be sufficient to develop quality programs and hire qualified personnel under guidelines established by the state. This individualized approach to funding ensures that districts have sufficient resources to accomplish their educational purposes.

With appropriate base funding, the districts must, as sketched earlier, be then held responsible for results, which depend upon their effective use of funds. This approach also makes it possible to provide direct incentives through financial rewards for good performance (again, on a value-added basis )—without bringing charges that we are only aiding the winners and not paying attention to those who need the most help.

To this discussion of funding, we must add a caveat. As important as the funding issue is, it must not be allowed to dominate the discussions of education reform. As we have made clear in preceding chapters, the question of whether schools have enough money to offer a good (or adequate) education has overshadowed other policy issues that are equally or more important, e.g., how money can be more effectively used. For many educators, there will never be enough money devoted to education, and alleged insufficient funding will always be an easy excuse for their failures, particularly the subpar performance of their students. Indeed, even very highly funded school districts, such as New York City, the Abbott districts in New Jersey, and Wyoming school districts, claim they do not have enough money and resources to do the job.[84] And in reality, given the lack of any consistent relationship between spending and achievement, no one can really say what "sufficient" funding is. Therefore, as a practical matter, deciding upon appropriate levels of funding remains a political question for our local, state, and federal leaders, and there it must be left. As the public and politicians gain a better understanding of what can be accomplished with effective use of funds, better decisions about the level of funding can be made.

These difficulties notwithstanding, schools cannot operate effectively without a funding base, and the state finance system must ensure that they have a reasonable level of funding without being held hostage each year to the schools' demands for more money and resources. Lack of sufficient funding is, in our view, not the principal problem in most states and school districts, and should not be accepted as an excuse for lack of progress, although the temptation will always be there to blame failure on lack of resources. Undoubtedly, parents, educators, and others will have to remain vigilant to ensure that appropriate levels of funding continue to be made available, but given their past success, this component of our proposal should be the least problematic.

One other aspect of overall funding deserves mention. If the funding of districts is highly volatile, if the rules change frequently, and if revenues are not known until after decisions about the next school year must be made, it is difficult for school administrators to develop solid, long-run programs. On this score, many legislatures have repeatedly failed. Therefore, the system should contain safeguards designed to provide timely information regarding resources and to ensure reasonable stability in their availability.[85]

NEEDS-ADJUSTED BASE FUNDING

A key element of the funding system is how it varies across districts. The guiding principle is that districts that face more difficult or costly educational challenges *for reasons not of their own doing* should receive extra funding. The finance system we propose relies on "needs-adjusted base funding." The system has similarities to common proposals for weighted-student funding, but it is not the same.[86] Funding needs vary not only with the student but also with the district, and the total funding includes incentives for teachers, administrators, and schools. Thus, funding depends on attributes of student needs (the object of weighted-student funding) and on circumstances related to the district and classroom (elements left out of weighted-student funding).

This needs-based approach would subsume a variety of current funding programs and rules, including most, if not all, categorical programs. Under this system, the current base funding would follow individual students across districts, eliminating the common usage of multiple categorical funding programs. These base funds would then be supplemented by additional amounts reflecting varying needs as determined by student weighting. For example, a typical student may receive a base funding of, say, $7,900 per year. A student with need of English language instruction may receive $8,500. Other categories of students, defined in terms of educational needs, may receive other amounts. But it is important that funding does not follow directly from latitude afforded district personnel to make more expensive choices. For example, if added funding depends on district identification of a particular student as, say, "learning disabled," often a very broadly defined category, then it is likely that districts will tend to overidentify learning disabled students. (We return to the case of special education funding later, because this is precisely what has occurred there.)

Categorical funding sometimes relates to individual needs (such as identified special education conditions) but more often relates to specific uses of funds, such as smaller class sizes, the use of guidance counselors, or the purchase of new textbooks. Thus, unlike needs-based funding, it prescribes how the money is to be used (regardless of any district priorities), and it invariably requires district reports confirming that the funds were used in the prescribed manner. Needs-based funding would provide resources where extra support is required but would allow local districts to establish the priorities for its use.

Three issues immediately arise: What needs should be recognized? How much should they affect funding? And, how should they be integrated into the base funding scheme? Past experience gives some guidance about the norms of different states, but the divergent positions across states give little sense that these are settled questions.

The obvious candidates to consider are: (1) students with special needs, with economic disadvantages, and with language deficits; (2) districts in more expensive labor markets; and (3) districts facing economies or diseconomies of scale. In each case, districts facing different circumstances might well get different results in terms of student achievement, and the funding system can be used to "level the playing field." And this suggests a criterion for answering the basic questions about the character of the needs-based component: adjust funding for specific students or districts so that the expected performance of students is equalized.

This abstract principle, however, breaks down because there is no reliable information on how extra funding for these factors translates into student outcomes. For example, federal funding for disadvantaged students under the federal Title 1 of the Elementary and Secondary Education Act has not been shown to reliably relate to improved achievement.[87] The same lack of evidence holds for the other identified factors.[88]

Our basic funding formula would assign weights to each of the factors. For example, an economically disadvantaged student may be counted as 1.25 students. In other words, an extra 25 percent of base funding would be added for a disadvantaged student. But there is little history of using the extra funding in particularly effective ways, i.e., ways that overcome the basic deficits. This makes any reliable determination of what is required beyond current capacities of scientific evaluations. Given this current knowledge, it is reasonable to view this as a political determination, where legislatures begin with a funding strategy—probably based on past funding patterns—that can be linked to student performance.

Our proposal uses this needs-based system to determine the funding that goes to each district. As a variety of people have suggested, it is obviously possible to take this further and to follow these funds down to school allocations.[89] One advantage of this approach is that it makes the funding that is available transparent, so that anyone can know what resources flow with each student— something that is not currently possible. It also eliminates accounting for and spending money in narrowly defined ways, thus offering the school leaders more flexibility in programmatic decisions.

We do not, however, believe that it is appropriate to enforce allocation of funds to individual schools based on these needs-based factors.[90] As we developed earlier, we strongly believe in local decision making—and such a central allocation rule would clearly violate this by determining what combination of inputs is used at each school. Providing information about variations in funding with different concentrations of identified students may help promote better and more equitable decision making. But, in our opinion, the appropriate policy focus should remain student outcomes and not the underlying funding or inputs to each school.

Simply defining what characteristics receive needs-based weights and how large each weight should be does not answer all of the questions. One of the principles of funding is ensuring that schools are not given incentives that are unrelated to outcomes and that lead them to do unproductive things. This principle particularly comes into play when considering funding for special education and programs for English language learners.

## THE SPECIAL CASE OF SPECIAL EDUCATION SERVICES

The provision of services for special needs students has been greatly enhanced by federal[91] and state laws, but the current system remains problematic in a number of ways. Many state funding approaches create pressure to overidentify students with special needs.[92] There are a variety of legal rules and procedural safeguards that interfere with the provisions of successful programs. And more importantly, there is often concern that special education and regular education unduly compete for resources.

One approach to solving these problems is to provide block grants, coupled with a form of insurance covering very expensive disabilities. Block grants would address a root problem with much of the funding of special education, which is that the "price" changes depending on the identification or classification of the students. If districts can come out financially ahead by identifying an additional student as needing more intensive services, they are encouraged to overidentify—particularly given the ambiguity of categories such as "learning disabilities." If, however, the district is given a fixed amount of money, say, based on the demographics of its population, which is not changed with each newly identified student, then the incentive to overidentify goes away. The insurance component would address the risk that some very expensive disabilities will put small, or even larger, districts in untenable financial circumstances. One or more blind and deaf students could overwhelm small districts—but not if the state fully insured districts for very expensive children by picking up those costs directly. (Note that the previous concerns about incentives to overidentify special education students mainly apply to more ambiguous conditions such as "learning disabilities" and that the very expensive conditions, such as blindness, are more readily audited and diagnosed.)

This block grant approach is not, however, the only option. One approach that has had success nationally is to provide scholarships—in essence, special education vouchers—to students with disabilities to be used at schools of their choice, including private schools. When these scholarships were offered in Florida, parents' satisfaction increased, and districts' concerns about how to allocate resources were eliminated. The amount of the scholarship varies with the identified condition and its severity. Because students will potentially leave with the scholarship, the district does not have an incentive to overidentify disabilities. These special education vouchers have proved to be very popular with both parents and school districts.[93]

A remaining problem with special education, no matter how funded, is a general lack of focus, particularly on student achievement. Much of the law and regulation about special education is best characterized as process oriented; student achievement is not a priority, nor are there many incentives for learning gains. We currently do not have much experience with either measuring or rewarding performance in special education, and both areas are clearly priorities for research and experimentation. NCLB requires the testing of special education students, but it has not fully developed how accountability in this area should proceed.

## ENGLISH LANGUAGE LEARNERS

Schools in many states need extra funding to help non-English-speaking students (commonly referred to as English Language Learners or ELL students) learn to read, write, and speak the language. However, if funding simply follows identification of students needing to learn English, the temptation to overidentify students once again rears its ugly head. Such a funding system perversely charges a price for success, since a district will lose funding for any child who learns English.

One approach to funding ELL students is this: determine a student's need, then set a fixed length of time to fund additional services—say, three years. Funds would continue to go to the district regardless of any placement into special programs. This kind of funding, of course, requires having a student information system that tracks individual students.

A particularly significant problem with ELL students is their high mobility across districts, because it leads to questions about which district is responsible for success. If funding is fixed for the student, e.g., for three years, one district could use up the funding without providing good English language instruction, leaving the student's subsequent district without further funding for that student. If, on the other hand, funding is calculated based on the student's participation in a district's ELL programs, the incentive to move transient students through the program may decline. The problem is that in either case, successful results are not rewarded.

One possible approach to funding ELL programs is to provide block grant funding for ELL students based on some set of student characteristics, and then establish incentives through the accountability system to ensure the appropriate students are being well served. If district rules required, for instance, that all students must be included in the testing and accountability programs after a certain number of years of instruction, then districts would have a direct incentive for making sure that these children learned English. However, the issues regarding transient students remain significant if each district is viewed independently; therefore, a database to track such students is an important element of such a system.

## Big City Schools

The principles of performance-based funding we promote in this book are applicable to schools across states and across varying circumstances. The core elements are designed to create an overall institutional structure within which local adaptation of the actual details and delivery systems can occur.

Nonetheless, we cannot fail to note that the large urban systems of the nation have unique attributes that provide added challenges. They are large and complicated. If a state, New York City would rank sixteenth in the nation in terms of student population, and Chicago would rank twenty-fifth.[94] Twenty-seven school districts had more than 100,000 students in 2005. Moreover, as we have already noted, the big city districts have disproportionate shares of poor children, of minorities, and of immigrants, leading to concentrations of disadvantaged students. Thus, a significant part of dealing with achievement gaps is dealing with the schooling in our urban areas.

Based on demographic factors alone, these districts face significantly greater educational challenges than the more affluent districts of the nation. But the challenges they face are larger than just the populations they serve. The size of the districts engenders large and cumbersome educational bureaucracies. Union strength and a commensurate increase in contractual rigidities grow with size, as does union influence over school boards.[95] The overall politics also become more contentious. These politics lead, among other things, to a lack of continuity of leadership as illustrated by an average tenure of three years for large city superintendents.[96]

One response currently in vogue is to have mayoral takeover of the schools, a pattern seen in New York, Los Angeles, Chicago, Cleveland, the District of Columbia, and others.[97] Another response is for the state to step in, such as New Jersey's takeover of Jersey City schools, Pennsylvania's takeover of Philadelphia schools, and California's takeover of Oakland schools.[98]

We do not yet know the results of the latest wave of "management change" in urban schools, although it is hard to be overly optimistic about it. These changes at the top take place within the existing structure and incentives of schools. While there may be a new leader who can make some marginal changes, the situation in our view demands more than marginal changes.

The proposals we have set out would, we believe, provide a framework that will make improvement in our big city school districts more likely. Perhaps the biggest issue weighing down urban districts is the rigidity of the personnel system—a salary structure that, if anything, encourages teachers to flee the most disadvantaged schools, a set of rules and practices that inhibit rational teacher assignments, the inability to replace ineffective teachers with more capable ones, and the like. These issues, while generally important for most districts, become more serious in urban districts where the magnitude of the problem pushes districts more toward management by rules. Our proposals, by recognizing the value added of teachers and principals, provide a very different set of incentives for everybody.

Transparency both in student achievement and in the fiscal flows of the district funds to schools also encourages more rational decision making in assignments and programs.[99] Transparency, when linked to both accountability and flexibility in personnel and programs, is likely to be a significant force for improvement.

We should be clear. We think that our proposals will aid in moving our big city schools forward. We have no illusions, however, that this task will be an easy one. The challenges, both with disadvantaged populations and with built-up rigidities in the schools, are formidable. At the same time, we are quite confident that doing the same kinds of things, even with more intensity, will not work, and that the gains that any particular leader might be able to get are likely to disappear without more structural changes in the operations of the schools.

## Conclusions

School finance cannot be divorced from school policy. If the objective is to raise the performance of students, the finance system must support that goal, and it must be thoroughly integrated with the overall educational goals and policies of the system. Unfortunately, many current finance systems do not focus directly or effectively on achievement goals. They represent a combination of historical practices, conflicting components, and elements that not only fix in place unproductive practices, but also, in some cases, actually work against higher achievement. If schools are to improve and if we are to meet our achievement goals, the finance system must be harmonized with the policy structure to provide both support for and incentives within the schools.

Four basic reasons account for low student achievement: students may be ill prepared for a variety of reasons unrelated to the education system; the school and its teachers may be doing a poor job educating their students; students and/or school personnel may not be sufficiently motivated; and schools may lack the resources to do an acceptable job.

Much of policy discussion attempts to make a global determination of which cause is dominant and then to establish policies that address that one cause. Yet different observers, faced with the same evidence, will emphasize different factors depending on their philosophy, politics, experience, affiliations, and a host of other factors. In fact, past attempts to find a solution to low achievement have focused largely on only one of these factors: insufficient resources.

In our view, all of these reasons may affect any given school to different degrees. While local personnel may be able to assess the importance of each, it is difficult from outside to differentiate between them or to determine which is dominant. The fundamental difficulty is the underlying heterogeneity across schools and dis tricts. Thus, we conclude that attempting to parcel out fault for poor student outcomes is often an exercise in futility. We assume instead that all four factors are at play to different degrees in most school districts, and that to succeed in raising student achievement, policymakers must address all four. Our answer, therefore, is to provide the resources and incentives to address all four factors in a broad and rational manner.

The performance-based funding system we lay out in this chapter is a substantial departure from the current school finance system in virtually every state. It is true that many of the components we propose already exist in most states. Certainly every state has adopted outcome standards of some nature, along with varying types of accountability systems. Some have begun to experiment with economic incentives, such as performance-based pay and school choice options, while others have begun to give local school leaders more discretion over the spending of their budgets. However, as we have emphasized, it is the combination of all of these elements that holds the key to the system's success. Working together as part of an integrated system, they are likely to produce long-awaited improvement in our schools (while solving the funding-achievement puzzle).

We acknowledge that the optimal way to design the various incentive schemes and finance arrangements remains unknown at this time. While our recommendations are consistent with economic principles and, most important, common sense, we still do not have enough information to support the full development of the "best" system. At this point, we also need to have a transition path that seeks to build the ability to structure, apply, and evaluate alternative incentives. Any reform of the finance/policy system must also include an explicit program for improving our knowledge of the outcomes it produces and for refining and readjusting the policies.

Several aspects of our recommendations are controversial and may be opposed by significant interest groups. Some will entail additional costs, although we believe those costs will pale beside the costs of most other reform strategies now in vogue, such as class size reduction programs.

Not undertaking real reform, however, also involves huge potential costs: continued stagnation of our education systems, the persistence of achievement (and income) gaps damaging to huge numbers of our citizens and to American democratic values, increasing harm to our economic well-being as individuals, families, and a society, and threatened loss of American leadership in the world and global economy. The stakes could not be much higher.

# 9 | Making Performance-Based Funding a Reality

The best ideas are of little value unless they are actually implemented. Therefore, in this concluding chapter, we address several subjects critical to implementing performance-based funding. Since the state legislatures are the key to bringing about the type of reforms we recommend, we reflect on the legislative process and whether it is "broken" in various states, as is often alleged. To the extent the courts remain a force in school finance matters, we posit a different and, we believe, more productive role for them. We then discuss likely opposition to performance-based funding by teachers' unions and other influential interest groups and explain why we nevertheless believe that the time is right to pursue such reform strategies. Finally, we offer some reasonable compromises that might be necessary in order to ease opposition and to make our proposal a reality.

## The Persistence of Illusory Spending Solutions

The principal message of the previous chapters is that continued funding increases unaccompanied by other, more fundamental, reforms are unlikely to solve the education problems that we face. Almost two generations of significant increases in national spending on K–12 education with no commensurate improvements in student performance tell the whole story. To be sure, the quadrupling of real spending over the past four decades has been accompanied by good intentions and lofty plans, but on average, even though the increased spending might have worked effectively in some schools, it has not led to overall improvements in achievement.

This simple picture has been reinforced by extensive analyses that underscore the educational bankruptcy of past "reforms." Even when added resources and programs appeared to offer promising results in one setting, it has been difficult to replicate those results elsewhere, either because of poor implementation or because those responsible for implementing the strategy did not generally accept it.

Again, our message is not that money never matters or that money cannot matter. Such statements—sometimes employed as straw men to distract from the painful history of educational policy—are obviously incorrect. But equally obvious is that simply spending more within the existing system is unlikely to produce any sizeable improvements in student outcomes. Rather, true reform, as laid out in our performance-based funding model, requires that the structure of public education be changed to encourage school officials to identify, implement, and retain effective programs and people, while at the same time discouraging those that are not well suited for the school district or that prove, after a reasonable probation period, to be ineffective.

We believe that the state legislatures must play the key role in reforming education finance and education policy. Not only do they have the authority to address a wide range of problems, both inside and outside the schools, but new and innovative measures, such as stronger accountability systems, charter schools, vouchers, and more effective means of compensating teachers, almost always emanate from them. Moreover, legislatures have enjoyed some notable successes. During the 1990s, Texas and North Carolina were generally recognized as the states that had done most to improve student achievement among poor and minority students. Lawsuits, court-ordered remedies, and significantly increased spending had little or nothing to do with their success. Instead, the credit was largely due to accountability and other innovative measures originating in the state legislatures.[1]

Nevertheless, some would still prefer that courts exercise more power over education policy and finance because, they argue, the legislative process for determining and allocating education appropriations is broken. For example, in New York, the CFE plaintiffs contended that the allocation of the state's education budget was decided every year by "three men in a room" (the governor, assembly speaker and senate president), and that the complicated state finance formulas were then manipulated to conform to the deal reached between them.[2] These criticisms strike a nerve in many people. Watching a state legislature at work is not always pretty, and often brings to mind the old Bismarck saying: "There are two things you never want to see; one is making sausage and the other is the legislature making laws."[3]

As evidence that the legislatures are broken, education advocates point to perilously low student performance in many quarters. They then seek to fix the problem by adding more money to school budgets. But this is precisely the area where legislatures and governors can legitimately claim "success." Spending on schools has risen noticeably faster than inflation or other governmental services, save perhaps health care.[4] In contrast, in the one area where the legislative process has failed—enacting policies and creating structures that effectively use appropriations to improve student achievement—little change is sought. This focus desperately needs to be altered.

Some argue that education appropriations are often determined by the amount of state revenues "left over" once other governmental needs are satisfied, and that lawmakers rarely attempt to relate such appropriations to what an "adequate" education actually costs. This belief has led many states to rely on costing-out studies by outside consultants to determine how much should be appropriated for K–12 education. But while the legislative process is not without its problems, it is misleading to suggest that the education appropriations decided upon through the deliberative process are arbitrary and bear no relationship to the cost of providing an education. Legislators do not write on a blank slate. Each state knows the base cost of operating K–12 schools from prior budgets. Legislators know how much is necessary to pay teachers, maintain school buildings, buy textbooks, and so on. The primary issues before them each year generally relate to how much funding is needed to (1) continue existing programs, taking into account possible personnel raises, inflationary price increases, and enrollment increases (called the "continuation budget" in some states), and (2) fund new programs. Every year the legislature and its various committees and subcommittees hold hearings and collect information from a number of sources—including the state departments of education, local school district officials, and other interested parties and experts—about what else is desired and how much it will cost. Each measure is debated and weighed against other demands, both inside and outside the education arena. Some are enacted and others are not. Some fail because they are not good ideas, others because the legislature, in its discretion, finds better uses for available funds, and still others because powerful political interests, such as teachers' unions or business groups, oppose them. But certainly the measures that do pass and the funding appropriated to support them bear a relationship to the educational process.

While it is safe to say that the education sector rarely gets everything it wants (who does?), to say that it gets what is "left over" after the other needs of government are satisfied is not accurate. If anything, given the high priority education has enjoyed in most states over the past several decades, it is more likely the other sectors of government that get what is "left over."[5] Spending on K–12 education has increased as a percentage of total state spending, while spending on higher education, transportation, and other governmental services has decreased over the last decade. From 1994 to 2004, the percentage of state spending devoted to elementary and secondary education increased more than any other major sector of state government.[6]

The "broken" legislature argument forms the foundation for inviting the courts into school finance: if the state has a constitutional obligation to provide schooling, and if poor student achievement makes clear that the legislature has failed in this obligation, the courts have a duty to strike down the ineffectual system and compel the legislature to come up with an effective one. Unfortunately, the remedy generally sought from the courts is, as we just pointed out, precisely where the legislature has actually succeeded: getting ever more money into the schools. But spending remedies make sense only if the added funds can be expected to bring about higher achievement, which has clearly not been the case in the past and is unlikely to be the case in the future, unless, of course, other fundamental reforms are also made. If enacting higher spending were the issue, the courts would be hard-pressed to find legislative failure in most states. It is a task most state legislatures have done well.

Importantly, citizens have been led to believe that the funding situation is much different. The media regularly produce stories about how budgets are being slashed. A sample of stories on the dire budget situation in 2008 gives a flavor for the standard newspaper alarm. For example, a featured article in *USA Today* proclaimed: "Fuel prices force schools to weigh class, staff cuts" and went on to indicate that "nearly one in three [of the surveyed superintendents] are eliminating teaching jobs."[7] The food service director indicates that, because of budget problems, he "is scaling back on some of the more expensive menu items such as fruit juice."[8] And the superintendent of public instruction in California issued a press release that was widely covered in the California news media stating: "School districts up and down this state are sending out pink slips to tens of thousands of hard-working, dedicated teachers, administrators, and school staff, not because our state faces a spending problem, but because we face a priorities problem."[9] The *Boston Globe* cites hikes in insurance and utilities as it pronounces, "Schools brace for teacher layoffs."[10] There is, of course, nothing special about this collection of news reports. Each year there are an uncountable number of articles proclaiming that "teachers face layoffs because of $X$," where about the only thing changing is what $X$ happens to be at the time.

From this deluge of publicity about the constant cuts in school budgets and impending elimination of teachers and programs, the public gets a distorted picture of spending on schools and its pattern over time. Political scientists William Howell and Martin West surveyed two thousand households about spending in their districts and found that "the average respondent's estimate was just 42 percent of actual spending levels in their district."[11] Remarkably, the same survey found that 40 percent of the sample reported that their school spent less than $1,000 per pupil per year, even after the respondents were prompted about the range of expenditures by schools.[12] Actual spending averaged over $10,000 per pupil in their districts. This low level of knowledge on what schools actually spend makes it easy to get a sympathetic reaction to calls for increased funding for schools. In fact, another survey that asked about willingness to raise taxes in order to increase school funding found that half of all nonteachers (and 63 percent of school personnel) supported more spending.[13]

In short, politics certainly plays a role in determining education appropriations. But while reasonable people can differ as to whether enough money has been appropriated for K–12 schools, a system that builds upon present and past experience, including funding levels, and takes into consideration other governmental needs, cannot be considered unreasonable. The real complaint with the legislative process, we suggest, is not that it is broken, but that it has not produced the revenue increases for K–12 education hoped for by powerful stakeholders.

## Support for the Status Quo and Resistance to Change

The huge public commitment to improve the schools has largely been confined to and contained within preexisting systems and institutions. In almost all states, policy changes have occurred only at the margins, with accordingly limited impact on student achievement. Despite substantial evidence that increases in spending have not been the answer to the nation's education woes, the debates in both courts and state legislatures invariably come back to just that approach: higher spending but within the existing structures of the public school system. Indeed, one appeal of class size reduction programs to current participants in the system is that it introduces substantial new resources without changing any aspect of the current structure—i.e., it deepens the current activities without changing any incentives, rewards, or basic operations. The prevailing attitude has been that spending more on people and programs is an appropriate route to reform as long as business is conducted as usual.

Why has it been so difficult for policymakers, in both the courthouses and the statehouses, to change the way schools are financed and operated? We think there are several reasons.

First and foremost, schools are public monopolies, and they do not feel the same pressures to perform that firms in the competitive sectors of the economy face every day. Productivity and effectiveness have little to do with a school's survival. Contrast this with other sectors of the economy, where firms that cannot earn enough to cover their costs and make a reasonable profit find it difficult to attract investors and to continue operating, and firms with products that are in demand thrive and expand. Feeling little pressure to compete, schools also feel little pressure to make public any information about their performance. Both policymakers and the consumers of their services—the parents and children—are kept in the dark. The result is that many parents do not realize how badly the schools are doing and continue to support the traditional mode of delivering and paying for education services.

Survey results demonstrate the natural affection most parents have for their children's schools. For example, in 2007, a majority of public school parents thought their own child's school deserved a grade of A or B.[14] At the same time, however, only 14 percent of the same parents thought the schools of the nation as a whole deserved an A or B grade, even though logically these percentages should be the same.[15] The feelings of parents are echoed by the general public. The United States is a nation built on public schooling, and most people are grateful for and think fondly of their experience in the public schools. Thus, despite signs of distress, the public schools are considered basically sound and without need for drastic changes.

These feelings of goodwill dovetail nicely with the self-interests of public school administrators and teachers. They have chosen a career in education based at least in part on the existing structure of pay and incentives, and many are against any radical changes. The result is a loose but natural coalition of parents and school personnel who emphasize gradual changes that tend only to reinforce the existing structure. Changes that significantly alter these structures, called by some political scientists "disruptive changes," are fiercely resisted.[16] Thus, policies that lighten teacher workload, reduce class sizes, increase the salaries of existing teachers, and the like resonate with both parents and school personnel, while changes that increase competition and pressure to perform and that disrupt the existing scheme of things do not.

Policymakers have done little to lead the public beyond the status quo. It is hard for legislators to push for a policy change whose influence may not be evident for years when their own planning horizon tends to be bounded by the next election. Moreover, the difficulty of determining how best to structure and implement new strategies puts policymakers in the position of recommending uncertain reforms against a known status quo, something most are loath to do.

Finally, and perhaps most importantly, powerful, entrenched interest groups strongly favor continuing current policies and vigorously oppose significant changes that threaten the benefits they receive under the existing system. Chief among these are the teachers and other school employee unions. A recent survey of experts ranked the teachers' unions number one in their power to influence public policy, ahead of trial lawyers, business organizations, doctors, insurance companies, utilities, bankers, environmentalists, and other labor unions.[17] As Professor Terry Moe, the head of Stanford's Department of Political Science, points out: "[T]he largest, most powerful union in the country is not the Teamsters or the United Auto Workers, but the National Education Association."[18] Teachers' unions wield power at all levels of government; they influence local school board elections, and are the largest contributors to political campaigns in the nation.[19] Politicians cross them at their own peril, especially Democrats, who receive almost all the political contributions made by the two national teachers' unions and who can be counted on to support union causes.[20] In the words of Moe, a Democrat would be "committing political suicide" by opposing the union agenda.[21]

Teachers' unions are especially invested in programs that increase the funding of schools and that call for more teachers. Class size reduction programs are particularly attractive to them, and it is not difficult to figure out why.[22] Smaller classes mean more teachers, and more teachers mean more dues-paying members, which in turn mean more money in the union coffers. For example, the costing-out study conducted by CFE called for roughly fifteen thousand *more* teachers in the New York City school district.[23] Union dues in 2000 were $1,100 per year per member.[24] Simple math shows that accepting CFE's cost study would mean another $16.5 million in revenue for the American Federation of Teachers (AFT) local in New York City.[25] Again, class size reduction does not upset any of the current operating procedures, pay determination, or the like that the union might oppose. Similarly, they oppose charter schools and vouchers for private schools because teachers in such schools are rarely unionized. Since such programs would disturb the incentives and the normal mode of operation in the schools, they are harshly denounced as "destroying our public schools."[26]

Most problematic has been staunch union opposition to reform measures designed to get better teachers into the classrooms, such as performance-based pay to attract and retain more highly qualified teachers, incentive pay to persuade good teachers to teach in difficult-to-staff schools, and differential pay to attract teachers in chronic shortage areas, such as math and science.[27] They have also opposed changes to tenure laws and rules needed to rid classrooms of incompetent teachers.[28] The position of the unions is not news to anyone. As labor unions, they are out to do what they believe is in the best interests of their members. When Al Shanker, the legendary head of the American Federation of Teachers for many years, was asked about the rights of children, he famously replied: "They don't pay the dues in this union."[29] Despite Shanker's blunt statement, however, teachers' unions are masters in public relations and have effectively used the public's natural respect for teachers and our nation's tradition of public education to convince many people that what is good for the union is also good for children. But this is demonstrably not true.[30] As former Secretary of Education Rod Paige has said: "They [the teachers' unions] often paint themselves as the champions of children and teachers, but this is deeply dishonest and highly misleading. When the big teachers' unions oppose change because it will upset the status quo—when they try to strangle every effort to better the current system —they are not doing children or even their teachers any favors."[31] How, for example, does the unions' unwavering support for the current lockstep, nondifferentiated approach to teacher pay based on degrees obtained and years served benefit children when most researchers agree those two factors bear little significant relationship to student achievement?[32]

Whether the interests of the unions themselves coincide with the interests of their teacher members is also open to question. Class size reduction programs have become popular with many parents frustrated with the public schools. Teachers also like them if for no other reason than they mean less work overall and more time spent with each student. But teachers also like higher salaries and, given the choice, might prefer pay raises to smaller classes. The unions, on the other hand, have an incentive to add members and so push to support the class size reductions that effectively swell their ranks.

Some quick calculations make clear the trade-offs between smaller classes and higher salaries. Between 1996 and 2004, pupil–teacher ratios fell nationally from 17.6 to 16.2.[33] This necessarily means that in 2004 over 240,000 additional teachers were needed solely to support the lower pupil–teacher ratios. If the funds used to pay these additional teachers had instead been used to increase existing teacher salaries, noticeably higher salaries would have been possible without any change in total expenditures. Although per-pupil expenditures (measured in constant dollars) have increased by 21 percent between 1996 and 2004, average teacher salaries have increased by much less. The salary for a teacher with three years of experience, for example, rose only 9 percent from 1994 through 2004.[34] If the 1996 pupil–teacher ratios had been held constant, these salaries could have increased by 19 percent in real terms with no additional educational spending. Figure 9.1 shows actual real salaries (in 2004 dollars) compared with projected salaries (assuming no pupil–teacher ratio reductions) for an average teacher with three years of experience.

This trend has been true even in those states that have significantly increased overall education spending as the result of a court

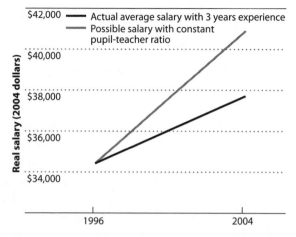

**9.1** Real Teacher Salaries, Three Years' Experience (projection with constant 1996 pupil–teacher ratio)

order. According to the salary surveys of the AFT, since 1990, teacher salaries, when adjusted for inflation, have not significantly increased in New Jersey, Kentucky, and Massachusetts, and have actually decreased in Wyoming and Maryland, despite huge increases in education spending in all five states as a result of court orders.[35] (Note, however, that the most recent spending increases in Wyoming may have finally filtered down to larger increases in teacher salaries.)[36]

The unions are not the only institutional opponents of change. Other members of the coalition to maintain the status quo include the nation's undergraduate and postgraduate schools of education, which have profited from the current system and seek, if anything, to expand their role. The reasons should be obvious. With increased pressure to reduce class size, significant numbers of new teachers will have to be hired. The need for more teachers means more tuition-paying students at the undergraduate schools of education. It means more students at the postgraduate schools trying to earn that next degree and the pay raise that comes with it (despite the evidence suggesting that these degrees bear no significant relationship to student performance). It means more money to be made by colleges and their professors offering a whole panoply of staff development courses to existing teachers, many for the purpose of rehabilitating teachers who might not be suited for the profession and would be let go were it not for the tenure rules. No wonder, then, that most colleges of education and their professors also oppose alternative entry routes to teaching, and that they largely embrace the current system.[37]

Finally, local school districts and local school boards are also highly vested in the current system. They are the direct recipients of increased state aid, and every year their superintendents or lobbyists visit the state capital seeking additional education appropriations. They have little stake in modifying a system that continues to supply them with a steady funding stream. Public school advocates, board of education members, and school administrators are particularly opposed to choice programs, such as charter schools or voucher programs. They argue that such programs divert money from public schools that badly need it, but in most cases, that statement is a red herring.[38] The public school districts may lose state or other funding for a student transferring to a charter school, but they also are relieved of the expense of providing such student's education. The opening of a charter school might cause some dislocation problems as the school district may be faced with fixed costs that cannot be readily reduced, but these should be relatively short-term transitional costs, assuming the school district adjusts its staffing levels to reflect reduced enrollment due to demand for the charter school.[39]

Political science teaches that the groups most interested in specific policies are decisive in policy development. They have important interests at stake and are personally willing to spend the energy and time to pursue them. On the other hand, the diffuse interests of others, such as taxpayers, concerned citizens, businesses, and even legislators, make them less likely to advocate and secure major changes, particularly when they do not coincide with the interests of powerful and influential interest groups. In fact, according to Moe and Chubb, perhaps the strongest power of unions is their ability to block any change that does not suit their own interests.[40] In this, schools of education that are responsible for the training of teachers are also heavily vested in the current system and provide further resistance to significant change.[41] All of these factors together constitute a powerful force against substantive changes that would disrupt the status quo in K–12 education. The natural pressures that have evolved favor "reform" initiatives that ruffle the fewest feathers, i.e., increased spending on personnel and programs.

## Some Current Countervailing Forces

The formidable pressures against true reform have, however, weakened in recent years. Most importantly, several elements of our performance-based funding proposal have begun to gain traction, and they have ancillary advantages in acting to break down the coalition protecting the status quo.

An important prerequisite to achieving change is for citizens and policymakers to understand fully how well or how badly the schools are doing. Many Americans are simply unaware of how their own schools stack up against those in other locations and countries.[42] They generally accept the idea that schools should be improved, but assume that their own are adequate as they are. But every state has now adopted academic standards that govern its school districts, as well as measures to hold schools and school districts accountable for meeting them or making appropriate progress toward them. At the federal level, NCLB codifies these fundamental concepts. As a result, information regarding performance of schools and school districts is increasingly available. Most states now issue "report cards" that not only describe the resources available in schools, but also chronicle the school's success or failure in comparison to achievement benchmarks, such as AYP under NCLB or statewide averages on academic tests. The increasing availability of international assessments also permits comparison of U.S. schools with those abroad.

Other key ingredients of adequate information disclosure are also enjoying growing support among the school community, education advocates, politicians, academicians, researchers, the media, and the public. For example, the idea of value-added assessment is catching on in a number of states. The Department of Education has approved use of similar "growth" models in all states for the purpose of assessing progress under NCLB.[43] Value-added assessments and growth modeling begin to relate the quality of schools and school personnel to student outcomes in a more informative and convincing way than mere achievement levels. The level of student achievement, as described in chapter 3, is affected by a range of factors outside the school, so it is a highly imperfect measure of the quality of local schools. This imperfect measure allows for many mistaken impressions of school quality and serves to reinforce the status quo and its supporters. Better and more relevant information about the school's performance would help make clear what changes are necessary to improve student performance.[44]

There is also broad support currently for driving more decision making down to lower levels, thereby giving local schools more say over how to spend their budgets.[45] This part of performance-based funding also works to weaken the coalition for the status quo, since local school districts and their teachers and principals are understandably as eager to have more flexibility in how to spend existing revenues as they are to generate new revenue streams. Furthermore, we do not envision that this aspect of performance-based funding will be opposed by the unions or other interest groups.

Opposition to merit-based pay and changes in the teacher tenure rules may also be easing. The arguments for paying teachers based on results and for easing tenure laws to terminate unfit teachers are so compelling, especially when it comes to serving mostly poor and minority enrollments, that movement toward a performance-based compensation system would seem almost inevitable. One of the few premises on which the scientific community agrees is that good teachers are the most important path, and perhaps the only consistent path, to improvements in student achievement. The international evidence also supports this critical finding. Countries that have done well on international assessments have policies that strongly support high-quality teachers and that do not tolerate bad teachers in classrooms for very long.[46] Such is not the case in the United States, where in some school districts it is virtually impossible to terminate incompetent teachers and where the single-salary schedule works against hiring and retaining exceptionally qualified teachers and worsens teacher shortages in areas such as math, science, and special education.

The public generally believes in linking pay to performance, seeing this kind of system working throughout the economy, although there is also some ambivalence by the public in applying this policy to teachers through state test scores. In 2007, 45 percent of those surveyed favored linking a teacher's salary in part to students' academic progress on state tests, while 31 percent did not favor such a policy.[47] Public reaction favoring performance pay has also gone even further, being the subject of public referenda in Oregon.[48]

Legislatures are increasingly recognizing this problem. Over twenty states have enacted programs experimenting with performance pay systems, despite often stiff opposition. Moreover, while the unions may oppose such programs, most of their own members clearly recognize the problem of unfit teachers propped up by the current pay and tenure system. In a recent survey by Public Agenda, 78 percent of teachers polled report "at least a few [teachers] in their school who are 'simply going through the motions.' "[49] Influential national organizations, such as Louis Gerstner's Teaching Commission, are calling for changes in the way teachers are paid. So are presidential candidates. In 2007, the Democratic presidential candidate Barack Obama told eight thousand delegates of the NEA that teachers should be paid based on their success in improving the performance of their students. He also called for more money for teachers in shortage areas, a policy that the NEA has stubbornly resisted for years.[50] The fact that the victorious Democratic candidate for president of the United States, in a speech to the largest and most powerful teachers' union in the country, would call for such reforms demonstrates perhaps better than anything the potency of the idea.

Movement is nonetheless not all in the same direction. In 2008, the New York teachers' unions convinced the legislature to pass a law that no information on student achievement could be used by schools in making teacher tenure decisions—apparently to thwart a move by New York City to introduce teacher value-added scores into such decisions.[51] (If student performance cannot be used in assessing teacher effectiveness, it would seem to imply that tenure decisions should be made on the basis of friendships and politics, just what unions have rightfully railed against regularly in their campaign against merit-based pay.)

School choice, an essential element of performance-based funding, is also gaining a foothold in many states through the expansion of charter schools.[52] Although public school administrators and board members often oppose charter schools, charters have, unlike vouchers, become very popular with the public and have flourished in a number of states. Indeed, the pressure to authorize more charter schools is so great in some states that even the unions are wavering in their opposition. For example, in New York City, the teachers' union itself has sponsored two charter schools.[53]

The importance of charter schools for changing the status quo is twofold. First, they complement performance-based funding by providing parents with a viable option (and threat) if their child's school does not perform. Second, choice options are critically important for any viable accountability system. Without choice, support for strong accountability measures is likely to weaken. Unions, school personnel, and others already dislike accountability systems because they shine a light directly on performance of the schools. Yet, because of the popularity of accountability and of increased information, they cannot directly attack the accountability systems themselves. Instead, they argue for "perfecting" the systems, a term that frequently means reducing the availability of information and therefore the ability of parents and others to judge the effectiveness of the public schools directly.[54] Charter schools, which provide options and benefits to parents dependent on information about school performance, will themselves act to preserve and improve the quality and integrity of accountability systems. (The same may be true of voucher programs, which, while far less popular than charters, have been very well received in the few places that have introduced them—notably Milwaukee—and the demand may increase as more information becomes available about them.)

The resistance to such reform measures has existed for decades and remains strong.[55] Yet both these steps and changing consumer sentiments bode well for further change. In the next section, we discuss ways to further facilitate such changes.

### Encouraging True Reform: Mutually Agreed Bargains

The most important area of reform, and perhaps one of the most feasible, involves hiring, selecting, and retaining effective teachers. We have already elaborated on the way that state tenure laws, reinforced by even stronger collective bargaining agreements, make it very hard to replace ineffective teachers,[56] and on the inability of schools to offer more pay to retain good teachers or to induce teachers to take various hard-to-fill positions. We note here also that many potential teachers are currently reluctant to enter the teaching profession because they doubt that their performance will be sufficiently rewarded.[57]

But teachers understandably value job security and will not lightly give up tenure. Therefore, some compromises are likely to be required. One possible compromise that has been advanced to clear this hurdle is that of a "grand bargain," or an agreement providing additional funds for higher teacher pay in return for concessions in tenure laws and union contracts.[58] For example, salary increases for teachers might be coupled with lengthening the time it takes to get tenure, serious evaluations of classroom success, and higher risk of termination. Under this bargain, current teachers would be compensated for changes in the contracts and employment conditions that they relied upon in making their career choice. This approach would be costly, but the money would be well spent since it would make it easier for principals to terminate unqualified teachers. The higher salaries could also be structured in a way to begin the transition to a system of performance pay, with higher pay raises directed toward the more successful teachers. The idea of a grand bargain in the context of schools recognizes that employment contracts are two-sided—involving both the employer and the employee—and that significant changes should contain an element of compromise to maintain harmony and a productive work environment.

However, the bargain must be enforceable and result in real change, something that has been missing from such bargains in the past. The case of Rochester, New York, is a good example. In 1986, the local teachers' union and the school district agreed to a highly publicized contract that granted large salary increases to teachers based upon their agreement to move toward a merit system linking salary with performance.[59] Unfortunately, the teachers, their union, and the school district never got to the point of adopting a merit-based system. After the teachers got their pay raises, they lost interest in the other half of the bargain.[60]

Other variants of the grand bargain offer more hope. For example, the states of Florida and Texas have made additional funds available to districts, provided they and their teachers agree to merit pay plans meeting certain broad requirements. These include limitations on the proportion of teachers that can receive merit pay (thereby ensuring that the pay incentives for the individual teachers will not be watered down by paying a little bit to most teachers) as well as the need to base a portion of the pay raise on the value added by the teacher.[61]

Another alternative that avoids conflict with existing teacher rights is to make a new performance-based contract mandatory for new teachers, but voluntary for existing teachers. If existing teachers do not opt for the new contract, they remain covered by the existing contract. The goal is to make the new contract sufficiently attractive in terms of merit-based salary increases that a substantial share of existing teachers will opt to choose it, rather than continuing under the old single-salary step contract, which may provide more security but less opportunity for substantial pay raises.[62] The new, riskier contract would have to offer higher expected salaries (for high-performing teachers) in order for existing teachers to accept it, but it seems clear that more money for effective teachers would be well worth it.[63]

We believe that a combination of bargaining for better contracts, compensation for accepting less job security, and voluntary (individual or group) acceptance of new contracts offers hope of implementing much needed reforms. But, we have not built up much of a record on what kinds of policies will be acceptable (and at what price).

## Changing the Focus of the Courts

It is an understatement to say that the courts have not, to date, had a very positive influence on education funding and policy. While courts may have an obligation to consider whether the schools of a state are meeting the requirements of the constitution, the approaches they have taken in most states inhibit, more than encourage, effective reform.

This is not the first time courts have struggled with finding effective remedies in education-related cases. The school desegregation cases illustrate both the successes and the difficulties courts have had in the remedial area. Under *Brown*, the federal courts relied upon their equitable powers to enjoin the operation of racially discriminatory laws, policies, and practices requiring and maintaining segregated schools. Most commentators agree that such injunctive orders were ultimately successfully in ending de jure, or official, governmental discrimination. Moreover, had the federal courts not intervened, it is doubtful that the southern states, and indeed many northern states, would have permitted repeal of laws and policies designed to segregate schoolchildren by race. Even after the Supreme Court's decision in *Brown*, governors and legislators throughout the South and elsewhere continued to resist school desegregation measures, knowing they would be voted out of office if they counseled compliance with the *Brown* decision.[64] Yet the federal district courts, shielded from this political influence through lifetime appointments, were finally able to end these discriminatory practices by using their authority to enjoin school officials from discriminating based on race.

But the courts' powers proved to be far less effective when used to order affirmative remedies. This was particularly true when the courts or defendants under their jurisdiction did not control all the participants necessary to effectuate the remedy. Thus, when remedies required the cooperation or participation of parents and students, they were often utter failures. Witness busing remedies, where federal court sought to integrate schools by reassigning white children to schools located in predominantly black neighborhoods and vice versa. This approach largely met with failure because neither the courts nor the school authorities could control parents, who chose to move out of the affected neighborhoods or place their children in private schools. "White flight," as it became known, severely compromised the effect of the court "busing" orders, and many inner-city school systems remained predominantly black despite decades of federal court orders designed to integrate them.[65]

Adequacy remedies in school finance cases face similar problems. The courts can, through their remedial decrees, influence the operation of the schools and state government, but their ability to control much of what happens within schools, let alone within the homes and neighborhoods that affect schools, is severely limited. Just as in the busing cases, the courts have limited authority and no effective means of addressing many factors affecting student achievement.[66]

While legislative bodies must deal with the same obstacles, unlike the courts, they have broader authority to address the adverse effects of home and neighborhoods and to alter the institutional structure of schools. Addressing some of the fundamental educational issues, however, may well be politically risky. That is why future court orders need to support legislators who want to address serious problems in education, but cannot do so because of strong political pressures protecting sacred cows. The courts can employ their considerable influence and prestige by (1) educating legislators on all of the problems that need to be addressed and (2) providing them with the specific data needed to get appropriate remedial measures enacted. Judges should—if they are to consider a remedy for a constitutional violation—identify all of the social, management, organizational, and financial problems adversely affecting the schools' ability to raise student achievement, without regard to the politics involved. Their fact-findings would be likely to carry weight with legislators and help proponents of change to convince their fellow lawmakers to address problems that have previously been left untouched because of politics.

A court, unburdened by political pressures, may be well positioned to point out where innovative solutions disruptive to the status quo are called for. Unfortunately, court orders in the past have been largely silent on inefficient use and waste of school funds, theorizing that *if* such problems exist they are also the state's responsibility to remedy. They have largely sided with the powerful forces favoring the status quo. If the courts were more specific in their findings about mismanagement, waste, inefficient practices, constraints imposed by collective bargaining agreements, state tenure laws, and so on, their decisions could provide leverage for those in the legislature who want to do something about them and thus contribute to solving rather than continuing the funding-achievement puzzle.

Consider the following examples where specific court findings might help to bring about systemic change.

### Teacher Tenure and Termination

If a trial court decided that significant numbers of incompetent teachers, protected from termination by lifetime tenure, were contributing to low student achievement in the state, the decision might significantly alter the political landscape and allow the lawmakers to pass new, more rational tenure initiatives.

### Collective Bargaining Agreements

Court opinions rarely mention any constraints arising from union contracts. In the *CFE* case, with one exception, none of the numerous trial and appellate court decisions dared question why the state should be ordered to pay more money to overcome inefficiencies resulting from a city-negotiated contract.[67] When the contract was renegotiated in 2005, none of the offending provisions were changed.[68] Had the court explored the ramifications of the collective bargaining agreement in the *CFE* case and placed the responsi-

bility for the problematic provisions squarely where they be-
longed—on the city of New York, which negotiated and agreed to
the contract—the 2005 contract might have been very different.

## School Consolidations

In many rural states, the elephant in the room when the efficient
use of funds is being deliberated is school consolidation. No small
town wants to lose its local school, regardless of how inefficient it
is to maintain and operate. But it is not clear that the state should
heavily subsidize local schools through their additional state aid.
If court decisions addressed this issue, legislatures might gain courage to do the fiscally sound if unpopular thing.

## Adverse External Influences

Courts have also taken the easy way out when it comes to addressing factors outside the schools that hurt student achievement,
such as poverty, crime, drugs, inadequate health care, and poor
parenting habits. Courts themselves often acknowledge that these
factors are enormously important for student achievement, but not
wishing to "blame the victim," they rarely deal with them in their
opinions. Instead, citing popular mottos like "All children can
learn" and the testimony of school superintendents that with more
resources all children can achieve at high levels, courts conclude
that these too are problems the state can solve with more resources
to the schools. Ignored in the process is forty years of experience
indicating that school funding increases have not led to a significant
closing of the achievement gap or otherwise significantly raised student performance.

These external influences need to be fully and honestly addressed
by court opinions so that legislative solutions outside the schools
can be sought. As argued by Richard Rothstein, the former education columnist for the *New York Times*:

It [closing the achievement gap] requires abandoning the illusion that school reform alone can save us from having to make the difficult economic and political decisions that the goal of equality inevitably entails. School improvement does have an important role to play, but it cannot shoulder the entire burden, or even most of it, on its own.[69]

Instead of disregarding or paying lip service to many of the real problems facing the schools, the courts should use their evidence-gathering powers to examine and make judgments about them, and they should also deal explicitly with them in their decisions. When the case is then returned to the state legislature, the legislators will be playing with a full deck and will be more likely to take appropriate action to address waste and mismanagement. Proceeding in this manner will also take advantage of the greatest strength of the judicial system: its general independence from political influences.[70]

One key element of judicial investigations should be consideration of the value added by the schools. To deal with this topic, the courts would necessarily have to focus on variations in the effectiveness of different schools, taking into account factors over which the school has little control, such as the performance level of the students upon entering the school, mobility of students, the support of their parents, and the like. Providing such information, after independent verification by the courts, would be very beneficial to school and district planners. Requiring it to be made available to parents and policymakers on an ongoing basis would be even more valuable.

This proposal would allow the courts to address politically difficult issues, but in a way that would not entangle them in either the running of the schools or the appropriation process. By using their investigative and fact-finding expertise and authority, the courts could empower legislators to address politically sensitive problems that otherwise would likely remain as obstacles to effective school reform. Frederick Hess of the American Enterprise Institute argues that "adequacy decisions create a 'policy window' for reform—an opportunity in which a public problem is defined, attention is focused, judicial cover is provided for legislative activity, and a variety of remedies are put forward."[71] These "windows" have been used mainly to push through higher funding, but there is no reason that court decisions could not also open a "window" during which other reforms, such as those discussed in this book, might also be enacted.

There is no question that this approach would make more work for judges. No longer would they be able to dismiss mismanagement, waste, inefficiency, and harmful external influences as the state's problem to remedy. They would have to make specific findings of fact on each of these subjects and determine the extent to which they contribute to the problem of low achievement or funding shortages. But, of course, more work should not deter judges. Currently, they go through the enormous time and expense of court proceedings without ever identifying and examining important parts of the problem. (Remember, the *CFE* trial judge took testimony in his courtroom for nine months.) If they are unwilling to address these central issues, then why not leave the subject to the legislature in the first place without the distractions and other costs of court intervention?

Some may conclude that the role we suggest for the courts violates the separation of powers doctrine by giving the courts even more control over the operations of the schools. If so, they misunderstand our proposal. The courts should no more order the legislature to enact specific remedies to prevent mismanagement than they should order certain amounts to be appropriated for K–12 education. Judicial intervention of that scale would be unprecedented, probably unconstitutional, and undoubtedly a disaster. Nor should courts take a partisan stance, favoring some school reform agendas over others. Courts should not order vouchers, for example, any more than they should order higher spending. What we urge is something else: having decided that they have jurisdiction to hear an adequacy case, and having then declared the system unconstitutional, courts should describe the specific shortcomings that rendered the system unconstitutional, and what caused them.[72]

At that point, the court's work is complete, and the fashioning of an appropriate remedy is for the legislative and executive branches.

We believe that this approach has two overwhelming advantages over the present strategy employed by many courts. First, court orders of the type we describe may persuade the legislature to adopt the more "disruptive" reforms that may actually lead to improvements in student achievement. Second, they will create less, not greater, strain on the relations between the judicial and legislative branches of government than the present orders, because they, unlike current orders, are not aimed at that most zealously guarded legislative prerogative: appropriations.

## Mobilizing for the Future

The answer to improving our schools lies not in spending more, but in spending more effectively. Schools must be funded by a system that encourages teachers, administrators, and others involved in education to make wise decisions that will benefit children—indeed, that makes it in their financial interest to do so. With that as our goal, we have proposed a system of performance-based funding for consideration by not only state legislators, but also parents, policymakers, public school employees, union members, and advocates everywhere of better public education.

We have recounted the difficulties our proposal will face in many states and why we nevertheless believe the time is ripe for passage of these reforms. Perhaps the most important development operating in favor of the changes we recommend is that the pressure from the courts to increase funding has diminished. For the last decade or more, legislatures in many states have been faced with demands to raise spending, sometimes by 30 to 45 percent, buttressed by the threat of court orders. But in the last few years, almost every pending adequacy lawsuit has been dismissed or reached a judgment favorable to the defense. None have ordered costing-out studies likely to call for vast increases in education spending. In states where court spending orders have long dominated the legislative agenda, the lawsuits have been resolved.[73] As a consequence, state legislatures have a window of opportunity to concentrate on real reform without a court order hanging over their heads. It is also important to note that there are fifty different state legislatures, and, while the defenders of the status quo are powerful in many states, they have less influence in others. The road to true reform has to start somewhere, and if performance-based funding is adopted and successful in even one state, that track record will provide the impetus for changes in other states looking for more promising solutions.

Performance matters, and the future of our nation depends on getting it right. Our economic well-being is dependent on the skills of our labor force, and actions taken today will have effects decades from now.

Some have asserted that everything is basically all right except for students at the very bottom of the learning curve.[74] The bottom is indeed extraordinarily important given our shared values about the importance of opportunity for all. The racial achievement gaps, for example, drive a variety of inequities in society along with imperiling our national economic future.[75] But this is not the whole story. We are also not doing well at the top. Many nations currently produce significantly more highly skilled people. We have been fortunate that other strengths of the U.S. economy have made up for our mediocre schooling, but there is reason to doubt that these other advantages will be sufficient to carry us into the future.[76]

In closing, for the last three decades the fifty states have stuck to the status quo, propping up the basic structures for delivering K–12 education that have been in place for decades with ever vaster sums of money. This massive financial investment should have catapulted our students to new levels of achievement appropriate for the twenty-first century, but that has not happened. Instead, they continue to perform at the same level they did in 1960. The idea of reform has been popular since the time of *Sputnik*, but the reality is that virtually all of the popular, widely promoted reform programs that have been implemented are ones that maintain and reinforce the current structures and poor incentives, albeit with more resources. If we continue along the same road, adding more money to the system every year but ignoring its underlying weaknesses, the country could well wake up forty years from now with its students still performing at 1960 levels. Change is long overdue, and we believe that performance-based funding is an essential ingredient in moving public education toward a goal everyone shares: significantly improved achievement for all children.

# Notes

1. Lippman et al. (2008).
2. Howell, West, and Peterson (2007), p. 24. Public school employees are only slightly more confident about this than citizens outside of the schools.

## CHAPTER 1
## JUST HOW IMPORTANT IS EDUCATION?

1. See the history of twentieth-century schooling in America and its relationship to earnings in Goldin and Katz (2008).

2. These comparisons hold across subcategories of people grouped by race, gender, and age. For example, the average thirty-five-year-old black male earned $25,410 if he had twelve years of schooling but only $20,427 if he had ten or eleven years of schooling. Yet, over 40 percent of the thirty-five-year-old black males with twelve years of schooling earned less than $20,427—the average earnings for ten or eleven years of schooling. The earnings overlap for different school completion levels tends to be larger for Hispanics (of both genders) than for whites or blacks. Over 40 percent of Hispanics with twelve years of schooling earn less than the average for Hispanics with just ten or eleven years completed (author's calculations from the 2000 Census of Population).

3. For a summary of relevant work, see Hanushek (2002). The consistency of the impact of achievement on earnings can be seen by comparing Lazear (2003), Mulligan (1999), and Murnane, Willett, Duhaldeborde, and Tyler (2000).

4. In technical terms, this movement corresponds to a one-half standard deviation difference in achievement scores. Moreover, these studies may actually underestimate the importance of schooling on earnings. Most measures of low income do not take into account the fact that some people have low incomes only because they are just beginning a career. Their lifetime income is likely to be much larger as they age, gain experience, and move up in their firms and career.

5. Rivkin (1995). Bishop (1991) and Hanushek, Rivkin, and Taylor (1996), in considering the factors that influence school attainment, find that individual achievement scores are highly correlated with continued school attendance. Neal and Johnson (1996) in part use the impact of achievement differences of blacks and whites on school attainment to explain racial differences in incomes. Behrman, Kletzer, McPherson, and Schapiro (1998) find strong achievement effects on

both continuation into college and quality of college. Moreover, the effects are larger when proper account is taken of the various determinants of achievement. Hanushek and Pace (1995) find that college completion is significantly related to higher test scores at the end of high school. Each of these investigations independently highlights the role of achievement in affecting the schooling choices and investment decisions of individuals.

6. See, for example, Leibowitz (1974), Haveman and Wolfe (1993, 1994), Brooks-Gunn, Duncan, and Aber (1997a, 1997b). The causal relationship has, however, been recently questioned by investigations of whether the causal agent is the mother's education or other things that are correlated with mother's education. See, for example, Black, Devereux, and Salvanes (2005) and the references in that article. Alternative analytical approaches provide different results, leaving this question open (Carneiro, Meghir, and Parey [2007]). However, none of these investigations has delved into the cognitive skills of parents, which are central to this discussion. Education is also seen as breaking the intergenerational cycle of welfare, although, again, little is known about the impact of cognitive skills per se (Coelli, Green, and Warburton [2007]).

7. See Hanushek (2002, 2003).

8. The official poverty line in 2006 was $10,294 for a single individual and $20,614 for a family of four. The official poverty line does not include in-kind benefits, such a food stamps or health programs, but these do not significantly change the overall picture.

9. This act also continued until the present and was the foundation for the No Child Left Behind Act of 2001. Title I of the Elementary and Secondary Education Act of 1965 established the federal government's role in compensatory funding for disadvantaged students. At the same time, the Office of Economic Opportunity began the Head Start program, which provided preschool education for disadvantaged three- and four-year-olds and experimented with other ways to raise achievement. See, for example, Vinovskis (1999).

10. An implication is a growing share of total income of those at the very top of the distribution and relative losses in the middle and below. See Lindert (2000), p. 201, and Goldin and Katz (2008), p. 48.

11. Murnane, Willett, and Levy (1995).

12. See, for example, O'Neill (1990); Juhn, Murphy, and Pierce (1991, 1993); Murphy and Welch (1992); Pierce and Welch (1996).

13. Identifying the changing impact of measured ability on the distribution of outcomes over time is also a very difficult problem, particularly given the structure of available data. See Cawley, Heckman, Lochner, and Vytlacil (2000), Heckman and Vytlacil (2001). See also Murnane, Willett, and Levy (1995).

14. See the discussion and references in Neal (2006).

15. See Barro and Sala-i-Martin (2004).

16. See, for example, Krueger (1974); Grossman and Helpman (1991); Parente and Prescott (1994, 1999).

17. The first work by Hanushek and Kimko (2000) involves economic growth between 1960 and 1990 for thirty-one countries. This research has been expanded upon by others. The more recent studies trace growth from 1960 to 2000 across fifty countries that have participated in one or more international tests. Jamison, Jamison, and Hanushek (2007), Hanushek and Woessmann (2008), Hanushek, Jamison, Jamison, and Woessmann (2008).

18. The academic literature has been concerned with questions of causation, i.e., whether measured achievement causes growth or is merely associated with it, while other factors are the actual cause of growth. For a discussion of this, see Hanushek and Woessmann (2008).

19. Hanushek, Jamison, Jamison, and Woessmann (2008).

20. See, for example, the discussion of testing in Koretz (2008).

21. Note, however, that most of the existing analysis has relied on test results where the scores might be regarded as a reflection of the student's true ability. It goes without saying that, if test scores were artificially inflated, say, by cheating or emphasizing just the mechanics of test taking, they would not reflect skill differences. In such a case, the relationship between measured scores and economic outcomes might disappear.

22. See, for example, Murnane, Willett, Braatz, and Duhaldeborde (2001), Cunha, Heckman, Lochner, and Masterov (2006), and Heckman, Lochner, and Todd (2006).

23. Bracey (2002) phrases his discussion in terms of "competitiveness," measured by the Current Competitiveness Index developed by the World Economic Forum. He correlates this index with current scores on the Third International Mathematics and Science Study (TIMSS). The most telling points, he believes, are that TIMSS scores are not perfectly correlated with this index and that the United States ranks highly on the index. He goes on to explain why the United States ranks well on the competitiveness index by essentially the factors discussed for growth rate differences: higher quantity of education, greater college attendance, retaining our scientists and engineers (while attracting foreign immigrants), securing favorable rankings of its economy by international businesspeople, and having greater innovative capacity.

24. In the 2007 academic rankings of the world's research universities by the Institute of Higher Education, Shanghai Jiao Tong University, the United States had seventeen of the top twenty universities and fifty-four of the top ninety-nine (see http://ed.sjtu.edu.cn/rank/2007/ARWU2007TOP500list.htm, accessed January 12, 2008). In a 2007 professional ranking by the Ecole des Mines de Paris based on graduates who were CEOs at Global Fortune 500 countries, U.S. institutions had ten of the top twenty-two places and twenty-four of the top fifty-nine

places (see http://www.ensmp.fr/Actualites/PR/EMP-ranking.html, accessed January 12, 2008).

25. See Romer (1990); Barro and Sala-i-Martin (2004).

26. Committee on Science Engineering and Public Policy (2005).

27. See, for example, the analysis and predictions in Friedman (2007).

CHAPTER 2
U.S. EDUCATION AT A CROSSROADS

1. See chapter 9.

2. Heckman and LaFontaine (2007).

3. Note that these graduation rates exclude GED recipients. While the GED rates make things look better over time, it is generally believed that the social and economic status of GED completers is much closer to high school dropouts than to high school graduates. See Cameron and Heckman (1993); Tyler, Murnane, and Willett (2000).

4. This figure is reproduced from Heckman and LaFontaine (2007), which provides details of the decisions about measuring graduation rates. Data for Hispanics that also include immigrants are excluded. Their calculations come from Census IPUMS 1970, 1980, 1990, and 2000. Census graduation rates are ages twenty to twenty-four or twenty-five to twenty-nine, depending on cohort, and do not include recent immigrants. Recent immigrants are those who entered the United States within the last ten years for twenty- to twenty-four-year-olds and within the last fifteen years for twenty-five to twenty-nine-year-olds. GED recipients are estimated for each cohort using GED testing service data and are deducted from the census high school completer totals. Those who report never having enrolled in school are excluded.

5. The graduation rates in figure 2.1 approximate the completion rates in figure 2.2 from 1975 forward. For example, the completion rate for twenty-five to twenty-nine-year-olds in 1975 in figure 2.2 corresponds roughly to the graduation rate shown in figure 2.1 for children born in 1946–50. As indicated in both figures, the graduation rate since 1975 has leveled off or gotten worse.

6. Bound, Lovenheim, and Turner (2007); Bound and Turner (2007); U.S. Department of Education (2004), Indicator 19.

7. Parsad and Lewis (2003); U.S. Department of Education (2004), Indicator 1.

8. While we do not spend much time on this topic, these discussions tend to concentrate on items of curriculum and standards as opposed to the amount of learning that is going on. See, for example, Arenson (2004) and ACT (2005, 2007). There clearly must be a balance between what is being taught and what level of proficiency a student attains, but our view is that levels of student proficiency or knowledge are the more important.

9. The Organisation for Economic Co-operation and Development (OECD) includes the developed countries in the world. The OECD has collected completion data using standardized data. It should be noted that a large number of OECD countries do not appear in the figure because the required data are unavailable (Austria, Australia, Belgium, Canada, Korea, Netherlands, New Zealand, Portugal, and the United Kingdom). Thus, the position of the United States in the rankings is probably even lower than the plot suggests.

10. NAEP categorizes student achievement into three categories—basic, proficient, and advanced. The lowest of these is the "basic" category, which is defined as follows: "Partial mastery of prerequisite knowledge and skills that are fundamental for proficient work at each grade." NAEP website at www.nces.ed.gov/ nationsreportcard/reading/achieve.asp., accessed November 12, 2007.

11. Some might think that current tests measure more complicated skills and that therefore comparisons over time would not be valid. However, NAEP also reports long-term trends using scores that are based only on those skill sets and questions that have been used consistently over the long term and that enable researchers to validly compare the performance of children over a long period (NAEP website at www.nces.ed.gov/nationsreportcard/ltt/moreabout.asp, accessed November 12, 2007).

12. At the beginning of this chapter we illustrated the current state of student achievement using achievement levels, as opposed to scale scores, because achievement levels (e.g., basic) are more understandable. However, scale scores are preferable for analyzing improvement over time because they measure real overall improvement, whereas a change in the percentage of students in one or more categories might not necessarily indicate a change in the overall scale scores. For that reason, NAEP does not even publish long-term trend information in anything but scale scores.

13. The National Center for Educational Statistics did not consider the average score for seventeen-year-olds "in 2004 . . . a significant change when compared to the score in either 1973 or 1999."

14. National Center for Education Statistics (2007b).

15. For an analysis of trends within states in state test scores, see Center on Education Policy (2008).

16. The leading treatises for this position include Bracey (1991) and his subsequent "Bracey Reports," Rothstein (1998), and Berliner and Biddle (1995). Some of this analysis is based on SAT scores and their trends. However, the SAT is a test voluntarily taken by a self-selected group of students intending to attend college, and the average scores can change from year to year solely because the percentage of students taking the test and differences between them change. See, for example, Congressional Budget Office (1986, 1987); Rothstein (1998).

17. In 1980, three-fourths of students were white, and this fell to three-fifths in 2004 (U.S. Department of Education [2007], table 16). This shift was the result of proportionate increases in Hispanic students (8.5 percent to 18 percent) and

other or multiple race students (2.5 percent to 7 percent). The math score gain for seventeen-year-olds between 1978 and 2004 of 6.4 scale points (roughly 0.2 standard deviations) would be approximately 2 scale points higher if the distribution had remained at the 1978 levels by race and ethnicity (i.e., if average scores by ethnicity were the same as observed in 2004 but whites were still three-quarters of the total, Hispanics were still 8.5 percent, and so forth).

18. Rothstein (1998) builds on the prior analysis of Grissmer, Kirby, Berends, and Williamson (1994).

19. Coleman et al. (1966) and Hanushek (1997a). The Coleman Report is discussed more extensively in chapter 3.

20. Grissmer, Kirby, Berends, and Williamson (1994) attempt to sort out the various factors in a crude way. Their analysis uses econometric techniques to estimate how various family factors influence children's achievement at a point in time. It then applies these cross-sectionally estimated regression coefficients as weights to the trended family background factors identified earlier. Their overall findings are that black students performed better over time than would be expected from the trends in black family factors. They attribute this better performance to improvements in schools. On the other hand, white students, who make up the vast majority of students, performed worse over time than would be expected, leading presumably to the opposite conclusion that schools for the majority of students actually got worse over time. There are, nonetheless, reasons to be skeptical about these statistical results. See Hanushek (2006b). A similar discussion of the difficulty of pinpointing the causal impact of family factors relates to family income. Mayer (1997).

21. Other researchers have reached the same conclusion. In a 2004 study, Jay Greene and Greg Forster relied on a "teachability index," which tracks sixteen predictors of student achievement, and concluded that students today are coming to school with fewer disadvantages than thirty years ago. Greene and Forster (2004).

22. Reading has been tested less frequently, in part because of the extra difficulty in developing a valid test of reading differences across languages. Further, while all of the international tests tend to be correlated, the previous analyses both of individual earnings and of economic growth concentrate on math and science performance because of its close relationship to productivity differences.

23. There have been twelve testing occasions (albeit under different sponsorship), combining results from a total of thirty-six separate test observations at different age levels and in different subjects. See Hanushek and Woessmann (in process) for comparisons of achievement levels across time. The testing of reading skills, while not available over as many years, does not change the picture.

24. As Koretz (2008) notes, a different group of countries has participated in the various international testing. Standardizing the scores for participation, however, still leaves the United States performing below the average for more

developed countries; see Hanushek, Jamison, Jamison, and Woessmann (2008) and Hanushek and Woessmann (in process).

25. See Welch and Light (1987); Clotfelter (2004); and Rivkin and Welch (2006).

26. U.S. Department of Education (2007), table 8.

27. Heckman and LaFontaine (in process).

28. Heckman and LaFontaine report that a significant portion of the convergence in the graduation rate gap reported by the U.S. Department of Education is due to the inclusion of black males obtaining a GED in prison—hardly a positive sign for our K–12 education systems. U.S. Department of Education (2007), pp. 8–9, 26–27; Heckman and LaFontaine (2007).

29. The continued existence of these gaps is also reflected in state-administered tests.

30. These differences in achievement are very similar to those found in the Coleman Report in 1966. Coleman et al. (1966).

31. U.S. Department of Education (2008), table 87. The top twenty-five districts have 12.2 percent of all students, while the top fifty districts have 16.4 percent.

## Chapter 3
### The Political Responses

1. School districts, scholars, colleges and universities, teachers and their unions, governors, state legislators, state education authorities, citizens, private foundations, advocacy groups, the courts, and many others have all, in one way or another, been involved in a massive effort to solve the problems outlined in earlier chapters. Examination of all of the various reforms and programs, including a long list of education fads, is beyond the scope of this book, and our review is therefore limited to the major responses of the three branches of government.

2. National Commission on Excellence in Education (1983).

3. National Commission on Excellence in Education (1983), p. 5.

4. National Commission on Excellence in Education (1983), p. 17. Some argued subsequently that the commission had overstated the case and that we should not really worry. For example, Bracey (2002) derided the commission and subsequent authors who warned that our economy was endangered by poor educational outcomes. In his words, "None of these fine gentlemen provided any data on the relationship between the economy's health and the performance of schools. Our long economic boom suggests there isn't one—or that our schools are better than the critics claim." He was correct that *A Nation at Risk* did not provide any convincing analysis. He was wrong in suggesting that there is no relationship between education and long-run economic conditions.

5. See Peterson (2003b) for a comprehensive review of the aftermath of *A Nation at Risk*.

6. These real spending calculations, put on a real 2007–6 dollar basis, employ adjustments for changes in the consumer price index (CPI) during a school year based on the number of students in average daily attendance (ADA). One could argue that a more appropriate inflation adjuster would be one based only on wages, since wages account for most school district spending. In general, wages rise faster than consumer prices; therefore, if the spending on schools were adjusted for wage increases, the increase would be somewhat less but still very large. For example, from 1984 to 2004, the average annual increase in the CPI was 2.99 percent, while the average annual increase in the employment cost index for private industry was 3.67 percent. Council of Economic Advisers (2006), tables B-48 and B-60. This suggests that the growth in spending deflated by wages would be 81 percent of that deflated by consumer prices. Applying this analysis to the entire 1960–2005 period, spending at the end of the period would be 3.1 times the initial level using the wage measure of inflation instead of 3.8 times. See also Hanushek (1997b), which discusses earlier consideration of price indices.

7. Another way that international spending comparisons have been done is to compare spending with gross domestic product (GDP). On these grounds, U.S. spending in 2004 on all levels of education of 7.4 percent noticeably exceeded the OECD mean of 5.8 percent. Only Iceland spent more. For elementary and secondary school spending, the United States at 4.1 percent of GDP exceeds the OECD mean of 3.8 percent but lags behind several OECD countries. See National Center for Education Statistics (2008a), Indicator 38.

8. Schools must compete with other industries to obtain teachers and other personnel. Because of productivity improvements, these competing industries have been able to pay higher salaries over time, putting pressure on schools that have not seen the same productivity increases (Scitovsky and Scitovsky [1959], Baumol and Bowen [1965], Baumol [1967]). Nonetheless, this phenomenon—often called "Baumol's disease"—cannot explain why schools have so dramatically expanded their hiring of teachers and other personnel.

9. Hanushek and Rivkin (1997) describe underlying forces in spending growth across the twentieth century, including the importance of staffing increases after 1970.

10. Hanushek, Kain, and Rivkin (2002) show that special education programs do appear effective in raising achievement, even if many special education students remain outside of the regular achievement testing.

11. The largest increases have come in "specific learning disabilities," on average a less expensive category for which to provide services. U.S. Department of Education (2007), tables 47 and 48.

12. The calculations are found in Hanushek and Rivkin (1997). See also Podgursky (2007). More recent expenditure estimates are lower (1.91 for 2000), implying that the calculations we use here may tend to overestimate the impact of special education. Chambers, Shkolnik, and Pérez (2003).

13. For New York State, Lankford and Wyckoff (1995) indicate slightly higher increases during the 1980s (and larger during the early 1990s). Berman, Davis, Koufman-Frederick, and Urion (2001) studied Massachusetts in the 1990s and found that special education expenditures grew much faster in that state than regular education expenditures, but that the share of special education to total spending increased from just 17.2 percent of total spending to 19.5 percent over the decade.

14. But not to all. For example, former Senate majority leader Dick Armey cynically observed: "If spending were the issue, DC [Washington, DC] would have a top-notch education system." Armey (2003) at http://www.freedomworks.org/informed/issues_template.php?issue_id=1490, accessed April 2, 2008. While the Washington, DC, school district spends more per pupil than almost any state (eclipsed only by New York and New Jersey), its achievement is so low it is almost off the charts when compared with the fifty states.

15. Judge Clark's order literally "allowed the District planners to dream" and "provided the mechanism for those dreams to be realized." *Jenkins III* (1995), pp. 79–80.

16. *Jenkins II* (1990).

17. Ciotti (1998); Evers and Clopton (2006).

18. Ciotti (1998).

19. Ciotti (1998).

20. For example, by 1991–92, per pupil expenditures in Kansas City had reached $9,412 versus $2,854 to $5,956 per student in the surrounding suburban districts. *Jenkins* (1994), p. 399.

21. Ciotti (1998); *Jenkins III* (1995), p. 79.

22. *Jenkins III* (1995), pp. 76–80; Ciotti (1998).

23. Magnet schools, which have been widely used in efforts to desegregate schools, typically have a specialty (e.g., college prep, the arts) and are designed to attract students from throughout a district. By breaking the linkage to residential location, they offer a potential means of having racial compositions that differ from the racial composition of neighborhood schools that reflected segregated housing patterns. See Armor (1995).

24. Ciotti (1998). See also Evers and Clopton (2006).

25. See expert report of Dr. John Murphy introduced during 2001 unitary hearing in *Berry v. School District of Benton Harbor*, Civil Action No. 4167-CV-9 (W.D. Mich. 2001) (Murphy was the court-appointed monitor of the Kansas City, Missouri, school district from 1997 to 2000). See also the data in Evers and Clopton (2006).

26. Ciotti (1998); Evers and Clopton (2006).

27. *Jenkins III* (1995), p. 24.

28. Ciotti (1998) and Evers and Clopton (2006) discuss a wider array of districts with virtually unlimited spending, such as Cambridge, Massachusetts, and

Sausalito, California, that have failed to turn increased funding into higher student achievement.

29. See, for example, Hanushek (2003, 2006b).

30. Coleman et al. (1966). This report provided one of the first attempts to apply statistical analyses to student achievement in what is now commonly referred to as "educational production functions." At the time of this report, Coleman was a professor at Johns Hopkins University.

31. Early discussions focused on whether the statistical analyses in the Coleman Report were valid. Bowles and Levin (1968); Cain and Watts (1970); Hanushek and Kain (1972). The Coleman Report gave little attention to racial composition of schools, the focus of *Brown* and subsequent court cases, but a follow-up report focused on this issue. U.S. Commission on Civil Rights (1967).

32. The results of prior studies can be found in Hanushek (2003, 2006b) and Hanushek and Rivkin (2006). Note that some studies use teacher–pupil ratios while others use actual class sizes. The results for studies of actual class sizes show, if anything, a weaker relationship between class size and achievement than those results for studies involving pupil–teacher ratios.

33. STAR is an acronym for student/teacher achievement ratio. The debates on the subject can be found in Word et al. (1990); Hanushek (1999a, 1999b, 2002a); and Krueger (2002).

34. Stecher and Bohrnstedt (1999) and Jepsen and Rivkin (2009).

35. For further discussion of teacher experience, see Hanushek and Rivkin (2007)and Murnane and Steele (2007).

36. Two aspects of these studies bear note. First, studies that compare achievement of schools in different states ignore any policy differences among the states, a fundamental concern given that most education policy is dictated by individual states. This neglect is potentially very serious in terms of biasing any statistical analyses, but is particularly damaging to statistical results when the underlying analysis is conducted using aggregate state data (such as state average spending per pupil). See Hanushek, Rivkin, and Taylor (1996). Second, when analyses consider just the level of achievement as opposed to the learning gains over time, the statistical results generally cannot allow for historical family and school factors that affect achievement. Hanushek (2003) shows that the studies supporting the positive impacts of resources are disproportionately afflicted with these two important methodological problems.

37. Hanushek and Rivkin (2006).

38. Some studies have found statistically significant positive effects of school spending, and people who wish to advocate for more spending tend to cite just these. Nonetheless, particularly with the spending studies, the relatively few studies finding a positive relationship with achievement tend to be the lowest-quality studies.

39. U.S. Department of Education (2007), table 170. Besides Utah, other low-spending states included Arizona, Oklahoma, Mississippi, Idaho, Nevada, and

Tennessee. The top spenders, in addition to New Jersey, were New York and the District of Columbia.

40. A common measure of variation is the coefficient of variation, defined as the standard deviation in spending divided by average spending. This measure was 0.20 in 1970, reached a peak of 0.27 in 1990, but fell to 0.225 in 2004. U.S. Department of Education (2007), table 170.

41. Adjustment for cost of living does change some of the state rankings. For example, Vermont replaces New Jersey as the top spender, while the District of Columbia would fall to seventh. Wyoming would move up from thirteenth in unadjusted spending to fourth when adjusted for cost of living differences. There are alternative ways to adjust for cost differences, although none is completely without problems. One approach is to adjust for average wage differences outside of schools. See Taylor and Fowler (2006) and Taylor (2006). Using this adjustment, which ranges from 0.91 in Montana to 1.48 in DC, the variation in spending across states is reduced by 30 percent.

42. An early expression of this appeared in 1997, when David Grissmer and his colleague, Ann Flanagan, conducted a study on behalf of the National Education Goals Panel, which monitored and reported annually on thirty-three indicators linked to eight national education goals. They found that Texas and North Carolina stood out among the fifty states for the progress they had made in improving student achievement. From 1990 to 1997, these two states had the highest average gains on the NAEP tests—gains also reflected in state assessments administered during the same period. Moreover, they found that the scores of disadvantaged students in the two states had improved more rapidly than those of more advantaged students. In assessing the reasons behind the so-called Texas miracle, as well as North Carolina's success, Grissmer and Flanagan found that increased spending and the resources commonly purchased with such spending were not associated with these remarkable gains. See Grissmer and Flanagan (1998). Their subsequent work, switching perspective and showing the fragility of these estimates, questioned some of their early conclusions, even though based on much of the same data. See Grissmer, Flanagan, Kawata, and Williamson (2000).

43. Hanushek and Raymond (2005).

44. The reverse is also true. Many districts get high student achievement while spending little. See Walberg (2006).

45. At least outside of courtrooms in school finance court cases (discussed later), most discussion of the "money never matters" debate, a controversy of a decade ago, has subsided. For the historical framing of the question, see the exchange in Hedges, Laine, and Greenwald (1994) and Hanushek (1994).

46. A variety of studies have pursued this general approach over the past four decades. See Hanushek (1971, 1992); Armor et al. (1976); Murnane (1975); Murnane and Phillips (1981); Aaronson, Barrow, and Sander (2007); Rockoff (2004); Rivkin, Hanushek, and Kain (2005); and Hanushek, Kain, O'Brien, and Rivkin (2005).

47. As discussed in the next chapter, because educational funding has not normally been viewed as a matter for federal courts, the discussion of equity has focused on the distribution of spending within each state. Nonetheless, in terms of the distribution of spending across students, the largest differences remain those across states. If differences in spending are decomposed into the component arising within states and that between states, the between-state component dominates. See Murray, Evans, and Schwab (1998) and National Center for Education Statistics (2007a), Indicator 39. In early debates about federal involvement in education, Senator Robert Taft, a conservative Republican from Ohio, even introduced the idea of federal policies to help equalize funding across states. See Cross (2004).

48. Another term that has been used to describe this type of equity is "parity plus." *Abbott* (1990), p. 385.

49. As with most aspects of state taxes and revenues, reliance on the property tax varies widely—from roughly 40 percent of local revenue (Alabama, Arkansas, and Louisiana) to virtually all (Connecticut, Montana, New Jersey, Massachusetts, and Vermont). It nevertheless remains an important component of school funding in all but a few states. U.S. Bureau of the Census (2007).

50. In a number of lawsuits, the arguments have implicitly been ones of taxpayer equity—that is, whether it is fair that some taxpayers must pay much higher tax rates than others in order to reach the same school spending levels. As discussed in the next chapter, however, the nature of the state constitutions clearly distinguishes issues of educational equity and taxpayer equity.

51. Coons, Clune, and Sugarman (1970).

52. Strayer and Haig (1923); Strayer (1934). This plan is sometimes referred to as the Strayer-Haig-Mort plan, recognizing the subsequent development of it by Paul Mort.

53. Although states differ on whether they do or do not require local districts to meet this level of tax effort, the local district will commonly be treated as if it has levied the base rate when calculating the amount of state aid to which it is entitled.

54. The possibility that the local district might have to turn over excess revenues to the state for redistribution to other districts is sometimes called "recapture."

55. This approach goes under a variety of alternative names including guaranteed tax base, percentage equalizing, variable matching grant, and guaranteed yield plan. Proposals of this type were advocated by Coons, Clune, and Sugarman (1970) and have been extensively analyzed. See, for example, Stern (1973), Feldstein (1975), and Inman (1978).

56. *Education Week* (2005) highlights that state use of categorical grants varies broadly, ranging in 2004 from zero in Alaska and Tennessee to fifty such grant programs in California. Assessing their importance and impact is difficult, however, as even the number of such programs is open to question. For example, the

2006 "Getting Down to Facts" studies for California schools identified not fifty, but over one hundred categorical programs representing over one-third of the state and local school spending. Loeb, Bryk, and Hanushek (2008).

57. Johns (1972).

58. Data on types of school finance plans come from *Education Week* (2005) at http://www2.edweek.org/ew/qc/2005/tables/pdf/17equity-t1.pdf (accessed September 10, 2007). As noted later on, however, some characteristics of finance systems are difficult to categorize accurately, such as state shares when the state completely controls overall district spending as it does in California. Also, the funding formulas in two states (New York and Rhode Island) defy simple description and categorization.

59. States vary widely in the proportion of school funding they provide. Two, Hawaii and the District of Columbia, rely wholly on state or federal funding. The other forty-nine states range from Minnesota and New Mexico (70 percent state funding) to Nevada (less than 30 percent). (Data on types of school finance plans come from *Education Week* [2005]; basic tables are available at http://www2.edweek.org/ew/qc/2005/tables/pdf/17equity-t1.pdf [accessed September 10, 2007].) Funding data can be found in U.S. Department of Education (2007), table 159. Federal funds, which tend to follow poverty rates in states because of their compensatory nature, also significantly differ by state, being less than 5 percent of total spending in New Jersey but over 15 percent in New Mexico and Alaska. The way in which state funding is reported can sometimes be misleading. For example, in California, local districts are identified as raising one-third of total funds, yet it is better thought of as full state funding, because variations in local revenues raised for base funding are all perfectly offset by state funding. It should be noted that these state variations in funding change over the years, sometimes dramatically. For example, New Hampshire went from 87 percent in locally raised funding in 1995 to 46 percent in 2004. Vermont experienced a similar change, going from 63 percent local funding in 1995 to 24 percent in 2004. Alabama went in the opposite direction, with 22 percent locally raised funds in 1995 to 42 percent in 2004. Regardless of these examples, largely having to do with court actions, the variation in state and local shares between states declined between 1995 and 2004.

60. Murray, Evans, and Schwab (1998) concluded that such litigation reduced disparities in spending within states by 19 to 34 percent from 1972 to 1992, mainly by increasing spending in poor districts. See also Berry (2007).

61. For example, in Georgia, the base rate under its foundation formula is only five mills, although the average tax rate in the state is about fifteen mills and some districts levy over twenty mills.

62. This situation was originally suggested by Tiebout (1956) and tested in a fiscal sense by Oates (1969). More recent investigations have separated the purely fiscal parts from elements of school quality. See, for example, Black (1999) or Weimer and Wolkoff (2001).

63. Some may believe that it is the wealthy who are paying such higher prices; however, the research indicates that people of similar means often make different housing choices based on the quality of the schools. Those who opt to purchase houses in communities with good schools over perhaps larger and nicer houses in other communities end up trading school quality for a more desirable house. See, for example, Epple and Nechyba (2004); Nechyba (2006); Hanushek and Yilmaz (2007).

64. One of the explanations for the passage of the spending limitation in California is the sharp restrictions on local choice of funding that resulted from the California funding equity lawsuit of *Serrano v. Priest* (discussed later). See Fischel (1989) and Silva and Sonstelie (1995).

65. California's ranking among the fifty states in spending per pupil declined from tenth in 1970 to eighteenth in 1980 to twenty-fourth in 1990 to twenty-ninth in 2000 and to thirtieth in 2005; U.S. Department of Education (2008), table 174. These figures are even more striking when adjusted by a comparable wage index for each state, which is based on the relative wages of nonteaching college graduates; see Taylor (2006) and Taylor and Fowler (2006). Then California falls to one of the lowest-ranking states in spending per pupil.

66. U.S. Department of Education (2008), table 88.

67. Such students are identified by a variety of acronyms, including LEP (limited English proficiency), ESL (English as a second language) and ELLs (English language learners). The acronym most used currently seems to be ELLs.

68. Thirty-eight states had some program to provide extra funding for poor children according to the 2001 survey in Carey (2002). Some states do not use a weighting system, and the actual amount will vary according to the importance of state funding versus local funding. An alternative set of estimates based on reviewing state finance formulas is found in Thompson and Silvernail (2001), who find essentially the same proportion of states with poverty-based funding.

69. Past evaluations of Title 1, the federal compensatory education program for disadvantaged students, have failed to show consistently positive achievement effects for students. See Borman and D'Agostino (1996) and Vinovskis (1999).

70. Variations in funding by poverty level of students in school districts can be found in National Center for Education Statistics (2007a).

71. The perception that poor students receive less funding is often promoted and encouraged by prominent authors on education reform. For example, in his recent book *Shame of the Nation*, well-known social critic Jonathan Kozol complains at length about unequal resources in America's mostly poor and minority inner-city schools. To support his central thesis—that significantly less is spent on the nation's poor students—he cites per-pupil spending differences between seven central city school districts surrounded by some of the wealthiest school districts in the country, while ignoring overall spending figures showing that children in the school districts with the most economically disadvantaged students, on the average, have the most, not the least, spent on their schools. Kozol (2005), pp. 321–25.

72. Ladd (1975) analyzes the impact of commercial and industrial properties on the ability of local communities to raise funds. A large property tax base that allows the residents to raise a portion of the school funds from people outside of the district, i.e., the owners of the commercial and industrial property, may not be entirely a windfall for the residents. Commercial and industrial property may not be desirable for aesthetics and other reasons. In fact, some communities with wealthy families attempt through zoning and other devices to limit the amount of such property in their communities. For a general discussion, see Fischel (2006).

73. See Georgia Department of Education website at www.app.doc.K12.ga.us/ows-bin/owa/fin_pack_revenue.display_proc, accessed November 12, 2007.

74. Roza and Hill (2006); Roza, Guin, Gross and Deburgomaster (2007).

75. Thomas B. Fordham Institute (2006); Ouchi (2003).

76. A key question surrounding such proposals is whether simply channeling the money directly to the schools, and bypassing the school district, without also changing the current institutional framework of, for example, hiring, assigning, removing, and compensating teachers and administrators, would result in more effective schools. Therefore, while this funding approach may result in a more equitable distribution of funds between schools based on student need, we are not confident that it alone, without other more fundamental changes giving school administrators more control over their school and teaching staffs, would lead to more efficient or effective use of school funds.

77. Others argue that adequate funding necessarily must come before equitable funding. Baker and Rebell (2006).

78. Maxwell (2007).

79. Downes (1992); Hanushek and Somers (2001); Flanagan and Murray (2004); Downes (2004); Cullen and Loeb (2004); Duncombe and Johnston (2004). See also Greene and Trivitt (2008). These findings are entirely consistent with the direct investigations of the implications for achievement of adding more resources to schools.

80. Smith and O'Day (1990); O'Day and Smith (1993).

81. Details of the history and substance of the national goals can be found at the website of the National Education Goals Panel. While this panel was dissolved by Congress, its website still provides relevant information. See http://govinfo.library.unt.edu/negp/index-1.htm.

82. Peterson (2006a) provides an overall evaluation of the program. Figlio and Rouse (2006) provide a detailed evaluation of student performance effects along with an attempt to sort out the causes for student gains.

83. Most state accountability systems emphasized rewards for good performance, while NCLB placed more emphasis on correcting poor performance. NCLB also introduced "adequate yearly progress," or AYP, as a measure of movement toward universal proficiency. Various aspects of this measure have proved to be the most controversial and have led to, among other things, consideration of value-added measurements.

84. The analysis of NAEP performance by Hanushek and Raymond (2005) incorporates consistent differences of states (using state fixed effects in the statistical analysis). It finds growth in performance with consequential accountability systems but not those having only report card systems. However, it also shows a widening of achievement gaps because performance gains by white students exceed those of blacks and Hispanics. Carnoy and Loeb (2002) use a different approach to identify the effects of accountability, relying on variations in the strength of the state accountability to estimate the impact. They also find that strong accountability measures lead to improved NAEP performance.

85. The Center on Education Policy (2007) assesses achievement growth in all states that have maintained a consistent testing program that allows direct comparisons since 2002. It finds that nine of the thirteen states with such data experienced more rapid growth after 2002 than before.

86. Center on Education Policy (2007).

87. Other concerns related to accountability measures have also been raised, including a potential narrowing of the curriculum, the possibility of cheating on tests, and the increased pressures on teachers and administrators. Jacob and Levitt (2003) and Chubb (2005).

88. Criterion-referenced tests are designed to indicate whether or not the particular standards are accomplished by students. The alternative testing structure is the norm-referenced test. These tests are generally not related to specific state content standards or curriculum but instead represent testing of general content that is assumed relevant across states. Norm-referenced tests typically provide information about how a given score relates to the distribution of results across the population, while scores on criterion-referenced tests can be thought of as what portion of the content standards has been mastered. As such, everybody could conceptually receive the highest score on a criterion-referenced test, while norm-referenced tests grade on the "curve."

89. One way to see the differences in performance is to compare state proficiency scores with proficiency according to the NAEP tests. The variation is startling, as seen in figure 3.8. National Center for Education Statistics (2007b).

90. Note again that there is no absolute standard of what "proficiency" means. The NAEP "proficient" standard is commonly thought to be a relatively high standard, beyond what most people envision should be for the requirements of NCLB.

91. National Center for Education Statistics (2007b).

92. Friedman (1962) and Friedman and Friedman (1980).

93. Extensive work by Thomas Nechyba and others shows that there are large gains in a society's welfare from breaking the link between residential location and school choice. See Nechyba (2006).

94. See Coons, Clune, and Sugarman (1970), pp. 256–68.

95. Coons and Sugarman (1978); Clune (1994).

96. Chubb and Moe (1990).

97. For a list of voucher programs in several states and cities, see the website of the National School Boards Association at www.nsba.org, accessed November 12, 2007.

98. *Holmes* (2006).

99. Greene and Winters (2007) and Greene (2007).

100. In Georgia, approximately nine hundred disabled students took advantage of a newly enacted voucher program in 2007—the program's first year. Stepp (2007).

101. See Rouse (1998); Witte (1999); Howell and Peterson (2002); Peterson (2003a). Being confident of identifying the causal impact of vouchers is often difficult, because the families choosing vouchers tend to differ in both observable and unobservable ways from those not choosing vouchers. One approach to separating the impacts of vouchers per se is to rely upon situations in which there is an excess number of people applying to the program and to compare students randomly admitted with those who applied for but were randomly excluded from the program.

102. Greene (2001a, 2001b); Figlio and Rouse (2006).

103. Finn, Manno, and Vanourek (2000); Hill (2006).

104. Hill (2009).

105. Center for Education Reform (2003).

106. Data on charter schools come through the Common Core of Data and can be found at http://nces.ed.gov/pubsearch/pubsinfo.asp?pubid=2007309 (accessed July 22, 2008).

107. National Center for Education Statistics (2007b), Indicator 32.

108. National Center for Education Statistics (2007b), Indicator 32.

109. See Hanushek, Kain, Rivkin, and Branch (2007) for an analysis of variations across schools and of the effects of age of the charter school involving Texas charter schools. The average North Carolina charter school appears less effective than the average traditional public school, whereas the average Florida charter school is on a par with the traditional government schools after a start-up phase of two to four years. Bifulco and Ladd (2006); Sass (2006). On the other hand, relying on comparisons between charter applicants in Chicago who were randomly accepted or randomly denied admission, Hoxby and Rockoff (2004) conclude that the city's charter schools significantly outperform their regular school counterparts.

110. Hoxby (2003). Jay Greene found similar effects resulting from the Florida Opportunity Scholarship program. Greene (2001a, 2001b).

111. A number of magnet schools grew out of desegregation of schools, since they offered a way of having more racially balanced schools without disturbing a general pattern of neighborhood schools. See Armor (1995).

112. Hoffman (2003). While more recent data exist for some states, it is not reliably reported for all; see http://nces.ed.gov/pubsearch/pubsinfo.asp?pubid=2007309 (accessed July 22, 2008).

113. Henke, Kaufman, Broughman, and Chandler (2000); Wirt et al. (2005), Indicator 3.

114. This research is reviewed and evaluated in Hanushek and Rivkin (2004, 2006).

115. Wayne and Youngs (2003) document the limitations of most studies on certification. Elements of the debate over the effectiveness of teacher certification can be traced through National Commission on Teaching and America's Future (1996); Abell Foundation (2001); Walsh (2002); Goldhaber and Brewer (2000, 2001); Darling-Hammond, Berry, and Thoreson (2001). Goldhaber and Brewer (2000) find, for example, that teachers with subject-matter certification in mathematics perform better than other teachers, while teachers with emergency certification perform no worse than teachers with standard certification, although Darling-Hammond, Berry, and Thoreson (2001) dispute the interpretation. Jepsen and Rivkin (2009) find small certification effects on teacher value added to mathematics and reading achievement.

116. Raymond, Fletcher, and Luque (2001); Raymond and Fletcher (2002); Decker, Mayer, and Glazerman (2004).

117. See, for example, Murnane et al. (1991), Grossman and Loeb (2008).

118. As discussed in chapter 9, these traditional teacher preparation programs have been heavily criticized.

119. Boyd et al. (2006); Kane, Rockoff, and Staiger (2006).

120. Further evidence shows that test scores in 1970 were significantly below those a decade earlier. See Congressional Budget Office (1986, 1987).

## Chapter 4
### Court Interventions in School Finance

1. The federal government played a minor role until the passage of the Elementary and Secondary Education Act of 1965, when for the first time significant federal funding was provided for K–12 education.

2. Some of the material in this chapter and chapter 5 is based upon Lindseth (2006).

3. *Brown I* (1954).

4. *Brown II* (1955), pp. 300–301.

5. Ferejohn (1995).

6. Because this is an active area of litigation, the legal landscape is always subject to change. Therefore, this discussion is necessarily based on the court rulings available through July 31, 2008, and the conclusions that can be drawn from them.

7. The extent of desegregation following *Brown* is analyzed in Welch and Light (1987); Clotfelter (2004); and Rivkin and Welch (2006).

8. *Milliken II* (1977), pp. 283–87.

9. *Jenkins III* (1995), p. 84.

10. *Jenkins III* (1995), p. 74.

11. *Milliken II* (1977).

12. *Milliken I* (1974), pp. 744–46.

13. *Milliken II* (1977), pp. 275–77.

14. *Milliken II* (1977), pp. 275–79.

15. *Milliken II* (1977), pp. 281–91.

16. See *Liddell* (1984). The St. Louis voluntary interdistrict transfer program was not imposed by the court, but was the result of a settlement agreement between the state, the city of St. Louis school district and a number of participating suburban school districts around St. Louis. The court did, however, order the state to pay the costs of the program. *Liddell* (1984), pp. 1301–1304.

17. *Little Rock* (1988), pp. 1307; *Little Rock* (1986), pp. 435–36.

18. *Brinkman* (1985) (Dayton); *Penick* (1981) (Columbus); *Reed* (1982) (Cleveland).

19. *Benton Harbor* (2002); see Haynes, Comer, and Hamilton-Lee (1988) about the program and its use.

20. *Yonkers Settlement* (2002). Total spending in the federal court case was obtained from the New York attorney general's office. With its federal court–ordered aid running out in June 2006, the Yonkers school district sued the state of New York in state court in an educational adequacy case in order to keep extraordinary state aid flowing. *Yonkers* (2005).

21. *Jenkins III* (1995), pp. 84–100.

22. *Jenkins III* (1995), pp. 100–103.

23. *Jenkins III* (1995), pp. 93–94.

24. *Jenkins III* (1995), pp. 101–2. With this handwriting on the wall, the Kansas City, Missouri, school district realized that it would be difficult to justify its remaining extraordinary state funding much longer, and negotiated a settlement with the state of Missouri that phased out any further special state payments over the next three years. *Jenkins* (1997), p. 595. At first, not wanting to give up its ability to levy a higher local property tax than other school districts in the state, the KCMSD did not want to be released from the supervision of the federal court. Later, however, state law was changed to permit the district to retain its high millage rate, and the district moved to have the case dismissed. Its motion was granted in 2003, thereby ending the Kansas City saga. *Jenkins* (2003).

25. *Yonkers Settlement* (2002); *Liddell Settlement* (1999); *Benton Harbor* (2002); *People Who Care* (2001).

26. Interestingly, with a few exceptions, such as *Hobson v. Hansen* in the District of Columbia, the federal court desegregation cases paid little attention in their remedial decrees to the allocation of funds between schools. In *Hobson v. Hansen*, the court monitored disparities in funding within the district and ruled that all schools had to spend amounts that fell within very narrow bands. *Hobson* (1967). At the time, the Washington, DC, schools were already overwhelmingly black, so the within-district distribution of funding had little to do with race.

27. The classic analysis of funding equity is Berne and Stiefel (1984). See also Murray, Evans, and Schwab (1998).

28. *Rodriguez* (1973). As with the evidence in many court cases, the extremes of the distribution are not very representative, even though they make the disparities vivid.

29. *Rodriguez* (1973), p. 37.

30. *Rodriguez* (1973), pp. 40–44.

31. *Rodriguez* (1973), p. 44.

32. *Rodriguez* (1973), p. 49.

33. *Rodriguez* (1973), p. 6.

34. It is important to note that *Rodriguez* (1973) addressed funding differences between school districts and not schools. Equality of funding of schools within a school district remained an important element of most school desegregation cases, and the federal courts did not hesitate to address such inequalities.

35. Coons, Clune, and Sugarman (1970).

36. *Serrano* (1976).

37. *Serrano* (1976), pp. 932–34.

38. *Serrano* (1976), p. 953.

39. *Serrano* (1976), pp. 948, 953, 958.

40. See history of New Jersey school finance litigation from 1970 through 1998 in *Abbott v. Burke* (1998), pp. 455–60.

41. See a state-by-state summary of school finance decisions in the website of the National Access Network at Teachers College, Columbia University, http://www.schoolfunding.info

42. See the analysis in Fischel (2006) and the separate studies by Hoxby (2001a) and Berry (2007).

43. The changes over time and their relationship to court decisions are traced in Murray, Evans, and Schwab (1998).

44. Equity lawsuits are still being filed in some states but normally as one count of a complaint that focuses primarily on "adequacy" claims. See, e.g., *Douglas County* (2003); *Williston* (2003); *Committee for Educational Equality* (2004); *Lobato* (2005); and *Abbeville County* (1999).

45. E.g., *Levittown* (1982); *Skeen* (1993); *McDaniel* (1981).

46. *Levittown* (1982), p. 50.

47. *Milliken I* (1974), p. 741.

48. See Hoxby (2001a).

49. Hoxby and Kuziemko (2004).

50. Fischel (1989, 2006).

51. Rebell (2001), p. 227; Heise (1995), p. 560.

52. *Levittown* (1982), p. 28. Part of the argument in the New York City adequacy case concerned "municipal overburden," or large demands for expenditures for things other than schools that limited the city's ability to fund its public

schools. This argument was rejected and has not been an important element of other suits. See Brazer and McCarty (1987).

53. In "adequacy" suits, even highly funded school districts may benefit. For example, in the late 1990s, the St. Paul and Minneapolis school districts both filed an adequacy suit against the state of Minnesota, even though both school districts enjoyed revenues for pupils significantly above the state average and among the highest of any school districts in the state. *St. Paul* (1999); *Minneapolis* (2000). In the most recent Missouri adequacy case, the city of St. Louis school district intervened to assert adequacy claims even though it is one of the highest-spending school districts in the state. See Missouri Department of Elementary and Secondary Education website, http://dese.mo.gov/divadm/Finance/historialindex.html, accessed October 10, 2007. According to recent statistics, New Jersey has the highest average per-pupil expenditures in the nation. *Education Week* (2005). The thirty-one Abbott districts that are the beneficiaries of the court's "adequacy" remedy spend almost $3,000 per pupil more than the "wealthy" school districts in the state. Mackey (2002), appendix A.4; see www.policy.rutgers.edu/cgs/PDF/NJPS02.pdf. Yet the New Jersey adequacy suit has gone on for over thirty years. E.g., *Abbott* (2002); see also *Millville* (2005).

54. Schrag (2003), p. 9.

55. Notwithstanding their different legal bases, the distinction between equity and adequacy cases is often blurred when evidence showing a lower level of resources in some districts than others is introduced to prove the inadequacy of the resources in the former districts. The courts have also used egalitarian measures, e.g., the opportunity to compete, in defining the standards of education required to meet constitutional mandates. Briffault (2007), pp. 27–28.

56. N.Y. Const. art. XI, §1 (New York) (emphasis added).

57. Mass. Const., part II, cl. 5, §2 (emphasis added).

58. Kan. Const., art. 6, §6 (emphasis added).

59. Wyo. Const. art. 7, §1 (emphasis added).

60. Wyo. Const. art. 7, §9 (emphasis added).

61. About one-fourth of state and local direct expenditure goes to K–12 education (along with another tenth for higher education). Most of state budgets for K–12 education are intergovernmental grants where the spending actually happens at the local level. U.S. Bureau of the Census (2007), tables 425 and 440.

62. In the federal court desegregation cases, there was no issue about the power of the federal courts to intervene in otherwise state and local matters. Under the supremacy clause, it was clear that when local laws, policies, and practices interfered with the plaintiffs' federal constitutional rights, they had to give way. See *Idaho* (2004), pp. 462–63, which distinguishes the powers of the federal courts to order appropriations or levy taxes from those of state courts under the supremacy clause and separation of powers doctrine.

63. *Pawtucket* (1995) (Rhode Island); *Edgar* (1996) (Illinois); *Coalition* (1996) (Florida); *Casey* (1979) (Pennsylvania); *Douglas County* (2007) (Nebraska);

*Oklahoma Education Association* (2007) (Oklahoma); *Pendleton* (2008) (Oregon); *Williams* (2007) (Kentucky); *Lobato* (2006) (Colorado). Courts in two other states, Alabama and Ohio, belatedly reached the same conclusion. Initially, the courts decided to hear the cases and, after trial, actually held that the education funding systems in those states were not adequate under their respective state constitutions. *DeRolph* (1997); *Harper* (1993). However, after struggling for a number of years with remedial issues, the highest court in both states ultimately decided that such questions were better left to the legislature, and dismissed the cases without ever deciding whether the violations had been remedied. *Lewis* (2003); *James* (2002).

64. E.g., *Chadha* (1983).

65. Hamilton (1788).

66. Home page of New York's Court of Appeals at http://www.courts.state.ny/ctapps/, accessed December 2, 2005.

67. Home page of Kansas Supreme Court at http://www.kscourts.org/supct/scbios.htm, accessed December 2, 2005.

68. See, for example, Volcansek (1981): "[M]any judges attain the office initially through midterm appointment and rarely leave due to electoral defeat." Even when the electoral structure provides retention elections as an opportunity to unseat judges, most judges are not ousted: in a ten-state study of judicial retention elections (in which voters were presented with a choice of allowing a sitting judge to remain in office or to be dismissed), researchers found that in 6,306 judicial retention elections held from 1964 through 1998, only fifty-six judges were not retained. Aspin (2007).

69. See Model Code of Judicial Conduct R. 4.1, comments 12–13 (2007).

70. The lower court judgment in the *CFE* case called for an additional $5.63 billion per year for operating funds and an additional $9.2 billion spread over five years for capital costs—implying that the legislature should make available an additional $7.4 billion each year. New York State had 7,119,000 households in 2003, yielding an average bill of over $1,000 per household (ignoring the fact that not all households pay taxes). Population figures come from U.S. Bureau of the Census (2006), table A-6.

71. *Montoy* (2004); *Robinson* (1976). Note the irony of this approach of the courts. They are saying that "if you do not give the schools more money, we will insist that they get no money."

72. N.Y. Const., art. VII, §7; Fla. Const., art. VII, §c. ("No money shall be drawn from the treasury except in pursuance of appropriation made by law"); Kan. Const., art. 2, §24 ("No money shall be drawn from the treasury except in pursuance of a specific appropriation made by law"); Kan. Const., art. 11, §5 ("No tax shall be levied except in pursuance of a law, which shall distinctly state the object of the same; to which object only such that shall be applied").

73. For papers on different strategies to close the achievement gap, see Peterson (2006b).

74. *Levittown* (1982), pp. 38–39. See also *Pawtucket* (1995), p. 57.

75. *Baker* (1962).

76. *Baker* (1962), p. 209.

77. *Edgar* (1996), p. 1183.

78. *Edgar* (1996), p. 1191.

79. *Coalition* (1996), p. 407.

80. E.g., *Montoy* (2005), p. 19. A common element of these decisions is that the court falls back on evidence from a "costing-out" study by experts who purportedly calculate the costs of a constitutionally adequate system. Thus, it is not the court itself that is saying what is needed, since it is relying on the experts. These studies are discussed in detail later.

81. *Lakeview* (2002), p. 507.

82. In the first Kentucky adequacy case, the court held: "To avoid deciding the case because of 'legislative discretion,' 'legislative function,' etc., would be a denigration of our own constitutional duty. To allow the General Assembly . . . to decide whether its actions are constitutional is literally unthinkable." *Rose* (1989), pp. 213–14. Apparently, this did not concern the court as much in the second go-around of adequacy litigation in Kentucky. It dismissed the second case brought a decade later on separation of powers grounds. *Williams* (2007).

83. *Rose* (1989) (Kentucky); *McDuffy* (1993) (Massachusetts); *Roosevelt* (1994) (Arizona—facilities only); *Campbell County* (1995) (Wyoming); *Claremont* (1997) (New Hampshire); *Abbott* (2002) (New Jersey); *DeRolph* (1997) (Ohio); *CFE II* (2003) (New York); *Montoy* (2005) (Kansas); *Lakeview* (2002) (Arkansas); *Columbia Falls* (2005) (Montana); *Harper* (1993) (Alabama); *Brigham* (1997) (Vermont); *Hoke County* (2004) (North Carolina); *Seattle* (1978) (Washington); *Kelly* (1979) (West Virginia); *Bradford* (1996).

84. *Brown I* (1954) and *Brown II* (1955) were concerned with intentional racial discrimination, which is not even an issue in either equity or adequacy lawsuits. No allegations, much less evidence, of racial or any other form of discriminatory conduct is required. All that plaintiffs must prove is that the education offered falls short of the court's interpretation of what constitutes an "adequate" education. Furthermore, in *Brown*, there were also no issues of coequal branches of government intruding on the rights and powers of other branches clearly granted to them under the constitution, such as the legislature's exclusive appropriations power under most state constitutions. Under the supremacy clause of the U.S. Constitution, the power of the federal courts to intervene in state and school district affairs to guarantee equal protection of the law to black students was clear.

85. See *DeGrasse I* (2001), p. 2.

86. *Baker* (1962). Michael Rebell, who led the plaintiffs' efforts in the New York adequacy case, credits the standards movement for much of the success of the adequacy movement: "The extensive education reform initiatives most states adopted to meet this challenge [low expectations] provided the courts workable criteria for developing the 'judicially manageable standards' that were necessary

to craft practical remedies in these litigations. . . . 'Adequate education' was no longer a vague notion that could be assumed almost in passing to describe almost any state education system." Rebell (2001). Indeed, Rebell (2004) goes further, claiming that "education adequacy lawsuits have become the driving force for achieving the aims of the standards-based reform movement."

87. "It is the clear policy of the State, as formulated by the Regents and SED, that all children can attain the substantive knowledge and master the skills expected of high school graduates." *DeGrasse I* (2001), pp. 35–36. See also *Montoy* (2003), pp. 84–85, 89.

88. P.L. 107–10, §1, 115 Stat. 1425, codified 20 USCS §6301 et seq.

89. E.g., *Columbia Falls* (2004), p. 25.

90. Outside of court, even adequacy proponents acknowledge that NCLB's ultimate achievement goals are "grossly unrealistic." Rebell and Wolff (2006), p. 16. See also Schaps (2007). Recently, one liberal-leaning group convened by the Economic Policy Institute began a public campaign to acknowledge that many other factors besides the schools were responsible for low achievement of disadvantaged students and that, instead of concentrating all of the attention of accountability on schools, attention should shift to these other basic factors. See "A Bolder, Broader Approach to Education," at http://www.boldapproach.org/statement.html [ accessed October 6, 2008].

91. Plaintiffs were less successful in Virginia, Wisconsin, and Oregon during this period. *Scott* (1994); *Kukor* (1989); *Vincent* (2000); and *Coalition for Equitable School Funding* (1991) (Oregon). In North Dakota, the supreme court decided, by a vote of three to two, that the state's funding system was unconstitutional. However, in that state, it takes a two-thirds vote to overturn a state statute; therefore, the state funding system survived the constitutional challenge. *Bismarck* (1994).

92. *West Orange-Cove* (2005); *Hancock* (2005).

93. *Williams* (2007); (Kentucky); *Pendleton* (2008) (Oregon); *Oklahoma Education Association* (2007) (Oklahoma); *Lobato* (2006) (Colorado). An Indiana lower court also dismissed an adequacy case on separation of powers grounds during this period, but the state supreme court reversed and reinstated the case. *Daniels* (2008).

94. *Crane* (2006).

95. *Campbell County III* (2008).

96. *Moore* (2007) (Alaska); *Committee for Educational Equality* (2007).

97. *Abbeville County* (2005); *Campbell County* (2006).

98. *CFE III* (2006), p. 13.

99. Actually, courts in both Washington and West Virginia struck down school financing systems in those states on adequacy grounds a decade earlier; however, no other courts followed suit until the sweeping decision in the *Rose* case. *Seattle* (1978); *Kelley* (1979).

100. For further background on the people involved in bringing the litigation, see Pankratz (2000), pp. 11–15.

101. *Rose* (1989), p. 562.

102. *Rose* (1989), p. 562.

103. *Rose* (1989), pp. 565–66.

104. *Rose* (1989), pp. 579–80.

105. E.g., *McDuffy* (1993), pp. 554–55.

106. *Rose* (1989), p. 211.

107. Hess (2007), p. 164.

108. The reforms enacted by the Kentucky legislature, together with the additional funding, ended the Kentucky case for almost a decade. However, in 2003, the Council for Better Education filed another adequacy suit, again "seeking adequate funding for elementary and secondary education." Relying on a cost study, plaintiffs claimed another $892 million a year was required to meet constitutional standards. ACCESS website, www.schoolfunding.Info/states/ky/2-23-04 Consolidated.php3. This second lawsuit, however, was dismissed on separation of powers grounds in 2006. *Williams* (2007).

109. The original 1997 court decision identifying the school districts entitled to the court remedy in *Abbott* initially named twenty-eight districts, but this number was subsequently expanded first to thirty and then to thirty-one.

110. *Abbott* (1990), p. 385.

111. *Abbott* (1998), pp. 473–74.

112. Goertz and Weiss (2007), p. 31: See also Mackey (2002), A.4. During the same year, the average school district in the country spent $8,044 per pupil.

113. Resch (2006). This does not count the billions of dollars of school construction aid the Abbott districts have also received.

114. Goertz and Weiss (2007), pp. 2, 10; see also Mackey (2002), p. 25. Interestingly, New Jersey has rated districts on the socioeconomic characteristics of their populations (including income, poverty status, education, and unemployment) since 1975. The Abbott districts are drawn from the lowest two rating categories, but some eighty other districts fall into the same categories but lack the Abbott designation. The distinguishing feature of Abbott districts was high academic failure rates, and this opens them up to much greater funding than available to the low-SES but non-Abbott districts. A listing of the Abbott districts is available at: http://www.state.nj.us/cgi-bin/education/abbotts/abbotturls .pl?string=code&maxhits=100 (accessed July 25, 2008). A description of the categories of SES backgrounds of districts, called District Factor Groups, is found at http://liberty.state.nj.us/education/finance/sf/dfg.shtml (accessed July 25, 2008). As previously indicated, Resch (2006) calculates that the Abbott districts spent $16,889 per pupil in 2004, compared to $11,952 by the other poor districts (all in 2000 dollars). In order to facilitate comparison to the calculations in chapter 3, the average Abbott district in 2004 was spending $20,336 when put in 2007 dollars.

115. Rural School and Community Trust (2003), p. 4; see http://www.ruraledu
.org/site/c.beJMIZOCIrH/b.497215/. In April 2007, plaintiffs also filed a motion
seeking additional funding for facilities in the Abbott districts. "Group Seeks Aid
for N.J. Facilities," *Education Week*, April 18, 2007, p. 18. In March 2008, the
state attorney general filed a motion seeking to end the case, contending that 2008
legislation addresses all the constitutional problems identified by the court. Plaintiffs, however, are likely to oppose it, and, in any event, it is not likely to be decided
by the court in the near future. "New Jersey A.G. Moves to Terminate Long-
Pending Abbott Litigation," ACCESS website at http://www.schoolfunding.info/
news/litigation/4-1-08Abbott.php3 (accessed April 2, 2008).

116. The case received attention all over the country. For example, the *CFE*
trial court's initial decision in favor of plaintiffs was cited almost a dozen times
by the Wyoming Supreme Court in its 2001 opinion, even though it is almost
unheard of for state supreme courts to cite the lower court decisions of other states
in their opinions. *Campbell County* (2001).

117. Accounts of the history of this case can be found in Williams (2005) and
Stern (2006).

118. Al Lindseth, one of this book's coauthors, headed up the Sutherland trial
team. In one of his prior cases, Lindseth had represented the state of Missouri in
negotiating an end to the state's involvement in the Kansas City school desegregation case. In a twist of irony, Missouri had previously been represented by Joel
Klein, who would become the chancellor of the New York City schools during
the *CFE* litigation.

119. *CFE I* (1995).

120. *CFE I* (1995), pp. 316–17.

121. Tr. 16234–35 (Murphy); ($9,500 per student for 1999–2000); Tr. 22728–
33 (Berne) (budget increases in 2000–2001); DX 19228, CFE trial record (hereafter citations to the testimony of witnesses in the trial of the *CFE* case will be by
transcript page number, e.g., Tr. 16234. Citations to trial exhibits will be by exhibit number, e.g., "DX10" for Defendants' Exhibit 10 and "PX5" for Plaintiffs'
Exhibit 5).

122. *DeGrasse I* (2001), p. 14. The *Economist*, commenting on the New York
*CFE* decision, wryly remarked that "this is a standard most congressmen probably
could not meet." *Economist* (November 7, 2004), p. 29.

123. *DeGrasse I* (2001).

124. With upstate Republicans controlling the senate and New York City Democrats the assembly and with the state facing a projected deficit of over $5 billion,
the legislature had been unable to agree upon any remedial legislation.

125. The CFE report was based on the Regents' Learning Standards, perhaps
the highest of the academic standards adopted by the fifty states, which CFE's
cost consultants had decided to use in conducting their study based on public
input at meetings held around the state. AIR/MAP Study, p. 4. Justice DeGrasse
approved the consultant's recommendations without reference to that part of the

*CFE II* ruling holding that the Regents' Learning Standards were not the appropriate standard. *DeGrasse IIA* and *IIB* (2005).

126. CFE, Report and Recommendations of Judicial Referees, November 30, 2004. Put another way, $17,200 per student translates into $344,000 for a class of twenty students.

127. *DeGrasse IIB* (2005), pp. 4–5.

128. *DeGrasse IIB* (2005), pp. 4–5.

129. *CFE III* (2006), p. 20.

130. Fessenden (2007). The political deal that resulted in this substantial increase in funding for New York City schools smacked of the political dealing condemned by CFE during the course of the litigation (referring to budget making largely controlled by the governor, the assembly speaker, and the senate majority leader). Although the new education finance formulas are purportedly "needs" based, the one-year budget deal in fact gave several wealthy "low needs" suburban districts some of the largest increases in state aid in return for the votes of their representatives in the state legislature.

131. *Edgewood* (1995).

132. For history of the school finance litigation in Texas to this point, see *West Orange-Cove* (2005), p. 12, and *Edgewood IV* (1995), pp. 726–29.

133. *West Orange-Cove* (2005), p. 5.

134. *West Orange-Cove* (2004).

135. *West Orange-Cove* (2004). Judge John Dietz's findings of fact on these issues are scattered throughout his 120-page opinion.

136. *West Orange-Cove* (2004), pp. 55–63.

137. *West Orange-Cove* (2005), p. 7.

138. *West Orange-Cove* (2005), p. 81.

139. *West Orange-Cove* (2005), p. 81.

140. *West Orange-Cove* (2005), p. 91.

141. *West Orange-Cove* (2005), p. 35.

142. *West Orange-Cove* (2005), p. 90.

143. *West Orange-Cove* (2005), p. 90.

144. *West Orange-Cove* (2005), pp. 88–89.

145. *West Orange-Cove* (2005), p. 89.

146. *West Orange-Cove* (2005), p. 47.

## CHAPTER 5
### PRACTICAL ISSUES WITH EDUCATIONAL ADEQUACY

1. *Rodriguez* (1973), p. 43.

2. See notes 56–60, chapter 4.

3. Dunn and Derthick (2007a), p. 331.

4. In California, for example, a voter referendum (Proposition 98) was adopted in 1988 to require a minimum annual funding level for the state's schools. For

a description of Proposition 98, see report of Legislative Analyst's Office dated February 2005 at www. lao.ca.gov/2005/prop-98-primer/prop-98-primer-020805 .htm. Similarly, Missouri has a constitutional requirement to put at least 25 percent of "state revenue" into "free public schools." *Committee for Educational Equality* (2007).

5. *CFE I* (1995), p. 317.

6. *CFE I* (1995), pp. 316–17.

7. *CFE I* (1995), pp. 316–17.

8. *DeGrasse I* (2001), p. 14.

9. *CFE II* (2003), p. 909.

10. The only cost study conducted during the litigation that relied on the actual court standard of adequacy was a professional judgment study conducted by Management Analysis and Planning, Inc. Based on the standard of adequacy taken from the *CFE I* opinion, the study concluded that the school district's existing budget was sufficient. This study was excluded on hearsay grounds by Justice DeGrasse, even though during the remedy phase he admitted and accepted the recommendations of similar studies based on the Regents' Learning Standards by the very same consultants. *Campaign for Fiscal Equity v. New York*, No. 111070 (N.Y. Sup. Ct. Apr. 13, 2000).

11. Hanushek (2003).

12. Other states get down to a level of micromanagement that few outside of the schools would believe. For example, state regulations in New Jersey ban the use of glossy paper for informational materials by districts. See Belluscio (2008).

13. Neira (2008) as found at: http://www.nysut.org/cps/rde/xchg/nysut/hs.xsl/ legislation_9423.htm (accessed July 25, 2008).

14. As noted, most adequacy cases also include an equity component, making it easy to combine the two when judging what is constitutionally required.

15. *Lakeview* (2002), p. 488.

16. Some more recent decisions have returned to these state minimum requirements. For example, in Texas, the court specifically cited accreditation standards and the ability of the school districts to meet them on existing revenue streams in denying adequacy claims. *West Orange-Cove* (2005), p. 47.

17. Wyo. Const. art. 7, §§1 and 9.

18. *Campbell County* (1995), p. 1279.

19. *Campbell County* (2001), p. 538.

20. During depositions of state experts prior to a 2005 trial in the Wyoming case, a common refrain was to ask them if there were not some "visionary" methods that had not yet been funded for Wyoming's schools. Interview with Wyoming Assistant Attorney General Michael O'Donnell, October 9, 2007.

21. *Education Week* (2006), p. 98. The referenced rankings are after per-pupil expenditures have been adjusted for regional cost of living differences.

22. *Campbell County III* (2008).

23. *Montoy* (2003), p. 10.

24. Hanushek (2007c); Armor (1995).

25. *Montoy* (2005A, 2005B). Faced with a court ready to close the state's schools if it did not comply, the Kansas legislature, after a protracted and bitter fight over two legislative sessions, increased K–12 education appropriations by approximately $755 million a year, which the court accepted in 2006. The case has been dismissed for the time being, but it remains to be seen whether it will be refiled if the ambitious outcome goals set by Judge Bullock are not achieved. *Montoy* (2006).

26. The use of state academic standards as the constitutional standard to both prove liability and "cost out" the remedy has led to what adequate litigation supporters call a "high minimum" standard. See Rebell (2006b), pp. 10–11. This is, of course, an oxymoron.

27. Rebell and Wolff (2006), p. 16.

28. Rebell (2006a), p. 49.

29. Costrell (2007), 281.

30. Heise (2007), pp. 266–67.

31. Costrell (2007), pp. 281–82.

32. See Ryan (2004); Hoff (2002); Tough (2006).

33. Rebell and Wolff (2006), pp. 7–8.

34. Peterson and Hess (2005); see also Rothschild (2005) (Kansas); "Governor's Commission Considers Watering Down Regents Standards," Campaign for Fiscal Equity website, 2003, at www.cfequity.org/10–1–03govcommission.htm (New York); Gewertz (2004) (New Jersey).

35. Arizona has been ordered to increase spending on facilities, *Roosevelt* (1994), but a similar suit to require it to raise spending for school operations was dismissed. *Crane* (2006).

36. Rebell (2001), p. 230 and p. 257, note 80.

37. Staros (1994), pp. 498–99. See, e.g., *Coalition* (1996), p. 405.

38. *Edgar* (1996); *Coalition* (1996); and *Honore* (2003).

39. Dunn and Derthick (2007), p. 334.

40. *Hancock* (2005), pp. 1150–51; see also *West Orange-Cove* (2005), p. 91.

41. Coleman et al. (1966).

42. Carneiro and Heckman (2003); Fryer and Levitt (2004).

43. For example, Caroline Hoxby of Stanford University has estimated that 93 percent of the variation in student test scores is attributable to family and neighborhood differences, with just a little over 3 percent due to school variables. Hoxby (2001b), p. 98.

44. *Freeman* (1992), p. 491.

45. *Milliken I* (1974), pp. 744–46.

46. *Jenkins III* (1995), pp. 101–2.

47. *CFE I* (1995), p. 318.

48. Not every court agrees with this approach. Ironically, the same day it was holding the state liable for failing to overcome these adverse socioeconomic influ-

ences in New York City, a majority of the New York Court of Appeals, in an opinion also written by Chief Judge Kaye, was doing the opposite in another adequacy case involving the Rochester, New York, schools. This time, after quoting the words of *CFE I* about the need to exercise "caution" in judging outcomes because of the "myriad of factors" influencing them, it ruled for the state, holding that the claims asserted did not rest on a lack of funding, but "on the failure to mitigate demographics." That, of course, is the very same thing the court was holding the state liable for in the *CFE* case the same day—the failure to mitigate the demographics of New York City's large poor and minority public school enrollment. *Paynter* (2003).

49. Even in those few instances that have claimed success in closing the gap, Richard Rothstein believes they are "upon examination, unfounded." Rothstein (2004), p. 83. Evidence from intensive study of California schools shows some schools that are relatively more successful than others, but none that can maintain an entire school at state proficiency levels for two years. Sonstelie (2007); Pérez et al. (2007).

50. U.S. Department of Education (2007), table 175.

51. Hanushek, Kain, and Rivkin (2004).

52. Rothstein (2004), pp. 146–47.

53. *Campbell County* (1995), pp. 1258–59; *Campbell County* (2001), p. 538.

54. When accused by the defense of "throwing" money at the problems, the New Jersey Supreme Court left no doubt as to what level of government was responsible for any waste: "[W]e require that the [State] Commissioner use his statutory and regulatory authority to ensure that the increased funding that we have ordered today be put to optimal educational use." *Abbott* (1997), p. 442.

55. *Montoy* (T.C. Order dated Dec. 2, 2003), pp. 79–80; *Hoke County* (2004), p. 16.

56. DX17098; Tr. 3033–35 (Tames testimony), CFE trial record; the National Commission on Teaching and America's Future, headed by plaintiffs' expert, Linda Darling-Hammond, echoed similar concerns, describing the board's hiring procedures as "dysfunctional and cumbersome." DX19469, p. 1, CFE trial record.

57. DX19469, p. 1, CFE trial record.

58. DX19182; *CFE App. Div.* (2002), p. 23.

59. Tr. 3320–22 (Ward testimony); PX2026A, ¶¶86–87 Zardoya witness statement, CFE trial record.

60. PX 1155; PX 1175; PX1246; Tr. 15396–98 (Donohue testimony) and Tr. 4139–41 (Spence testimony), CFE trial record.

61. PX 1167; PX 3159; PX 3160B, ¶¶ 80–81; Tr. 15409–11 (Donohue testimony), CFE trial record.

62. Einhorn (2006).

63. DX 11170, CFE trial record.

64. Tr. 19959–21650, CFE trial record. Lawyer Edward Stancik headed a staff of sixty that did nothing but investigate fraud and corruption in the New York City schools.

65. *New York Post* (2004); Schrag (2003), p. xi.

66. There have been exceptions to this general trend. For example, in New Hampshire, the court displayed some deference to the legislature by first instructing it to define "adequacy" before conducting a costing-out study to determine how much it would cost to provide. *Londonderry* (2006). In Montana, the court also directed the legislature to define adequacy, but qualified its delegation of authority by also stating that, in its opinion, any legitimate definition would require additional funding. *Columbia Falls* (2005). Both states have now enacted legislation defining "adequacy." How much deference the courts will give these definitions remains undecided.

67. Cost studies have been a central part of the remedial orders in all these states. Yet in none of these cases have the courts ordered studies to determine if existing funds were being utilized in an "efficient" manner, despite the explicit requirement in several of their constitutions that the system of financing education be, among other things, "efficient." The constitutions of the states of Arkansas, Kentucky, Maryland, New Jersey, West Virginia, and Wyoming, along with six other states, all use the term "efficient" to describe, at least in part, the education systems they require.

68. See *Montoy* (2003) ("that dog won't hunt"), p. 93; *Lakeview* (2002), pp. 488–89.

69. E.g., Augenblick, Myers, Silverstein, and Barkis (2002).

70. Some courts, such as those in Kansas City, New Jersey, and Wyoming, have not been shy when it comes to involvement in the local decisions—but it has not been confrontational. In these cases, the courts have retained control of the remedy phase of the trial and have pegged the spending that is ordered to court testimony on the costs of achieving the goals of the judgment. In these, the local districts have essentially submitted programmatic requests to be funded by the state.

71. *CFE II* (2003), pp. 919–20. Dissenting Judge Read had no problem seeing through this faulty reasoning, stating: "Plaintiffs' proof of a causal link amounts to nothing more than an article of faith; the New York City public school system is not what we would like it to be or what it needs to be, and more money is always better; therefore, the system's shortcomings are attributable to inadequate funding, for which the State is necessarily responsible because of the obligations placed upon it by the Education Article." As Judge Read recognized, "This is not proof of a causal connections, it is a recipe for 'limitless litigation.' " *CFE II* (2003), p. 956 (Dissent).

72. Will (2005).

73. Starr (2007), p. 314.

74. See, for example, *Carlson v. City of Helena*, 101 P. 163 (Mont. 1909): "[A]ny attempt by a mere colorable dispute to obtain the opinion of the court

upon a question of law which a party desires to know for his own interest or his own purposes when there is no real or substantial controversy between those who appear as adverse parties to the suit, is an abuse which courts of justice have always reprehended, and treated as a punishable contempt of court" (citation omitted).

75. In those few states where the state education authorities line up on the state's side, it makes a significant difference in the defense of the case. In both Texas and Massachusetts, the state education agencies supported their respective state-level systems of education. That support was undoubtedly critical in convincing the appellate courts that their respective "systems of education" were adequate.

76. Plaintiffs are also supported in their effort by the nation's education schools. Because they are beholden to the public school establishment, most research from education schools supports the existing system of delivering education services. See Moe (2001c). It is a rare professor of education who is brave enough to bite the hand that feeds him. Therefore, while plaintiffs have their pick of local and state educators to testify about the need for more money or university professors to testify about programs that could, according to them, solve everything if only the state was willing to pay for them, defendants do not have that advantage. The state will almost always have a difficult time in finding both lay and expert witnesses willing to take on the educational establishment.

77. PX519, pp. 2–3; Tr. 994 (Sobol), CFE trial record.

78. DX19529, p. 705260.

79. Thomas Sobol, Robert Berne, Henry Levin, David Monk, and Linda Darling-Hammond.

80. *Grand Forks Herald* (2005).

81. Tom Decker deposition, in *Williston* (2003), pp. 291–95. The National Access Network is housed at Teachers College, Columbia University. Its activities are described at http://www.schoolfunding.info/index.php3 (accessed September 24, 2008).

82. The "State," represented by the attorney general, argued that the $140 million increase in education appropriations was within the proper discretion of the legislature and was therefore constitutional; the governor was represented by another lawyer from the attorney general's office, who took the opposite position, contending the increased appropriation was insufficient. The state board and commissioner of education, represented by still other lawyers, "strongly" disagreed with portions of the legislation, but were willing to accept the extra $140 million as an interim measure (the "bird in the hand" theory) pending another "cost study." *Montoy* (2005), pp. 4–5.

83. *Crane* (2002).

84. *Consortium* (2005), Hoff (2006).

85. *Crawford* (2007).

86. In an exception to this general rule, taxpayers were allowed to intervene in the Missouri school finance case. *Committee for Educational Equity* (2007) (order dated Nov. 8, 2006). Perhaps because of the added defense against the suit, the lower court dismissed the case completely.

## CHAPTER 6
### THE EFFECTIVENESS OF JUDICIAL REMEDIES

1. Frederick Hess of the American Enterprise Institute perhaps put it best: "When it comes to practical outcomes, we know little about the actual impact of adequacy suits on student achievement, education policy, education decision making, or the shape of school reform. At best, proponents can document an increase in school spending in particular locales." Hess (2007), p. 161.

2. For example, in an op-ed piece extolling the benefits of adequacy lawsuits, Michael Rebell cites more resources, "sweeping educational improvements," and "important new approaches," but remains silent as to whether such lawsuits have resulted in improved student achievement in any state in which they have been brought. Rebell (2004).

3. More attempts have been made to study the results of equity cases. Downes (1992) investigates whether the early alterations in California arising from the *Serrano v. Priest* case had any impact on variations in student test performance but finds no significant impact on performance. Hanushek and Somers (2001) pursue a different tack. They consider whether variations in spending within a state are ultimately reflected in earnings variations when the students progress into the labor market, again finding little or no impact. A series of specific state studies consistently show small and insignificant effects of court orders on achievement. Flanagan and Murray (2004); Downes (2004); Cullen and Loeb (2004); Duncombe and Johnston (2004).

4. The source of all the NAEP scores cited in this chapter is the National Center for Education Statistics, which can be accessed at http://nces.ed.gov/nationsreportcard/.

5. The growth in NAEP scores over time for these samples is consistent with the prior discussion of long-term trends in scores. Looking back to the longer time series, gains in both reading and math are smallest for seventeen-year-olds (and negative for science), larger for thirteen-year-olds, and largest for nine-year-olds. In other words, any gains in younger grades appear to be temporary and have not resulted in higher achievement for students at the end of their schooling. This pattern is very consistent with the results from international tests, where U.S. students score highly in lower grades compared to other developed countries but slip dramatically in relative terms in testing in later grades. No state-level data on seventeen-year-olds exist, forcing us to concentrate just on younger grades.

6. This is one of the major premises of NCLB that requires the reporting of state test results for a number of different categories of students, including eth-

nicity, family economic circumstances, and other characteristics, so that low performance by any group will not be masked by overall student averages.

7. See, for example, Schrag (2003), p. xvii (*Rose* case "most successful in attaining equity or adequacy in funding" and "great model for the national movement").

8. Poggio (2000). Others have cited some test score increases in Kentucky, although they acknowledge difficulty in determining how significant the increases have been or in attributing them to Kentucky's reform efforts because of assessment changes in 1999. They also acknowledge a failure to close the achievement gap between black and white students. Lusi and Goldberg (2000), pp. 231–32. Others have found no improvement. Clark (2003).

9. Koretz and Barron (1998).

10. Poggio (2000), pp. 78–80.

11. Average scale scores are used for the analysis because they reflect actual improvements or declines from year to year. Using other measures, such as changes in the percentage deemed "proficient," to assess long-term trends can be misleading because the same overall increases in scale scores can lead to widely varying results in the percentage deemed "proficient." See Goertz and Weiss (2007), pp. 22, 33–34, for an explanation as to why it is preferable to use scale scores in analyzing achievement trends.

12. We have not relied on test scores for economically disadvantaged students in our evaluation since NAEP did not separately report such scores until after the remedy had been in place almost a decade.

13. Weston and Sexton (2007), p. 13, table 5.

14. There are also serious questions about whether the accountability and other changes instituted after the *Rose* decision have had much impact, which may be one of reasons for the relative lack of improvement in student achievement. Hess (2007).

15. Spending data are found in U.S. Department of Education (2008), table 174. State cost differences come from the National Center for Education Statistics, "Comparable Wage Index Data Files and Documentation," found at: http://nces.ed.gov/edfin/adjustments.asp (accessed July 23, 2008).

16. The court judgment in Wyoming required that the legislature commission a cost study every five years. In 2005, a change in methodology to the "evidence-based" approach was introduced, and the resulting study called for substantial increases in resources. See Odden et al. (2005). This methodology is discussed in the next chapter, along with how the Wyoming school districts actually used the added funding.

17. Odden et al. (2008); Barron (2006)

18. Barron (2006).

19. Hanushek (2006c), p. 298.

20. For the sake of consistency, we have used the 1992 scores as the pre-remedy score, although the significant additional funding did not begin to flow until 1996. With one exception, they are the latest NAEP latest scores available prior to the funding of the remedy, and enable us to compare NAEP scores in Wyoming during the trial of the *Campbell County* case with recent post-remedy test scores. 1994 test scores are available for fourth grade reading, but do not materially change the trends found using test scores from 1992 through 2007.

21. Hanushek (2006c).

22. This figure is not adjusted for state cost differences. Doing so would push all of the state lines higher relative to the national average, although the comparisons across the states would remain essentially the same. U.S. Department of Education (2008), table 174.

23. Hanushek (2006c).

24. *Education Week* (2007c), p. 48. Kentucky did even worse, ranking thirty-fifth out of fifty states. Massachusetts, much to its credit and consistent with our findings, ranked very well, finishing first among the fifty states. New Jersey also did well, finishing second, but since the remedy there was not statewide, but limited to thirty-one school districts, no clear conclusions can be drawn from the comparisons. The high ranking there may be more attributable to improvements in the non-Abbott districts than in those districts benefiting from the remedy.

25. Montana, North Dakota, and South Dakota have also been the subject of adequacy suits. In South Dakota, the case had not been decided at this writing. In Montana, the court ruled for plaintiffs, but the funding increases possibly attributable to the influence of the court order have been insignificant compared to those in Wyoming. North Dakota has also experienced recent increases in education appropriations, albeit not as a result of any court order. In any event, these relatively small increases have been very recent, and it is too early to determine whether they are having any impact on student achievement. *Columbia Falls* (2005); *Williston* (2003).

26. In 2008, the Wyoming Supreme Court dismissed the adequacy case, finding that the state legislature was funding the "thorough and efficient" education required by the state constitution. Focusing almost entirely on inputs and resources, the court's discussion about whether the massive resource increases in Wyoming resulted in any improvement in student outcomes is confined to a single sentence of its fifty-four-page decision, in which it stated only that "Wyoming ranked as one of the highest states in the nation for schools making adequate yearly progress under the federal No Child Left Behind program." *Campbell County III* (2008), p. 28. Yet, as we have just shown, Wyoming, especially in comparison to its lower-funded neighbors, has in fact made very little, if any, progress according to the NAEP.

27. Mackey (2002), p. A.4; Goertz and Weiss (2007), p. 12.

28. In 2005, New Jersey's per-pupil expenditures were $14,117, more than any other state and over 60 percent higher than the national average. When adjusted for state wage cost differences, its spending ranked third highest of the fifty states (behind Vermont and Wyoming) but still 60 percent more than the national average. U.S. Department of Education (2008), table 174, and Taylor and Fowler (2006).

29. Mackey (2002), p. A.4.

30. *Education Week* (2005), p. 41.

31. Evers and Clopton (2006), p. 136, and Resch (2006).

32. Evers and Clopton (2006), pp. 133–36.

33. Coate and VanderHoff (1999).

34. Schrag (2003), p. 121.

35. Goertz (2007), p. 2.

36. Both the governor and commissioner of education attribute the large gains in 2007 to the preschool and other early childhood programs funded by, among other things, the court remedy. See "New Jersey Fourth-Graders Among Top Readers in Nation," a press release issued by the New Jersey Department of Education, September 25, 2007. However, other important developments have also taken place in the last several years, such as the realignment of the curriculum in the Abbott districts to conform to the state academic standards, that could account for the more recent improvements in test scores. As state Commissioner of Education David C. Hespe said in 2001, in remarking on revised math and language arts tests being implemented in 2003: "Greater gains can and will be achieved as schools continue to align their curriculum with our new higher standards." "New Jersey, A Court Fight over Funding Has Melded with the Standards Movement to Shape State Policy," in *Education Week* (2001), p. 156.

37. In their 2007 study of New Jersey achievement based primarily on state test results, Margaret Goertz and Michael Weiss also found some improvement in NAEP scores at the fourth grade level between 1994 and 2005, but little or no improvement at the eighth grade level during the same period. However, several assumptions introduce questions about the validity of these conclusions. First, it assumes the "central city" scores are those of the Abbott districts, which may not be true. Second, it looks only at all student test scores, and not at the scores of minority groups that make up most of the enrollment of the Abbott districts. Most important, it only compares "central city" NAEP scores in New Jersey with the scores of the "urban fringe" or suburban areas and the state as a whole, which tells us nothing about whether the unprecedented remedial efforts in New Jersey have increased the achievement of its poor and minority students relative to the rest of the country. Goertz and Weiss (2007), p. 26.

38. Goertz and Weiss (2007), pp. 21–24. Interestingly, using a different approach to investigate the changes in performance of Abbott districts, Resch (2006) finds some evidence of improved performance of the top achievers on eighth grade

state assessments. She finds no impacts, however, on high school tests and negative performance changes on the SAT.

39. Again, the simple picture on high school examinations is consistent with the more sophisticated analysis in Resch (2006).

40. Fine et al. (2007), p. 15. See http://ielp.rutgers.edu/docs/SRA_Policy_Brief _final.pdf (accessed July 30, 2008).

41. Gewertz (2006).

42. Greene and Winters (2005); National Center for Education Statistics (2008a), Indicator 21.

43. Rebell (2007), p. 33.

44. Gewertz (2006); see also Cooperman (2007) who states that the "numbers are cooked" on New Jersey graduation rates. As noted previously, in the labor market, the characteristics of GED recipients appear to be closer to dropouts than to graduates.

45. Goertz and Weiss (2007), pp. 26, 32.

46. Costrell (2007), p. 278.

47. To put this gain into the perspective of chapters 1 and 2, it amounts to approximately one-half standard deviation of performance—the kind of gain that would move the United States to the top-scoring countries on the international tests.

48. See note 24, chapter 6. As previously noted, *Education Week* ranked Massachusetts first among the fifty states in its success at improving K–12 education.

49. *Hancock* (2005), pp. 1149–51.

50. The decision in *Hancock* (2005), pp. 1142–45, suggested that Massachusetts also abolished the practice of teacher tenure. This appears to be largely a matter of semantics, however. Ballou and Podgursky (1997), pp. 121–24, note that Massachusetts officially eliminated tenure, but that they effectively just renamed it. There are a few conditions for continued employment, but they are easy to meet.

51. *Hancock* (2005), pp. 432, 438–42. Kentucky also enacted accountability and other nonfinancial measures to go along with increases in education funding. However, while Massachusetts has been vigorous in its enforcement of standards, Kentucky has been less so. Hess (2007).

52. While several states have no doubt experienced substantial increases in K–12 education expenditures as the result of adequacy litigation, the net financial effect of such decisions is not as clear on a nationwide basis. According to a recent study by Dr. Christopher Berry of the Harris School of Public Policy at the University of Chicago, what he refers to as "school finance equalization court decisions" in favor of plaintiffs have resulted in a substantial increase in *state* spending on K–12 education. However, he is uncertain as to how much these increases in state aid have been offset by reductions in local dollars spent on education. Therefore, he concludes that "it is not certain whether local changes in education revenue

after school finance judgments offset increases partially or completely." Berry (2007), pp. 214, 223.

1. John Myers, partner in Augenblich & Myers consulting firm, stated: "Historically adequacy was determined politically using input measures and available resources. . . . Now adequacy is technically determined and output oriented" (Dunn and Derthick [2007b]). Indeed, consultants do not limit themselves to determining "needed" inputs. They also decide upon the desired outcomes in most such studies. For example, in the New York study sponsored by CFE, the outcomes on which the study was based were specified by the consultants after obtaining input from public forums organized by CFE, and bore little, if any, relationship to the constitutional standard enunciated by the court.

2. The same rules apply to making decisions in other policy areas, although the actual application is generally beyond current knowledge. For example, one could conceptually judge whether spending more on education is better than spending a dollar more on health care by comparing the gain in society's well-being from a dollar spent on education and health care. But in reality we have poor measures of society's "well-being" and how well-being is affected across areas. Thus, we ask legislatures to make their best judgments about how limited public money should be allocated between, among other things, education and health care.

3. See, for example, Slavin (2007).

4. A review of past costing-out studies can be found in *Education Week*'s annual report for 2005, *Education Week* (2005). See also the ACCESS Project website (www.schoolfunding.info), a project of the Campaign for Fiscal Equity (CFE), the plaintiffs in the New York City adequacy case.

5. This explains why the websites for advocacy organizations give top billing to costing-out studies. For an example, see the ACCESS Project website.

6. See, e.g., *CFE II* (2003); *CFE III* (2006); *Montoy* (2005A).

7. Augenblick & Myers, who have conducted costing-out studies in more than twenty states, were hired by the Kansas legislature, and concluded that an "adequate" education in Kansas would cost approximately $850 million over what the state was spending at the time. The study and its results were introduced into evidence at trial, and the court held they were binding against the state, ruling that they showed the state was underfunding education to the tune of about $850 million. The Kansas Supreme Court also held the state to the study's conclusions and affirmed Judge Bullock's order. *Montoy* (2005). Subsequently, the amount required was reduced to approximately $755 million based on the results of another costing-out study. *Montoy* (2006).

8. See, for example, the discussion and analysis of poverty and California school performance in Sonstelie (2007) and Loeb, Bryk, and Hanushek (2008).

9. Hanushek (2003).

10. As noted, the research on spending and achievement does not imply, as some critics say, that "money never matters" or that "money cannot matter."

11. An early and insightful discussion of the importance of skill differences is found in Murnane and Nelson (1984).

12. Health care, on the other hand, has many parallels to education. Not surprisingly, the best way to provide health care services is subject to many of the same controversies.

13. An example of this is Augenblick Palaich & Associates (2003), p. II-3.

14. Examples of this approach include the following costing-out study reports: Augenblick & Myers (2002b); Augenblick, Myers, Silverstein, and Barkis (2002); Augenblick Palaich & Associates (2003); AIR/MAP (2004); Picus, Odden, and Fermanich (2003); Verstegen and Associates (2003). A majority of these reports are available from the websites of the relevant states.

15. Often the consultants will enhance the teacher salaries if they believe the prevailing salary schedules are lower than the surrounding states, e.g., Augenblick Palaich & Associates (2003). Such an approach is obviously arbitrary (but one-sided since it always involves raising salaries). As noted, variations in teacher salaries are unrelated to effectiveness in the classroom, and little research suggests that changing the average salary will affect student outcomes. See Hanushek and Rivkin (2004, 2006); Hoxby and Leigh (2004).

16. For example, Augenblick & Myers (2002a), appendix D-1 (instructions to professional Judgment School Site Panel members).

17. *Campbell County* (1995), p. 1279.

18. Augenblick Palaich & Associates (2003), p. IV-15.

19. The terms *cost, cost efficiency,* and *efficiency* are often used interchangeably to indicate the minimum spending required to achieve a given outcome. For example, in comparing different programs that are designed to achieve the same outcome, the cost-efficient one would be that requiring the least spending. It is important, however, to understand that the cost-efficient choice applies only to alternative ways of achieving the same objective. If one wished to, say, compare programs that yielded different outcomes, the efficient one would not necessarily be the one with the smallest expenditure.

20. See notes 16 and 18, this chapter.

21. *Hancock* (2004), p. 283.

22. Augenblick and Myers (2003), p. IV-5.

23. Interview with Deidre Roney, counsel for state during Hancock trial.

24. *Hancock* (2004), pp. 283–84.

25. AIR/MAP (2004), p. 3, note 12. This "warning label" contrasts sharply with the claim in the November 2002 AIR/MAP proposal that their study would answer the question, "What does it actually cost to provide the resources that

each school needs to allow its students to meet the achievement levels specified in the Regents' Learning Standards?" See Hanushek (2006c).

26. Augenblick Palaich & Associates (2003).

27. *Committee for Educational Equality* (2004), State Exhibits 761, 766.

28. AIR/MAP Study, p. 7.

29. Williams (2005), p. 28; Williams (2007), p. 202.

30. See Odden, Fermanich, and Picus (2003).

31. See Odden, Picus, Goetz, and Fermanich (2006). This analysis is similar to an earlier study conducted by the same consultants for the state of Wyoming. Odden et al. (2005).

32. For more detail on the problems with these analyses, see Hanushek (2007a).

33. Odden, Picus, Goetz, and Fermanich (2006) provide information about the "effect size" of each program they select. The effect size indicates how large of a change in student outcomes could be expected from the program, where change is measured in standard deviations of the outcome. The figure simply translates these changes into movements in the overall performance distribution. For example, a change of one standard deviation would move a person at the middle of the distribution to the 84th percentile of the distribution.

34. Odden, Picus, Goetz, and Fermanich (2006) report that class size reduction would improve student achievement by 0.34 standard deviations. We simply report the implied change in achievement. This magnitude of change is equivalent to moving up 13 percentiles in the distribution—the result shown in the figure.

35. The technical basis for this conclusion comes from their assessment of the "effect sizes," or the predicted standard deviations of improvement in achievement. Their model school is reported to have a total effect size of 3.0 to 6.0 standard deviations, a completely implausible outcome that would place the average beyond the 99.9 percentile of the prior distribution.

36. The consultants often justify their inclusion of all the recommended programs as being required to achieve "adequacy." However, the notion that the *average* student in a state must score at, for example, the 99th percentile, in order for the education to be "adequate" is ludicrous.

37. Odden et al. (2008) reports on the results of a study for the Wyoming legislature about district spending after acceptance of their prior study on an evidence-based funding for Wyoming schools (Odden et al. 2005). The follow-up study is available at: http://legisweb.state.wy.us/2008/interim/schoolfinance/schoolfinance.htm (accessed July 24, 2008). A similar analysis for Arkansas supports the same general findings.

38. Odden et al. (2008).

39. The same question, of course, arises with the professional judgment model, where there is little reason to believe that schools actually array themselves in the ways chosen by the panels. One difference, however, is that the professional judgment panels seldom get into any programmatic detail but instead stop at ge-

neric descriptions of numbers of people of specific kinds and perhaps numbers of computers and the like.

40. See, for example, Augenblick & Myers (1997); Myers and Silverstein (2005); Standard & Poor's School Evaluation Service (2004).

41. In some instances, there may be a considerable difference between spending levels in the "successful" districts, and the issue arises as to whether the high spenders, or a portion of them, should be eliminated because they are not efficiently using the funds available to them. This was a major issue in the CFE case. While the trial court rejected the use of an "efficiency screen," the New York Court of Appeals reversed and approved the state's cost study, which eliminated the top half of the spenders in calculating the spending levels needed to be a "successful" district. *CFE III* (2006), pp. 18–20.

42. Another potentially important issue is whether the analysis has identified schools that are truly successful. The test score measures that are used to pinpoint those schools doing well are often fraught with error. As pointed out in terms of school accountability, this can lead to some schools being identified as good during one year and bad during another. See Kane and Staiger (2002) and Peterson and West (2003).

43. Thompson and Silvernail (2001); Carey (2002).

44. Bruce Baker, who reviewed weights for the evaluation of school finance systems by *Education Week*, stated: "Rarely is there any empirical evidence to influence weighting. . . . [T]here are many layers of arbitrary and political decisions applied in each weight" (Park 2005). Even Michael Rebell, a strong proponent of costing-out studies, acknowledges that such weightings have little empirical or scientific basis. Rebell (2006b), pp. 56–57.

45. *Hancock* (2004), p. 280.

46. In economics and other quantitative sciences, one variable is said to be a function of another if its level is shown to vary, whether positively or negatively, in response to changes in another variable. For example, when the price of gas increases, demand for gas goes down; demand for gas is therefore a function of price. The cost function label reflects the assumption made in these studies that the level of required spending in a district varies predictably along with various observable characteristics of its students and the desired achievement level.

47. Cost function analyses generally employ standard regression models but at times use alternative methods that weight certain districts, those presumed to be more efficient in their spending, more heavily. See, for example, Gronberg, Jansen, Taylor, and Booker (2004). These alternatives also suffer from a series of problems, but they are not explicitly discussed here. For a critique of cost function studies, see Costrell, Hanushek, and Loeb (2008).

48. Guthrie and Rothstein (1999), p. 223.

49. Duncombe (2006) argues that one way to assess these models is measurement of "predictive validity." Thus, if the predicted spending by districts in years other than those on which the estimation is based is close to actual spending levels,

he would say the models are validated. However, this only shows a continuation of the school spending patterns of the past, and not that such funding was needed to reach any particular achievement levels. The validity of cost functions should be based not on their ability to predict future expenditures but on the ability to predict the outcome improvements that would result from different levels of spending.

50. Hanushek (2003). These studies are generally referred to as "production function" analysis. They are statistical analyses (using many of the same approaches as the "cost function" analyses discussed here), except they generally try to explain variations in achievement across students, schools, and districts. The cost function studies try to explain variations in spending.

51. A more complete description of the problems of the cost function estimation and the comparison with the production function approach is found in Costrell, Hanushek, and Loeb (2008).

52. The studies into the finance and governance of California schools were part of an overall evaluation of how to improve the state's schools. See Loeb, Bryk, and Hanushek (2008).

53. Imazeki (2007, 2008).

54. Guthrie and Springer (2007a), p. 106.

55. Imazeki (2007, 2008) and Loeb, Bryk, and Hanushek (2008).

56. There is nothing special about the subject, the grade, or the state, and using a different grade or test would still yield a picture qualitatively similar to figure 7.3.

57. Baker (2006) included measures for state aid/pupil, income/pupil, the resident tax ratio, and the population aged sixty-five or greater in order to eliminate differences in the efficiency of spending across districts. Duncombe (2007) included measures of the fiscal capacity of the district and voter turnout.

58. Both methods have to deal with the fact that typically there are no districts that achieve at the performance levels defined as adequate. In such cases, the consultants typically assume that the relationship between spending and achievement they identify remains the same regardless of achievement level. That is, if they observe proficiency levels to be increasing by ten percentage points for every additional $1,000 per pupil spent in a set of districts with a maximum proficiency rate of 60 percent, they assume that the relationship remains unchanged as districts near the target of 100 percent proficiency. There is, of course, no way to know whether that is true.

59. Cost function analyses make assumptions about the way in which various factors based on student characteristics, such as the percentage of low-income students in a district, affect required costs. However, it is unclear, for example, whether the evidence from Westchester County is at all informative about how to improve student achievement in the Bronx or about precisely what adjustments would have to be made to account for the many differences in the two locations. Yet that is exactly the kind of analytic leap of faith that a cost function study

conducted in New York State was forced to make, leading one study to conclude, apparently seriously, that New York City needed to spend 3.5 times as much per student to obtain the same level of achievement as other districts in New York State. Duncombe and Yinger (1998). Their subsequent estimates of adequacy for New York City are lower but still far above those of the other costing-out studies for New York. See, for example, Duncombe and Yinger (1998), pp. 129–53.

60. The studies were done at different times. To ensure that he was not comparing apples with oranges, he adjusted the results of each study to reflect the dollar amounts deemed necessary to achieve adequacy in 2004 dollars.

61. *Education Week* (2005), p. 39.

62. Augenblick & Myers (2003), p. ES-3.

63. *Education Week* (2005), p. 36.

64. E.g., *Williston*, Deposition of Tom Decker, August 17, 2005, p. 312.

65. Guthrie and Springer (2007b).

66. The state of Maryland actually used such a study as the basis for its school finance system; however, whether the system will ever be fully funded remains to be seen. Wyoming may be an exception where the court, until its recent change of direction, ordered the legislature to fully fund the consultants' cost function results. See chapter 6.

67. See the discussion in the text of the AIR/MAP (2004) study and note 25, this chapter.

68. See note 37, this chapter.

69. For example, in 2002, two constitutional amendments were passed in Florida, one requiring class size reductions and the other requiring the implementation of preschool programs. Fla. Constitution, art. IX, §1.

70. For a history of comprehensive school reform, see Borman, Hewes, Overman, and Brown (2003). The Abbott school districts in New Jersey were, for example, required to adopt an approved whole school reform model.

71. For a history of the New American Schools, see Mirel (2001).

72. Evaluations of the implementation and success of these schools can be found in American Institutes for Research (1999) and a series of RAND reports including Berends, Kirby, Naftel, and McKelvey (1996) and Glennan (1998). In 1994 its demise was complete when it was absorbed into the American Institutes for Research; see Olson (2004).

73. Gramlich and Koshel (1975).

74. The analytical portions of this section are elaborated on in Hanushek (1999a). A broad independent assessment of class size policies can be found in Ehrenberg, Brewer, Gamoran, and Willms (2001a, 2001b).

75. That is, smaller classes provide these gains if teachers actually change how they teach and how they interact with the class as class size is reduced. It also assumes that the necessary hiring of additional teachers that goes along with a general class size reduction policy brings in new teachers who are equally effective as the existing teachers. These important matters are discussed later.

76. A description of the program and the results can be found in Word et al. (1990). The original design also investigated regular classrooms with teacher aides, but this portion was abandoned after initial investigation showed that the aides added nothing to student performance.

77. See Mosteller (1995) on the advantages of this design for studying class size reduction.

78. An analysis of the quality of the experiment is found in Hanushek (1999b).

79. For a discussion of the range of issues in the experiment and policy debate, see Mishel and Rothstein (2002).

80. The exact class sizes required are specified in detail. For example, the classes had to average near twenty between September and April, even if larger than twenty students in some month. Schools could implement it in some but not all grades K–3, but they had to start with all first and second grades. None of these details materially affect the discussion, however.

81. See the evaluation of the California program in Stecher and Bohrnstedt (1999).

82. Data from the state website: http://www.ed-data.k12.ca.us/welcome.asp (accessed December 31, 2007).

83. Calculating the cost of class size reduction is actually a complicated process that depends on the range of changes that take place with it. See Brewer, Krop, Gill, and Reichardt (1999).

84. As noted, the costing-out studies such as Odden, Picus, Goetz, and Ferman-ich (2006) do not attempt to address these issues (see Hanushek 2007a). There are questions about the cost of increasing teacher quality, but most analyses suggest that it would be less than the cost of the large-scale class size reductions of Tennessee. See, for example, Hanushek, Kain, O'Brien, and Rivkin (2005); Hanushek (2004).

85. The pattern of legislative changes across the states can be found in Zinth (2005).

86. Heckman (2006); Heckman and Masterov (2007); Carneiro and Heckman (2003) .

87. Schweinhart et al. (2005) and Witte (2007). A comprehensive review of different pre-K programs and their evaluations can be found in Besharov, Ger-manis, Higney, and Call (2008).

88. Gramlich (1986); Barnett (1992); Galinsky (2006); Belfield, Nores, Bar-nett, and Schweinhart (2006).

89. *Abbeville County* (2000) (on appeal); *Abbott* (1998), pp. 473–74.

90. Campbell and Ramey (1995) and Campbell et al. (2001).

91. An extensive reanalysis of the data from these programs has been conducted by Anderson (2007). He attempts to correct for attrition and multiple outcome evaluations along with statistical innovations.

92. Reynolds, Temple, Robertson, and Mann (2002). The evaluation of the program relies on matching participants with comparable students in similar

schools. The validity of this approach requires that the students similar on a few measured characteristics provide a good comparison group for what might happen if the program students were not in the program—an uncertain assumption.

93. Gormley, Gayer, Phillips, and Dawson (2005).

94. Anderson (2007).

95. The impact of differences in criminal activity are particularly important in the case of the benefit-cost analyses; see Gramlich (1986). The females did, nonetheless, generally have positive school completion results; Anderson (2007).

96. Cost estimates and programmatic comparisons are found in Witte (2007). Children actually participated one or two years, and the cost figure represents an average for the actual program. For a new program, costs would presumably be larger per child if all students participated two years.

97. Campbell and Ramey (1995).

98. Costs reflect per-child costs over preschool years. See Belfield and Schwartz (2007).

99. Early action is estimated to be very important in saving future costs of remediation and special education. For example, Lyon and Fletcher (2001) conclude that addressing early reading problems can substantially reduce subsequent special education costs.

100. Gormley et al. (2005), p. 873.

101. For a sense of the disagreements about programs and purposes, see Kirp (2007), Fuller (2007), and Finn (2009).

102. Fuller (2007), chapter 6.

103. The Chicago Parent-Child Centers is a public program, and thus differs from the other programs discussed, but its research design is notably weaker than the randomized experiments. Thus, the evidence marshaled to support broader adoption of preschool programs generally focuses on the experimental but nonpublic programs.

104. Head Start Bureau (2005).

105. Besharov, Myers, and Morrow (2007).

106. Relevant studies include Fryer and Levitt (2004); Currie and Thomas (1995, 2000); Garces, Thomas, and Currie (2002); Administration for Children and Families (2005).

107. Gormley, Phillips, and Gayer (2008) consider the impact of preschool for a special sample of students in Tulsa, Oklahoma, and conclude that the Tulsa program had positive impacts, ones that were larger than for Head Start. Lisa Snell, policy analyst at the Reason Foundation, observes nonetheless that students in Oklahoma have actually lost ground in fourth grade reading on the NAEP tests since universal preschool was introduced (Snell 2008).

108. This is not to say that the benefits—particularly in areas outside of cognitive achievement—are insufficient to potentially justify some types of public programs.

109. Texas, California, Illinois, New York, New Jersey, Ohio, Michigan, Oklahoma, Missouri, Nebraska, and Pennsylvania. U.S. Department of Education (2007), table 85.

110. U.S. Department of Education (2007), table 89.

111. The research papers under the Getting Down to Facts project on the condition of education in California had a common theme of the inappropriateness of central regulation. Loeb, Bryk, and Hanushek (2008).

112. The "going to scale" problem is often associated with imperfect identification of causal forces. For example, analyses of class size reduction that do not consider variations in teacher quality are likely to mistake the impact of these programs when applied to different circumstances with different teacher quality inputs.

113. McNeil (2007); Odden, Picus, and Mangan (2006); Odden et al. (2008).

114. See, for example, discussions of the evidence and debates over charter schools in Henig (2008).

115. Tyack and Cuban (1995) see the policy process as political, and the cycles (fads) of policies seem very natural to them from the sweep of history. In their words, "While some lament that educational reform is an institutional Bermuda Triangle into which intrepid change agents sail, never to appear again, others argue that public education is too trendy, that entirely too many foolish notions circulate through the system at high velocity. Are schools too resistant to change or too faddish? Viewed over the course of history, they may seem to be both correct" (p. 4).

116. Various angles on the linkage of research and policy are displayed vividly in Hess (2008).

117. The evaluations of the What Works Clearinghouse (WWC) can be found at http://ies.ed.gov/ncee/wwc/ (accessed March 31, 2008). Its goal, epitomized by its own description, is to be "A central and trusted source of scientific evidence for what works in education."

118. The WWC provides an assessment of the amount and quality of evidence available, with strong emphasis on evidence from studies employing randomized or quasi-random designs. It also indicates the magnitude of any effects found. So, for example, the study of Instructional Conversations and Literature Logs found that students improved an average of twenty-nine percentile points with the program, but there were only two studies conducted by the program developers. See http://ies.ed.gov/ncee/wwc/reports/english_lang/icll/ (accessed March 31, 2008).

119. Manna and Petrilli (2008).

## Chapter 8
### A Performance-Based Funding System

1. The Getting Down to Facts project involved over $2 million and produced twenty-two separate investigations of different aspects of finance, governance, and performance of California schools. The overview of the results can be found

in Loeb, Bryk, and Hanushek (2008), and the complete set of papers can be found at: http://irepp.stanford.edu/projects/cafinance.htm.

2. Governor's Committee on Educational Excellence (2007a).

3. One running concern about the No Child Left Behind Act of 2001 is that it gave responsibility for developing proficiency standards to each state and also created some incentives to promulgate relatively low-level definitions of proficiency. We believe that high-level standards matching those of our international competitors should be the goal of all states and that the federal government and regional consortia of states can aid in setting these standards. It is also possible to provide incentives for states to develop meaningful standards. See, for example, the suggestions for lengthening the time to proficiency for states that have particularly high standards in Hoxby (2005). In addition, NCLB and state systems have been heavily criticized because various assessments are too narrow, measure just low-level skills, and distort some instruction. In general, we agree with these diagnoses. Better assessments are readily possible to develop—and some already exist. Our purpose is not, however, to enter into these detailed debates. Instead, on that front, we simply acknowledge the need for improvement and build into our thinking of how we might proceed with more appropriate assessments.

4. Sanders and Horn (1994, 1995); Hanushek and Rivkin (2004, 2006).

5. Hanushek and Raymond (2001, 2003); Chubb (2005).

6. While there is an academic debate about the best way to separate the value added of schools and teachers and about the specifics of reward systems, a variety of approaches offer practical alternatives. See the overview in Rivkin (2007).

7. Hoff (2007).

8. Hanushek and Raymond (2005), for example, show that states that have accountability systems that attach consequences to performance do better than states without such systems.

9. By disaggregating results by race, ethnicity, and poverty status, it is not possible to mask the poor performance of one group by the good performance of another.

10. Peterson and West (2006).

11. Peterson (2006a) provides an overall evaluation of the program. Figlio and Rouse (2006) provide a detailed evaluation of student performance effects along with an attempt to sort out the causes for student gains.

12. Resch (2006) provides a description and a summary of the resource differences among poor districts.

13. Greene (2001a, 2001b); Figlio and Rouse (2006).

14. The term "Blaine amendments" refers to provisions in many state constitutions that forbid state aid to educational institutions that have any religious affiliation, and are named after James Blaine, a former Speaker of the U.S. House of Representatives, who led a failed campaign in 1875 to have a similar provision added to the U.S. Constitution. In recent years, they have been used by antivoucher groups to resist governmental aid to private schools. Gedicks (2004).

15. The California Education Code can be found at http://www.cde.ca.gov/re/lr/cl/. Examples come from this website, accessed on March 29, 2008.

16. Some people in fact believe that all of the major decisions should be made at the school building. However, the evidence on "site-based management" is currently mixed, in part reflecting the inconsistent incentives and authority across different places where it has been attempted. For a discussion of successful site-based interventions and the underlying conceptual framework, see Ouchi (2003). See also Hill and Bonan (1991) and Summers and Johnson (1996).

17. We do not take up the issue of whether federal standards that apply across the states should be developed. For the most part, these discussions, with their strong advocates on both sides, are a distraction from the main message that we have about the nature of the policy process.

18. Governor's Committee on Educational Excellence (2007b). See also Rose, Sengupta, Sonstelie, and Reinhard (2008) for a more detailed description of California school funding.

19. Sample programs for 2008 as found at http://www.cde.ca.gov/fg/aa/ca/ (accessed March 29, 2008).

20. *DeGrasse I* (2001), p. 50. In a typical year, only about one of ten thousand teachers is fired for incompetence in the New York City public schools (ten out of a total teaching force of eighty thousand in 2006–7) (Honawar 2007). See also the general responses of California administrators in Loeb, Bryk, and Hanushek (2008).

21. Honawar (2007)

22. See DX19469, p. 1, CFE trial record, about "rubber rooms" filled with teachers waiting to be terminated. For more details concerning the difficulty of terminating tenured teachers, see Schweizer (1999) at: http://www.hoover.org/publications/digest/3506971.html (accessed February 5, 2008).

23. In an effort on the same ballot to limit the union's political pull, Proposition 75 required member approval to spend dues on political causes. It also was defeated. Hogen-Esch (2006), pp. 4–5; Hirsch (2005); Sack (2005).

24. PX 1155; see also Moe (2001b), p. 162. For a full discussion on how the New York City union contract interferes with principals in the running of their schools, see Ballou (1999).

25. Schrag (2003), p. 186. Some commentators have estimated that such rules increase the cost of operating schools from 8 to 15 percent, without any consensus that they help improve student achievement at all. Moe (2001a), p. 166.

26. Loeb, Bryk, and Hanushek (2008), p. 9.

27. Moe (2001b), p. 165.

28. The relationship between school quality and property values falls under the economist's heading of "capitalization," as discussed earlier in chapter 3. Specifically, good-quality schools lead to a bidding up of house prices as additional people want to participate in the high-quality schools. Indeed, people who are shopping to buy a house are often directed to areas with good schools, even

though they might have been able to buy a comparable house for less in another, less well-functioning school district. See Oates (1969); Hanushek (1991); Hoxby and Kuziemko (2004); Fischel (2006).

29. For the reasons outlined in the previous note, the spending of localities should not be fully equalized because the effects of school quality on housing prices and the tax base provide important incentives for districts to perform well.

30. On competition, see Friedman (1962), Hoxby (2003), and Greene (2001a, 2001b).

31. Public opinion on charters can be found in surveys by Howell, West, and Peterson (2007), p. 18. Extensive descriptions of regulations of charters can be found in Center for Education Reform (2003). Smarick (2008), p. 41, finds that twenty-five states have some sort of cap on the number of charters, with eight of them inhibiting new entry in 2008.

32. Hoxby and Rockoff (2004); Sass (2006); Bifulco and Ladd (2006); Booker, Gilpatric, Gronberg, and Jansen (2007); Hanushek, Kain, Rivkin, and Branch (2007). For a discussion of the best charter schools and their role in reform, see Thernstrom and Thernstrom (2003).

33. There is mixed evidence on public attitudes on vouchers. Moe (2001a) finds considerable support for choice by parents, at least before the blitz of negative campaigning typically preceding referenda over vouchers. Bolick (2008). Other surveys find that opinions on vouchers are more divided than opinions on charters. Howell, West, and Peterson (2007), p. 17. The conclusions and results of surveys on the subject are very sensitive to how questions are phrased, so one must be very careful in interpreting them (Moe 2002).

34. Friedman (1962). See also Chubb and Moe (1990) who develop the idea of targeted vouchers.

35. As part of our proposal, we recommend that more authority to approve charter schools be vested in the state, which does not have the same perverse incentives to oppose charter school applications. At the same time, the state should be prepared to help local school districts deal with the short-term costs associated with the sudden loss of significant numbers of students.

36. Clint Bolick, a leading proponent of vouchers, acknowledges that, in challenging yet to be operational programs, unions have never lost at the ballot box, including voucher measures in Washington, California, Michigan, and Kansas. One of the reasons for such losses, he contends, is the specter raised by union opponents that approval of such measures will harm the public schools. Bolick (2008), pp. 49, 51.

37. Private schools have been found to be a viable and beneficial force in the poorest of countries, reinforcing the importance of choice and options. Tooley (2001); Tooley and Dixon (2005).

38. Christensen and Horn (2008), p. 19. See also Christensen, Horn, and Johnson (2008). A similar call for developing innovation outside of the traditional

public schools, relying on Christensen's former analysis of private industry, is developed by Kolderie (2004).

39. Moe and Chubb (2009).

40. Student motivation is obviously a crucial issue. Having consequential central examinations for students, for example, encourages them to work harder. See Bishop (2006), Woessmann (2005, 2007).

41. While we concentrate on compensation, this is largely for exposition of the general principle. It is possible, as we describe later, to accomplish much the same as we suggest in this section by having the current structure of pay but making much more selective decisions about hiring and retention of people.

42. Hanushek and Rivkin (2004, 2006).

43. Podgursky and Springer (2007a, 2007b); Hanushek (2007b).

44. Quote from Stern (1997). Bailey left the AFT to join the alternative Association of American Educators, an organization built more on professional goals than traditional union representation and bargaining goals. It has, however, yet to make much of a dent in the representation of the National Education Association or the American Federation of Teachers.

45. Hoxby and Leigh (2004).

46. Teaching Commission (2004), p. 23.

47. A variety of approaches have been used to find the value added of individual teachers; see reviews in Hanushek and Rivkin (2004); Hanushek and Rivkin (2006); Rivkin (2007); and Sanders and Horn (1995, 1998). The various methods are the subject of lively debate—see, for example, the conference at the Center for Analysis of Longitudinal Data in Educational Research (CALDER) at: http://www.caldercenter.org/events/valueadded.cfm (accessed July 30, 2008). The key is achieving a balance between the objective and subjective evaluations—something that private industry understands well. And, as with different firms, the best decisions on the balance are likely to be made in local school districts, as we stress in the need to have decentralized decision making.

48. Some evidence shows that principals are able to identify these poor performers. See, for example, Murnane (1975); Armor et al. (1976); or Jacob and Lefgren (2006). It also is almost certainly true that other teachers and parents recognize these ineffective teachers. In the survey of teachers in Duffett, Farkas, Rotherham, and Silva (2008), p. 2, "[A]lmost half of teachers (46 percent) say they know a teacher in their own building who is past the probationary period but who is clearly ineffective and shouldn't be in the classroom." It seems to be simply a lack of will to act on readily available information.

49. Toch and Rothman (2008).

50. A wide range of research continually points to the same outcome. See, for example, the collection of essays in Loeb, Rouse, and Shorris (2007). See also Hanushek and Rivkin (2004).

51. Duffett, Farkas, Rotherham, and Silva (2008).

52. Tr. 3002–7 (Tames); PX 1191, CFE trial record.

53. PX 1191, PX 1270, CFE trial record.

54. Hanushek, Kain, O'Brien, and Rivkin (2005).

55. Kershaw and McKean (1962).

56. Finn (2001). The term "gadfly" derives from his weekly column in the *Education Gadfly*, a weekly bulletin of news and analysis from the Thomas B. Fordham Institute (http://www.edexcellence.net/gadfly/index.cfm). See also Finn (2008).

57. Again, the majority of teachers appears to disagree with this policy position of their unions. Duffett, Farkas, Rotherham, and Silva (2008).

58. Hanushek and Rivkin (2004); Hanushek (2007b).

59. This argument is made forcefully by Vigdor (2008).

60. See Ballou and Podgursky (2002); Lankford and Wyckoff (1995).

61. Calculations are based on the 2005 New York City teachers' contract salary schedule. For example, new teacher pay increases from $39,000 to $41,172 under the new November 1, 2005, schedule, a 5.6 percent increase. The salary of a teacher with a master's degree and twenty-two years of experience increased from $76,445 to $85,141, an 11.4 percent increase.

62. Ciotti (1998).

63. Most teachers are part of a defined benefit retirement plan that determines retirement pay on the basis of the highest salaries obtained. See Costrell and Podgursky (2008).

64. For an excellent review of plans found in 2007, see Podgursky and Springer (2007a).

65. See http://www.talentedteachers.org/.

66. Descriptions of the initial Florida plan can be found in Hanushek (2006d); various programs from 2007 are described in *Education Week* (2008b).

67. Keller and Honawar (2008).

68. Silva (2008).

69. See the press release of the New York City schools, Department of Education (2007), found at http://schools.nyc.gov/Offices/mediarelations/NewsandSpeeches/2007-2008/20071218_performance_pay.htm (accessed March 29, 2008).

70. Podgursky and Springer (2007a), p. 943.

71. The situation is not as stark as this suggests. The entering knowledge for students of the high school physics teacher might be measured by prior math scores of students. The high school world history performance might be related to prior students' performance in other history and general social studies courses.

72. The estimates of the impact of the least effective teachers in Hanushek (2009) are based on observed variations in teacher effectiveness discussed in Rivkin, Hanushek, and Kain (2005).

73. These estimates indicate that eliminating the bottom 6 to 10 percent of teachers would lead to improvements of test scores of one-half standard deviation, roughly the difference between the United States and Canada on international

tests. The implications of such a change are graphically illustrated in chapter 1. Hanushek (2009).

74. Barber and Mourshed (2007).

75. National Association of State Boards of Education (1997); National Council on Teacher Quality (2007).

76. Toch and Rothman (2008).

77. As noted in Brunner and Imazeki (2008), salaries already adjust to differences in employment risk. Districts in states with longer probationary periods tend to have higher salaries, other things being equal.

78. Ballou (2001); Ballou and Podgursky (1997). Performance pay is also used extensively in higher education and, although the evaluations are limited, there is evidence of considerable success in improving teacher effectiveness at the university level. Brickley and Zimmerman (2001).

79. See Cohen and Murnane (1986) and Hatry, Greiner, and Ashford (1994) for discussion of these systems and the conclusions about their impact. As Cohen and Murnane describe, the historic merit pay plans come under continual pressure from unions, and they tend to devolve into either very uniform rewards across teachers or extra pay for extra work. Some people also argue that such rewards are ill-conceived because they do not evoke positive responses by individuals (e.g., Kohn [1999]). This view, however, is not found in other sectors of the economy, particularly competitive sectors.

80. The Data Quality Campaign is an effort of a large number of organizations to improve the quality of current decision making through better data (http:// www.dataqualitycampaign.org/). Its website describes the elements it recommends for a sound state data system.

81. See the discussion in Jepsen and Rivkin (2009).

82. An evaluation was conducted by the American Institutes for Research and the RAND Corporation, but it was doomed from the beginning because there was no control group to allow reliable investigation of the effects on achievement. It could, however, document some of the teacher moves and teacher shortages. Stecher (1999).

83. For a discussion of evaluation in schools, including the use of randomization of treatments, see Mosteller and Boruch (2002) and Bloom (2005).

84. Another example of this sometimes insatiable demand for additional funding is Massachusetts. Although that state's spending on its public schools soared from $3 billion to $10 billion and its students perform better than those of almost every other state, that record did not stop school districts in the state from filing a new lawsuit, a decade after their win in *McDuffy*, seeking still greater funding. See *McDuffy* (1993); *Hancock* (2005).

85. The funding volatility and late availability of budget information are frequently the result of other financial and political problems in states. For example, in 2008, California, faced with a large overall deficit at the state level, could not reach any agreement on the state budget until several weeks after the opening of

schools. Such a situation is clearly a management nightmare for the schools and leads to a variety of unfortunate decisions that are not in the long-term interest of developing effective school operations and, by implication, not in the interests of the students.

86. The term "weighted student funding" has been applied in very different ways with very different objectives and proposals. For a common description, see Thomas B. Fordham Institute (2006). As described, however, it is not possible to collapse our performance-based funding into a simple set of student weights.

87. Past evaluations are reviewed in Vinovskis (1999).

88. See note 44, chapter 7.

89. See, for example, Roza, Guin, Gross, and Deburgomaster (2007); Roza and Hill (2006).

90. Some versions of "weighted student funding" would make funding of schools in such a way a mandatory part of state plans, following the idea that this practice would force districts to make decisions that better served disadvantaged populations.

91. The legislative history and important policies of the federal government can be found at: http://www.ed.gov/about/offices/list/osers/policy.html (accessed March 30, 2008). Discussions of relevant policy issues can be found in Finn, Rotherham, and Hokanson (2001) and the included references. See also President's Commission on Excellence in Special Education (2002).

92. Cullen (2003).

93. Greene (2007).

94. U.S. Department of Education (2007), tables 33 and 89.

95. Moe (2005, 2009).

96. Council of Great City Schools (2006) indicates a slight lengthening of the typical tenure of superintendents in the larger cities, but it is yet to be seen whether these changes are truly significant. The circumstances behind superintendent turnover vary widely, but the Miami/Dade Country experience is illustrative of one element. When urban school boards are divided along distinct, often ethnic lines, a change of a single board position can lead to a new superintendent, as with the dismissal of Rudy Crew in 2008. See Gewertz (2008).

97. See Wong and Shen (2005). Among the largest one hundred central city districts, those with mayoral control had not shown a consistent systematic impact on fiscal or staffing outcomes by 2002.

98. Note that state takeover has occurred more frequently because of financial problems than because of academic problems. Such was the case in Oakland, which ran up a $100 million deficit in 2003 (see Murphy [2003]), but the financial takeover often leads to actions directly related to academic issues. Early state takeovers for academic reasons took place in Jersey City (Walsh [1993]) and Philadelphia (Gill, Zimmer, Christman, and Blanc ([2007]).

99. The inequitable distribution of resources within urban districts has been well documented (e.g., Roza and Hill [2006], Roza, Guin, Gross and Deburgo-

master [2007]). Current systems neither keep track of the flow of funds on a regular basis nor provide much alternative even if known. As we have argued, without the ability to choose teachers, replacing ineffective teachers with more effective ones, and without flexibility on salaries, management by fiscal equity across schools is unlikely to lead to achievement gains or more equity in achievement outcomes.

## Chapter 9
### Making Performance-Based Funding a Reality

1. See note 42, chapter 3.

2. It is often the case that one's opinion as to whether a political compromise is part of the democratic process or a corrupt backroom deal lies more in whose ox is being gored, rather than upon any reasoned principle. Interestingly, when the *CFE* litigation ended and Governor Spitzer was able to push through record spending increases for the New York City schools through a "political" deal with several Long Island representatives, there were no complaints from New York City that the system was corrupt or broken. See note 130, chapter 4.

3. Attributed to Otto von Bismarck, the famous "Iron Chancellor" of Germany, 1871–90.

4. As noted previously, there have been some ups and downs in the growth of K–12 education funding, such as the lull during the early 1990s, but these have not changed the basic trend of vastly expanded resources for public schools.

5. See chapter 3.

6. National Association of State Budget Officers (2004), "Table 3. Comparison of Shares of State Spending, Fund Sources, Fiscal 1994 to 2004."

7. Toppo (2008).

8. Oppenheim (2008).

9. Press release of March 14, 2008: California Department of Education (2008), http://www.cde.ca.gov/nr/ne/yr08/yr08rel31.asp (accessed July 30, 2008). The governor had warned of massive budget deficits in his January address to the legislature (McKinley [2008]). The California budget deficit was estimated in the summer of 2008 to be some $15 billion, and the $143 billion state budget (including the education appropriations) was not passed until late September 2008—a record eighty-five days late and well after the beginning of the school year (Steinhauer [2008]).

10. Rosenberg (2008), http://www.boston.com/news/local/articles/2008/01/24/schools_brace_for_teacher_layoffs/ (accessed July 30, 2008).

11. Howell and West (2008), p. 38.

12. Half of the sample, randomly chosen, was offered a prompt to encourage them to consider the full range of costs associated with educating a child in order to ensure that they were not erroneously focusing on just part of the spending of schools. These respondents were then told that "individual student costs go to-

ward teacher and administrator salaries, building construction and maintenance, extracurricular activities, transportation, etc." Howell and West (2008), p. 38.

13. Howell, West, and Peterson (2007), p. 23.

14. Rose and Gallup (2007).

15. There is some evidence that these rosy perceptions may be changing. Parents giving their own child's school an A or B slipped from 56 to 53 percent between 2006 and 2007, a period coinciding with the increased availability of information about student achievement flowing from the added accountability in the schools. Rose and Gallup (2007).

16. Hess (2007).

17. Moe (2001b), p. 171.

18. Moe (2001b), p. 159.

19. Moe (2001b), p. 159. The role of teachers' unions in school board elections is particularly important. School boards are often elected in special elections, where very few voters turn out. Those that turn out are often those with a stake in the current system, including parents of current student children and the school personnel themselves. In a report based on a survey of California districts, Moe (2005) provides a description of the various roles of unions in school board elections and politics, including endorsing and supporting candidates, giving them money, recruiting potential candidates, mobilizing members to canvas neighborhoods, and the like. Importantly, these activities increase dramatically with district size and are near ubiquitous in districts with over twenty-five thousand students. And the result, according to Moe (2006), is that unions heavily influence school board elections, getting their candidates elected. In a related finding, Moe (2006) found that teachers voted in school board elections about the same rate as the general public if they lived in a district different from the one where they worked. If, however, they lived and worked in the same district, they voted at a remarkably higher rate.

20. Moe (2001b), p. 172.

21. Moe (2001b), p. 183. Republicans have also experienced the wrath of the teachers' unions. During the 1996 presidential campaign, Republican senator Bob Dole challenged the teachers' unions on their opposition to school choice, but abandoned his stance when it was interpreted as a criticism of teachers. Chubb (2001). More recently, Governor Arnold Schwarzenegger's attempt to buck the unions over teacher tenure was soundly rebuffed in California. See chapter 8.

22. Ironically, the most recent class size reduction craze was started by Governor Pete Wilson of California. A Republican with no love for teachers, he jumped on class size reduction as a way of keeping extra funding for teachers off the bargaining table and out of salary increases for teachers. He grossly underestimated the value to the teachers' unions of the large increases in their membership resulting from the reduction of class sizes, and consequent hiring of more teachers.

23. Under the CFE-sponsored study, class sizes would be significantly reduced, requiring the hiring of additional teachers. For example, maximum class sizes in

"high-poverty" New York City elementary schools would be fourteen students. In addition, every two classrooms in such schools would also be allocated an extra teacher, besides the ones already assigned to the classroom. Extra teachers would also be assigned for every 2.2 "core classroom teachers" in middle and high schools. AIR/MAP (2004), pp. 33–34.

24. See United Federation of Teachers website at http//:www.uft.org/member/money/tax/uft.dues (accessed July 30, 2008).

25. In addition to dues, the city of New York also pays $1,245 per teacher, or over $87 million, into the union's "Welfare Fund," which is mainly used to provide additional benefits for union members. An additional fifteen thousand teachers would mean almost $19 million a year more for the fund. Randi Weingarten deposition, July 21, 1999, pp. 45–70, CFE trial record; Agreement between the Board of Education of the City of New York et al. and the United Federation of Teachers (New York City Local) et al. covering teachers, October 16, 1995, through November 15, 2000, p. 9.

26. Chubb (2001), p. 21. Unions, however, may be willing to compromise when the state requires charter school teachers to join the union. For example, when Governor Eliot Spitzer proposed increasing the number of charter schools in New York State from 100 to 250 schools, the American Federation of Teachers opposed it until the governor changed his proposal to require that charter schools with more than 250 students automatically become union shops after two years. *New York Post* (2007).

27. Peterson (2003b). The president of the NEA recently affirmed his union's long-standing opposition to merit pay linked to any kind of test results. Weaver (2007). The union's priorities are most evident in New York City. After negotiations that had gone on for years, New York City, its board of education, and the local teachers' union finally agreed on a new contract in 2005. Although Mayor Bloomberg and Joel Klein, the chancellor of the New York City public schools, had promised at the outset of their terms to eliminate the old salary schedule with its automatic step raises, the 2005 contract retained it. Merit or performance-based pay was not mentioned. Wolf (2005). In 2007, however, Mayor Bloomberg announced a plan whereby teachers in some two hundred high-poverty schools would be eligible for bonuses, supported by private funds, if test scores improved. This plan, which provides money to schools, was supported by Randi Weingarten, the UFT union head. See Chan (2007) and Medina (2008).

28. Examples of union reaction to proposals to eliminate tenure are plentiful. See, for example, the reaction to earlier attempts to change teacher tenure in Richardson (1995).

29. Glazer (2008), p. 82.

30. A recent analysis by Terry Moe relates the restrictiveness of union contracts to student outcomes in California and finds that contract restrictions are negatively related to student performance (Moe [2009]). His conclusion is: "The bottom line is that the interests of teachers (and unions) are *not aligned* with the

interests of children, and the organizational arrangements pursued by unions will ultimately *diverge* from those that are best for students." In an analysis of California schools, Koski and Horng (2007), however, do not find that seniority rules adversely affect the distribution of certified teachers across schools.

31. Paige (2006), p. 190.

32. For example, Hanushek (2003); Hanushek and Rivkin (2004); Rivkin, Hanushek, and Kain (2005).

33. U.S. Department of Education (2007), tables 33 and 60.

34. Changes in teacher salaries are often difficult to accurately calculate. Because there have been large changes in the demographics of the teacher populations resulting from waves of new hiring and aging of the teacher force, the average change in salaries can be misleading. For example, average real salaries of all teachers increased by just 2 percent between 1996 and 2004, reflecting these compositional changes (U.S. Department of Education 2007, table 71). Additionally, the increase in salaries for teachers with a given experience level does not reflect the increase in pay that any given teacher will see, because pay also goes up with experience and because, over time, additions to teacher retirement have led to even faster increases in total compensation for teachers. See Podgursky (2003) and Costrell and Podgursky (2008). This trend has been true even in those states that have significantly increased overall education spending as the result of a court order.

35. National Center for Education Statistics (2008b), table 78, for 2001–2. See also Hess (2007), pp. 181–85.

36. Odden et al. (2008).

37. National Board for Professional Teaching Standards (1991); National Commission on Teaching and America's Future (1996).

38. One suspects that the real motive of many school districts in opposing charters is not the loss of money, but the fear that the charter schools will show failings of the public schools.

39. Some additional state funding might be provided for a transition period to help alleviate this problem, but it should not continue indefinitely. As discussed earlier, public schools have been resistant to cutting staff in the face of significantly reduced enrollments.

40. Moe and Chubb (2009).

41. We have previously discussed the role of the union contracts and related work rules. Many also fault our teacher training institutions. For example, in describing the role of postgraduate schools of education in a 2005 report, Arthur Levine, then president of Columbia University Teachers College and head of the Education Schools Project, delivered a scathing assessment of the nation's graduate schools of education, stating: "Everybody benefits from the current system, except our children" (Toppo 2005). A later report also found massive problems in the country's undergraduate schools of education. For a description of these problems and a discussion of changes, see Levine (2005). His solution (p. 105)

resonates well with our perspective: "RECOMMENDATION TWO: Focus on student achievement as the primary measure of teacher education program success." Larabee (2004) is even stronger in his criticism of education schools: "But the most important fact that belies the ed school's importance in teacher education is the consistent finding in the research on teacher education that these programs exert remarkably little impact on the way their graduates teach" (p. 174).

42. Surprisingly, the problem of imperfect knowledge is perhaps most severe in middle- and upper-income communities. There the public often sees reports of assessment scores that show high proficiency levels in their schools, at least relative to those in less advantaged areas, and credit their schools with doing a good job. But these statistics may be very misleading when it comes to the value added by the schools. While some high-performing schools are adding a lot to the learning of students, others are not. Instead they are simply riding on the strong preparation that more advantaged parents and classmates provide. In fact, many surprises occur when a state or locality switches from rating schools on their average performance and instead rates them partially or totally on the gains in performance—something that comes closer to measuring the contribution of the schools. Such was the case in Florida and New York when new grading systems for the schools were introduced (Figlio and Lucas 2004). See also Peterson and West (2006).

43. Starting with an experiment in the use of growth models, two states (North Carolina and Tennessee) were initially permitted calculations using student achievement growth. This was soon expanded to six other states; see *Education Week* (2007a). In December 2007, the possibility was opened to all states that had the capacity. Hoff (2007). Even New York City is experimenting with value-added measures by issuing letter grades to each of its elementary schools. Gewertz (2007).

44. Peterson and West (2006).

45. This movement is partly related to notions of accountability and standards-based reform. Specifically, if local schools and districts are to be held responsible for outcomes, they should have the flexibility to decide which educational programs will be effective in their schools.

46. Barber and Mourshed (2007).

47. Howell, West, and Peterson (2007), p. 22. The 2008 results for the Education Next/PEPG survey with the same question provided virtually the same results for attitudes on performance pay. The 2008 survey, however, disaggregated the survey results for teachers, who displayed very different reactions: 17 percent favored performance pay, while 71 percent opposed it. (Results of the 2008 survey were scheduled to appear in the May 2009 edition of *Education Next*, and these data were reported in personal correspondence.)

48. Hudetz (2008).

49. Hess (2007).

50. *Education Week* (2007b); Obama (2007), pp. 162–63.

51. Hakim and Peters (2008); *Education Week* (2008a).

52. For discussions of charter schools, see Nathan (1996); Finn, Manno, and Vanourek (2000); and Hill (2006).

53. "Union-Run Charter Schools Show What Works," *New York Teacher*, October 19, 2006 (see http://www.nysut.org/ops/cps/rde/xchg/nysut/hs.xsl/newyorkteacher_5175.htm).

54. "Perfecting" frequently also means eliminating or reducing any sanctions for lack of performance.

55. Advocates for fundamental changes in finance and policy still remain over-powered by forces in favor of the existing structure in most states and must be vigilant to prevent backsliding. While eliminating accountability measures or ending all charter schools is unlikely, weakening or crippling them is not out of the question. For these reasons, more active policies to move forward performance-based funding are required if backsliding is to be prevented.

56. For example, in New York, state law grants tenure to teachers after five years of continuous service, but in New York City this period is effectively reduced to three years under the union contract. Ballou (1999).

57. Hoxby and Leigh (2004).

58. Miller (2003).

59. The Carnegie Forum on Education and the Economy (1986) recommended raising teacher salaries to those of highly paid professionals in exchange for a greater relationship between salary and performance.

60. Marshall and Tucker (1992).

61. See Peterson (2006c).

62. In most states, teachers' contracts are negotiated locally, even though many states establish a salary schedule that typically sets a floor that can be negotiated upward. There is good reason for this because states cannot devise optimal contracts for hundreds of districts with different circumstances, opportunities, and preferences. However, while leaving the details to the local districts, the state can achieve its goal of an incentive-based system by conditioning a district's right to additional funding on negotiating contracts and pay systems that complement and support the goal of achieving better outcomes.

63. Here, again, however, teachers' unions have opposed such changes, pre-sumably because the unions believe that they lose control when the contract openly allows for differentiation among members. When Michelle Rhee, the reform-minded superintendent of the District of Columbia, attempted to establish just such a bargain, she was rebuffed by the teachers' union, leading her to move toward more aggressive dismissal policies in the fall of 2008. See Turque (2008). Using outside private funds of $200 million, she had offered a more lucrative contract to teachers who would agree to a one-year probationary policy. The union was unhappy with the possibility that existing tenured teachers might be let go during this probationary period, leading the superintendent to eschew the

bargaining process and rely on unilateral actions. As of this writing, the ultimate outcome of this dance in the District of Columbia was unknown.

64. For example, many southern legislatures enacted "segregation laws" discouraging or preventing any integration of the schools. See, for example, 1955 Ga. Laws 174 (no state and local funds could be appropriated, except for "schools in which the white and colored races are separately educated").

65. Rossell (1990); Welch and Light (1987); Clotfelter (2004).

66. For a full discussion of the institutional difficulties impacting the ability of the courts to bring about social change, see Horowitz (1977); Rosenberg (1991); Sandler and Schoenbrod (2003); and Dunn and Derthick (2007a).

67. The lone exception was the first decision of the appellate division, which reversed Justice DeGrasse's trial ruling. It ruled that the problems with assigning the least-qualified teachers to the schools with the neediest students were attributable to the union contract and not the state funding system. CFE, (2002), pp. 32–33. This point was disregarded by the New York Court of Appeals when it overturned the appellate division's ruling in CFE II (2003).

68. Wolf (2005).

69. Rothstein (2004), p. 149.

70. Courts are by no means immune from political pressures. A number of researchers have found that judges' party affiliations prior to their appointments have been "significant predictors of case outcomes in court" and concluded that "politics matter in education funding litigation." See deMoss (2004). As Sol Stern put it in referring to Justice DeGrasse, the trial judge in the CFE case: "[T]he reality is that no one gets on the bench [in Manhattan] who would be likely to question the standard Democratic Party approach to public policy issues, including education." Stern (2006), p. 1. See also Williams (2007), p. 211. In perhaps the most obvious example of politics at work in adequacy litigation, the plaintiffs dismissed a case filed in 2004 challenging the adequacy of Georgia's public schools on the eve of trial because it had been reassigned to a new judge with Republican leanings. The new judge had been appointed by a Republican governor and had previously been the chairman of the state Republican Party. Prior to the new judge making any rulings in the case, the plaintiffs declared they could not get a "fair trial" from him and dismissed the case, vowing to refile it in a friendlier court. Diamond (2008). More generally, see Ferejohn (1995).

71. Hess (2007), p. 161.

72. Legal scholars may argue that we are asking the courts to render "advisory opinions," which they are loath to do. However, that is not the case. We are simply asking the courts to describe the failures in the system responsible for low achievement, lack of funding, or other problems, as they would normally do in the course of ruling on a request for a declaratory judgment.

73. As of the writing of this book, only a few educational adequacy cases were pending and had not yet been decided. South Dakota Coalition of Schools (2006) went to trial in fall 2008, while the Washington case, McCleary (2007), was sched-

uled for trial but had not yet begun. The Indiana case, *Daniels* (2007), was returned for trial, but no decision had been made. An adequacy case in Georgia was scheduled for trial in October 2008 but was dismissed by the plaintiffs on the eve the trial (see note 70, chapter 9). *Consortium* (2008).

74. Mathews (2008) cites a variety of people espousing such a view.

75. Hanushek and Woessmann (2008) present evidence that national growth is dependent upon both a high level of basic skills and a substantial group of high performers.

76. Friedman (2007).

# Legal Citations

### FEDERAL COURT CASES
### (ARRANGED IN ALPHABETICAL ORDER)

Baker (1962): *Baker v. Carr*, 369 U.S. 186, 209 (1962).

*Benton Harbor* (2002): *Berry v. School District of the City of Benton Harbor*, 195 F. Supp.2d 971 (W.D. Mich. 2002).

*Brinkman* (1985): *Brinkman v. Gilligan*, 610 F. Supp. 1288 (S.D. Ohio 1985).

*Brown I* (1954): *Brown v. Board of Education*, 347 U.S. 483 (1954).

*Brown II* (1955): *Brown v. Board of Education*, 349 U.S. 294, 300–301 (1955).

*Hobson v. Hansen*, 269 F. Supp. 401 (D.D.C. 1967).

*Chadha* (1983): *I.N.S. v Chadha*, 462 U.S. 919, 963 (1983).

*Freeman* (1992): *Freeman v. Pitts*, 503 U.S. 467, 491 (1992).

*Jenkins II* (1990): *Missouri v. Jenkins*, 495 U.S. 76 (1990).

*Jenkins* (1994): *Jenkins v. Missouri*, 19 F.3d 393 (8th Cir. 1994).

*Jenkins III* (1995): *Missouri v. Jenkins*, 515 U.S. 70 (1995).

*Jenkins* (1997): *Jenkins v. Missouri*, 122 F.3rd 588, 595 (8th Cir. 1997).

*Jenkins* (2003): *Jenkins v. School District of Kansas City, Missouri*, No. 77–0420-CV-W-DW (W.D. Mo. Aug. 13, 2003).

*Liddell* (1984): *Liddell v. Missouri*, 731 F.2d 1294 (8th Cir.), *cert. denied*, 469 U.S. 816 (1984).

*Liddell* (1987): *Liddell v. Missouri*, 822 F.2d 1446 (8th Cir. 1987).

*Liddell Settlement* (1999): *Liddell v. The Board of Education of the City of St. Louis, et al.*, Case No. 72–0100C(6) (E.D. Mo., Order dated Mar. 12, 1999).

*Little Rock* (1986): *Little Rock Sch. Dist. v. Pulaski County Special Sch. Dist.*, 778 F.2d 404, 435–36 (8th Cir. 1985), *cert. denied*, 476 U.S. 1186 (1986).

*Little Rock* (1988): *Little Rock Sch. Dist. v. Pulaski County Special Sch. Dist., et al.*, 839 F.2d 1296, 1307 (8th Cir.), *cert. denied, Arkansas State Bd. of Educ. v. Little Rock Sch. Dist.*, 488 U.S. 869 (1988).

*Milliken I* (1974): *Milliken v. Bradley*, 418 U.S. 717, 744–46 (1974).

*Milliken II* (1977): *Milliken v. Bradley*, 433 U.S. 267, 283–87 (1977).

*Penick* (1981): *Penick v. Columbus Bd. of Educ.*, 519 F. Supp. 925 (S.D. Ohio 1981), *aff'd*, 663 F.2d 24 (6th Cir. 1981).

*People Who Care* (2001): *People Who Care v. Rockford Board of Education School District No. 205*, 246 F.3d 1073 (7th Cir. 2001).

*Reed* (1982): *Reed v. Rhodes*, 500 F. Supp. 404 (N.D. Ohio 1980), *aff'd*, 662 F.2d 1219 (1981), *cert. denied*, 455 U.S. 1018 (1982).

*Rodriguez* (1973): *San Antonio Independent School District v. Rodriguez*, 411
U.S. 1 (1973).
*Yonkers* (1980): *United States of America v. Yonkers Board of Education*, Docket
No. 80-CIV-6761 (S.D.N.Y.).
*Yonkers Settlement* (2002): *United States of America, et al. v. Yonkers Board of
Education, et al.*, Docket No. 80-CIV-6761 (LBS) (S.D.N.Y., Order approving
Settlement Agreement dated Mar. 28, 2002).
*Yonkers* (2005): *Citizens for Yonkers, et al. v. State of New York, et al.*, Index No.
08850/05 (Sup. Ct. Westchester Cnty, N.Y., 2005).

## STATE COURT CASES
### (ARRANGED BY STATE AND, WITHIN STATES, CHRONOLOGICALLY)

### Alabama

*Harper* (1993): *Harper v. Hunt, Op. of Justices*, 624 So.2d 107 (Ala. 1993).
*James* (2002): *Alabama Coalition for Equity v. Fob James, et al.*, 836 So.2d 813
(Ala. 2002).

### Alaska

*Alaska* (2007): *Kristine Moore, et al. v. State of Alaska*, Case No. 3AN-04–9756
Civil (Sup. Ct. Anchorage, Alaska, June 21, 2007).

### Arizona

*Crane* (2002): *Crane Elementary School District, et al. v. State of Arizona, et al.*,
CV2001–016305 (Sup. Ct., Maricopa Cnty, Ariz., Order dated May 13, 2002).
*Crane* (2006): *Crane Elementary School District, et al. v. State of Arizona*, Case
No. CV2001–016305 (Ct.App., Ariz., Nov. 22, 2006).
*Roosevelt* (1994): *Roosevelt Elementary School District v. Bishop*, 877 P.2d 806
(Ariz. 1994).

### Arkansas

*Lakeview* (2002): *Lakeview School District v. Huckabee*, 91 S.W.3d 472 (Ark.
2002).

### California

*Serrano* (1976): *Serrano v. Priest*, 557 P.2d 929 (Calif. 1976).

### Colorado

*Lobato* (2006): *Anthony Lobato, et al. v. The State of Colorado, et al.*, Case No.
05CV4794 (Dist. Ct. Denver, Colo., Order dated March 2, 2006); *cert. denied,*

*Anthony Lobato, et al. v. The State of Colorado, et al.*, Case No. 065C598 (S.Ct. Colo., Oct. 23, 2006).

## Connecticut

*Sheff* (1997): *Sheff v. O'Neill*, 678 A.2d 1267 (Conn. 1996).

## Florida

*Coalition* (1996): *Coalition for Adequacy and Fairness in School Funding v. Chiles*, 680 So.2d 400 (Fla. 1996).

*Holmes* (2006): *Holmes v. Bush*, No. 04–2323 (Fla. Jan. 5, 2006).

*Honore* (2003): *Honore, Faith L. v. Board of Education of State of Florida, et al.*, Civil Action No. 000017 (Sup. Ct. Leon County, Fla., June 16, 2003).

## Georgia

*Consortium* (2005): *Consortium for Adequate School Funding in Georgia, Inc., et al. v. The State of Georgia*, Civil Action No. 2004CV91004 (Sup. Ct., Fulton Cnty, Ga., Sept. 25, 2005).

*Consortium* (2006): *Consortium for Adequate School Funding in Georgia, Inc., et al. v. State of Georgia, et al.*, Civil Action No. 2004CV91004 (Sup. Ct. Fulton Cnty, Ga., Nov. 21, 2006).

*Consortium* (2008): *Consortium for Adequate School Funding in Georgia*, Civil Action No. 2003CV91004 (Sup. Ct. Fulton Cnty, Ga., Sept. 16, 2008).

*McDaniel* (1981): *McDaniel v. Thomas*, 248 Ga. 632 (1981).

## Idaho

*Idaho* (2004): *Idaho Schools for Equal Educational Opportunity v. State of Idaho*, 97 P.3d 453, 462–463 (Idaho 2004).

## Illinois

*Edgar* (1996): *Committee for Education Rights v. Edgar*, 672 N.E.2d 1178 (Ill. 1996).

## Indiana

*Daniels* (2007): *Philip-Anthony Bonner, et al. v. Mitch Daniels, Governor of the State of Indiana, et al.*, 885 N.E.2d 673 (Ind. 2008).

## Kansas

*Montoy* (2003): *Montoy v. State*, Case No. 99-C-1738 (Kan. Dist. Ct., Dec. 3, 2003).

*Montoy* (2004): *Montoy v. State*, 2004 WL 1094555 (Kan. Dist. Ct.).

*Montoy II* (2005): *Montoy v. State*, 279 Kan 817, 112 P.3d 923 (Kan. 2005).
*Montoy* (2006): *Montoy v. State of Kansas*, No. 92032 (S.Ct. Kan. 2006).

## Kentucky

*Rose* (1989): *Rose v. Council for Better Education*, 790 S.W.2d 186 (Ky. 1989).
*Williams* (2003): *Council for Better Education, Inc. v. David L. Williams*, Civil No. 03-CI-1152 (Franklin Cir. Ct., Ky., complaint filed Sept. 17, 2003).
*Williams* (2007): *Young v. Williams*, Case No. 03-CI-00055 (Cir. Ct., Franklin County, Ky., Order dated Feb. 12, 2007).

## Maryland

*Bradford* (1996): *Bradford v. Maryland*, Case No. 94340058CE189672 (Cir. Ct., Baltimore City, Md., Consent Order dated Nov. 26, 1996).

## Massachusetts

*Hancock* (2004): *Julie Hancock and others v. David P. Driscoll and others*, Superior Court C.A. No. 02–2978 (SJC, Suffolk County, Mass., Apr. 26, 2004).
*Hancock* (2005): *Hancock, et al. v. Commissioner of Education, et al.*, 443 Mass. 428 (Mass. 2005).
*McDuffy* (1993): *McDuffy v. Secretary, Executive Office of Education*, 615 N.E.2d 516 (Mass. 1993).

## Minnesota

*Skeen* (1993): *Skeen v. State*, 505 N.W.2d 299 (Minn. 1993).
*St. Paul* (1999): *Independent School District No. 625, St. Paul Minnesota v. Minnesota*, No. C2–96–9356 (Dist. Ct. Ramsey Co. Minn., 1999).
*Minneapolis* (2000): *NAACP v. Minnesota*, No. 95–14800 (Dist. Ct. Hennepin Co. Minn., 2000).

## Missouri

*Committee for Educational Equality* (2007): *Committee for Educational Equality, et al. v. State of Missouri, et al.*, Case No. 04CV323022 (Circuit Ct. of Cole County, Mo., Oct. 17, 2007).

## Montana

*Columbia Falls* (2005): *Columbia Falls Elem. School Dist. No. 6, et al. v. The State of Montana*, No. 04–390 (Mont. S. Ct., Mar. 22, 2005).

## Nebraska

*Douglas County* (2003): *Douglas County School District, et al. v. Michael Johanns, et al.*, Doc. 1028, No. 017 (District Court of Douglas County, Neb. 2003).

*Douglas County* (2007): *Douglas County School District, et al. v. Johanns*, Case No. 017 (S. Ct., Neb., May 11, 2007).

## New Hampshire

*Claremont* (1997): *Claremont School District v. Governor*, 703 A.2d 1353 (N.H. 1997).

*Londonderry* (2006): *Londonderry School District SAU#12, et al. v. State of New Hampshire*, Case No. 2006–0258 (N.H. Sept. 8, 2006).

## New Jersey

*Robinson* (1976): *Robinson v. Cahill*, 360 A.2d 400 (N.J. 1976).

*Abbott* (1990): *Abbott v. Burke*, 119 N.J. 287, 575 A. 2d 359 (N.J. 1990).

*Abbott* (1997): *Abbott v. Burke*, 149 N.J. 145, 693 A.2d 417 (N.J. 1997).

*Abbott* (1998): *Abbott v. Burke*, 153 N.J. 480, 710 A.2d 450 (N.J. 1998).

*Abbott* (2002): *Abbott v. Burke*, 170 N.J. 537, 790 A.2d 842 (N.J. 2002).

*Abbott* (2002): *Abbott v. Burke*, 172 N.J. 294, 798 A.2d 602 (N.J. 2002).

*Millville* (2005): *Bd. of Educ. of City of Millville v. NJ Dept. of Ed.*, 183 N.J. 264 (2005).

*Crawford* (2007): *Crawford v. Daney*, Docket No. C-137–06, slip op. and order (N.J. Super Ct., Ch. Div., Oct. 4, 2007).

## New York

*Anderson* (1981): *Anderson v. Regan*, 52 N.Y.2d 356, 365 (1981).

*CFE I* (1995): *Campaign for Fiscal Equity v. State of New York, et al.*, 86 N.Y.2d 307, 655 N.E.2d 661 (1995).

*CFE App. Div.* (2002): *Campaign for Fiscal Equity v. State*, No. 5330, 2002 N.Y. App. Div. LEXIS 7252 (N.Y. App. Div. June 25, 2002).

*CFE II* (2003): *Campaign for Fiscal Equity v. New York*, 100 N.Y.2d 893, 801 N.E.2d 326 (N.Y. 2003).

*CFE III* (2006): *Campaign for Fiscal Equity v. New York*, No. 136 (Ct. App., Nov. 20, 2006).

*DeGrasse I* (2001): *Campaign for Fiscal Equity v. State of New York, et al.*, 187 Misc.2d 1 (Sup. Ct. New York County, N.Y., 2001).

*DeGrasse IIA* (2005): *Campaign for Fiscal Equity v. State of New York, et al.* (Order dated Feb. 14, 2005).

*DeGrasse IIB* (2005): *Campaign for Fiscal Equity v. State of New York, et al.* (Order dated Mar. 16, 2005).

*Levittown* (1982): *Bd. of Educ. v. Nyquist*, 57 N.Y.2d 27, N.E.2d 359 (N.Y. 1982).

*Paynter* (2003): *Amber v. Paynter, et al. v. State of New York, et al.*, 100 N.Y.2d 434, 797 N.E.2d 1225 (N.Y. 2003).

*Yonkers* (2005): *Citizens for Yonkers, et al. v. State of New York, et al.*, Index No. 08850/05 (Sup. Ct. Westchester County, N.Y.).

## North Carolina

*Hoke County* (2004): *Hoke County Bd. of Educ., et al. v. State of North Carolina*, 358 N.C. 605, 599 S.E.2d 365 (2004).

## North Dakota

*Williston* (2003): *Williston Public School District No. 1, et al. v. State of North Dakota, et al.*, Civil No. 03-C-507 (Dist. Ct., Northwestern Judicial Circuit, N.D., 2003).

*Bismarck* (1994): *Bismarck Public School Dist. No. 1 v. State*, 511 N.W. 2d 247 (N.D. 1994).

## Ohio

*DeRolph* (1997): *DeRolph v. State*, 677 N.E.2d 733 (Ohio 1997).

*Lewis* (2003): *State ex rel. State v. Lewis*, 789 N.E.2d 195 (Ohio 2003), *cert. denied*, 124 S.Ct. 432 (2003).

## Oklahoma

*Oklahoma Education Association* (2007): *Oklahoma Education Association, et al. v. State of Oklahoma, ex rel.*, Case No. 103,702 (Okla. S.Ct., May 8, 2007).

## Oregon

*Coalition for Equitable School Funding* (1991): *Coalition for Equitable School Funding, Inc. v. State*, 811 P. 2d 116 (Ore. 1991).

*Pendleton* (2008): *Pendleton School District 16R, et al. v. State of Oregon*, 185 P.3d 471 (Ore. 2008).

## Pennsylvania

*Casey* (1979): *Danson v. Casey*, 399 A.2d 360 (Pa. 1979).

## Rhode Island

*Pawtucket* (1995): *City of Pawtucket v. Sundlun*, 662 A.2d 40 (R.I. 1995).

## South Carolina

*Abbeville County* (1999): *Abbeville County Sch. Dist. v. State*, 515 S.C. 535 (1999).

*Abbeville County* (2005): *Abbeville County School District, et al. v. The State of South Carolina*, Case No. 93-CP-31–0169 (Ct. Common Pleas, 3rd Jud. Cir., S.C., Dec. 29, 2005).

## South Dakota

*South Dakota Coalition of Schools* (2006): *South Dakota Coalition of Schools, et al. v. The State of South Dakota, et al.*, Civ#06–244 (6th Jud. Cir., S.D., Complaint filed June 21, 2006).

## Texas

*Edgewood* (1989): *Edgewood Independent School District v. Kirby*, 777 S.W.2d 391 (Tex. 1989).

*Edgewood* (1995): *Edgewood Independent School District v. Kirby*, 917 S.W.2d 717 (Tex. 1995).

*West Orange-Cove* (2004): *West Orange-Cove Consolidated Independent School District, et al. v. Shirley Neeley, et al.*, No. GV-100528 (Dist. Ct., Travis County, Tex., Nov. 30, 2004).

*West Orange-Cove* (2005): *Shirley Neely, et al. v. West Orange-Cove Consolidated Independent School District, et al.*, Case No. 04–1144 (Tex. 2005).

## Vermont

*Brigham* (1997): *Brigham v. State*, 692 A.2d 384 (Vt. 1997).

## Virginia

*Scott* (1954): *Scott v. Commonwealth*, 443 S.E. 2d 138 (Va. 1994).

## Washington

*Seattle* (1978): *Seattle Sch. Dist. v. Steele*, 585 P.2d 71 (Wash. 1978).

*McCleary* (2007): *McCleary v. State of Washington*, Case No. 07-2-02–02323–2SEA (Sup. Ct. King Cnty, Wash., Complaint filed Jan. 11, 2007).

## West Virginia

*Kelly* (1979): *Pauley v. Kelly*, 255 S.E.2d 859 (W.Va. 1979).

## Wisconsin

*Kukor* (1989): *Kukor v. Grover*, 436 N.W. 2d 568 (Wisc. 1989).

*Vincent* (2000): *Vincent v. Voight*, 614 N.W. 2d 388 (Wisc. 2000).

## Wyoming

*Campbell County* (1995): *Campbell County School District v. Wyoming*, 907 P.2d 1238 (Wyo. 1995).

*Campbell County* (2001): *Campbell County School District v. State*, 19 P.3d 518 (Wyo. 2001).

*Campbell County* (2006): *Campbell County School District, et al. v. State of Wyoming, et al.*, Docket No. 129–59 (1st Jud. Dist., Wyo., Jan. 31, 2006).

Campbell County (2008): *Campbell County School District, et al. v. State of Wyoming, et al.*, Docket No. 2008 WY 2 (S.C., Wyo., Jan. 8, 2008).

# Sources for Figures and Tables

Tables

| 1.1 | Day and Newburger (2002), adjusted to 2007 with consumer price index |
|------|------|
| 2.1 | http://nationsreportcard.gov/ |
| 2.2 | U.S. Bureau of the Census, Current Population Reports, various issues; U.S. Bureau of the Census (2007), table 223 |
| 3.1 | U.S. Department of Education (2007), Table 61, 66, and 167 |
| 3.2 | Authors calculations from 1962 Munich school yearbook and http://www.dpi.state.nd.us/dpi/reports/profiles/0607/10019.htm |
| 4.1–4.2 | Author calculations from decisions through July 2008 |
| 6.1 | U.S. Department of Education (2008), tables 12, 20, and 40 |
| 6.2 | Author calculations based on http://nationsreportcard.gov/ |
| 6.3 | NCHEMS Information Center: http://www.higheredinfo.org/ |

# References

Aaronson, Daniel, Lisa Barrow, and William Sander. 2007. Teachers and student achievement in the Chicago public high schools. *Journal of Labor Economics* 25, no. 1 (January): 95–135.

Abell Foundation. 2001. *Teacher certification reconsidered: Stumbling for quality.* Baltimore, MD: Abell Foundation.

ACT. 2005. *Crisis at the core: Preparing all students for college and work.* Iowa City, IA: ACT.

———. 2007. *ACT national curriculum survey, 2005–2006.* Iowa City, IA: ACT.

Administration for Children and Families. 2005. *Head Start impact study: First year findings.* Washington, DC: U.S. Department of Health and Human Services (May).

AIR/MAP. 2004. *The New York adequacy study: Determining the cost of providing all children in New York an adequate education.* Vol. 1, *Final report.* American Institutes for Research and Management Analysis and Planning (March).

American Institutes for Research. 1999. *An educators' guide to schoolwide reform.* Washington, DC: American Institutes for Research.

Anderson, Michael. 2007. Multiple inference and gender differences in the effects of preschool: A reevaluation of the Abecedarian, Perry Preschool, and Early Training Projects. Minneapolis, MN, DP-109, University of Minnesota and Federal Reserve Bank of Minneapolis (February).

Arenson, Karen W. 2004. Study of college readiness finds no progress in decade. *New York Times*, October 14.

Armey, Dick. 2003. A chance for freedom's advance: Let's put freedom to work in public education. (July 17). at http://www.freedomworks.org/informed/issues_template.php?issue_id=1490 [accessed September 22, 2008]

Armor, David J. 1995. *Forced justice: School desegregation and the law.* New York: Oxford University Press.

Armor, David J., Patricia Conry-Oseguera, Millicent Cox, Niceima King, Lorraine McDonnell, Anthony Pascal, Edward Pauly, and Gail Zellman. 1976. *Analysis of the school preferred reading program in selected Los Angeles minority schools.* Santa Monica, CA: RAND Corporation.

Aspin, Larry. 2007. Judicial retention election trends 1964–2006. *Judicature* 90, no. 5 (March–April): 208–13.

Augenblick & Myers. 2002a. *Calculation of the cost of a suitable education in Montana in 2001–2002.* Augenblick & Myers (August).

———. 2002b. *Calculation of the cost of an adequate education in Indiana in 2001–2002 using the professional judgment approach. Prepared for Indiana State Teachers Association.* Augenblick & Myers (September).

———. 2003. *Calculation of the cost of an adequate education in Missouri using the professional judgment and the successful school district approaches.* Augenblick & Myers (February).

Augenblick, John, and John Myers. 1997. *Recommendations for a base figure and pupil-weighted adjustments to the base figure for use in a new school finance system in Ohio.* Augenblick & Myers (July).

Augenblick, John, John Myers, Justin Silverstein, and Anne Barkis. 2002. *Calculation of the cost of a suitable education in Kansas in 2000–2001 using two different analytical approaches: Prepared for Legislative Coordinating Council.* Denver, CO: Augenblick & Myers (March).

Augenblick Palaich & Associates. 2003. *Calculation of the cost of an adequate education in North Dakota in 2002–2003 using the professional judgment approach.* Bismarck, ND: North Dakota Department of Public Instruction (September).

Baker, Bruce D. 2006. *Missouri's school finance formula fails to guarantee equal or minimally adequate educational opportunity to Missouri schoolchildren.* Report prepared on behalf of Committee for Educational Equality. Lawrence: University of Kansas.

Baker, Bruce D., and Michael A. Rebell. 2006. Robbing Peter to pay Paul: Weighted-student funding is not the "100 percent solution." *Education Week*, November 29, 30–31.

Ballou, Dale. 1999. The New York City teachers' union contract: Shackling principals' leadership. Civic Report No. 6, Center for Civic Innovation, Manhattan Institute (June).

———. 2001. Pay for performance in public and private schools. *Economics of Education Review* 20, no. 1 (February): 51–61.

Ballou, Dale, and Michael Podgursky. 1997. *Teacher pay and teacher quality.* Kalamazoo, MI: W. E. Upjohn Institute for Employment Research.

———. 2002. Returns to seniority among public school teachers. *Journal of Human Resources* 37, no. 4 (Fall): 892–912.

Barber, Michael, and Mona Mourshed. 2007. *How the world's best-performing school systems come out on top.* McKinsey.

Barnett, W. Steven. 1992. Benefits of compensatory preschool education. *Journal of Human Resources* 27, no. 2 (Spring): 279–312.

Barro, Robert J., and Xavier Sala-i-Martin. 2004. *Economic growth.* 2nd ed. Cambridge, MA: MIT Press.

Barron, Joan. 2006. Schools face high expectations. *Casper Star-Tribune*, March 24.

Baumol, William J. 1967. Macroeconomics of unbalanced growth: The anatomy of urban crisis. *American Economic Review* 57, no. 3 (June): 415–26.

Baumol, William J., and William G. Bowen. 1965. On the performing arts: The anatomy of their economic problems. *American Economic Review* 55 (May): 495–502.

Behrman, Jere R., Lori G. Kletzer, Michael S. McPherson, and Morton Owen Schapiro. 1998. The microeconomics of college choice, careers, and wages: Measuring the impact of higher education. *Annals of the American Academy of Political and Social Science* 559 (September): 12–23.

Belfield, Clive R., Milagros Nores, Steve Barnett, and Lawrence J. Schweinhart. 2006. The High/Scope Perry Preschool Program. *Journal of Human Resources* 41, no. 1 (Winter): 162–90.

Belfield, Clive R., and Heather Schwartz. 2007. The cost of high-quality preschool education in New Jersey. Education Law Center (December).

Belluscio, Frank. 2008. New state regulations likely to increase school administrative costs. *Daily Journal*, July 11.

Berends, Mark, Sheila Nataraj Kirby, Scott Naftel, and Christopher McKelvey. 1996. *Implementation and performance in New American Schools: Three years into scale-up*. Santa Monica, CA: RAND Corporation.

Berliner, David C., and Bruce J. Biddle. 1995. *The manufactured crisis: Myths, fraud, and the attack on America's public schools*. Boston: Addison-Wesley.

Berman, Sheldon, Perry Davis, Ann Koufman-Frederick, and David Urion. 2001. The rising costs of special education in Massachusetts: Causes and effects. In *Rethinking special education for a new century*, edited by Chester E. Finn Jr., Andrew J. Rotherham, and Charles R. Hokanson,183–211. Washington, DC: Thomas B. Fordham Foundation.

Berne, Robert, and Leanna Stiefel. 1984. *The measurement of equity in school finance: Conceptual, methodological, and empirical dimensions*. Baltimore, MD: Johns Hopkins University Press.

Berry, Christopher. 2007. The impact of school finance judgments on state fiscal policy. In *School money trials: The legal pursuit of educational adequacy*, edited by Martin R. West and Paul E. Peterson, 213–40. Washington, DC: Brookings Institution Press.

Besharov, Douglas J., Justus A. Myers, and Jeffrey S. Morrow. 2007. Costs per child for early childhood education and care: Comparing Head Start, CCDF child care, and prekindergarten/preschool programs (2003/2004). Washington, DC: American Enterprise Institute for Public Policy Research (August).

Besharov, Douglas J., Peter Germanis, Caeli Higney, and Douglas M. Call. 2008. Summaries of twenty-four early childhood evaluations. Welfare Reform Academy. College Park, Maryland School of Public Affairs (July).

Bifulco, Robert, and Helen F. Ladd. 2006. The impacts of charter schools on student achievement: Evidence from North Carolina. *Education Finance and Policy* 1, no. 1 (Winter): 50–90.

Bishop, John H. 1991. Achievement, test scores, and relative wages. In *Workers and their wages*, edited by Marvin H. Kosters,146–86. Washington, DC: AEI Press.

———. 2006. Drinking from the fountain of knowledge: Student incentive to study and learn—Externalities, information problems, and peer pressure. In *Handbook of the economics of education*, edited by Eric A. Hanushek and Finis Welch, 909–44. Amsterdam: North-Holland.

Black, Sandra E. 1999. Do better schools matter? Parental valuation of elementary education. *Quarterly Journal of Economics* 114, no. 2 (May): 577–99.

Black, Sandra E., Paul J. Devereux, and Kjell G. Salvanes. 2005. Why the apple doesn't fall far: Understanding intergenerational transmission of human capital. *American Economic Review* 95, no. 1 (March): 437–49.

Bloom, Howard S., ed. 2005. *Learning more from social experiments: Evolving analytic approaches*. New York: Russell Sage Foundation.

Bolick, Clint. 2008. Voting down vouchers: Lessons learned from Utah." *Education Next* 8, no. 1 (Spring): 46–51.

Booker, Kevin, Scott M. Gilpatric, Timothy Gronberg, and Dennis Jansen. 2007. The impact of charter school attendance on student performance. *Journal of Public Economics* 91, no. 5–6 (June): 849–76.

Borman, Geoffrey D., and Jerome V. D'Agostino. 1996. Title I and student achievement: A meta-analysis of federal evaluation results. *Educational Evaluation and Policy Analysis* 18, no. 4 (Winter): 309–26.

Borman, Geoffrey D., Gina M. Hewes, Laura T. Overman, and Shelly Brown. 2003. Comprehensive school reform and achievement: A meta-analysis. *Review of Educational Research* 73, no. 2 (Summer):125–230.

Bound, John, Michael F. Lovenheim, and Sarah Turner. 2007. Understanding the increased time to the baccalaureate degree. Stanford, Discussion Paper No. 06–43, Stanford Institute for Economic Policy Research (August).

Bound, John, and Sarah Turner. 2007. Cohort crowding: How resources affect collegiate attainment. *Journal of Public Economics* 91, no. 5–6 (June): 877–99.

Bowles, Samuel, and Henry M. Levin. 1968. The determinants of scholastic achievement: An appraisal of some recent evidence. *Journal of Human Resources* 3, no. 1 (Winter): 3–24.

Boyd, Don, Pam Grossman, Hamilton Lankford, Susanna Loeb, and James Wyckoff. 2006. How changes in entry requirements alter the teacher workforce and affect student achievement. *Education Finance and Policy* 1, no. 2 (Spring): 176–216.

Bracey, Gerald W. 1991. Why can't they be like we were? *Phi Beta Kappan* (October): 104–17.

———. 2002. Why do we scapegoat the schools? *Washington Post*, May 5, B01.

Brazer, Harvey E., and Therese A. McCarty. 1987. Interaction between demand for education and for municipal services. *National Tax Journal* 40, no. 4 (December): 555–66.

Brewer, Dominic J., Cathy Krop, Brian P. Gill, and Robert Reichardt. 1999. Estimating the cost of national class size reductions under different policy alternatives. *Educational Evaluation and Policy Analysis* 21, no. 2 (Summer): 179–92.

Brickley, James A., and Jerold L. Zimmerman. 2001. Changing incentives in a multitask environment: Evidence from a top-tier business school. *Journal of Corporate Finance* 7: 367–96.

Briffault, Richard. 2007. Adding adequacy to equity. In *School money trials: The legal pursuit of educational adequacy,* edited by Martin R. West and Paul E. Peterson, 25–54. Washington, DC: Brookings Institution Press.

Brooks-Gunn, Jeanne, Greg J. Duncan, and J. Lawrence Aber, eds. 1997a. *Neighborhood poverty: Context and consequences for children,* vol. 1. New York: Russell Sage Foundation.

——, eds. 1997b. *Neighborhood poverty: Policy implications in studying neighborhoods,* vol. 2. New York: Russell Sage Foundation.

Brunner, Eric, and Jennifer Imazeki. 2008. Probation length and teacher salaries: Does waiting pay off? (mimeo) Quinnipiac University (June).

Cain, Glen G., and Harold W. Watts. 1970. Problems in making policy inferences from the Coleman Report. *American Sociological Review* 35, no. 2 (April): 328–52.

California Department of Education. 2008. *State schools chief Jack O'Connell, teachers, support staff, administrators announce more than 20,000 teachers and support staff getting layoff notices due to budget crisis.* Sacramento, CA: California Department of Education (March 14).

Cameron, Stephen V., and James J. Heckman. 1993. The nonequivalence of high school equivalents. *Journal of Labor Economics* 11, no. 1, pt. 1 (January): 1–47.

Campbell, Frances A., Elizabeth P. Pungello, Sharon Miller-Johnson, Margaret Burchinal, and Craig T. Ramey. 2001. The development of cognitive and academic abilities: Growth curves from an early childhood educational experiment. *Developmental Psychology* 37, no. 2: 231–42.

Campbell, Frances A., and Craig T. Ramey. 1995. Cognitive and school outcomes for high-risk African-American students at middle adolescents: Positive effects of early intervention. *American Educational Research Journal* 32, no. 4 (Winter): 743–72.

Campbell, Jay R., Catherine M. Hombo, and John Mazzeo. 2000. *NAEP 1999 trends in academic progress: Three decades of student performance.* Washington: National Center for Education Statistics.

Carey, Kevin. 2002. *State poverty-based education funding: A survey of current programs and options for improvement.* Washington, DC: Center on Budget and Policy Priorities (November 7).

Carnegie Forum on Education and the Economy. 1986. *A nation prepared: Teachers for the 21st century.* Carnegie Forum on Education and the Economy.

Carneiro, Pedro, and James J. Heckman. 2003. Human capital policy. In *Inequality in America: What role for human capital policies?* edited by Benjamin M. Friedman, 77–239. Cambridge, MA: MIT Press.

Carneiro, Pedro, Costas Meghir, and Matthias Parey. 2007. Maternal education, home environments and the development of children and adolescents. London, WP15/07 (September).

Carnoy, Martin, and Susanna Loeb. 2002. Does external accountability affect student outcomes? A cross-state analysis. *Educational Evaluation and Policy Analysis* 24, no. 4 (Winter): 305–31.

Cawley, James, James J. Heckman, Lance Lochner, and Edward Vytlacil. 2000. Understanding the role of cognitive ability in accounting for the recent rise in the economic return to education. In *Meritocracy and economic inequality*, edited by Kenneth Arrow, Samuel Bowles and Steven Durlauf, 230–65. Princeton, NJ: Princeton University Press.

Center for Education Reform. 2003. *Charter school laws across the states: Ranking score card and legislative profiles.* Washington, DC: Center for Education Reform (January 2003).

Center on Education Policy. 2007. *Answering the question that matters most: Has student achievement increased since No Child Left Behind?* Washington, DC: Center on Education Policy (June).

———. 2008. *Has student achievement increased since 2002?* Washington, DC: Center for Education Policy.

Chambers, Jay G., Jamie Shkolnik, and María Pérez. 2003. *Total expenditures for students with disabilities, 1999–2000: Spending variation by disability.* Palo Alto, CA: American Institutes for Research (June).

Chan, Sewell. 2007. Mayor announces plan for teacher merit pay. *New York Times*, October 17.

Christensen, Clayton M., and Michael B. Horn. 2008. How do we transform our schools? *Education Next* 8, no. 3 (Summer): 12–19.

Christensen, Clayton M., Michael B. Horn, and Curtis W. Johnson. 2008. *Disrupting class: How disruptive innovation will change the way the world learns.* New York: McGraw-Hill.

Chubb, John E. 2001. The system. In *A primer on America's schools*, edited by Terry M. Moe, 15–42. Stanford, CA: Hoover Institution Press.

———, ed. 2005. *Within our reach: How America can educate every child.* Stanford: Rowman & Littlefield.

Chubb, John E., and Terry M. Moe. 1990. *Politics, markets and America's schools.* Washington, DC: Brookings Institution Press.

Ciotti, Paul. 1998. Money and school performance: Lessons from the Kansas City desegregation experiment. Washington, no. 298, Cato Institute (March).

Clark, Melissa. 2003. Education reform, redistribution, and student achievement: Evidence from the Kentucky Education Reform Act. Mathematica Policy Research (October).

Clotfelter, Charles T. 2004. *After* Brown: *The rise and retreat of school desegregation*. Princeton, NJ: Princeton University Press.

Clune, William H. 1994. The shift from equity to adequacy in school finance. *Educational Policy* 8, no. 4 (December): 376–94.

Coate, Douglas, and James VanderHoff. 1999. Public school spending and student achievement: The case of New Jersey. *Cato Journal* 19, no. 1 (Spring/Summer): 85–99.

Coelli, Michael B., David A. Green, and William P. Warburton. 2007. Breaking the cycle? The effect of education on welfare receipt among children of welfare recipients. *Journal of Public Economics* 91, no. 7–8 (August): 1369–98.

Cohen, David K., and Richard J. Murnane. 1986. Merit pay and the evaluation problem: Understanding why most merit pay plans fail and a few survive. *Harvard Educational Review* 56, no. 1 (February): 1–17.

Coleman, James S., Ernest Q. Campbell, Carol J. Hobson, James McPartland, Alexander M. Mood, Frederic D. Weinfeld, and Robert L. York. 1966. *Equality of educational opportunity*. Washington, DC: U.S. Government Printing Office.

Committee on Science Engineering and Public Policy. 2005. *Rising above the gathering storm: Energizing and employing America for a brighter economic future*. Washington, DC: National Academies Press.

Congressional Budget Office. 1986. *Trends in educational achievement*. Washington, DC: Congressional Budget Office.

———. 1987. *Educational achievement: Explanations and implications of recent trends*. Washington, DC: Congressional Budget Office.

Coons, John E., William H. Clune, and Stephen D. Sugarman. 1970. *Private wealth and public education*. Cambridge, MA: Belknap Press of Harvard University Press.

Coons, John E., and Stephen D. Sugarman. 1978. *Education by choice: The case for family control*. Berkeley: University of California Press.

Cooperman, Saul. 2007. Good families make good schools and other lessons of urban reform learned in New Jersey (and in life). *Education Week*, January 24, 38–39.

Costrell, Robert M. 2007. The winning defense in Massachusetts. In *School money trials: The legal pursuit of educational adequacy*, edited by Martin R. West and Paul E. Peterson, 278–304. Washington, DC: Brookings Institution Press.

Costrell, Robert M., Eric A. Hanushek, and Susanna Loeb. 2008. What do cost functions tell us about the cost of an adequate education? *Peabody Journal of Education*. 83, no. 2:198–223.

Costrell, Robert M., and Michael Podgursky. 2008. Peaks, cliffs, and valleys. *Education Next* 8, no. 1 (Winter): 22–28.

Council of Economic Advisers. 2006. *Economic report of the president*. Washington, DC: Council of Economic Advisers (February).

Council of Great City Schools. 2006. Urban school superintendents: Characteristics, tenure, and salary fifth survey and report. *Urban Indicator* 8, no.1 (June).

Cross, Christopher T. 2004. *Political education: National policy comes of age.* New York: Teachers College, Columbia University.

Cullen, Julie B. 2003. The impact of fiscal incentives on student disability rates. *Journal of Public Economics* 87, no. 7–8 (August): 1557–89.

Cullen, Julie B., and Susanna Loeb. 2004. School finance reform in Michigan: Evaluating Proposal A. In *Helping children left behind: State aid and the pursuit of educational equity,* edited by John Yinger, 215–249, Cambridge, MA: MIT Press.

Cunha, Flavio, James J. Heckman, Lance Lochner, and Dimitriy V. Masterov. 2006. Interpreting the evidence on life cycle skill formation. In *Handbook of the economics of education,* edited by Eric A. Hanushek and Finis Welch, 697–812. Amsterdam: Elsevier.

Currie, Janet, and Duncan Thomas. 1995. Does Head Start make a difference? *American Economic Review* 85, no. 3 (June): 341–64.

———. 2000. School quality and the longer-term effects of Head Start. *Journal of Human Resources* 35, no. 4 (September): 755–74.

Darling-Hammond, Linda, Barnett Berry, and Amy Thoreson. 2001. Does teacher certification matter? Evaluating the evidence. *Educational Evaluation and Policy Analysis* 23, no. 1 (Spring): 57–77.

Day, Jennifer Cheeseman, and Eric C. Newburger. 2002. *The big payoff: Educational attainment and synthetic estimates of work-life earnings.* Current Population Reports, P23–210. Washington, DC: U.S. Bureau of the Census (July).

Decker, Paul T., Daniel P. Mayer, and Steven Glazerman. 2004. The effects of Teach for America on students: Findings from a national evaluation. Discussion Paper No. 1285–04, Institute for Research on Poverty (July).

deMoss, Karen. 2004. Political contexts and education finance litigation: Toward a methodology for comparative state-level analyses. In *Money, politics, and law: Intersections and conflicts in the provision of educational opportunity,* edited by Karen deMoss and Kenneth Wong, 47–60. Larchmont, NY: Eye on Education.

Department of Education. 2007. Chancellor Klein announces 86% of eligible schools opt to participate in performance pay program (press release, December 18).

Diamond, Laura, 2008. Rural schools withdraw suit against Georgia. *Atlanta Journal-Constitution,* September 16.

Downes, Thomas A. 1992. Evaluating the impact of school finance reform on the provision of public education: The California case. *National Tax Journal* 45, no. 4 (December): 405–19.

———. 2004. School finance reform and school quality: Lessons from Vermont. In *Helping children left behind: State aid and the pursuit of educational equity,* edited by John Yinger, 284–313. Cambridge, MA: MIT Press.

Duffett, Ann, Steve Farkas, Andrew J. Rotherham, and Elena Silva. 2008. Waiting to be won over: Teachers speak on the profession, unions, and reform. Washington, D.C.: Education Sector (May).

Duncombe, William. 2006. Responding to the charge of alchemy: Strategies for evaluating the reliability and validity of costing-out research. *Journal of Education Finance* 32, no. 2 (Fall): 137–69.

———. 2007. *Estimating the cost of meeting student performance standards in the St. Louis public schools.* Report prepared for the board of education, City of St. Louis (January).

Duncombe, William, and Jocelyn M. Johnston. 2004. The impacts of school finance reform in Kansas: Equity is in the eye of the beholder. In *Helping children left behind: State aid and the pursuit of educational equity*, edited by John Yinger, 148–93. Cambridge, MA: MIT Press.

Duncombe, William, and John Yinger. 1998. Financing higher standards in public education: The importance of accounting for educational costs. Policy Brief No. 10/1998, Syracuse University.

Dunn, Joshua, and Martha Derthick. 2007a. Adequacy litigation and the separation of powers. In *School money trials: The legal pursuit of educational adequacy*, edited by Martin R. West and Paul E. Peterson, 322–44. Washington, DC: Brookings Institution Press.

———. 2007b. Judging money: When courts decide how to spend taxpayer dollars. *Education Next* 7, no. 1 (Winter): 68–74.

*Education Week.* 2001. *Quality counts 2001: A better balance.* January 11 ed. Washington, DC: Education Week.

———. 2005. *Quality counts 2005: No small change: Targeting money toward student performance.* January 6 ed. Washington, DC: Education Week.

———. 2006. *Quality counts 2006.* January 6 ed. Washington, DC: Education Week.

———. 2007a. Alaska, Arizona OK'd for "growth models." *Education Week*, July 18, 25.

———. 2007b. Coalition spells out "essentials" of plans for performance pay. *Education Week*, August 1, 6.

———. 2007c. *Quality counts 2007.* January 6 ed. Washington, DC: Education Week.

———. 2008a. Lawmakers in N.Y. bar student scores in weighing tenure. *Education Week*, April 23, 20.

———. 2008b. States experiment with pay for performance. In *Equality counts 2008: Tapping into teaching.* Washington, DC: Education Week.

Ehrenberg, Ronald G., Dominic J. Brewer, Adam Gamoran, and J. Douglas Willms. 2001a. Class size and student achievement. *Psychological Science in the Public Interest* 2, no. 1 (May): 1–30.

———. 2001b. Does class size matter? *Scientific American* (November): 83–89.

Einhorn, Erin. 2006. Klein: We gotta keep the rejects. *New York Daily News*, September 6.

Epple, Dennis, and Thomas Nechyba. 2004. Fiscal decentralization. In *Handbook of regional and urban economics*, edited by J. Vernon Henderson and Jacques-François Thisse, 2423–80. Amsterdam: Elsevier.

Evers, Williamson M., and Paul Clopton. 2006. High spending, low performing school districts In *Courting failure: How school adequacy lawsuits pervert judges' good intentions and harm our children*, edited by Eric A. Hanushek, 103–94. Stanford: Education Next Books.

Feldstein, Martin S. 1975. Wealth neutrality and local choice in public education. *American Economic Review* 65, no. 1 (March): 75–89.

Ferejohn, John. 1995. Law, legislation, and positive political theory. In *Modern political economy: Old topics, new directions*, edited by Jeffrey S. Banks and Eric A. Hanushek. New York: Cambridge University Press.

Fessenden, Ford. 2007. For some schools and taxpayers, a big relief. *New York Times*, April 22, 6.

Figlio, David N., and Maurice E. Lucas. 2004. Do high grading standards affect student performance? *Journal of Public Economics* 88, no. 9–10 (August): 1815–34.

Figlio, David N., and Cecilia Elena Rouse. 2006. Do accountability and voucher threats improve low-performing schools? *Journal of Public Economics* 90, no. 1–2 (January): 239–55.

Fine, Michelle, Liza Pappas, Stan Karp, Lesley Hirsch, Alan Sadovnik, Andre Keeton, and Mary Bennett. 2007. New Jersey's special review assessment: Loophole or lifeline? New York, CUNY Graduate Center (August).

Finn, Chester E., Jr. 2001. Getting better teachers—and treating them right. In *A Primer on America's schools*, edited by Terry M. Moe, 127–50. Stanford: Hoover Institution Press.

———. 2008. *Troublemaker: A personal history of school reform since sputnik*. Princeton, NJ: Princeton University Press.

———. 2009. *Reroute the pre-school juggernaut*. Stanford, CA: Hoover Institution Press.

Finn, Chester E., Jr, Bruno V. Manno, and Gregg Vanourek. 2000. *Charter schools in action: Renewing public education*. Princeton, NJ: Princeton University Press.

Finn, Chester E., Jr, Andrew J. Rotherham, and Charles R. Hokanson, Jr., eds. 2001. *Rethinking special education for a new century*. Washington, DC: Thomas B. Fordham Foundation and Progressive Policy Institute.

Fischel, William A. 1989. Did Serrano cause Proposition 13? *National Tax Journal* 42 (December): 465–74.

———. 2006. The courts and public school finance: Judge-made centralization and economic research. In *Handbook of the economics of education*, edited by Eric A. Hanushek and Finis Welch, 1277–1325. Amsterdam: North-Holland.

Flanagan, Ann E., and Sheila E. Murray. 2004. A decade of reform: The impact of school reform in Kentucky. In *Helping children left behind: State aid and the pursuit of educational equity*, edited by John Yinger, 195–214. Cambridge, MA: MIT Press.

Friedman, Milton. 1962. *Capitalism and freedom*. Chicago: University of Chicago Press.

Friedman, Milton, and Rose Friedman. 1980. *Free to choose: A personal statement*. San Diego, CA: Harcourt.

Friedman, Thomas L. 2007. *The world is flat: A brief history of the twenty-first century*. Release 3.0 ed. New York: Picador/Farrar, Strauss & Giroux.

Fryer, Roland G., Jr., and Steven D. Levitt. 2004. Understanding the black-white test score gap in the first two years of school. *Review of Economics and Statistics* 86, no. 2 (May): 447–64.

Fuller, Bruce. 2007. *Standardized childhood: The political and cultural struggle over early education*. Stanford, CA: Stanford University Press.

Galinsky, Ellen. 2006. *Economic benefits of high-quality early childhood programs: What makes the difference?* New York: Committee for Economic Development (February).

Garces, Eliana, Duncan Thomas, and Janet Currie. 2002. Longer-term effects of Head Start. *American Economic Review* 92, no. 4 (September): 999–1012.

Gedicks, Frederick Mark. 2004. "Reconstructing the Blaine Amendments." *First Amendment Law Review* 2:85–106.

Gewertz, Catherine. 2004. N.J. panel to weigh in on constitution convention. *Education Week*, December 1, 20.

———. 2006. Raising bar in N.J. includes closing test loophole. *Education Week*, October 18, 1, 14.

———. 2007. N.Y.C. district issues. *Education Week*, November 14, 6.

———. 2008. Miami board buys out leader's contract. *Education Week*, September 17, 6.

Gill, Brian, Ron Zimmer, Jolley Christman, and Suzanne Blanc. 2007. *State takeover, school restructuring, private management, and student achievement in Philadelphia*. Santa Monica, CA: RAND Corporation.

Glazer, Nathan. 2008. The good, the bad and the ugly, an honest look at union hero Albert Shanker. *Education Next* 8, no. 3 (Summer): 82–83.

Glennan, Thomas K., Jr. 1998. *New American Schools after six years*. Santa Monica, CA: RAND Corporation.

Goertz, Margaret E., and Michael Weiss. 2007. Money order in the court: The promise and pitfalls of redistributing educational dollars through court mandates: The case of New Jersey. Paper presented at *Annual meeting of the American Education Finance Association*. Baltimore, MD.

Goldhaber, Dan D., and Dominic J. Brewer. 2000. Does teacher certification matter? High school teacher certification status and student achievement. *Educational Evaluation and Policy Analysis* 22, no. 2 (Summer): 129–45.

Goldhaber, Dan D., and Dominic J. Brewer. 2001. Evaluating the evidence on teacher certification: A rejoinder. *Educational Evaluation and Policy Analysis* 23, no. 1 (Spring): 79–86.

Goldin, Claudia, and Lawrence F. Katz. 2008. *The race between education and technology.* Cambridge, MA: Harvard University Press.

Gormley, William T., Jr., Deborah Phillips, and Ted Gayer. 2008. The early years: Preschool programs can boost school readiness. *Science* 320 (June 27): 1723–24.

Gormley, William T., Jr., Ted Gayer, Deborah Phillips, and Brittany Dawson. 2005. The effects of universal pre-K on cognitive development. *Developmental Psychology* 41, no. 6:872–84.

Governor's Committee on Educational Excellence. 2007a. *Students first: Renewing hope for California's future.* Sacramento, CA: Governor's Committee on Educational Excellence (November).

———. 2007b. *Students first: Renewing hope for California's future: Technical report.* Sacramento, CA: Governor's Committee on Educational Excellence (November).

Gramlich, Edward M. 1986. Evaluation of education projects: The case of the Perry Preschool Program. *Economics of Education Review* 5, no. 1:17–24.

Gramlich, Edward M., and Patricia P. Koshel. 1975. *Educational performance contracting.* Washington, DC: Brookings Institution Press.

*Grand Forks Herald.* 2005. Schools lawsuit over ND finance progresses. *Grand Forks Herald,* November 16.

Greene, Jay P. 2001a. An evaluation of the Florida A-Plus Accountability and School Choice Program. New York: Center for Civic Innovation, Manhattan Institute (November).

———. 2001b. The looming shadow: Florida gets its "F" schools to shape up. *Education Next* 1, no. 4 (Winter): 76–82.

———. 2007. Fixing special education. *Peabody Journal of Education* 82, no. 4:703–23.

Greene, Jay P., and Greg Forster. 2004. The teachability index: Can disadvantaged students learn? New York, Education Working Paper No. 6, Manhattan Institute (September).

Greene, Jay P., and Julie R. Trivitt. 2008. Can judges improve academic achievement? *Peabody Journal of Education* 83, no. 2 (April):224–37.

Greene, Jay P., and Marcus A. Winters. 2005. Public high school graduation and college-readiness rates: 1991–2002. New York, Education Working Paper No. 8, Manhattan Institute (February).

———. 2007. Debunking a special education myth: Don't blame private options for rising costs. *Education Next* 7, no. 2 (Spring): 67–71.

Grissmer, David, and Ann Flanagan. 1998. *Exploring rapid achievement gains in North Carolina and Texas.* Washington, DC: National Goals Panel (November).

Grissmer, David W., Ann Flanagan, Jennifer Kawata, and Stephanie Williamson. 2000. *Improving student achievement: What NAEP state test scores tell us.* Santa Monica, CA: RAND Corporation.

Grissmer, David W., Sheila Nataraj Kirby, Mark Berends, and Stephanie Williamson. 1994. *Student achievement and the changing American family.* Santa Monica, CA: RAND Corporation.

Gronberg, Timothy J., Dennis W. Jansen, Lori L. Taylor, and Kevin Booker. 2004. *School outcomes and school costs: The cost function approach.* Mimeo, Texas A&M University.

Grossman, Gene M., and Elhanan Helpman. 1991. *Innovation and growth in a global economy.* Cambridge, MA: MIT Press.

Grossman, Pam, and Susanna Loeb. 2008. *Alternative routes to teaching: Mapping the new landscape of teacher education.* Cambridge, MA: Harvard Education Press.

Guthrie, James W., and Richard Rothstein. 1999. Enabling "adequacy" to achieve reality: Translating adequacy into state school finance distribution arrangements. In *Adequacy in education finance: Issues and perspectives,* edited by Helen F. Ladd, Rosemary Chalk and Janet S. Hansen, 209–59. Washington, DC: National Academy Press.

Guthrie, James W., and Matthew G. Springer. 2007a. Courtroom alchemy: Adequacy advocates turn guesstimates into gold. *Education Next* 7, no. 1 (Winter): 20–27.

———. 2007b. Politicization of the school finance legal process. In *School money trials: The legal pursuit of educational adequacy,* edited by Martin R. West and Paul E. Peterson, 102–30. Washington, DC: Brookings Institution Press.

Hakim, Danny, and Jeremy W. Peters. 2008. Legislators balk at tying teacher tenure to student tests. *New York Times.* April 9.

Hamilton, Alexander. 1788. Federalist Paper No. 78. June 14.

Hanushek, Eric A. 1971. Teacher characteristics and gains in student achievement: Estimation using micro data. *American Economic Review* 60, no. 2 (May): 280–88.

———. 1991. When school finance "reform" may not be good policy. *Harvard Journal on Legislation* 28, no. 2 (Summer): 423–56.

———. 1992. The trade-off between child quantity and quality. *Journal of Political Economy* 100, no. 1 (February): 84–117.

———. 1994. Money might matter somewhere: A response to Hedges, Laine, and Greenwald. *Educational Researcher* 23, no. 4 (May): 5–8.

———. 1997a. Assessing the effects of school resources on student performance: An update. *Educational Evaluation and Policy Analysis* 19, no. 2 (Summer): 141–64.

———. 1997b. The productivity collapse in schools. In *Developments in school finance, 1996,* edited by William J. Fowler Jr., 185–95. Washington, DC: National Center for Education Statistics.

Hanushek, Eric A. 1999a. The evidence on class size. In *Earning and learning: How schools matter*, edited by Susan E. Mayer and Paul E. Peterson, 131–68. Washington, DC: Brookings Institution Press.

———. 1999b. Some findings from an independent investigation of the Tennessee STAR experiment and from other investigations of class size effects. *Educational Evaluation and Policy Analysis* 21, no. 2 (Summer): 143–63.

———. 2002. Publicly provided education. In *Handbook of public economics*, edited by Alan J. Auerbach and Martin Feldstein, 2045–141. Amsterdam: Elsevier.

———. 2003. The failure of input-based schooling policies. *Economic Journal* 113, no. 485 (February): F64–98.

———. 2006a. Alternative school policies and the benefits of general cognitive skills. *Economics of Education Review* 25, no. 4 (August): 447–62.

———. 2006b. School resources. In *Handbook of the economics of education*, edited by Eric A. Hanushek and Finis Welch, 865–908. Amsterdam: North-Holland.

———. 2006c. Science violated: Spending projections and the "costing out" of an adequate education. In *Courting failure: How school finance lawsuits exploit judges' good intentions and harm our children*, edited by Eric A. Hanushek, 257–311. Stanford: Education Next Books.

———. 2006d. Teacher compensation. In *Reforming education in Florida*, edited by Paul E. Peterson,149–63. Stanford, CA: Hoover Institution Press.

———. 2007a. The confidence men: Selling adequacy, making millions. *Education Next* 7, no. 3 (Spring): 73–78.

———. 2007b. The single salary schedule and other issues of teacher pay. *Peabody Journal of Education* 82, no. 4 (October): 574–86.

———. 2007c. Some U.S. evidence on how the distribution of educational outcomes can be changed. In *Schools and the equal opportunity problem*, edited by Ludger Woessmann and Paul E. Peterson, 159–90. Cambridge, MA: MIT Press.

———. 2009. Teacher deselection. In *Creating a new teaching profession*, edited by Dan Goldhaber and Jane Hannaway. Washington, DC: Urban Institute Press.

Hanushek, Eric A., Dean T. Jamison, Eliot A. Jamison, and Ludger Woessmann. 2008. Education and economic growth: It's not just going to school but learning that matters. *Education Next* 8, no. 2 (Spring): 62–70.

Hanushek, Eric A., and John F. Kain. 1972. On the value of "equality of educational opportunity" as a guide to public policy. In *On equality of educational opportunity*, edited by Frederick Mosteller and Daniel P. Moynihan, 116–45. New York: Random House.

Hanushek, Eric A., John F. Kain, Daniel M. O'Brien, and Steve G. Rivkin. 2005. The market for teacher quality. Working Paper No. 11154, National Bureau of Economic Research (February).

Hanushek, Eric A., John F. Kain, and Steve G. Rivkin. 2002. Inferring program effects for specialized populations: Does special education raise achievement for students with disabilities? *Review of Economics and Statistics* 84, no. 4 (November): 584–99.

———. 2004. Why public schools lose teachers. *Journal of Human Resources* 39, no. 2:326–54.

Hanushek, Eric A., John F. Kain, Steve G. Rivkin, and Gregory F. Branch. 2007. Charter school quality and parental decision making with school choice. *Journal of Public Economics* 91, no. 5–6 (June): 823–48.

Hanushek, Eric A., and Dennis D. Kimko. 2000. Schooling, labor force quality, and the growth of nations. *American Economic Review* 90, no. 5 (December): 1184–1208.

Hanushek, Eric A., and Richard R. Pace. 1995. Who chooses to teach (and why)? *Economics of Education Review* 14, no. 2 (June): 101–17.

Hanushek, Eric A., and Margaret E. Raymond. 2001. The confusing world of educational accountability. *National Tax Journal* 54, no. 2 (June): 365–84.

———. 2003. Lessons about the design of state accountability systems. In *No Child Left Behind? The politics and practice of accountability,* edited by Paul E. Peterson and Martin R. West, 127–51. Washington, DC: Brookings Institution Press.

———. 2005. Does school accountability lead to improved student performance? *Journal of Policy Analysis and Management* 24, no. 2 (Spring): 297–327.

Hanushek, Eric A., and Steven G. Rivkin. 1997. Understanding the twentieth-century growth in U.S. school spending. *Journal of Human Resources* 32, no. 1 (Winter): 35–68.

———. 2004. How to improve the supply of high quality teachers. In *Brookings papers on education policy 2004,* edited by Diane Ravitch, 7–25. Washington, DC: Brookings Institution Press.

———. 2006. Teacher quality. In *Handbook of the economics of education,* edited by Eric A. Hanushek and Finis Welch, 1051–78. Amsterdam: North-Holland.

———. 2007. Pay, working conditions, and teacher quality. *Future of Children* 17, no. 1 (Spring): 69–86.

Hanushek, Eric A., Steven G. Rivkin, and Lori L. Taylor. 1996. Aggregation and the estimated effects of school resources. *Review of Economics and Statistics* 78, no. 4 (November): 611–27.

Hanushek, Eric A., and Julie A. Somers. 2001. Schooling, inequality, and the impact of government. In *The causes and consequences of increasing inequality,* edited by Finis Welch, 169–99. Chicago: University of Chicago Press.

Hanushek, Eric A., and Ludger Woessmann. 2008. The role of cognitive skills in economic development. *Journal of Economic Literature* 46, no. 3 (September): 607–68.

———. In process. *The human capital of nations.*

Hanushek, Eric A., and Kuzey Yilmaz. 2007. The complementarity of Tiebout and Alonso. *Journal of Housing Economics* 16, no. 2 (June): 243–61.

Hatry, Harry P., John M. Greiner, and Brenda G. Ashford. 1994. *Issues and case studies in teacher incentive plans*. 2nd ed. Washington, DC: Urban Institute.

Haveman, Robert, and Barbara Wolfe. 1993. Children's prospects and children's policy. *Journal of Economic Perspectives* 7, no. 4 (Fall): 153–74.

————. 1994. *Succeeding generations (on the effects of investments in children)*. New York: Russell Sage Foundation.

Haynes, Norris M., James P. Comer, and Muriel Hamilton-Lee. 1988. The school development program: A model for school improvement. *Journal of Negro Education* 57, no. 1 (Winter): 11–21.

Head Start Bureau. 2005. *Biennial report to Congress: The status of children in Head Start programs*. Washington, DC: U.S. Department of Health and Human Services.

Heckman, James J. 2006. Skill formation and the economics of investing in disadvantaged children. *Science* 312, no. 5782 (June 30): 1900–1902.

Heckman, James J., and Paul A. LaFontaine. 2007. The American high school graduation rate: Trends and levels. Working Paper No. 13670, National Bureau of Economic Research (December).

————. In process. The GED and the problem of noncognitive skills in America. Chicago: Department of Economics, University of Chicago.

Heckman, James J., Lance J. Lochner, and Petra E. Todd. 2006. Earnings functions, rates of return and treatment effects: The Mincer equation and beyond. In *Handbook of the economics of education*, edited by Eric A. Hanushek and Finis Welch, 307–458. Amsterdam: North-Holland.

Heckman, James J., and Dimitriy V. Masterov. 2007. The productivity argument for investing in young children. *Review of Agricultural Economics* 29, no. 3:446–93.

Heckman, James J., and Edward Vytlacil. 2001. Identifying the role of cognitive ability in explaining the level of and change in the return to schooling. *Review of Economics and Statistics* 83, no. 1 (February): 1–12.

Hedges, Larry V., Richard D. Laine, and Rob Greenwald. 1994. Does money matter? A meta-analysis of studies of the effects of differential school inputs on student outcomes. *Educational Researcher* 23, no. 3 (April): 5–14.

Heise, Michael. 1995. State constitutions, school finance litigation, and the "third wave": From equity to adequacy. *Temple Law Review* 1151 (Fall).

————. 2007. Adequacy litigation in an era of accountability. In *School money trials: The legal pursuit of educational adequacy*, edited by Martin R. West and Paul E. Peterson. 262–77. Washington, DC: Brookings Institution Press.

Henig, Jeffrey R. 2008. *Spin cycle: How research is used in policy debates—The case of charter schools*. New York: Russell Sage Foundation.

Henke, Robin R., Phillip Kaufman, Stephen P. Broughman, and Kathryn Chandler. 2000. *Issues related to estimating the home-schooled population in the*

*United States with national household survey data*. Washington, DC: National Center for Education Statistics (September).

Hess, Frederick M. 2007. Adequacy judgments and school reform. In *School money trials: The legal pursuit of educational adequacy*, edited by Martin R. West and Paul E. Peterson, 159–94. Washington, DC: Brookings Institution Press.

———, ed. 2008. *When research matters: How scholarship influences education policy*. Cambridge, MA: Harvard Education Press.

Hill, Paul T., ed. 2006. *Charter schools against the odds*. Stanford, CA: Hoover Institution Press.

———. 2009. *School choice: Why is it so slow?* Stanford, CA: Education Next Books.

Hill, Paul T., and Josephine Bonan. 1991. *Decentralization and accountability in public education*. Santa Monica, CA: RAND Corporation.

Hoff, David. 2002. States revise the meaning of "proficient." *Education Week*, October 9.

———. 2006. N.Y. judge denies request by mother for tuition aid. *Education Week*, February 22, 6.

———. 2007. "Growth" pilot now open to all states. *Education Week*, December 12, 1, 20.

Hoffman, Lee McGraw. 2003. *Overview of public elementary and secondary schools: School year 2001–02*. Washington, DC: National Center for Education Statistics (May 2003).

Honawar, Vaishali. 2007. New York City taps lawyers to weed out bad teachers. *Education Week*, December 5, 13.

Horowitz, Donald L. 1977. *The courts and social policy*. Washington, DC: Brookings Institution Press.

Howell, William G., and Paul E. Peterson. 2002. *The education gap: Vouchers and urban schools*. Washington, DC: Brookings Institution Press.

Howell, William G., and Martin R. West. 2008. Is the price right? Probing Americans' knowledge of school spending. *Education Next* 8, no. 3 (Summer): 36–41.

Howell, William G., Martin R. West, and Paul E. Peterson. 2007. What Americans think about their schools: The 2007 Education Next–PEPG survey. *Education Next* 7, no. 4 (Fall): 12–26.

Hoxby, Caroline Minter. 2001a. All school finance equalizations are not created equal. *Quarterly Journal of Economics* 116, no. 4 (November): 1189–1231.

———. 2001b. If families matter most, where do schools come in? In *A primer on America's schools*, edited by Terry M. Moe, 89–125. Stanford, CA: Hoover Institution Press.

———. 2003. School choice and school productivity (or could school choice be a tide that lifts all boats?). In *The economics of school choice*, edited by Caroline Minter Hoxby. Chicago: University of Chicago Press: 287–341.

Hoxby, Caroline Minter. 2005. Adequate yearly progress: Refining the heart of the No Child Left Behind Act. In *Within our reach: How America can educate every child*, edited by John E. Chubb. Stanford: Hoover Institution Press: 79–94.

Hoxby, Caroline Minter, and Ilyana Kuziemko. 2004. Robin Hood and his not-so-merry plan: Capitalization and the self-destruction of Texas' school finance equalization plan. Working Paper No. 10722, National Bureau of Economic Research (September).

Hoxby, Caroline Minter, and Andrew Leigh. 2004. Pulled away or pushed out? Explaining the decline of teacher aptitude in the United States. *American Economic Review* 94, no. 2 (May): 236–40.

Hoxby, Caroline Minter, and Jonah E. Rockoff. 2004. The impact of charter schools on student achievement. Mimeo, Harvard University (November).

Hudetz, Mary. 2008. Oregon measure seeks merit-based pay for teachers. *Boston Globe*, September 29.

Imazeki, Jennifer. 2007. Assessing the costs of K–12 education in California public schools. IREPP Research Summary. Institute for Research on Education Policy and Practice, Stanford University.

———. 2008. Assessing the costs of adequacy in California public schools: A cost function approach. *Education Finance and Policy* 3, no. 1 (Winter): 90–108.

Inman, Robert P. 1978. Optimal fiscal reform of metropolitan schools. *American Economic Review* 68, no. 1 (March): 107–22.

Jacob, Brian A., and Lars Lefgren. 2006. When principals rate teachers. *Education Next* 6, no. 2 (Spring): 59–69.

Jacob, Brian A., and Steven D. Levitt. 2003. Rotten apples: An investigation of the prevalence and predictors of teacher cheating. *Quarterly Journal of Economics* 118, no. 3 (August): 843–77.

Jamison, Eliot A., Dean T. Jamison, and Eric A. Hanushek. 2007. The effects of education quality on mortality decline and income growth. *Economics of Education Review* 26, no. 6 (December): 772–89.

Jepsen, Christopher, and Steve G. Rivkin. 2009. Class reduction and student achievement: The potential trade-off between teacher quality and class size reduction. *Journal of Human Resources*, Winter.

Johns, Thomas L. 1972. *Public school finance programs, 1971–72*. Washington, DC: U.S. Department of Health, Education, and Welfare.

Juhn, Chinhui, Kevin M. Murphy, and Brooks Pierce. 1991. Accounting for the slowdown in black-white wage convergence. In *Workers and their wages*, edited by Marvin H. Kosters, 107–43. Washington, DC: AEI Press.

———. 1993. Wage inequality and the rise in returns to skill. *Journal of Political Economy* 101, no. 3 (June): 410–42.

Kane, Thomas J., Jonah E. Rockoff, and Douglas O. Staiger. 2006. What does certification tell us about teacher effectiveness? Evidence from New York City. Working Paper No. 12155, National Bureau of Economic Research (April).

Kane, Thomas J., and Douglas O. Staiger. 2002. Volatility in school test scores: Implications for test-based accountability systems. In *Brookings papers on education policy 2002*, edited by Diane Ravitch, 235–69. Washington, DC: Brookings Institution Press.

Keller, Beth, and Vaishali Honawar. 2008. Performance-pay setup in Texas shows promise. *Education Week*, March 12, 1.

Kershaw, Joseph A., and Roland N. McKean. 1962. *Teacher shortages and salary schedules.* New York: McGraw-Hill.

Kirp, David L. 2007. *The sandbox investment: The preschool movement and kids-first politics.* Cambridge, MA: Harvard University Press.

Kohn, Alfie. 1999. *Punished by rewards: The trouble with gold stars, incentive plans, A's, praise, and other bribes.* Boston: Houghton Mifflin.

Kolderie, Ted. 2004. *Creating the capacity for change: How and why governors and legislatures are opening a new-schools sector in public education.* Bethesda, MD: Education Week Press.

Koretz, Daniel M. 2008. *Measuring up: What educational testing really tells us.* Cambridge, MA: Harvard University Press.

Koretz, Daniel M., and Sheila I. Barron. 1998. *The validity of gains in scores on the Kentucky Instructional Results Information System (KIRIS).* Santa Monica, CA: RAND Corporation.

Koski, William S., and Eileen L. Horng. 2007. Facilitating the teacher quality gap? Collective bargaining agreements, teacher hiring and transfer rules, and teacher assignment among schools in California. *Education Finance and Policy* 2, no. 3 (Summer): 262–300.

Kozol, Jonathan. 2005. *The shame of the nation: The restoration of apartheid schooling in America.* New York: Three Rivers Press.

Krueger, Alan B. 2002. Understanding the magnitude and effect of class size on student achievement. In *The class size debate*, edited by Lawrence Mishel and Richard Rothstein, 7–35. Washington, DC: Economic Policy Institute.

Krueger, Anne O. 1974. The political economy of the rent seeking society. *American Economic Review* 64, no. 3 (June): 291–303.

Ladd, Helen F. 1975. Local educational expenditures, fiscal capacity, and the composition of the property tax base. *National Tax Journal* 28:145–58.

Lankford, Hamilton, and James Wyckoff. 1995. Where has the money gone? An analysis of school district spending in New York. *Educational Evaluation and Policy Analysis* 17, no. 2 (Summer): 195–218.

Larabee, David F. 2004. *The trouble with ed schools.* New Haven: Yale University Press.

Lazear, Edward P. 2003. Teacher incentives. *Swedish Economic Policy Review* 10, no. 3:179–214.

Leibowitz, Arleen. 1974. Home investments in children. *Journal of Political Economy* 82, no. 2, pt. 2 (March–April): S111–31.

Levine, Arthur. 2006. *Educating school teachers*. Washington, DC: Education Schools Project (September).

Lindert, Peter H. 2000. Three centuries of inequality in Britain and America. In *Handbook of income distribution*, edited by Anthony B. Atkinson and Francois Bourguignon, 167–216. Amsterdam: Elsevier.

Lindseth, Alfred A. 2006. The legal backdrop to adequacy. In *Courting failure: How school finance lawsuits exploit judges' good intentions and harm our children*, edited by Eric A. Hanushek, 33–78. Stanford: Education Next Books.

Lippman, Laura, Lina Guzman, Julie Dombrowski Keith, Rebecca Shwalb, and Peter Tice. 2008. *Parent expectations and planning for college*. Washington, DC: U.S. Department of Education.

Loeb, Susanna, Anthony S. Bryk, and Eric A. Hanushek. 2008. Getting Down to Facts: School finance and governance in California. *Education Finance and Policy* 3, no. 1 (Winter): 1–19.

Loeb, Susanna, Cecilia Rouse, and Anthony Shorris. 2007. Excellence in the classroom: Introducing the issue. *Future of Children* 17, no. 1 (Spring): 3–14.

Lusi, Susan Follett, and Patricia Davis Goldberg. 2000. A new mission for the Department of Education. In *All children can learn: Lessons from the Kentucky reform experience*, edited by Roger S. Pankratz and Joseph M. Petrosko. San Francisco: Jossey-Bass: 225–43.

Lyon, G. Reid, and Jack M. Fletcher. 2001. Early warning system: How to prevent reading disabilities. *Education Matters* 1, no. 2 (Summer): 23–29.

Mackey, Phillip E. 2002. *New Jersey's public schools: A biennial report for the people of New Jersey*. New Brunswick, NJ: Public Education Institute.

Manna, Paul, and Michael J Petrilli. 2008. Double standard? "Scientifically based research" and the No Child Left Behind Act. In *When research matters: How scholarship influences education policy*, edited by Frederick M. Hess, 63–88. Cambridge, MA: Harvard Education Press.

Marshall, Ray, and Marc Tucker. 1992. *Thinking for a living: Education and the wealth of Nations*. New York: Basic Books.

Mathews, Jay. 2008. Bad rap on the schools. *Wilson Quarterly* (Spring).

Maxwell, Lesli. 2007. Mayor backs off plan for school funding Method in N.Y.C. *Education Week*, May 2, 8.

Mayer, Susan E. 1997. *What money can't buy: Family income and children's life chances*. Cambridge, MA: Harvard University Press.

McKinley, Jesse. 2008. Schwarzenegger acts on California's big deficits. *New York Times*, January 9.

McNeil, Linda M. 2007. As budgets swell, spending choices get new scrutiny. *Education Week*, March 28, 1.

Medina, Jennifer. 2008. City to give $14.2 million in bonuses to teachers at schools with improved report cards. *New York Times*, September 19.

Miller, Matthew. 2003. *The 2% solution: Fixing America's problems in ways liberals and conservatives can love*. New York: Public Affairs.

Mirel, Jeffrey. 2001. *The evolution of the New American Schools: From revolution to mainstream*. Washington, DC: Thomas B. Fordham Foundation.

Mishel, Lawrence, and Richard Rothstein, eds. 2002. *The class size debate*. Washington, DC: Economic Policy Institute.

Moe, Terry M. 2001a. *Schools, vouchers, and the American public*. Washington, DC: Brookings Institution Press.

———. 2001b. Teachers unions and the public schools. In *A primer on America's schools*, edited by Terry M. Moe, 151–83. Stanford, CA: Hoover Institution Press.

———, ed. 2001c. *A primer on America's schools*. Stanford, CA: Hoover Institution Press.

———. 2002. Cooking the questions. *Education Next* 2, no. 1 (Spring): 71–77.

Mosteller, Frederick. 1995. The Tennessee study of class size in the early school grades. *Future of Children* 5, no. 2 (Summer–Fall): 113–27.

Mosteller, Frederick, and Robert Boruch, eds. 2002. *Evidence matters: Randomized trials in education research*. Washington DC: Brookings Institution Press.

Mulligan, Casey B. 1999. Galton versus the human capital approach to inheritance. *Journal of Political Economy* 107, no. 6, pt. 2 (December): S184–224.

Murnane, Richard J. 1975. *Impact of school resources on the learning of inner city children*. Cambridge, MA: Ballinger.

Murnane, Richard J., and Richard R. Nelson. 1984. Production and innovation when techniques are tacit: The case of education. *Journal of Economic Behavior and Organization* 5:353–73.

Murnane, Richard J., and Barbara Phillips. 1981. What do effective teachers of inner-city children have in common? *Social Science Research* 10, no. 1 (March): 83–100.

Murnane, Richard J., Judith D. Singer, John B. Willett, James J. Kemple, and Randall J. Olsen. 1991. *Who will teach? Policies that matter*. Cambridge, MA: Harvard University Press.

Murnane, Richard J., and Jennifer L. Steele. 2007. What is the problem? The challenge of providing effective teachers for all children. *Future of Children* 17, no. 1 (Spring): 15–43.

Murnane, Richard J., John B. Willett, M. Jay Braatz, and Yves Duhaldeborde. 2001. Do different dimensions of male high school students' skills predict labor market success a decade later? Evidence from the NLSY. *Economics of Education Review* 20, no. 4 (August): 311–20.

Murnane, Richard J., John B. Willett, Yves Duhaldeborde, and John H. Tyler. 2000. How important are the cognitive skills of teenagers in predicting subsequent earnings? *Journal of Policy Analysis and Management* 19, no. 4 (Fall): 547–68.

Murnane, Richard J., John B. Willett, and Frank Levy. 1995. The growing importance of cognitive skills in wage determination. *Review of Economics and Statistics* 77, no. 2 (May): 251–66.

Murphy, Dean E. 2003. Dream ends for Oakland school chief as state takes over. *New York Times*.

Murphy, Kevin M., and Finis Welch. 1992. The structure of wages. *Quarterly Journal of Economics* 107, no. 1 (February): 285–326.

Murray, Sheila E., William N. Evans, and Robert M. Schwab. 1998. Education-finance reform and the distribution of education resources. *American Economic Review* 88, no. 4 (September): 789–812.

Myers, John L., and Justin Silverstein. 2005. *Successful school districts study for North Dakota*. Augenblick Palaich & Associates (August 15).

Nathan, Joe. 1996. *Charter schools: Creating hope and opportunity for American education*. San Francisco: Jossey-Bass.

National Association of State Boards of Education. 1997. Teacher tenure. *Policy Updates 5*, no. 3 (February): 1.

National Association of State Budget Officers. 2004. *2003 state expenditure report*. Washington, DC: NASBO.

National Board for Professional Teaching Standards. 1991. *Toward high and rigorous standards for the teaching profession*. 3rd ed. Detroit, MI: NBPTS.

National Center for Education Statistics. 2007a. *The condition of education 2007*. Washington, DC: U.S. Department of Education.

———. 2007b. *Mapping 2005 state proficiency standards onto the NAEP scales*. Washington, DC: U.S. Department of Education (June).

———. 2008a. *The condition of education 2008*. Washington, DC: U.S. Department of Education.

———. 2008b. National public education financial survey data. In *Common Core of Data* (CCD). Washington, DC: NCES.

National Commission on Excellence in Education. 1983. *A nation at risk: The imperative for educational reform*. Washington, DC: U.S. Government Printing Office.

National Commission on Teaching and America's Future. 1996. *What matters most: Teaching for America's future*. New York: NCTAF.

National Council on Teacher Quality. 2007. *State teacher policy yearbook, 2007*. Washington, DC: National Council on Teacher Quality.

National Education Association. 2003. *Status of the American public school teacher, 2000–01*. Washington: National Education Association (August).

Neal, Derek. 2006. Why has black-white skill convergence stopped? In *Handbook of the economics of education*, edited by Eric A. Hanushek and Finis Welch, 511–76. Amsterdam: North-Holland.

Neal, Derek A., and William R. Johnson. 1996. The role of pre-market factors in black-white differences. *Journal of Political Economy* 104, no. 5 (October): 869–95.

Nechyba, Thomas J. 2006. Income and peer sorting in public and private schools. In *Handbook of the economics of education*, edited by Eric A. Hanushek and Finis Welch, 1327–68. Amsterdam: North-Holland.

Neira, Maria. 2008. Testimony on K–12 physical education 2008. Albany, NY: Assembly Standing Committee on Education.

*New York Post*, 2004. Mike: Albany must pick up school tab. December 3, 15.

———. 2007. Spitzer's school sellout. March 31, 18.

O'Day, Jennifer A., and Marshall S. Smith. 1993. Systemic school reform and educational opportunity. In *Designing coherent policy*, edited by Susan H. Fuhrman, 250–312. San Francisco: Jossey-Bass.

O'Neill, June. 1990. The role of human capital in earnings differences between black and white men. *Journal of Economic Perspectives* 4, no. 4 (Fall): 25–46.

Oates, Wallace E. 1969. The effects of property taxes and local public spending on property values: An empirical study of tax capitalization and the Tiebout hypothesis. *Journal of Political Economy* 77, no. 6 (November–December): 957–71.

Obama, Barack. 2007. *The audacity of hope: Thoughts on reclaiming the American dream*. New York: Three Rivers Press.

Odden, Allan, Mark Fermanich, and Lawrence O. Picus. 2003. *A state-of-the-art approach to school finance adequacy in Kentucky*. Lawrence O. Picus & Associates (February).

Odden, Allan, Lawrence O. Picus, Michael Goetz, and Mark Fermanich. 2006. *An evidence-based approach to school finance adequacy in Washington*. Lawrence O. Picus & Associates (June 30).

Odden, Allan, Lawrence O. Picus, Michael Goetz, Mark Fermanich, Richard C. Seder, William Glenn, and Robert Nelli. 2005. *An evidence-based approach to recalibrating Wyoming's block grant school funding formula*. Lawrence O. Picus & Associates (November 30).

Odden, Allan, Lawrence O. Picus, and Michelle Turner Mangan. 2006. *Level and use of resources in Arkansas: Are use patterns consistent with doubling student performance?* Lawrence O. Picus & Associates (June 15, revised).

Odden, Allan, Lawrence O. Picus, Michelle Turner Mangan, Mike Goetz, and Anabel Aportela. 2008. *The use of educational resources in Wyoming*. Lawrence O. Picus & Associates (February 14, 2008).

Olson, Lynn. 2004. Research Group, New American Schools merge. *Education Week*, May 5.

Oppenheim, Jamie. 2008. School lunches pinched by budget. *Novato Advance*.

Organisation for Economic Co-operation and Development. 2008. *Education at a glance: OECD indicators 2008*. Paris: Organisation for Economic Co-operation and Development.

Ouchi, William G. 2003. *Making schools work: A revolutionary plan to get your children the education they need*. New York: Simon & Schuster.

Paige, Rod. 2006. *The war against hope: How teachers' unions hurt children, hinder teachers, and endanger public education*. Nashville, TN: Thomas Nelson.

Pankratz, Roger S. 2000. The legal and legislative battles. In *All children can learn: Lessons from the Kentucky reform experience*, edited by Roger S. Pankratz and Joseph M. Petrosko, 11–28. San Francisco: Jossey-Bass.

Parente, Stephen L., and Edward C. Prescott. 1994. Barriers to technology adoption and development. *Journal of Political Economy* 102, no. 2 (April): 298–321.

———. 1999. Monopoly rights: A barrier to riches. *American Economic Review* 89, no. 5 (December): 1216–33.

Park, Jennifer. 2005. Targeted spending. In *Quality counts 2005: No small change*: *Education Week* 24, no. 17 (January 6): 46.

Parsad, Basmat, and Laurie Lewis. 2003. *Remedial education at degree-granting postsecondary institutions in fall 2000*. Washington, DC: National Center for Education Statistics (November).

Perez, Maria, Priyanka Anand, Cecilia Speroni, Thomas Parrish, Phil Esra, Miguel Socias, and Paul Gubbins. 2007. Successful California schools in the context of educational adequacy. Stanford, Institute for Research on Education Policy and Practice.

Peterson, Paul E. 2003a. "The theory and practice of school choice." In *The legacy of Milton and Rose Friedman's Free to Choose: Economic liberalism at the turn of the twenty-first century*, edited by Mark A. Wynne, Harvey Rosenblum, and Robert L. Formaini. Dallas, TX: Federal Reserve Bank of Dallas: 37–54.

———, ed. 2003b. *Our schools and our future: Are we still at risk?* Stanford, CA: Hoover Institution Press.

———. 2006a. The A+ plan. In *Reforming education in Florida*, edited by Paul E. Peterson, 49–66. Stanford, CA: Hoover Institution Press.

———, ed. 2006b. *Generational change: Closing the test score gap*. Lanham, MD: Rowman & Littlefield.

———, ed. 2006c. *Reforming education in Florida*. Stanford, CA: Hoover Institution Press.

Peterson, Paul E., and Frederick M. Hess. 2005. Johnny can read . . . in some states. *Education Next* 5, no. 3 (Summer): 52–53.

Peterson, Paul E., and Martin R. West. 2006. Is your child's school effective? Don't rely on NCLB to tell you. *Education Next* 6, no. 4 (Fall): 77–80.

———, eds. 2003. *No child left behind? The politics and practice of accountability*. Washington, DC: Brookings Institution Press.

Picus, Lawrence O., Allan Odden, and Mark Fermanich. 2003. *A professional judgment approach to school finance adequacy in Kentucky*. Lawrence O. Picus & Associates (May).

Pierce, Brooks, and Finis Welch. 1996. Changes in the structure of wages. In *Improving America's schools: The role of incentives*, edited by Eric A. Hanushek and Dale W. Jorgenson, 53–73. Washington, DC: National Academy Press.

Podgursky, Michael J. 2003. Fringe benefits. *Education Next* 3, no. 3 (Summer): 71–76.

——. 2007. Is teacher pay adequate? In *School money trials: The legal pursuit of educational adequacy*, edited by Martin R. West and Paul E. Peterson, 131–55. Washington: Brookings Institution Press.

Podgursky, Michael J., and Matthew G. Springer. 2007a. Teacher performance pay: A review. *Journal of Policy Analysis and Management* 26, no. 4:909–49.

——. 2007b. Credentials versus performance: Review of the teacher performance pay research. *Peabody Journal of Education* 82, no. 4:551–73.

Poggio, John P. 2000. Statewide performance assessment and school accountability. In *All children can learn: Lessons from the Kentucky reform experience*, edited by Roger S. Pankratz and Joseph M. Petrosko. San Francisco: Jossey-Bass.

President's Commission on Excellence in Special Education. 2002. *A new era: Revitalizing special education for children and their families*. Washington, DC: U.S. Department of Education.

Raymond, Margaret E., and Stephen Fletcher. 2002. Teach for America. *Education Next* 2, no. 1 (Spring): 62–68.

Raymond, Margaret E., Stephen Fletcher, and Javier A. Luque. 2001. *Teach for America: An evaluation of teacher differences and student outcomes in Houston, Texas*. Stanford University: CREDO.

Rebell, Michael A. 2001. Educational adequacy, democracy, and the courts. In *Achieving high educational standards for all*, edited by Timothy Ready, Jr. Christopher Edley, and Catherine E. Snow, 227. Washington, DC: National Research Council.

——. 2004. Why adequacy lawsuits matter. *Education Week*, August 11, 40.

——. 2006a. Professional rigor, public engagement, and judicial review: A proposal for enhancing the validity of education adequacy studies. Paper presented at *Annual meeting of the American Education Finance Association*. Denver, CO.

——. 2006b. Professional rigor, public engagement, and judicial review: A proposal for enhancing the validity of education adequacy studies. *Teachers College Record*.

Rebell, Michael A., and Jessica R. Wolff. 2006. Opportunity knocks: Applying lessons from the education adequacy movement to reform the No Child Left Behind Act. Policy Paper No. 2, Teachers College, Columbia University (March).

Resch, Alexandra M. 2006. The effects of the Abbott school finance reform on student achievement in New Jersey. Paper presented at *APPAM Fall Research Conference*. Madison, WI: Association for Public Policy Analysis and Management.

Reynolds, Arthur J., Judy A. Temple, Dylan L. Robertson, and Emily A. Mann. 2002. Age 21 cost-benefit analysis of the Title I Chicago Child-Parent Centers. *Educational Evaluation and Policy Analysis* 24, no. 4:267–303.

Richardson, Joanna. 1995. Critics target state teacher-tenure laws. *Education Week*, March 1.

Rivkin, Steven G. 1995. Black/white differences in schooling and employment. *Journal of Human Resources* 30, no. 4 (Fall): 826–52.

Rivkin, Steven G. 2007. Value-added analysis and education policy. Brief 1, Center for Analysis of Longitudinal Data in Education Research, Washington, DC (November).

Rivkin, Steven G., Eric A. Hanushek, and John F. Kain. 2005. Teachers, schools, and academic achievement. *Econometrica* 73, no. 2 (March): 417–58.

Rivkin, Steven G., and Finis Welch. 2006. Neighborhood segregation and school integration. In *Handbook of the economics of education*, edited by Eric A. Hanushek and Finis Welch, 1019–49. Amsterdam: North-Holland.

Rockoff, Jonah E. 2004. The impact of individual teachers on student achievement: Evidence from panel data. *American Economic Review* 94, no. 2 (May): 247–52.

Romer, Paul. 1990. Endogenous technological change. *Journal of Political Economy* 99, no. 5, pt. 2:S71–102.

Rose, Heather, Ria Sengupta, Jon Sonstelie, and Ray Reinhard. 2008. Funding formulas for California schools: Simulations and supporting data. San Francisco, Public Policy Institute of California (January).

Rose, Lowell C., and Alec M. Gallup. 2007. The 39th annual Phi Delta Kappa/Gallup poll of the public's attitudes toward the public schools. *Phi Delta Kappan* (September): 33–48.

Rosenberg, Gerald N. 1991. *The hollow hope: Can courts bring about social change?* Chicago: University of Chicago Press.

Rosenberg, Steven. 2008. Schools brace for teacher layoffs—Hikes in insurance, utilities blamed. *Boston Globe*, January 24.

Rossell, Christine H. 1990. *The carrot or the stick for school desegregation policy: Magnet schools or forced busing*. Philadelphia: Temple University Press.

Rothschild, Scott. 2005. Lower bar for schools advised. *Lawrence Journal-World*, August 10.

Rothstein, Richard. 1998. *The way we were? The myths and realities of America's student achievement*. New York: Century Foundation Press.

———. 2004. *Class and schools: Using social, economic, and educational reform to close the black-white achievement gap*. Washington, DC: Economic Policy Institute.

Rouse, Cecilia Elena. 1998. Private school vouchers and student achievement: An evaluation of the Milwaukee Parental Choice Program. *Quarterly Journal of Economics* 113, no. 2 (May): 553–602.

Roza, Marguerite, Kacey Guin, Betheny Gross, and Scott Deburgomaster. 2007. Do districts fund schools fairly? *Education Next* 7, no. 4 (Fall): 69–73.

Roza, Marguerite, and Paul T. Hill. 2006. How can anyone say what's adequate if nobody knows how money is spent now? In *Courting failure: How school adequacy lawsuits pervert judges' good intentions and harm our children*, edited by Eric A. Hanushek, 235–55. Stanford: Education Next Books.

Rural School and Community Trust. 2003. *The rural school funding report*. Rural School and Community Trust.

Ryan, James E. 2004. The perverse incentives of the No Child Left Behind Act. *New York University Law Review* 79, no. 3 (June): 932–89.

Sack, Joetta L. 2005. Calif. teachers rally against ballot measures. *Education Week* (October 26): 25.

Sanders, William L., and Sandra P. Horn. 1994. The Tennessee Value-Added Assessment System (TVAAS): Mixed-model methodology in educational assessment. *Journal of Personnel Evaluation in Education* 8:299–311.

———. 1995. The Tennessee Value-Added Assessment System (TVAAS): Mixed model methodology in educational assessment. In *Teacher evaluation: Guide to effective practice*, edited by Anthony J. Shinkfield and Daniel L. Stufflebeam, 337–76. Boston: Kluwer Academic Publishers.

———. 1998. Research findings from the Tennessee Value-Added Assessment System (TVAAS) database: Implications for educational evaluation and research. *Journal of Personnel Evaluation in Education* 12:247–56.

Sandler, Ross, and David Schoenbrod. 2003. *Democracy by decree*. New Haven, CT: Yale University Press.

Sass, Tim R. 2006. Charter schools and student achievement in Florida. *Education Finance and Policy* 1, no. 1 (Winter): 91–122.

Schaps, Eric. 2007. Why the No Child Left Behind Act is unsalvageable. *Education Week*, May 9, 32–33.

Schrag, Peter. 2003. *Final Test: The battle for adequacy in America's schools*. New York: New Press.

Schweinhart, Lawrence J., Jeanne Montie, Zongping Xiang, W. Steven Barnett, Clive R. Belfield, and Milagros Nores. 2005. *Lifetime effects: The High/Scope Perry Preschool study through age 40*. Ypsilanti: High/Scope Press.

Schweizer, Peter. 1999. The dance of the lemons. *Hoover Digest* 1.

Scitovsky, Tibor, and Anne Scitovsky. 1959. What price economic progress? *Yale Law Review* 49 (Autumn): 95–110.

Silva, Elena. 2008. The Benwood plan: A lesson in comprehensive teacher reform. Washington, DC: Education Sector (April).

Silva, Fabio, and Jon Sonstelie. 1995. Did Serrano cause a decline in school spending? *National Tax Journal* 48, no. 2 (June): 199–215.

Slavin, Robert E. 2007. The What Works Clearinghouse: Time for a fresh start. *Education Week*, December 19, 36, 27.

Smarick, Andy. 2008. Wave of the future: Why charter schools should replace failing urban schools. *Education Next* 8, no. 1 (Winter): 38–45.

Smith, Marshall S., and Jennifer O'Day. 1990. Systemic school reform. In *The politics of curriculum and testing*, edited by Susan H. Fuhrman and Betty Malen, 233–67. London: Falmer Press.

Snell, Lisa. 2008. *Failing public schools wipe out any preschools gains*. Reason Foundation (June 6).

Sonstelie, Jon. 2007. Aligning school finance with academic standards: A weighted-student formula based on a survey of practitioners. Stanford, Institute for Research on Education Policy and Practice.

Standard & Poor's School Evaluation Service. 2004. *Resource adequacy study for the New York State Commission on Education Reform* (March).

Staros, Barbara J. 1994. School finance litigation in Florida: A historical analysis. *Stetson Law Review* 23, no. 2 (Spring): 497–520.

Starr, Kenneth. 2007. "The uncertain future of adequacy remedies." In *School money trials: The legal pursuit of educational adequacy*, edited by Martin R. West and Paul E. Peterson. Washington: Brookings: 77–101.

Stecher, Brian M., and George W. Bohrnstedt. 1999. *Class size reduction in California: Early evaluation findings, 1996–98*. Palo Alto, CA: American Institutes for Research.

Steinhauer, Jennifer. 2008. California budget is signed, 85 days late and despised. *New York Times*, September 23.

Stepp, Diane R. 2007. Controversial voucher program making headway. *Atlanta Journal-Constitution*, November 1.

Stern, David. 1973. Effects of alternative state aid formulas on the distribution of public school expenditures in Massachusetts. *Review of Economics and Statistics 55*, no. 1 (February): 91–97.

Stern, Sol. 1997. How teachers' unions handcuff schools. *City Journal*, Spring.

———. 2006. *Campaign for Fiscal Equity v. New York:* The march of folly. In *Courting failure: How school adequacy lawsuits pervert judges' good intentions and harm our children*, edited by Eric A. Hanushek, 1–31. Stanford: Education Next Books.

Strayer, George D. 1934. The ability and the obligation of the state to support education. *Teachers College Record 35*, no. 7:580.

Strayer, George D., and R. M. Haig. 1923. *The financing of education in the state of New York*. New York: Macmillan.

Summers, Anita A., and Amy W. Johnson. 1996. The effects of school-based management plans. In *Improving America's schools: The role of incentives*, edited by Eric A. Hanushek and Dale W. Jorgenson, 75–96. Washington, DC: National Academy Press.

Taylor, Lori L. 2006. Comparable wages, inflation, and school finance equity. *Education Finance and Policy* 1, no. 3 (Summer): 349–71.

Taylor, Lori L., and William J. Fowler. 2006. *A comparable wage approach to geographic cost adjustment*. Washington, DC: National Center for Education Statistics (May).

Teaching Commission. 2004. *Teaching at risk: A call to action*. New York: Teaching Commission.

Thernstrom, Abigail, and Stephan Thernstrom. 2003. *No excuses: Closing the racial gap in learning.* New York: Simon & Schuster.

Thomas B. Fordham Institute. 2006. *Fund the child: Tackling inequity and antiquity in school funding.* Washington, DC: Thomas B. Fordham Institute.

Thompson, A. Mavourneed, and David L. Silvernail. 2001. States' provisions of extra funding for economically-disadvantaged students. Gorham, ME: Maine Education Policy Research Institute (October).

Tiebout, Charles M. 1956. A pure theory of local expenditures. *Journal of Political Economy* 64, no. 5 (October): 416–24.

Toch, Thomas, and Robert Rothman. 2008. Rush to judgment: Teacher evaluation in public education. Washington, DC: Education Sector (January).

Tooley, James. 2001. *The global education industry: Lessons from private education in developing countries.* 2nd ed. Washington, DC: Institute of Economic Affairs.

Tooley, James, and Pauline Dixon. 2005. *Private education is good for the poor: A study of private schools serving the poor in low-income countries.* Washington, DC: Cato Institute.

Toppo, Greg. 2005. Training programs for principals inadequate. *USA Today,* March 15.

———. 2008. Survey: Fuel prices force schools to weigh class, staff cuts. *USA Today,* July 29, 2A.

Tough, Paul. 2006. Still left behind: What it will really take to close the education gap. *New York Times Magazine,* November 26.

Turque, Bill. 2008. Long battle expected on plan to fire teachers: D.C. union being aided by national organization. *Washington Post,* October 25, B01.

Tyack, David, and Larry Cuban. 1995. *Tinkering toward utopia: A century of public school reform.* Cambridge, MA: Harvard University Press.

Tyler, John H., Richard J. Murnane, and John B. Willett. 2000. Estimating the labor market signaling value of the GED. *Quarterly Journal of Economics* 115, no. 2 (May): 431–68.

U.S. Bureau of the Census. 2006. *State and metropolitan area data book: 2006.* 6th ed. Washington, DC: U.S. Bureau of the Census.

———. 2007. *Statistical abstract of the United States: 2007.* Washington, DC: U.S. Government Printing Office.

———. Various years. Current Population Reports, Series P-20, P-60. Washington, DC: U.S. Bureau of the Census.

U.S. Commission on Civil Rights. 1967. *Racial isolation in the public schools.* Washington, DC: U.S. Government Printing Office.

U.S. Department of Education. 2004. *The condition of education 2004.* Washington, DC: National Center for Education Statistics.

———. 2007. *Digest of education statistics, 2006.* Washington, DC: National Center for Education Statistics.

U.S. Department of Education. 2008. *Digest of Education Statistics, 2007.* Washington, DC: National Center for Education Statistics.

Verstegen & Associates. 2003. *Calculation of the cost of an adequate education in Kentucky: Prepared for the Council for Better Education* (February).

Vigdor, Jacob. 2008. Scrap the sacrosanct salary schedule: How about more pay for new teachers, less for older ones? *Education Next* 8, no. 4 (Fall): 36–42.

Vinovskis, Maris A. 1999. Do federal compensatory education programs really work? A brief historical analysis of Title I and Head Start. *American Journal of Education* 107, no. 3 (May): 187–209.

Volcansek, Mary L. 1981. Explaining outcomes of judicial elections: An exploration. *Western Political Quarterly* 572, no. 4:572–77.

Walberg, Herbert J. 2006. High-poverty, high performance schools, districts, and states. In *Courting failure: How school adequacy lawsuits pervert judges' good intentions and harm our children*, edited by Eric A. Hanushek, 79–101. Stanford, CA: Education Next Books.

Walsh, Kate. 2002. Positive spin: The evidence for traditional teacher certification, reexamined. *Education Next* 2, no. 1 (Spring): 79–84.

Walsh, Mark. 1993. State takeover of Jersey City schools seen yielding significant improvements. *Education Week*, February 17.

Wayne, Andrew J., and Peter Youngs. 2003. Teacher characteristics and student achievement gains: A review. *Review of Educational Research* 73, no. 1 (Spring): 89–122.

Weaver, Reg. 2007. NEA favors more pay—but not tied to test scores. *Education Week*, October 17, 29–30.

Weimer, David L., and Michael J. Wolkoff. 2001. School performance and housing values: Using non-contiguous district and incorporation boundaries to identify school effects. *National Tax Journal* 54, no. 2 (June): 231–53.

Welch, Finis, and Audrey Light. 1987. *New evidence on school desegregation.* Washington, DC: U.S. Commission on Civil Rights.

Weston, Susan Perkins, and Robert F. Sexton. 2007. Substantial and yet not sufficient: Kentucky's effort to build proficiency for each and every child. In *Symposium of Equal Educational Opportunity: What Now?* Teachers College.

Will, George. 2005. Judges and "soft rights." *Newsweek*, February 28.

Williams, Joe. 2005. The legal cash machine: A New York adequacy case tests the limits of fiscal coherence. *Education Next* 5, no. 3 (Summer): 27–33.

———. 2007. Non-implementation of New York's adequacy judgment. In *School money trials: The legal pursuit of educational adequacy*, edited by Martin R. West and Paul E. Peterson, 195–212. Washington, DC: Brookings Institution Press.

Wirt, John, Susan Choy, Patrick Rooney, William Hussar, Stephan Provasnik, Gillian Hampden-Thompson, Barbara Kridl, and Andrea Livingston. 2005. *The condition of education: 2005.* NCES 2005–094. Jessup, MD: National Center for Education Statistics (June).

Witte, John F. 1999. *The market approach to education*. Princeton, NJ: Princeton University Press.

———. 2007. A proposal for state, income-targeted, preschool vouchers. *Peabody Journal of Education* 82, no. 4:617–44.

Woessmann, Ludger. 2005. The effect heterogeneity of central examinations: Evidence from TIMSS, TIMSS-Repeat and PISA. *Education Economics* 13, no. 2 (June): 143–69.

———. 2007. International evidence on school competition, autonomy and accountability: A review. *Peabody Journal of Education* 82, no. 2–3–3: 473–97.

Wolf, Andrew. 2005. The UFT agreement. *New York Sun*, October 4.

Wong, Kenneth K., and Francis X. Shen. 2005. "When mayors lead urban schools: Assessing the effects of takeover." In *Beseiged: School boards and the future of education politics*, edited by William G. Howell. Washington, DC: Brookings Institution Press: 81–101.

Word, Elizabeth, John Johnston, Helen Pate Bain, B. DeWayne Fulton, Jayne Boyd Zaharies, Martha Nannette Lintz, Charles M. Achilles, John Folger, and Carolyn Breda. 1990. *Student/teacher achievement ratio (STAR), Tennessee's K–3 class size study: Final summary report, 1985–1990*. Nashville: Tennessee State Department of Education.

Zinth, Kyle. 2005. *State class-size reduction measures*. Denver, CO: Education Commission of the States (March).

# Index